Loyal Subjects

LOYAL SUBJECTS

Bonds of Nation, Race, and Allegiance in
Nineteenth-Century America

ELIZABETH DUQUETTE

Rutgers University Press
NEW BRUNSWICK, NEW JERSEY, AND LONDON

Copyright © 2010 by Elizabeth Duquette

All rights reserved

No part of this book may be reproduced or utilized in any form or by any means, electronic or mechanical, or by any information storage and retrieval system, without written permission from the publisher. Please contact Rutgers University Press, 100 Joyce Kilmer Avenue, Piscataway, NJ 08854–8099. The only exception to this prohibition is "fair use" as defined by U.S. copyright law.

Visit our Web site: http://rutgerspress.rutgers.edu

Manufactured in the United States of America

LIBRARY OF CONGRESS CATALOGING-IN-PUBLICATION DATA

Duquette, Elizabeth, 1963–
  Loyal subjects : bonds of nation, race, and allegiance in nineteenth-century America / Elizabeth Duquette.
      p. cm. — (American literatures initiative)
  Includes bibliographical references and index.
  ISBN 978-0-8135-4780-0 (hardcover : alk. paper)
  ISBN 978-0-8135-4781-7 (pbk. : alk. paper)
    1. American literature—19th century—History and criticism.   2. United States—History—Civil War, 1861–1865—Literature and the war.   3. National characteristics, American, in literature.   4. Loyalty in literature.   5. Allegiance in literature.   6. Nationalism in literature.   7. Nationalism and literature—United States—History—19th century.   I. Title.
  PS217.N38D87   2010
  810.9'358735—dc22

2009043151

A British Cataloging-in-Publication record for this book is available from the British Library.

A book in the American Literatures Initiative (ALI), a collaborative publishing project of NYU Press, Fordham University Press, Rutgers University Press, Temple University Press, and the University of Virginia Press. The Initiative is supported by The Andrew W. Mellon Foundation. For more information, please visit www.americanliteratures.org.

In memory of my mother, Marie H. Duquette

Contents

	Acknowledgments	ix
	Introduction: Pledging Allegiance	1
1	Loyalty, Oaths, and the Nation	17
2	One Big Happy Family, Again?	61
3	Pledging Allegiance in Henry James	100
4	Loyalty's Slaves	137
5	Philosophies of Loyalty	179
	Afterword	219
	Notes	223
	Index	263

Acknowledgments

I am grateful for the many people and institutions that have supported me over the years, and for the opportunity to acknowledge them in print. A fellowship at the Illinois Program for Research in the Humanities (IPRH) at the University of Illinois let me develop an observation into a book-length project, while a year at the Tanner Humanities Center at the University of Utah allowed that project to become an actual book. In between, a grant from the Gilder Lehrman Foundation funded archival research on the Loyal Publication Society. Gettysburg College provided both time and money for the writing process.

My editors at Rutgers University Press, Leslie Mitchener and Rachel Friedman, ably assisted by Katie Keeran, have provided excellent feedback, and timely reminders. Hearty thanks are due, as well, to Tim Roberts, of the American Literatures Initiative, and Robert Burchfield, who were instrumental in getting the manuscript ready for publication. I am truly delighted that the project found such a congenial institutional home. I am grateful, as well, to Oxford University Press for the permission to reprint portions of chapter 5, which appeared in an earlier iteration in *American Literary History* 16 (2004): 29–57.

Throughout the years, I have benefited enormously from the encouragement and example of numerous colleagues, friends, and teachers, including Steve Brauer, Lawrence Buehl, Chris Castiglia, Russ Castronovo, Erin Forbes, Anselm Haverkamp, Christopher Johnson, Caroline Levander, Stacey Margolis, Sam Otter, Mary Poovey, Joan Saab, Xiomara Santamarina, Pam Schirmeister, Bill Solomon, Lisa Steinman, and Tina

Zwarg. Any missteps the book contains are despite their very best efforts. At the IPRH, Suvir Kaul and Matti Bunzl created an atmosphere that encouraged the lively exchanges through which the argument took shape; Chris Catanzarite guaranteed that the resources were in place so all the fellows could thrive. Sophia Mihic intervened in my thinking at key moments, and her influence is evident throughout the book. The excellent feedback I received while in residence at the University of Utah from Vincent Cheng, Stacey Margolis, Howard Horwitz, and the Tanner Ladies—Michaele Ferguson and Kathrin Koslicki—helped me to refine and clarify the book's thesis. My colleagues in the English Department at Gettysburg also deserve thanks for their unflagging and exuberant encouragement.

In the midst of all this support, however, one person stands out as exemplary. Serving variously and often simultaneously as an advocate, an enthusiast, a mentor, and a friend, Bob Levine has cheered this project at every turn. I do not exaggerate when I say that I'm not sure if this book would exist today if it weren't for his generosity and kindness.

And then there are those who have endured me as I learned how to finish a book: Peter Chapin, Katja Garloff, David Garrett, Deborah Hellman, Alex Hrycak, Virginia King, Karen Kligerman, Karen Lubell, Kate Nicholson, Allison Pease, Bill Ray, Brady Rymer, Bridget Clark Rymer, Adrienne and John Scott, and Kim Smith. The McDermotts, Michelle and Bob, kindly opened their home to a scholar seeking to extend her fellowship dollars. I am both deeply grateful and incredibly lucky to have such a patient and caring group of friends. This good fortune includes, as well, a family—my father and stepmother, Tom and Connie, and brother, John—that has supported me emotionally through the years. A special thanks is due to the Silver Spring Breens (Ali, Danny, Molly, and Sean) for intervening at moments when it seemed that the project would never end.

Two names are notably absent from the above lists. Shaindy Rudoff, a brilliant scholar and dedicated friend, died too soon in the summer of 2006. As I have worked through the end of this book, I have keenly missed her warmth and wit. Even more difficult was the sudden loss of my mother, Marie H. Duquette, in the early days of 2007. I dedicate this book, which she would have loved to have seen in its completed form, to her memory and to all the things she taught me over the years.

Yet my debt and gratitude alike are greatest to Michael Breen, my first, most exacting reader and closest friend. His unwavering conviction that I can do anything, even when it is glaringly obvious that I cannot, makes the very best version of me possible.

Introduction: Pledging Allegiance

Tens of thousands of American children recited the Pledge of Allegiance for the first time on October 21, 1892. Planned to correspond with the dedication ceremony for the Columbian World Exposition in Chicago, the Pledge of Allegiance was one part of a pedagogical program designed by the staff at the *Youth's Companion* to inculcate patriotic habits among American children.[1] Like the fair itself, which Charles Eliot Norton likened to "a great promise, even a great pledge," the "1892 Columbus Day Programme" was designed to honor "what the flag ... stood for, the *reason* for loyalty," its writer, Francis Bellamy, later explained.[2] In addition to reciting the pledge—"I pledge allegiance to my Flag and to the Republic for which it stands—one Nation indivisible—with Liberty and Justice for all"—the children involved read an ode ("Columbia's Banner"), listened to an address ("The Meaning of the Four Centuries"), and sang the "Song of Columbus Day."[3]

In "The Meaning of the Four Centuries," Bellamy developed the political ideas condensed in the Pledge of Allegiance, couching them in a language appropriate to a child's celebration of "true Americanism." Reviewing the nation's history,

> We see hardy men with intense convictions, grappling, struggling, often amid battle smoke, and some idea characteristic of the New World always triumphing. We see settlements knitting together into a nation with singleness of purpose. We note the birth of the modern system of industry and commerce, and its striking forth

into undreamed of wealth, making the millions members one of another as sentiment could never bind. And under it all, we fasten on certain principles ever operating and regnant—the leadership of manhood; equal rights for every soul; universal enlightenment as the source of progress. These last are the principles that have shaped America; these principles are the true Americanism.[4]

It is "a singleness of purpose" that unites Bellamy's America, even if "battle smoke" makes these shared "principles hard to see." Notably, these "principles," coupled with "the modern system of industry and commerce," establish ties that are more effective than those that "sentiment" could create. In a program designed to foster national pride and patriotism in American schoolchildren, why would Bellamy suggest that "sentiment" is insufficient to bind Americans to the nation?

Recalling the central role played by sentiment in the construction of actual and imagined bonds of affiliation for eighteenth- and nineteenth-century Americans makes Bellamy's assertion even odder.[5] Scholars have convincingly established its importance, figured through the concept of sympathy, in both the early national and the antebellum periods. "Between the 1790s and the Civil War," one historian asserts, references to the nation were often couched in "familial and domestic terms."[6] In 1821, for example, John Quincy Adams noted "the tie which binds us to our country" originates in the "sympathies of domestic life."[7] "In writings spanning nearly a hundred years," Elizabeth Barnes explains, "and including authors as diverse as Thomas Paine and Harriet Beecher Stowe, sympathy—expressed as emotional, psychological, or biological attachment—is represented as the basis of democracy, and therefore as fundamental to the creation of a distinctly 'American' character."[8] Equally important was sympathy's value in the shaping of both political and moral "character"; drawing on Adam Smith's influential *The Theory of Moral Sentiments*, particularly the idea that people are naturally sympathetic, the moral value of sentiment, and its seminal role in the creation of various kinds of allegiance, was widely accepted.

But for Bellamy, writing at the end of the nineteenth century, sentiment was not "natural" enough to secure national allegiance. In an 1891 essay, he argued instead for the importance of "mutual obligations," not feelings, in the constitution of the nation. It is imperative to recognize, he continued, that "no individual can claim isolation and independency. Let him make the most of his individuality; yet, as Aristotle said, 'Man is a political animal'; his nature apart from the nation is incomplete;

sundered from that to which he belongs he seems a freak. The nation, then, is not an artificial binding of units; it is a natural relationship."[9] The nation has "self-consciousness and moral personality," and what is "natural" about our relationship to it are "obligations," reflection, and moral reasoning. Rather than draw a parallel to the family or our "domestic sympathies," Bellamy consistently stresses the significance of moral principle and personal commitment to a corporate whole.[10] Note that the children do not pledge any particular emotion in the pledge he writes for the "Columbus Day Programme."

Bellamy admits to finding his inspiration for his Pledge of Allegiance in "the Civil War period," especially the importance then placed on "the great word" "allegiance," which is one reason that he would have sought something besides sentiment to secure the individual's affiliation to the nation.[11] Whereas sentiment and sympathy grounded earlier allegiances, the years leading up to the war, as well as the violent conflict itself, made abundantly clear that emotions could just as easily pull people apart as bind them together. The assertion of affective norms was inadequate to contain or prevent the often-brutal social disruptions associated with the mounting passions of sections moving toward war. One sees in the 1860s, therefore, a precipitous decline in the cultural value of emotion and its related structure of sympathetic identification, an unsurprising realignment of priorities, Philip Fisher suggests, for a culture predicated on middle-class values like control, regularity, and order.[12] In this chaotic environment, Northerners turned to a new structure for organizing allegiance and affiliation, one they hoped would contain rebellious feelings and provide the means of securing both national and personal safety. Loyalty, their chosen model, is a structure for describing and prescribing relations between people, and, as defined by Union writers and thinkers, it organized these relations through rational commitment to shared abstract principles. So understood, loyalty corrected the promiscuous excesses associated with sympathy and, in the process, simultaneously altered the cultural value of reason and emotion during the period. That the Civil War restructured assumptions about allegiance, replacing sympathy with loyalty, is the fundamental claim of this book. Its specific project is tracking how this change influenced the ways that structures of allegiance were understood and used from 1861 to 1909, as well as the implications of their fluctuating connotations for the articulation of national belonging, moral authority, and racial characteristics during the period. Only by understanding the importance of loyalty as an alternative to sympathy in the discourse of allegiance can we appreciate what it meant for postbellum Americans to reconstruct the nation in both fact and fiction after 1865.

In arguing for the importance of loyalty as an alternative model for understanding human ties, I do not mean to suggest that sympathy did not remain a critical concept.[13] To the contrary, loyalty may have replaced sympathy in the articulation of Union, and later national, allegiance, but it also enabled sympathy's reconstruction later in the century as an important means of organizing and camouflaging racist hierarchies.[14] Despite the attention lavished on colonial and antebellum sympathy, its postbellum history remains largely untold, a fact that is somewhat odd given Lauren Berlant's influential work detailing how a liberal commitment to public sentiment continues to dominate and organize U.S. political and public discourse.[15] As I will show, one explanation for the ongoing inability to construct a viable alternative to what Berlant has aptly called "the unfinished business of sentimentality" is the ease with which purportedly abstract models for affiliation are redefined, reconstructed even, by the adaptation to sentimental forms.[16]

The Civil War is, in part, responsible for our inability to see the ways in which antebellum structures and concepts are perpetuated in, and reimagined by, postbellum Americans. Because of its unprecedented devastation and the important structural changes associated with both the war and Reconstruction, literary scholars have tended to understand the period, not unreasonably, as radically rupturing the fabric of American society; this break finds its literary expression in the shift from sentimentality and romance to realism, deemed more appropriate to the new conditions of American culture. Two things get lost in this compelling narrative, however: substantial engagement with the war itself and the possibility of connections between ante- and postbellum culture. We may have problematized Walt Whitman's assertion that "the real war will never get in the books," but our hesitation to challenge the critical paradigms that claim authorized persists.[17] With a few notable exceptions, scholars have been slow to consider literary productions during the war, the ongoing importance of sentimentality during the rise of realism, and how the war reconstructed the cultural valuation of affect, the connotations of sympathy, or definitions of national identity.[18]

This study thus begins with the Civil War and the newly negative associations for sympathy that its outbreak introduced. Rather than a measure of moral excellence, sympathy became for Union partisans not merely dangerous but potentially treasonous. As I argue in chapter 1, this new and overtly political connotation significantly destabilized existing forms of affiliation in previously unexamined ways. Horrified at the result of emotions seemingly out of control, the Union embraced the ideal of loyalty as the means of denoting what proper allegiance to the nation entailed and required. Both structures of affiliation between people—sympathy and loyalty—configure human relations in overlapping, yet different, ways. Beginning with personal feelings, and presupposing the possibility of an intimate imaginative interchangeability, sympathy's affiliations move from the individual—his or her interests, sentiments, hopes, and values—into a shared or communal space. Sympathy's "egalitarian experience" is best understood, in other words, as metaphoric, in that it establishes commonalities, sometimes surprising ones, amid differences.[19] The conception of loyalty operative in the North during the Civil War, however, is more like synecdoche than metaphor.[20] Conflating registers of affiliation—familial, political, religious—loyalty subordinates the importance of individual feeling to the coherence associated with bonds defined both more abstractly and more absolutely. This diminution of difference between public and private registers in loyalty denies as well the kind of surprising commonality central to the sympathy narrative of attachment; this part of loyalty's definition enabled its eventual conversion to an even more conservative tool of social organization, consistent with an emotionally shrill fanaticism. In the 1860s, however, loyalty's emphasis on a corporate whole, of which individuals are equally and interchangeably a part, seeks to narrow the interpretive difference between word and deed. If sympathy's narrative is characterized by embodied signs and displays of affect, loyalty relies heavily on the promissory mode, on narrative structures that reduce contingency and diminish the potential difference between both persons and moments in time.

As important as loyalty became to Northern, and eventually national, discourse, however, it is impossible to understand the ways in which the concept functioned without juxtaposing it with sympathy. In making this claim, I diverge from the views of the influential historian George Frederickson, whose work provides an important foundation for this study. In *The Inner Civil War* (1965), Frederickson considers the war as an intellectual event, focusing on its "ideological, philosophical, and aesthetic" influence on Northern intellectuals rather than its military, political, or economic import. Tracing the competing impulses that shaped Union thinking before and during the war, Fredrickson maintains that Northern thinkers fought "not only against the South but among themselves for possession of the ideological meaning of the conflict and, more than this, to determine the meaning of America and the dominant style of American thought." Those who believed "that the advance of democracy in the world depended on the preservation of the American nation" and were willing to accept the consequences of this position were, Fredrickson explains, the most successful in establishing their position as hegemonic. Associating this position with the "doctrine of loyalty," which he argues becomes important in 1863 as a result of a series of dreadful military defeats and in response to Copperhead antiwar polemics, Fredrickson explains that elite attempts to "give [loyalty] a firm philosophical ground" resulted in "a harvest of political thought" that should count as some of the "most interesting intellectual products of the war."[21] For Fredrickson, loyalty is primarily a product of elite writing and thinking; he does not connect the development of this ideology either to sympathy or to the larger moral context in which both sympathy and loyalty should be considered.

Loyal Subjects revises Fredrickson's argument in three important ways. First, I argue that loyalty becomes important in Union discourse before 1863, providing a critical means of distinguishing Union from Confederate allegiance from the very beginning of the war. In stressing a rational loyalty, and denigrating an indulgent sympathy as treasonous, the ideological work loyalty could do was more sweeping than Fredrickson acknowledges because its assault on affect involved a reorientation of the principles of sentimental right-feeling upon which antebellum Americans had articulated moral norms and values—and which were equally basic to the idea of the United States from its inception. Second, loyalty may have been an important concept for Northern elites, but, as I will show, it was equally critical to popular writings of the period. Rather than abandon established fictive models, Union writers adapted familiar sentimental conventions to articulate changed political values and priorities. In this regard, my study is indebted to the work of Alice Fahs, who thoroughly traces a number of themes through the literary production of both North and South between 1861 and 1865 (though I do not share her interest in overlapping elements of Union and Confederate writing).[22] Finally, I argue that loyalty was not only the standard model of Union allegiance but provided the norm for allegiance to the United States during and after Reconstruction. Loyalty, and its proper performance, is thus a crucial, but unstudied, element of the Civil War's influence on wartime and postbellum literature.[23]

* * *

Looking back on the event it had organized, the *Youth's Companion* is full of praise for the Columbus Day celebrations, particularly its unforgettable "lesson of thoughtful patriotism":

> That united salute makes an episode in American history. The marching of the army of eager children with drilled precision of steps, and with enthusiastic pride as the appointed bearers of their country's banner on this greatest of American days, was a prophetic picture of gladness and solemnity to all the people.
>
> No triumphal procession of victorious armies was ever so benign and appealing as this review of our nation's pupils, the citizens of the new century, at the opening of that century.[24]

As each child participates in exactly the same way—reciting the same words and walking "with drilled precision of steps"—the future is imagined as characterized by certainty, uniformity, and predictability. The passage seeks, in other words, to reassure readers that the world to come will be secure and legible, a message that is mirrored in the activity of pledging itself. Although rote repetition could seem problematic, Bellamy nonetheless associates the pledge with thought and reflection. This is a way, he maintains, to demonstrate a rational attachment to the nation. If we recall that the pledge was inspired by the Civil War, however, the emphatic certainty of the above passage takes on a new kind of meaning, evoking the anxieties associated with testing and securing allegiance, especially through loyalty oaths. In the late nineteenth century, such concerns may have been comparatively "benign," but no such comfort was associated with the loyalty oaths that provided an important historical antecedent for the Pledge of Allegiance.

Test oaths played an important role during the Civil War. They were used to police Union allegiance by "compel[ling] citizens to affirm supreme loyalty to the national Constitution as opposed to the states" and, later, to determine if Confederates could be readmitted to the nation as citizens.[25] During and after the war, oaths were crucial to the reconstruction of the Southern states, and, as a result, they haunted the national psyche, particularly in the South, decades after they were withdrawn, their constitutionality challenged. A potent example of their lingering importance is evident in Margaret Mitchell's *Gone with the Wind* (1936). In the 1939 film version, Scarlett O'Hara's father falls to his death in a riding accident: in the novel, however, he is killed by the Ironclad Test Oath, an oath introduced during the Civil War and deployed, to Southern horror, in its aftermath as a means of establishing the juror's absolute—past, present, and future—loyalty. Describing the events surrounding Gerald O'Hara's death to Scarlett, Will Vereen says,

> "I took [Suellen] to Jonesboro [and] she run into Mrs. MacIntosh ... [who] gave herself a lot of airs and said as how her husband had put in a claim with the Federal government for destroyin' the property of a loyal Union sympathizer who had never given aid and comfort to the Confederacy in any shape or form.... Anyway, the government gave them, well—I forget how many thousand dollars.... That started Suellen. She thought about it all week and ... that damned white trash, Hilton, gave her a passel of new ideas. He pointed out that your pa warn't even born in this country, that he hadn't fought in the war and hadn't had no sons to fight, and hadn't held no office under the Confederacy. He said they could strain a point about Mr. O'Hara bein' a loyal Union sympathizer. He filled her up with such truck and she come home and begun workin' on Mr. O'Hara. Scarlett, I bet my life your pa didn't even know half the time what she was talkin' about. That was what she was countin' on, that he would take the Iron Clad oath and not even know it."

But Suellen miscalculates: Gerald O'Hara recognizes the oath and refuses to swear, even after his daughter plies him with whiskey. His broken neck is thus the direct result of an attempt to have him swear a false oath. Even as she mourns her father's death, Scarlett admits to herself that "she couldn't blame Suellen," for the $150,000 bounty overwhelms her "horror" at the idea of her father's pretending to be loyal to the Union: "What a lot of money that was! And to be had for the mere signing of an oath of allegiance to the United States government, an oath stating that the signer had always supported the government and never given aid and comfort to its enemies. One hundred and fifty thousand dollars! That much money for that small a lie!"[26] The issue motivating Scarlett's reflection—the relationship between sincerity, veracity, and oaths of allegiance—is at the core of much Civil War–era writing about loyalty and the nation, although too often it has been edited out of accounts of that era in a manner that replicates the choices made in adapting *Gone with the Wind* to the screen. Political oaths are introduced during the Civil War as a mechanism for policing individual allegiance to the nation and patrolling its internal borders; as the century progresses, they continue to be used to establish bonds of allegiance.[27]

In turning critical attention to political oaths, my work corrects this oversight, while complementing recent studies on the role of promises in literature, indicating an additional way in which we might explore how words are used to create obligations and responsibilities between people. As a poem written for the 1876 Philadelphia Centennial Exposition indicates, verbal pledges—oaths and promises—create affiliations not just between people but also across time:

> Come back across the bridge of time
> And swear an oath that holds you fast,
> To make the future as sublime,
> As is the memory of the past![28]

For literary texts, in other words, an emphasis on the promise has more than thematic implications because promises enact with them a particular temporality. Note, for example, that Bellamy's "The Meaning of the Four Centuries" ends in a hopeful pledge "that the flag shall not be stained; and that America shall mean equal opportunity and justice for every citizen, and brotherhood for the world."[29] The excess of the students' doubled pledging—first in the Pledge of Allegiance and then again in the address—captures the instability often associated with pledging, especially in the wake of the Civil War.[30] Formally, this anxiety is manifested through repetition, as in the remarriages that lead to the "new birth of freedom" explored in chapter 2 or the return to (and revision of) antebellum figures examined in chapter 4.[31]

There is, however, an even more basic way that repetition is introduced by promises and oaths, namely through the understanding of time they enact. In *Arranging Grief*, Dana Luciano carefully explains how texts dealing with mourning and grief "*make time appear*"; promissory obligations strive to do the opposite—to make time disappear.[32] The promise's future is shaped by structures of intention and desire as past, present, and future are correlated, with an associated diminution of the always precarious distinction between fact and fiction, history and fantasy. Rather than questions of accuracy or verisimilitude, oaths or promises give voice to concerns about the importance of the future to the past, diminishing distinctions between history and fantasy while establishing obligations between people across time and space.

The frequency with which promises and oaths appear in postbellum narrative, particularly relative to the construction of consent, suggests that thinking through the basis of affiliation or allegiance, and of the moral issues associated with them, was at the core of the process of reconstruction, especially in those instances when authors were less than sanguine about the kind of nation created through the violence of the Civil War. A focus on loyalty, and the promises or oaths used to secure it, reveals, finally, an important structuring principle for postbellum fiction. As George Fletcher explains in *Loyalty: An Essay on the Morality of Relationships*, there is a particular "matrix" to the narrative representation of dilemmas associated with loyalty:

> There are always three parties, A, B, and C, in a matrix of loyalty. A can be loyal to B only if there is a third party C (another lover, an enemy nation, a hostile company) who stands as a potential competitor to B, the object of loyalty. The competitor is always lurking in the wings, rejected for the time being, but always tempting, always seductive. The foundational element in loyalty is the fact not present—the counterfactual conditional statement that if the competitor appears and beckons, the loyal will refuse to follow.[33]

Fletcher's explanation of the narrative structure associated with loyalty anticipates two important concerns for this study: first, the ways in which desire, fantasy, and fear—various "fact[s] not present"—become determinative for narratives of loyalty; and, second, why narratives in which allegiance is a central concern turn to the structure of promissory obligations to control the anxieties they necessarily create.[34]

Not only does this study expand our appreciation of the kind of work promissory structures can do in literary texts, it also complicates our understanding of their legal correlate, the contract. So important was the contract to Gilded Age economic, legal, political, and even social arrangements that scholars have dubbed these years the "Age of Contract."[35] For this aspect of my argument, two studies have been critical. Brook Thomas and Gregg Crane have convincingly established that the contract is equally important to postbellum narrative, influencing the works of preeminent realists like Mark Twain, William Dean Howells, and Henry James. Working within the larger "framework of contractarian thought," Thomas argues that postwar realism enacts the promise, fragile and often illusory, inherent in "contractarian thought" to depict the world as accurately as possible. Whereas Thomas's study focuses specifically on the postwar period, Crane's reading of contract is related to his analysis of higher law argument and the moral consensus it could mobilize, revealing how contract could be used "broadly as a means of and trope for human relations."[36] "Like any tool, contract, of itself, does nothing," he notes, "it is a language of intent (promises, statements of capability and agency, actions and words betokening assent) that may be used by powerful parties to expand their fortunes at the expense of the weaker parties or may be used between equals to structure their relations as equitably as they deem possible."[37] Yet while contracts bind people legally in relations of exchange, promises and oaths create structures that are less balanced and that do not necessarily assume reciprocal obligations, a point that is crucial to the kinds of dilemmas that emerge in the wake of the Civil War.

Even as I register the distinction between the promise and the contract, though, it is important to note that some postbellum Americans saw them as connected. Theodore Woolsey, for example, held that the predominance of the contract reflected its association with issues of morality. "A contract," he writes in *Political Science* (1878),

> is a transaction in which at least two persons, or parties, acting freely, give to one another rights and impose on one another obligations which relate wholly or partly to some performance in the future. . . . Contract thus derives much of its importance from the connection between present and future time. Man is no longer a creature of the present, but draws his motives from, and affects his desires by that part of life which is yet to come. He brings considerations from the future into the present, and thus brings permanent purpose, foresight, control over present impulse, into his character.

These "social transaction[s]" are essential, on Woolsey's view, to the development of "human society," and the obligations they create thus cannot be justified by reference to free will alone. It is not that free will is unimportant, but it cannot establish a "moral foundation" commensurate with contract's importance to "human intercourse." "That moral foundation," Woolsey argues, "is the sacredness of truth and the necessity of trust for all virtues that look heavenward, or towards men who could have no fellowship with one another if separated by distrust, but would be suspicious and suspecting, hateful and hating one another. If the expression may be allowed, a man by an engagement to another creates truth and can never rightly create a lie in his mind. Truth and trust are the props without which 'the pillared firmament is rottenness and earth's base built on stubble.'" Returning to the temporal dimensions of contracts, Woolsey reiterates the intimate relationship between "universal morality," "the sacredness of truth," and the contract that "unites present and future" and provides "a source of union among men." Promises, and other "*quasi contracts*," may lack the "formal" structure of contracts proper, he concludes, but are no less binding.[38]

On Woolsey's view, the contract is as important to the ethical life of a society, dependent upon standards of truth and trust, as it is to that society's legal system. Writing in 1897, Oliver Wendell Holmes Jr. takes a position directly opposed to Woolsey. It is a mistake, Holmes forcefully contended, to "confound morality with law." "Morals," he argues, "deal with the actual internal state of the individual's mind, what he actually intends," whereas intention is relatively unimportant in evaluating the legality of a contract.[39] "Holmes sought to keep ethics and law—as well as promises and contracts—separate," Melissa Ganz usefully notes.[40] Holmes's objections to confounding contracts with issues of morality may make sense for legal professionals, but they fail to address the ways in which promises, pledges, and oaths—all *"quasi contracts"*—function in fictional narratives, particularly given the ways in which these works construct the importance of intent.

* * *

The book pursues its argument along three methodological tracks. My study relies substantially on primary sources to establish how loyalty was defined, disseminated, and resisted during the Civil War and Reconstruction; philosophical analyses of promises and oaths to evaluate the ways in which they influenced the nation's reconstruction as a community; and literary texts to trace how these ideas were disseminated and contested. In seeking to understand how Northerners and other Union partisans understood their relationship to the United States, it builds from, and contributes to, historical analysis of the period, but the addition of a philosophical perspective enables a more critical appreciation of the problems facing nineteenth-century Americans, as well as the solutions they devised to them. Most important, however, this is a book of literary analysis, and throughout I seek not only to juxtapose historical, philosophical, and literary arguments but to show how philosophical analysis can complement and complicate our interpretation of various cultural moments and the aims of U.S. literature in the decades after the Civil War.

Yet individual chapters vary in the extent to which they prioritize history, philosophy, and literature. Whereas the first chapter moves through a significant amount of material to establish the wide use of loyalty in rendering Union allegiance both specific and precise, the third lingers with a single novel—Henry James's *The Bostonians* (1886)—to capture the philosophical richness of James's reading of the Civil War's legacy. In each instance, I have selected materials and texts to dramatize the breadth of thinking about loyalty, as well as to show how this concept altered understandings of allegiance, morality, race, and, more generally, the role of abstraction in American culture. Shifting modes of analysis allow the strengths of the disparate disciplines, which proceed differently despite a shared reliance on narrative, to emerge more robustly. At the same time, however, the book is grounded methodologically in the practice, and even promise, of close reading, seemingly necessary to a study that investigates competing assessments of the power of words to wound or mend individuals, to protect or destabilize nations.

One thing this book does not do, however, is provide an explicit paradigm for reinterpreting realism. This is, in part, a necessary result of an argument that suggests the importance of relations of similitude and repetition across time, structures that diminish the difference often associated with narrative genres. To the extent that the book is invested in interrogating generic claims, its focus would fall on sentimentality, particularly the ways in which it is reconstructed during and after the Civil War to accommodate both changing conditions and the desire for sameness. I must thus register my dissent from Brook Thomas's claim that paying attention to structures associated with contract allows us to differentiate clearly between sentimental and realist fiction. Arguing that an emphasis on a transcendental or vertical organizing principle is a hallmark of sentimental narrative, Thomas contends that an investment in contract reveals a repudiation of this principle as lives are assumed to be organized horizontally, represented through exchange or negotiation.[41] Once we recognize the structural importance of loyalty in determining relations between people during and after the Civil War, however, particularly loyalty's celebration of an abstract "organizing principle," the opposition for which Thomas argues dematerializes.

In the first chapter, I locate the concept of loyalty in the Civil War era, while showing how it resuscitated and reinterpreted republican ideals of duty, responsibility, and rationality and therefore addressed both political and moral concerns. Perhaps most important, loyalty facilitated a stark contrast with a Confederacy that could thus be discounted as emotional, irrational, and illegal. According to James Russell Lowell's pithy definition, loyalty had "its seat in the brain and not the blood."[42] His emphasis on the brain, and with it a sense that reason—not instinct—should provide the basis for affiliation, shifts assumptions about the body in ways that, at their best, provide the conditions of possibility for overcoming and resisting abjected forms of embodiment. Nathaniel Hawthorne's "Chiefly About War-Matters"(1862), Edward Everett Hale's "The Man without a Country" (1863), and Louisa May Alcott's "Love and Loyalty" (1864) anchor the chapter, which ranges widely to capture the extent of loyalty's reach and the complex moral and political issues it was used to resolve. The chapter brings together literary analysis, historical materials on loyalty oaths, and philosophical interrogation of the anxieties about certainty, context, temporality, and race such oaths provoked.

Union partisans held that loyalty would subordinate the heart to the head, disciplining both wayward emotions and rebellious citizens. Nonetheless, the most popular postbellum narrative mode for imagining a "re-United States" was the romance of reunion, a genre that posited the resolution of sectional antagonism through right feeling. In the second chapter, I look at two early examples of the genre—John W. De Forest's *Miss Ravenel's Conversion from Secession to Loyalty* (1867) and Elizabeth Stuart Phelps's *The Gates Ajar* (1868)—and demonstrate how this narrative goal was accomplished without abandoning the principles of loyalty outlined in the first chapter. Both authors, I explain, argue for a model of consent that can only be fully realized through the benign coercion of an authoritative guide. Adopting a position that is closer to Thomas Hobbes than John Locke, De Forest and Phelps alike contend that without careful supervision, individuals cannot be sure to act so as to secure either their own happiness or the safety of the nation. In *Miss Ravenel's Conversion*, it is the professional man who is most likely to create the conditions of possibility for democracy; Phelps locates this oversight in a vision of a domesticated heaven ruled by a caring god. The loving and inclusive families they depict are created through remarriage, potently underscoring the importance of self-discipline and calamity in the eventual creation of a "more perfection union."

While reunion romances rely on an analogy between marital and political unions, *The Bostonians* predicts that both will be "far from brilliant" thanks to the replacement of consent with coercion. In place of the balanced exchange of promises and pledges that mark the return of sectional peace in the romance of reunion, Henry James suggests that a different story of conflict resolution—the captivity narrative—better depicts the war's legacy in American culture. Diverging from many of his contemporaries, James expresses concern about the power of abstraction to breed fanaticism and fantasies of absolute allegiance, as well as the tendency of sympathy to confound an individual's beliefs and feelings. Completing James's consideration of the Civil War's aftermath is a penetrating analysis of the power of language, particularly its focus on pledges and oaths. Critics have carefully detailed the importance of the novel's thematic engagement with public speech; this chapter builds on that work, while arguing that it has nonetheless obscured the novel's basic engagement with questions concerning the nature of speech itself, particularly commissive speech acts.

The first three chapters trace loyalty from its origins in the Civil War, through its early implementation during Reconstruction, to the thorough critique of its precepts in *The Bostonians*. The fourth and fifth chapters shift the book's trajectory, exploring a different dimension of loyal ideology and loyalty, more broadly understood. In the popular postbellum trope of the loyal slave, the bleak captivity depicted at the end of *The Bostonians* acquires a nostalgic veneer. Turning first to plantation narratives and then to African American rebuttals of their sentimental representations of slavery, I demonstrate how the trope was deployed to alleviate concerns that loyalty might impoverish the individual will. Writers of the plantation school argued simultaneously for a return to an affect-based social organization and a notion of loyalty that protected white Americans from the implication that the individual's submission to the nation was a form of slavery. African Americans responded by detailing the complexities arising from competing claims of allegiance, like loyalty to the nation and loyalty to the race. Using Charles Chesnutt's "The Wife of His Youth" (1898) and Paul Dunbar's "Nelse Hatton's Vengeance" (1898), I chart the articulation of a loyal counternarrative that stresses choice and reason as fundamental qualities of American citizenship and offers African American loyalty as its exemplar.

Josiah Royce and W. E. B. Du Bois likewise investigate the linked issues of loyalty, race, and violence in their writings, arguing powerfully for a flexible yet committed understanding of moral abstractions. The different means they use to forward their claims—Royce in lectures of popular philosophy and in scholarly treatises and Du Bois in a biography of John Brown—reflect their diverse conclusions about the role of particular details—facts, bodies, narratives—in the development of abstract thought. The legacy of the Civil War may seem more explicit in Du Bois's biography, but both thinkers are engaged in the philosophical reconstruction of individual and national values. Their arguments for the positive interventions made possible by abstract categories and concepts not only update the Civil War ideal of loyalty but, more broadly, suggest new ways of thinking about how we negotiate the competing, but not contradictory, claims of emotion and reason, particulars and abstractions.

The motivating question for *Loyal Subjects* is a simple one: when one nation becomes two, or when two nations become one, what does national affiliation mean or require? The answers to this question open up a range of complex issues in nineteenth-century U.S. literature and culture. It might be fairer to say, in fact, that the answers themselves are more questions: What are our responsibilities to one another, and how should we act upon them? How do promises about the future determine the shape of the past? What are the conditions of possibility for freedom, consent, and personal expression? How does the interplay between memory and history limit or enable these possibilities? Seeking for answers to these enduring queries inspires the works examined in *Loyal Subjects*, even if the answers they posit are provisional and partial.

1 / Loyalty, Oaths, and the Nation

When he signs the contract with Captains Bildad and Peleg, Ishmael consents to join the *Pequod*'s crew, assuming a share of the responsibilities and earning a percentage of the profits. Through this scene, and its protracted haggling over what Ishmael will earn on the voyage, Herman Melville provides the reader of *Moby-Dick* (1851) with an example of consent characterized by choice and reflection. It is not long, however, before a second model of consent supplants the first. After the *Pequod* has set sail, Captain Ahab demands the crew agree to a new mission—the quest to destroy the white whale. Gone in this second scene is any ability to withhold consent, as well as the sense that deliberation or reflection is part of the crew's acceptance of their revised charge. Instead, Ishmael indicates an overpowering "feeling" guides his actions:

> I, Ishmael, was one of that crew; my shouts had gone up with the rest; my oath had been welded with theirs; and stronger I shouted, and more did I hammer and clinch my oath, because of the dread in my soul. A wild, sympathetical feeling was in me; Ahab's quenchless feud seemed mine. With greedy ears I learned the history of the murderous monster against whom I and all the others had taken our oaths of violence and revenge.[1]

Rather than the act of individual choice, Ishmael's "oath" results from a "wild, sympathetical feeling" that weakens his sense of self as he becomes "welded" to a "feud" that seems to be his own. Later in the novel, Starbuck recalls this moment, concluding that, on Ahab's view, because "the men have vow'd [the] vow," we are "all of us are Ahabs" (587). While one can wonder with Ishmael "what evil magic" allows Ahab to possess "their souls," the oath they swear refounds the *Pequod*'s community, replacing its commercial voyage with a search for revenge, individual sailors with a crew of Ahabs (154).[2] With one exception: from a secluded corner of the ship, Pip observes, "there they go, all cursing, and here I don't" (151). Pip is not the only black shipmate on the *Pequod*, but his explicit nonparticipation establishes race as pertinent to the novel's representation of consent, allegiance, and oaths.

When the *Pequod* sinks in the novel's closing pages, one might want to surmise that Melville's point is that only contracts openly and freely negotiated can float a ship of state, yet the novel resists that interpretation, desirable though it might be.[3] Far from a rational decision, Ishmael's determination to go whaling is motivated by an "everlasting itch for things remote" (22). Indeed, the novel's opening chapters are relentless in their discussion of Ishmael's disordered feelings, as they establish that his choice to go to sea depends as much on this nearly instinctive "itch" as on a calm or rational state of mind. Notably, even his selection of the *Pequod* is the work of a mere moment. That is to say, although the shipboard scene may *seem* more coercive, closer inspection reveals the novel's commitment to a more complicated position, specifically that consent, no matter how configured, is never wholly free, that it is always saturated with, even undermined by, affect. The therapeutic benefits Ishmael derives from his sympathetic bond with Queequeg must be juxtaposed, in other words, with Ahab's manipulation of sympathy to accomplish totalitarian ends.[4] Although the novel antedates the events that drove the sections, already alienated and tense, into war, as Starbuck contemplates armed rebellion or Ishmael reflects on the nature of the oath he has sworn, Melville captures the chaos at the core of Civil War era–politics, the obligations of American citizenship, and the states (or acts) of feeling that created and maintained them both.[5]

Anatomizing what it means to give one's consent—to sign or swear—Melville joins a long line of thinkers who have associated the very possibility of political organization with the ability to explain, argue, and promise. Since Aristotle's definition of humans as the "political animal" with the unique capacity to speak, philosophers, politicians, and writers have regularly identified language as "the great instrument and common tie of society."[6] According to Locke, although not all should be seen as creating a "Body Politick," the agreement to "make themselves Members of some Politick Society" "by their own Consents" constitutes the "Promises and Compacts," as "Promises and Compacts" are crucial to this incorporation.[7] These verbal contracts "defend the community against excessive individualism," providing the conditions of possibility for "civil society."[8] The framers of the U.S. Constitution clearly agreed, carefully specifying the oath required of the president and detailing which legislators and jurists would likewise be required to pledge their allegiance. In the wake of the Civil War, the Fourteenth Amendment once again returned to the problem, establishing the preeminence of national oaths.[9]

It is the fact that promises and oaths correlate the individual's relationship between past, present, and future that makes them so crucial in the political and the ethical realms. Dependent on the regularization of human interaction, both are rooted in the human capacity to speak, to remember, to reason, and to make verbal contracts, processes that all presuppose a measured temporality. As Friedrich Nietzsche explains:

> In order to have this kind of command over the future in advance, man must first have learned to separate the necessary from the accidental occurrence, to think causally, to see and anticipate what is distant as if it were present, to fix with certainty what is end, what is means thereto, in general to be able to reckon, to calculate,—for this man himself must first of all have become *calculable, regular, necessary*, in his own image of himself as well, in order to be able to vouch for himself *as future*, as one who promises does!

The ability to impress one's will on the future and the possibility to remember the past are both elements of the promise or the contract, which Nietzsche carefully notes is easily ruptured by violence: "Whoever can give orders, whoever is 'lord' by nature, whoever steps forth violently, in deed and gesture—what does he have to do with contracts!"[10] Melville shares this insight as *Moby-Dick* shows that "step[ping] forth violently" ultimately sinks the ship of state. Indeed, whereas Publius insists in *Federalist* XXII that "THE CONSENT OF THE PEOPLE" is the "pure, original, fountain of all legitimate authority," Melville proposes instead that consent is fragile and open to easy coercion; that violence and command muddy the "pure" "fountain" of the political; that "legitimate authority" is often indistinguishable from illegitimate authority; and that consensual bonds are as often the result of impulsive emotion as careful reflection.[11]

Melville's depictions of consent raise important questions about the role emotions can and should play in the formation of (political) communities. According to Locke's well-known and influential premise, people "joyn and unite into a Community" so they can experience "a secure Enjoyment of their Properties, and a greater Security against any that are not of it."[12] Drawing out the implications of Locke's position, Elaine Scarry asserts that "the fundamental logic of th[e] consensual act" is emotionally laden, for, from its early articulations, it stresses "the protection of persons, the prevention of injury."[13] The feelings that motivate consent—fear about security and anxiety over the future—may differ in degree from the "dread" that accompanies Ishmael's act of joining Ahab's community, but they do not differ in kind. Not only is the political community partially constituted through emotion, one of its first tasks is instituting means of policing the "passionate heats" that constitute the "State of Nature."[14] To what extent do strong emotions like fear, anxiety, or dread impede the careful reflection that we associate with a legitimate example of consent? What objections—affective, rational, or both—should count as a withdrawal of consent? What does, or should, consent feel like? If affective states influence decisions about consent, when do these emotions render them suspect? What kind of affective affiliations are appropriate for peace and necessary for war?[15]

My purpose in this chapter is to examine how people understood and negotiated the complex relationship between consent, feeling, and allegiance during the Civil War era. For residents in both the U.S.A. and the C.S.A., the dilemmas Melville dramatizes in *Moby-Dick* were not just the stuff of fiction, and the responses they crafted to the above questions help us to grasp more fully how nineteenth-century Americans understood the comparative (and always changing) significance of reason and emotion, the power of language, and the morality of political belonging. In the pages that follow, I argue that the cultural value of emotion declined precipitously for Northerners during the Civil War, resulting in significant changes to the assumptions underwriting modes of affiliation. For a country that had long associated morality with sympathy for others, the realization that emotions could careen violently out of control was deeply disturbing. Consuming passions had overwhelmed staid senators, rendering the very house of government unsafe: how were similar feelings, equally out of control, to be contained in the population at large?

Long before Harriet Beecher Stowe penned *Uncle Tom's Cabin*, affective consent, which Jay Fliegelman defines as "the operations of sympathy, the faculty that put individuals beyond themselves and their own self-interest into the realm of mutuality of feelings," had been accepted as crucial to American understandings of political authority.[16] "In writings spanning nearly a hundred years," Elizabeth Barnes explains, "and including authors as diverse as Thomas Paine and Harriet Beecher Stowe, sympathy—expressed as emotional, psychological, or biological attachment—is represented as the basis of democracy, and therefore as fundamental to the creation of a distinctly 'American' character."[17] Central to political *and* moral relations, sympathy organized a wide range of interpersonal affiliations. The structural similitude thus engendered provides one explanation for the moral tumult I maintain results from the Civil War. Separate from any of the significant ethical problems raised by the devastating violence before, during, and after the conflict, the Civil War forced Americans on both sides of the Mason-Dixon Line to reevaluate their basic assumptions about what could or should unite a people and to reflect seriously on the relationship between morality and politics.

Nor was this an issue that could wait. With the outbreak of the Civil War, finding a different model of affiliation was imperative as sympathetic identification quickly transformed from a moral necessity to a national peril. The very quality that had led Senator Bird to feel Eliza's plight might now encourage Northern citizens to sympathize with Southern rebels. To the extent that sympathy provided "aid and comfort" to the South, it corresponded to the constitutional definition of treason.[18] While sympathy for the slaves had the potential to galvanize some segments of the Northern population eager to fight for the end of a national sin, racial prejudice was just as likely to harden resistance to the war, as the 1863 New York Draft Riots demonstrate. In this overwrought environment, it was no longer certain that emotions provided "the basis of democracy," and other qualities—reason and rationality—rapidly rose in political and moral value. On both sides of the Mason-Dixon Line, the very future of the nation seemed to depend on being able to cultivate and control proper political sentiments. As Anthony Smith reminds us, "No 'nation-to-be' can survive without a homeland or a mythos of common origins and descent," and a corollary to this claim might be that two nations cannot entirely share the *same* "mythos of common origins and descent."[19]

Paradoxically, this problem may have been even more pressing for the Union. In the North, navigating these competing conditions required the careful negotiation between two opposed positions: first, that the Confederates were the enemy and, as such, dangerously other; and, second, that the Confederates were U.S. citizens and consequently both familial and familiar. Whereas the Confederacy obviously needed to articulate a unique identity quickly, decades of smoldering resentment at perceived Northern domination helped to unite the South's diverse population long enough to bring the state into existence.[20] Laying claim to the authority conferred by the United States' revolutionary heritage, Southern politicians maintained that their rights had been suppressed in a manner reminiscent of George III, and, as a result, they were entirely justified in withdrawing from the nation. In his inaugural address to the Confederacy, Jefferson Davis asserted that the actions of the Southern states "illustrate[] the American idea that governments rest on the consent of the governed and that it is the right of the people to alter or abolish them at will whenever they become destructive of the ends for which they were established." Because the U.S. government had been "perverted" from these ends, Davis had no doubt about either "the rectitude" of Southern conduct or the eventual vindication of history.[21] John L. O'Sullivan, writing in the North, echoed this opinion in an 1863 pamphlet: denying to the South "the inherent right of any and every great mass of human population ... to choose and change at will its form of government" was fundamentally un-American, he claimed. Even if the North were to win the war, how could Northerners imagine that Southerners would consent, in any substantive sense, to rejoin the United States?[22] Historical precedent notwithstanding, Northerners espoused an interpretation of the founding contract that rejected the idea that it could be severed "at will" (or indeed at all).

But to establish the citizen's primary allegiance as national required the articulation of a more coherent model of national allegiance. Complicating the situation, the relationship of many Americans "to their national polity was characterized by distance and distrust," Melinda Lawson writes, which is why "the relationship of individual Americans to the national state would become one of the dominant themes of Civil War nation-building."[23] Whereas sympathy had provided antebellum Americans with a moral norm that also had political implications, Union partisans now claimed that loyalty—defined by James Russell Lowell as having "its seat in the brain and not the blood"—was the appropriate structure for organizing proper American allegiance. Loyalty had specific moral implications, most notably the ability to control the precariously indiscriminate emotionalism of sympathetic identification.[24] Not only did loyalty particularize Union allegiance for U.S. citizens, it also provided a way of differentiating between Union and Confederate affiliations, to which I turn in a moment. As I show in this chapter, loyalty provided a model for Union allegiance that prioritized the importance of abstract ideals—the moral force of right thinking—in the construction of national and personal bonds. Consistently opposed to sympathy's poor politics and local allegiances, loyalty encouraged a movement of both moral norms and political practices away from feeling by suggesting that rational reflection provided a more stable basis for national affiliation.

To appreciate how this new model of affiliation came to prominence in Northern discourse during the 1860s, and in national discourse in the following decades, it is necessary to consider the intertwined connotation of loyalty and sympathy during the Civil War. This chapter charts this movement in several ways. After establishing what Nathaniel Hawthorne describes as the "anomaly of allegiance" in the United States, its originary confusion, I show how sympathy's treasonous dimensions, exacerbated by its association with Confederate nationalism, changed its meaning and use for Union citizens. In its stead, Northerners lauded the virtue of loyalty, defined against a caricatured version of sympathy as arbitrary, contingent, and uncontrolled.

One of the basic assumptions of this book is the need to understand ideas and structures as operating within a dynamic conceptual context defined by neither simple dichotomies nor reified keywords. Put differently, even as I trace the ways in which loyalty organized Union allegiance, it is imperative to note that assertions about consensus were often mere words; there had been much uncertainty about the meaning of the Union before the conflict began, and the outbreak of open conflict definitely did not silence all opposition. In the arguments for, and the fictions of, consensus, one sees the attempts to create its unanimity and to establish its certainty. The chapter begins with sympathy for two reasons: it is the more familiar of the two concepts, and, more important, loyalty's definition arises as an alternative to the established principles associated with sympathy's use in American culture.

There is a second component to this chapter's discussion of Union loyalty during the Civil War. Union partisans paired the definition of loyalty's content with an articulation of its proper performance. While there were many potential ways of demonstrating one's allegiance, the chapter focuses on the loyalty oath, identified in the period (as at other times) as a seemingly powerful means of generating the security necessary to create, defend, and perpetuate a community. As Sanford Levinson observes, "Oaths are mixtures of pure form and substantive content."[25] A political version of the promise, the loyalty oath formalizes the bond of allegiance, ratifying the idea that language was fundamental to the maintenance of a successful state and mediating between individual and communal commitment. To use Hannah Arendt's formulation, the assumption subtending the loyalty oath is that politics originates with "the faculty" to make promises and "to keep [them] in the face of the essential uncertainties of the future."[26] The "image of voluntary oath-taking (or -giving) at some level captures what we might mean by a government predicated on the 'consent' of the governed," Levinson notes. "After all, how better to test the presence of consent than by seeking evidence of an overt oath manifesting it?"[27]

Yet as *Moby-Dick* illustrates, and as wartime writers soon concluded, the oath's ability to measure allegiance is far from an infallible measure. The ease with which a person can be led to break an oath, swayed by events or feelings, reveals its instability, the ease with which political consent can be compromised or coerced. An oath provides a means of ritually performing allegiance, but its larger purpose—calming worries about allegiance and trust—is often left unfulfilled because without a preexisting condition of security it is difficult to trust a promise. Promissory structures negotiate, as Arendt indicates, between present and future, between the time of the promise and its fulfillment. Rather than calming anxiety, fraught by its own temporality problems, promises and oaths often exacerbate the very conditions they are introduced to manage.[28] Nonetheless, the promissory mode enables the imagined continuation of a nation in pieces, structured around an ideal of loyalty.

* * *

"We are so young a people," George T. Strong mused privately in 1854, "that we feel the want of nationality, and delight in whatever asserts our 'national' existence. We have not, like England or France, centuries of achievements or calamities to look back on; we have no 'record' of Americanism and we feel its want."[29] The beginning of hostilities—and the need to articulate not just one national existence but two—doubled this "want."[30] Yet as Nathaniel Hawthorne's "Chiefly About War-Matters" makes clear, fulfilling these various needs was complicated by what he calls the "anomaly of two allegiances"—to one's home state and to the nation as a whole.[31] The political problem of differentiating two national identities and the military necessity of being able to accurately distinguish friend from foe generated situations that, Hawthorne explains, were full of unanticipated, and thoroughly deplorable, consequences. "There never existed any other Government against which treason was so easy, and could defend itself by such plausible arguments as that of the United States," he observes (48). As if to demonstrate the ease with which allegiance could be complicated, Hawthorne published the essay under a pseudonym—"A Peaceable Man"—and wrote a series of footnotes in a second voice—an anonymous editor—criticizing the contents of the essay.[32] Although Hawthorne's own political priorities can be determined from his previous work, the reader of "Chiefly About War-Matters" is left uncertain about how to adjudicate between the opposing positions, the very problem the essay identifies as key.

Visiting Washington, the Peaceable Man finds himself wondering repeatedly "what proportion" of the people he encountered, "whether soldiers or civilians, were true at heart to the Union, and what part were tainted, more or less, with treasonable sympathies, even if such had never blossomed into purpose" (61). While Northern readers might be inclined to assume that all Southern partisans are traitors, the Peaceable Man offers an alternate interpretation of the situation, including the suggestion that time and circumstance may have *involuntarily* "converted" "honest people" by into "traitors":

> In the vast extent of our country,—too vast by far to be taken into one small human heart,—we inevitably limit to our own State, or, at farthest, to our own section, that sentiment of physical love for the soil which renders an Englishman, for example, so intensely sensitive to the dignity and well-being of his little island, that one hostile foot, treading anywhere upon it, would make a bruise on each individual breast. If a man loves his own State, therefore, and is content to be ruined with her, let us shoot him, if we can, but allow him an honorable burial in the soil he fights for. (48–49)

It is the special problem of the United States, in other words, that we expect a person to have allegiance to a state, which "comes nearest home to a man's feelings, and includes the altar and the heart," and a national government, which "claims his devotion only to an airy mode of law, and has no symbol but a flag." The situation that ensues is "exceedingly mischievous" because "it has converted crowds of honest people into traitors, who seem to themselves not merely innocent, but patriotic, and who die for a bad cause with as quiet a conscience as if it were the best" (48–49). In a contest between domestic sentiments (those that are "nearest home") and abstract loyalties ("too vast by far to be taken into one small human heart"), the disparity of scale explains any seemingly treasonous choice, Hawthorne suggests. The limits of the heart, the "sentiment of physical love" for the familiar, and the ease with which local causes can come to seem not just good but "patriotic" combine to create a state of mischief in which it may be *right* to wage war but it is also *moral* to honor the feelings that led to that war. "It is a strange thing in human life, that the greatest errors both of men and women often spring from their sweetest and most generous qualities," Hawthorne writes, "and so, undoubtedly, thousands of warm-hearted, sympathetic, and impulsive persons have joined the Rebels, not from any real zeal for the cause, but because, between two conflicting loyalties, they chose that which necessarily lay nearest the heart" (48). While one can say that Southerners "chose," Hawthorne persists in his distinction between a choice that it is independent, based on ideas or "real zeal," and one that is coerced ("necessarily") by their "sweetest and most generous qualities."

How, he continues, will such a situation end? "We woo the South 'as the Lion wooes his bride,'" he observes, and hope that "love and a quiet household may come of it at last" (even if the "courtship" is "rough"). If the North were to abandon the idea of reunification, to "stop short of that blessed consummation," Hawthorne notes with reference to Milton, "heaven was heaven still." "After Lucifer and a third part of the angels had seceded from its golden palaces," heaven was "perhaps all the more heavenly, because so many gloomy brows, and soured, vindictive hearts, had gone to plot ineffectual schemes of mischief elsewhere" (61).[33] Reinforced by layers of literary antecedents, Hawthorne concludes the essay by quietly pointing to the tragic dimensions of the standard Union position that reunification was the war's most desirable outcome. Relying on the marital analogy regularly deployed in discussions of the national compact (to which I turn in chapter 2), and identifying the conversion war can enact on the individual heart (from "warm" to "soured"), Hawthorne suggests that the war has turned the country into a state of nature, where consent has been subordinated to force. Is it reasonable, he asks, to assume that this will yield "a quiet household"? Why not make, instead, the "heavenly" compromise and let the "soured, vindicated hearts" go "elsewhere"?

These are the conclusions the Peaceable Man draws from the "anomaly" of American allegiance, but they are not the final words on the subject in "Chiefly About War-Matters." From the footnotes, the "editor" scolds the Peaceable Man for lacking proper "*reverence*" for Lincoln, deploring his "abominable sentiment[s]," "reprehensible" tone, and "impolitic" tendency (47, 54, 49), and correcting the essay by offering an alternate conclusion:[34]

We regret the innuendo in the concluding sentence. The war can never be allowed to terminate, except in the complete triumph of Northern principles.... We should be sorry to cast a doubt on the Peaceable Man's loyalty, but he will allow us to say that we consider him premature in his kindly feelings towards traitors and sympathizers with treason. As the author himself says of John Brown, (and, so applied, we thought it an atrociously cold-blooded *dictum*,) "any common-sensible man would feel an intellectual satisfaction in seeing them hanged, were it only for their preposterous miscalculation of possibilities." There are some degrees of absurdity that put Reason herself into a rage, and affects us like an intolerable crime,—which this Rebellion is, into the bargain. (61)

The imaginary editor pretends to be "sorry" to "doubt" the Peaceable Man's loyalty, maintaining that the author's "kindly feelings"—his sympathies—have led him astray intellectually and politically, the same judgment the Peaceable Man makes about Southern partisans. Here, however, "kindly feelings" are a "crime" that enrages "Reason," reenacting the affect of the rebellion, also a crime. What is entirely clear by the end of "Chiefly About War-Matters" is that Northern opinion makes no allowances for "kindly feelings," which are entirely "intolerable."

As the Peaceable Man indicates, Confederates were seen by their Northern opponents as valuing the allegiance "nearest [to] the heart." Nor was this just perception, as Southern nationalists defined the relationship between citizen and nation as rooted in, even dependent on, a domestic ideal: the homeland Dixie.[35] According to New Orleans minister Benjamin Palmer, the Confederate "country" means

> our homes and the cheerful firesides, and the prattling babes that gather round the paternal knee; it means sweet neighborhood and friendship, and the tender charities which solace life from the cradle to the tomb; it means the memories of our youth as they grow fresh again in the twilight of age; it means ancestry and the proud recollection of honored sires, who bequeathed their blessing with the names we inherit; it means our altars and sanctuaries where we have worshipped God and held communion with his saints on earth; it means the graves where our loved ones are lying, consecrated by the tears of a bitter parting when they were laid out of sight forever; it means all that the human heart can remember and love; all the associations which spread their secret network over human life; all the scattered leaves on which are written the sorrows and the joys through which man travels onward to his rest above.[36]

FIGURE 1. Cartoon from *Harper's Weekly*, December 6, 1862. The caption reads "OLD MR. SECESH, from his Housetop in Richmond, Va., looking out for the *Sympathy promised by some supporters of* GOV. SEYMOUR." (Courtesy HarpWeek, LLC)

By associating Southern nationalism with "cheerful firesides" and the defense of "prattling babes," Southerners enacted the opposition so often deployed in sentimental novels between a debased commercial world beyond the home—the materialistic Yankee was an established figure in the Southern imagination before the war—and an idealized home space governed by the moral ties of sympathy. Despite his rejection of Adam Smith's political economy, George Fitzhugh's defense of slavery in *Cannibals All! or Slaves without Masters* (1857) had already depicted the entire South as a domestic space thanks to its peculiar distribution of power and rights. "It is delightful to retire," Fitzhugh explains, both in terms of his argument and his life, "from the outer world, with its competitions, rivalries, envyings, jealousies, and selfish war of the wits, to the bosom of the family, where the only tyrant is the infant—the greatest slave the master of the household. You feel at once that you have exchanged the keen air of selfishness, for the mild atmosphere of benevolence."[37]

Using sympathy to specify Confederate affiliation addressed one of the signal challenges facing the fledgling nation: instilling an attachment substantial enough to justify the kinds of sacrifices that would have to be undertaken for the new nation. Stressing home and hearth helped ensure that Southerners, like Robert E. Lee, honored local, over national, bonds.[38] Acknowledging his "devotion to the Union and the feeling of loyalty and duty of an American citizen," Lee nonetheless asserted, "I have not been able to make up my mind to raise my hand against my relatives, my children, my home."[39] "When a Southron's home is threatened," an Alabama lawyer wrote, "the spirit of resistance is irrepressible." "I would give all I have got just to be in the front rank of the first brigade that marches against the invading foe who now pollute the sacred soil of my native state with their unholy tread," another soldier observed.[40] The concrete and familiar symbols from which Southern nationalism was shaped spoke across state and class boundaries, while building from what has been argued was the "most salient quality of the Southern mind," "the primacy of the concrete over the abstract, of action over contemplation."[41] The further hope was that the Confederate celebration of local "sentiments" would prove "aggressive upon the mind" of recalcitrant Southern residents, sympathetic persons in the North, and foreign nations.[42] Adapting the abolitionist image of the kneeling slave, a Union cartoon from 1862 (fig. 1) satirically challenges the Southern reliance on sympathy, drawing subtle attention to the assumption of Anglo-Saxon racial superiority fundamental to Confederate nationalism. Providing a racialized rhetoric of affiliation that complemented the Confederacy's "cheerful firesides," Southern nationalism unabashedly argued that the homes and hearths of Southern national identity were defined by a clear racial hierarchy and sustained by bonds forged through intimate particularity and domestic sympathy.[43]

Even as Confederate propagandists deployed sympathy to define their national affiliation, Union partisans were asserting that sympathetic feelings for the rebels were dangerous and traitorous. Even though sympathy had been lauded in countless antebellum tracts, novels, and sermons, Northern partisans derided those identifying with the plight of the South as overly emotional, unbalanced, even hysterical. "Appeals that indicate sympathy, or almost friendship" are "profoundly" disgusting to the loyal person, Horace Bushnell writes nearly in the voice of Hawthorne's "editor," because "the instinct of a loyal heart is wonderfully singular."[44] General George Thomas is regularly "accused of treason," Adam Gurowski wrote, "undoubtedly" because he "vibrat[ed] between loyalty . . . and sympathy with [the] rebels."[45] Given its antebellum cultural value, this newly negative connotation presented a significant challenge to established moral norms.⁴⁶ Sympathy's danger derived directly from its former value—the ability to reveal the similitude between seemingly disparate persons and situations—now inappropriate politically and indicative of poor character. This new recognition of sympathy's *political* impact built from the realization that the identification fundamental to its operation not only replaced reason with emotion but also worked by overwhelming the individual and his or her established beliefs or values.⁴⁷

"An insanity now rules in one portion of our land," Henry Ward Beecher asserted in a sermon preached two weeks after South Carolina seceded from the nation. Elizabeth Keckley's repetition of Varina Davis's assertion—"The South is impulsive"—provided authoritative evidence from the First Lady of the Confederacy for an established Union belief.⁴⁸ "Many of us," an 1863 writer observed, "entertained the belief that the South would early return to reason and loyalty.... Experience soon banished this delusive hope."⁴⁹ For the main character in James K. Hosmer's *The Thinking Bayonet* (1865), realizing that his Southern friend had been touched by a "barbarian taint" that disrupted the possibility of virtue through "ruthless violence and untempered appetite" inspires the Northern youth to enlist in the Union army; his new comrades are "rough," but they nonetheless display "fine sense and admirable intelligence."⁵⁰ Beecher summarizes the position when he asserts the North was "the *brain* of this nation," "the thinking part of this country."⁵¹

As a corollary to the idea of the North as "the *brain*," some commentators made a virtue of what had been before the war a failing. With the luxury of hindsight, John Draper could comfortably note that, contrary to expectations, the "love of homestead" would never have sufficed for a strong national sentiment in the North:

> [Northern] children leave their father's hearth without reluctance, for he is perpetually anticipating leaving it himself. It might have been feared—perhaps was feared by many observant persons—that this loss of local patriotism would imply the loss of national sentiment, but the experience of the civil war has shown the incorrectness of such a foreboding. The history of the world can not furnish a more splendid example of unwavering fortitude, unshrinking self-sacrifice, in vindication of national life.⁵²

Far from weakening the North, Horace Bushnell argued that this loss of "local patriotism" freed citizens to establish the kinds of affective ties to the ideals and principles sufficient to sustain "unwavering fortitude" and "unshrinking self-sacrifice."

> A national feeling, too, was growing up, silently and imperceptibly to ourselves, and the state feeling was subsiding into a more nearly domestic of household sentiment. Both kinds of allegiance are dear to us, but the higher allegiance raises a higher devotion; even as the flag which represents it everywhere, in every sea and clime and field of common battle, becomes a symbol more significant and sacred than the flags of the states.[53]

Here, as in the Hawthorne essay, there are two kinds of allegiance and two related kinds of "feeling." Whereas Hawthorne sees an obvious conflict between them, however, Bushnell experiences no such doubt, easily identifying the "higher" allegiance. Despite the frequency with which sentimental conventions were invoked in popular narratives—young men dreaming of their mothers on the battlefield was an especially common revision of the sentimental emphasis on maternal bonds—Bushnell dismissed "household sentiment[s]," surpassed by the "higher devotion" represented "everywhere" by the flag. Similarly, the anonymous poet who penned "Our Country" reminded Union soldiers and sailors that national allegiance "Is more than Home or Hearth":

> No narrow State in this dread hour
>   Shall dare to claim your birth,
> Allegiance to the Federal power
>   Is more than Home or Hearth.
> This broad land, this whole land, this free land is
>   yours,—
> It is the noble Union your Loyalty secures![54]

* * *

Early volleys in the Civil War were fired over history, with both nations claiming the legacy of the founders to secure the justice of their divergent arguments.[55] Secessionists cited the colonial example to justify Southern withdrawal from a government they likened to England in its tyranny: the Revolution had established "Liberty and freedom in this western world," a Texas soldier noted, and the Confederacy was "now enlisted in 'The Holy Cause of Liberty and Independence' again."[56] "Do you believe George Washington, were he living, would now be able to live one day in the city of Charleston," Beecher countered, "if he uttered the sentiments that he used to hold? He would not. He would be denounced as a traitor, and swung up on the nearest lamp-post."[57] A rebel like George Washington would be, in this new war, loyal to the Union partisans like Beecher claimed. Yet to provide a model for national unity effective enough to motivate significant sacrifice, loyalty had to counter Southern claims to Revolutionary legitimacy and distinguish its tenets from the loyalists who clung to King George III in the eighteenth century.[58] Could loyalty be made consistent with *both* the ideals of the framers *and* the defense of the Union?

Complicating efforts to shake off negative revolutionary-era associations was the lingering sense that loyalty was fundamentally antithetical to democratic values. For example, in "Self-Reliance," Ralph Waldo Emerson had written that loyalty is a "hieroglyphic" that "only obscurely signified" the ways in which rights could be determined and discerned.[59] "A strictly old-world word," loyalty would seem to "suppos[e] . . . some kind of hereditary magistracy, such as belongs, in other nations, to royal and princely orders," Horace Bushnell acknowledged in his wartime essay "The Doctrine of Loyalty."[60] Given its heredity, how could loyalty provide the North with a model of appropriate national allegiance? Further, how could such a broad term be made specific enough to motivate action? Having surveyed the falling fortunes of sympathy, it is now possible to examine loyalty directly, particularly how loyalty was defined as opposed both to tyranny and to sympathy's affective ties.

In a July 4, 1861, lecture, Henry James Sr. introduced distinctions *in* loyalty that would prove increasingly critical over the next few years.[61] Except for those citizens "immersed in abject spread-eagleism," a phrase he repeats to characterize extreme national sentiment as pornographic, James maintains that national pride is rooted in the character of American institutions and citizens, rather than national reputation or the people holding political office. "Loyalty," he states, "is a strictly personal sentiment" and even in England had long since been supplanted by "patriotism, which is a much more rational sentiment."[62] Loyalty replaces devotion to ideals and principles with an attachment to individuals and leaders, mirroring the relationship between superstition and religion. "We are the descendants," he reminds his audience, "not of English loyalists by any means, but of English patriots exclusively," conveniently ignoring the fact that as many as 20 percent of the colonists would have preferred to retain the association with England.[63]

Despite this seeming denunciation of loyalty as personal and narrow,

James's oration takes a sudden turn when he asserts that the national allegiance evident in the United States is, in fact, a "glorified" and "regenerate" form of loyalty: "And this English patriotism, which was itself a regenerate loyalty, or a love of country purified of all personal allegiance, has itself become glorified in our veins into a still grander sentiment,—that is, from a love of country has become exalted into a love of humanity."[64] "Regenerate loyalty" resolves the overly personal limitations of *degenerate* loyalty, replacing love of an individual with love for humanity at large: it is this "still grander sentiment" that one finds in the United States. Or at least in the North, for in James's analysis, slavery, a "slimy purulent ooze," is "the king of all evil pent up in human nature," destroying proper national sentiment with its self-interested and hypocritical demands. The coming conflict, which would pit Northern "patriots" against Confederates tainted by monarchical ambitions, would liberate the nation from the tyranny of "adroit political knaves," allowing it to return to the ideals upon which "man's real peace, his true prosperity, and his abiding wealth reside."[65]

James's oration moves from rejecting loyalty as overly personal and appropriate to monarchy to embracing its "glorified" form as a sentiment stripped of its personal ties, attached to an ideal rather than a person. Motivated by something "grander" than self-interest, James's regenerate loyalty recognizes that "real peace" is found in the renunciation of particular desires or aims. Although the association of loyalty and monarchy persisted among segments of the Northern population, especially with persons associated with the Democratic Party,[66] the assertion of an anonymous *Harper's Weekly* contributor—that loyalty is "a purely impersonal emotion"—is typical of Northern assumptions:

> When Mr. Fernando Wood and Mr. G. Ticknor Curtis sneer at loyalty, as a word which has no meaning in a popular government, what do they mean? When they say or insinuate that it is an emotion known only in monarchies, they merely say what every experience of every moment contradicts.... The general British loyalty to the monarch, for instance, is like the Romish reverence for the Pope. The Briton knows nothing and cares nothing about the woman Victoria. It is the Queen who is the object of his loyalty; just as the Holy Father may be personally a scamp or a criminal; but the Pope must be infallible.[67]

Like James, the *Harper's Weekly* contributor explains that loyalty is wrongly understood when it is fixed on a single person; the proper object of loyalty is the "Nation" or "Government," substantial abstractions that compel respect because of the principles and values they represent:

> It is the national glory and grandeur—in one word, it is the Nation—which, in any civilized modern people, is the object of the emotion called loyalty. It is blended of pride and fidelity. And as in this country there is no separate and permanent representative of the nation, independent of the parties in the nation, the feeling attaches itself to the Government lawfully constituted and represented. He is a loyal man who stands by it, and votes and fights for it.[68]

Repeatedly, Northerners explained that loyalty prized national ideals over personal interests, the principles outlined by the framers rather than the aristocratic pretensions of Southern planters. (Cartoons representing the Confederacy as a monarchy, and Jefferson Davis as King Jeff, made sure this belief was widely disseminated.[69]) At the same time, Union partisans, like Samuel Osgood, stressed that loyalty, if it is "to amount to anything," "must be not merely a sentiment but a principle."[70] A reasonable sentiment, loyalty retained the affective dimension of allegiance but made its object an abstract ideal, not an individual person or specific (and local) place.

Although Hawthorne worried that loyalty's appeal was unrealistic, too dependent on "an airy mode of law" to compete with "the sentiment of physical love" for state or section, many in the North were adamant that abstract affiliations were better suited to the unique character of the United States—and that the flag was fully adequate to its representation.[71] Such claims build from Daniel Webster's stirring 1830 reply to Robert Hayne during the South Carolina nullification crisis:

> I hope that I may not see the flag of my Country, with its stars separated or obliterated, torn by commotion, smoking with the blood of civil war.... I hope I shall not see written, as its motto, *first* Liberty, and *then* Union. I hope I shall see no such delusion and deluded motto on the flag of that Country. I hope to see spread all over it, blazoned in the letters of light, and proudly floating over Land and Sea that other sentiment, dear to my heart, "Liberty *and* Union, now and forever, one and inseparable!"[72]

The feelings "dear" to Webster's "heart" are the abstractions of "Liberty *and* Union," making his position consistent with those articulated during the Civil War. "We have, as republicans,... our flag," a more apt symbol than an individual could ever prove to be, Bushnell claimed thirty years later, which

> represents everything, the nation itself, the history, the laws, the successes, the honors of the past, the promises of the great future un-

known, all that we have been, all that we can be. We make no idol of a poor rag in three colors, but we take it as the one all-sufficient symbol. No royal person could signify as much with as little confusion. Most royal persons have bad passions, weaknesses, meannesses, vices, that awfully mar the symbol-force of their persons; flags have none.[73]

Purified of dangerous and "bad passions," the "symbol-force" of the flag suffered from neither confusion nor contradiction. As Beecher enthused in 1861, "Our flag means... all that our fathers meant in the Revolutionary War; it means all that the Declaration of Independence meant; it means all that the Constitution of our people, organizing for justice, for liberty, and for happiness, meant. Our flag carries American ideas, American history, and American feelings."[74] As Beecher's verb tenses demonstrate, the flag's symbolic power could project past meaning into the present and the future, without the distorting impact of opinion or interpretation, condensing plurality into a simple, single object. A like logic is operative in Lincoln's 1863 address in Gettysburg, which Dana Luciano has shown equates "nationalist action" with the "process of becoming symbolic" because "it enables citizens to mimic the temporal transcendence of the symbol" and to rise "above particularities."[75] The "transcendence" Luciano identifies in Lincoln's speech is part of a larger narrative that sought to replace sentiments and interests, as defined by individuals, with supra-individual loyalties. That each citizen—man, woman, and child—could function as a symbol fused, finally, the representation of individual actions with these more abstract implications; even as celebrations of the flag were replaced by other kinds of narratives, the ideological implications remained constant.[76]

As the preceding paragraphs have made clear, loyalty was regularly defined as opposed to individual interests. Although some claimed it was a mistake to see loyalty as incompatible with an individual's self-interest, a position consistent with the classic tenets of liberalism, loyal ideology more usually drew on republican ideas that associated the possibility of freedom with restraint and self-control. Seeking to align loyalty with liberalism, then, some suggested that only a mistaken understanding of what constituted "interest" could lead to the assumption that there was an inherent conflict between the two; instead, loyalty could be said to serve one's *true* interests. The conflation of private with public aims was, in fact, central to loyalty's totalizing logic. "This is not wholly a world of eating and drinking, and dressing—of houses, and farms, and stocks—of peace, and plenty, and laughter and tears," Henry Bellows observed. "It is also a world of ideas and principles, of obligations and duties."[77] Believing that food and drink constituted self-interest, while "ideas and principles" did not, misconstrued what was, or should be, meant by the word. Because the nation would shelter and protect both the rights and the interests of its citizens, it was clearly *in* their interests to support the nation. Such claims about the basis of interest were far from new; throughout the 1850s a variety of authors extolled the virtues of sacrifice, duty, and restraint as critical to the moral and political health of the nation. From Charles Eliot Norton ("that self-interest is short-sighted and imperfect which does not see that the pursuit of material comfort is a folly, when disjoined from the practice of virtue") to Henry David Thoreau to Lydia Sigourney, authors had railed against self-interested tyranny, which encouraged materialism and mediocrity.[78] Harriet Beecher Stowe's *Dred* (1856), for example, exhaustively demonstrates the damage that self-interest could wreak on society, causing one reviewer to complain that she had stopped writing novels "to perform the work of a political philosopher."[79] Consistent with this line of reasoning, Bellows held that if interests were divorced from a narrow sense of self-regard, they could be pursued without damage to the community. The position many wartime writers advocated in recuperating the concept of self-interest was that an individual's interests—and, just as important, feelings—were nourished *through* subordination. The personal value of submission to authority, a central tenet of, variously, republic ideology as well as sentimental fiction and the politics it authorized, is likewise crucial to the rhetoric of national identity during the Civil War.[80] As Deak Nabers has recently argued, the "Union's prosecution of the Civil War relied upon, if it did not in fact require," a particular "mixture of passivity and authority," a mixture I maintain is associated with loyalty.[81]

The adaptation of a sentimental ideal of submission was facilitated by arguments fusing loyalty and religion.[82] As Fredrickson has compellingly shown, the conservative elites who embraced loyalty explicitly underscored the parallels between national affiliation and religious devotion. "For what is religion but loyalty to God," Horace Bushnell asks, "and if there were no letting down of our great nature by sin, how grandly and heroically would it stand, taking sides eternally with god!"[83] What Fredrickson fails to note, however, is the parallel operation evident in sentimental and reform discourse, which enabled the arguments made by Northern propagandists. "Our very nature is political," Bushnell opined, "just as it is domestic; configured to the state as to the family, craving after loyal emotion, even as after family love. Without this political equipment, we should not even be complete men."[84] Bushnell's claims about the parallels between nations and families relies on a traditional association in political philosophy, including early American national materials, but finds its particular origin in his own theory of Christian nurture, articulated in numerous antebellum volumes.[85] According to Bushnell, individuals in communities—be they small, like families, or large, like nations or races—exerted conscious and unconscious influence on one another. No one lives isolated from the community, Bushnell suggested, even if individualistic philosophies maintained the contrary. Bushnell's publications during the Civil War hammered this point, arguing for the need of a national community that would develop both civic character and personal morality.[86] His arguments sometimes recall the example of Ahab with which this chapter opened. Dismissing consent as a fallacy, Bushnell, perhaps the most strident of loyalty's proponents, contended that political legitimacy is dependent on "the historic order," the set of conditions that allow a certain structure of power to emerge; like Ahab, Bushnell found in this historic success evidence of divine sanction, although the minister was less convinced that it appertained to him alone than the fictional sea captain.[87]

Despite the emphasis on rationality and control in Union definitions of loyalty, much writing on the topic concerned sentiment, especially how loyalty achieved a proper balance between head and heart. "There is, too," Moncure Conway wrote, "a tone of feeling to be created and sustained, every pulse of which throbs at the seat of government, and runs along the lines of our army; and this every man, woman, and child may help to make true, intense, and fervent."[88] Like sympathy, in other words, loyalty was an affect, but one that coupled rational commitment to an ideal with a sentimental attachment to one's country. "Do you call this sentimental patriotism?" W. G. Eliot asked. "It is not so. It is but the just and reasonable love of country, which every honest man should cherish, and without which honesty is seldom long maintained. The love of country, loyalty, patriotism, is the foundation of all social virtues, the corner stone on which society is built." Some might misidentify this sentiment as "enlarged selfishness," but in so doing they mistake selfishness for "self-sacrifice and heroism."[89]

As this summary has made clear, there were some significant differences in the way loyalty was defined, even as it was being widely disseminated as the proper model of allegiance. Before turning to the problem of performance, there are two other sources of conflict to consider. For some, loyalty was best understood as being faithful to the Constitution. People holding this position, mainly but not exclusively Copperheads, denounced "Abe" and suggested that his constitutional policies made him as much a traitor as "Jeff."[90] Their Republican opponents ridiculed this position as "law-alty." "The law has nothing whatever to do with loyalty," Bushnell explained in "The Doctrine of Loyalty," because loyalty is not "in any sense, a legal subject," for it instead "belongs entirely to the moral department of life."[91] Of course, those who were moral would be inclined by their nature to obey the law, but this propensity was misunderstood when taken as the basis of loyalty itself.

At the same time, others argued that loyalty presupposed the moral necessity of emancipation. Frederick Douglass, for example, argued that loyalty was dependent upon the abolition of slavery. On Douglass's view, only those who had a full commitment to the abolition of slavery and to citizenship rights for black Americans could be deemed loyal: those who advocated "putting down the rebellion . . . without abolishing slavery" failed to understand the true parameters of loyalty.[92] In May 1862, Charles Sumner introduced a resolution in the Senate asking Americans "without distinction of color" to manifest their loyalty by "ceasing to fight or labor for the Rebels," acts that Sumner hoped would inspire the government to recognize the rights of all men, also "without distinction of color."[93] That is to say, Douglass and Sumner hoped that the war would awaken Northerners from their moral lethargy, replacing complacency with a horror at the moral wrongs that had gone too long uncorrected. Loyal people understood, Douglass held, that the war's mission was millennial in character and thus supported "putting down the rebellion by putting down slavery upon every rod of earth which shall be made sacred by the footprints of a single loyal soldier."[94]

* * *

There was "no official public relations office to rally the people" during the Civil War, Melinda Lawson reminds us, and thus the task of defining national allegiance "fell largely to private individuals or associations, each with their own motives and methods."[95] As the self-appointed nationalists sought out means of disseminating the "doctrine of loyalty," they turned to materials already in place, particularly the literary tools of popular control. During the Civil War, reading was itself "suffused" with "nationalistic aims," changing it from "a private act" to "a vital part of a larger, public, patriotic culture."[96] Deploying popular genres, propagandists worked to influence their readers' priorities, particularly by replacing sympathy with loyalty, the new moral imperative. Sentimental conventions, proven successful at naturalizing specific values, were adopted and adapted to accommodate the Union's revised position on the importance of emotion. Nor was much revision required, for although sentimentality's investment in affect is regularly underscored, the careful distinctions it proposes between kinds of emotion receives less sustained attention; *Uncle Tom's Cabin* lauds *right* feeling, not *all* feeling. The hierarchy of affective states, already an important component of sentimental fiction, enabled the conversion of the antebellum sentimental novel into a key element of Union nationalism.[97] Like its antebellum precursor, wartime propaganda disciplined wayward emotions; the values it prized—renunciation, submission, duty, and civic nationalism—were inflected by a distrust of emotion and a privileging of the more abstract principles associated with loyalty, however. As the speaker in Lucy Larcom's "A Loyal Woman's No" explains in refusing a marriage proposal, she cannot marry a man who puts his interests before those of the nation;

> The men and women mated for that time
> Tread not the soothing mosses of the plain;
> Their hands are joined in sacrifice sublime;
> Their feet set in upward paths of pain.
>
> For me, I do not walk these hills alone:
> Heroes who poured their blood out for the Truth,
> Women whose hearts bled, martyrs all unknown,
> Here catch the sunrise of immortal youth
>
> On their pale cheeks and consecrated brows!
> It charms me not,—your call to rest below:
> I press their hands, my lips pronounce their vows:
> Take my life's silence for your answer: NO![98]

If the particular power of sentimentalism is "its ability to make forceful, in every sense, a set of ideals about human compassion and relations," then it is not hard to see how Larcom's speaker uses its tools to articulate a new "set of ideals" predicated on abstract values (like "Truth," or "Liberty" and "Law," also mentioned in the poem) and "sacrifice sublime."[99] In short, sentimentality proved an effective tool in disseminating the moral norms and political ideas for the nation at war, because it assumed, contra transcendental celebrations of the individual, that adaptation to cultural norms was the most assured route to personal and communal happiness.

Rather than proliferate examples, I will linger with one tale—Louisa Alcott's "Love and Loyalty" (1864)—to show how sentimental paradigms were used to instill loyalty. Like many tales of the period, "Love and Loyalty" pits North against South, brother against brother; it differs, however, in that the fraternal conflict between the Stirling men, Richard and Robert, is romantic, not political. Both are in love with a "rebel beauty," Rose, who demands, as the story opens, that Robert renounce his national allegiance or lose her love. "Remember what you ask, what I offer," she says in a "slow, sweet voice" the narrator labels "dangerous."[100] "I ask nothing of you but the relinquishment of a mistaken duty," and in return she vows to share with him her life of "luxury and power" (198). Inverting familiar carpe diem conventions, it is Rose who reminds Robert that "youth was made for happiness" and should not be wasted "in a quarrel which time alone can end" (199). Because "no one can serve two mistresses," she insists he choose between these competing claims on his allegiance (201). On the verge of succumbing to Rose's considerable charms, Robert hears a stanza from "The Battle Hymn of the Republic" and abruptly chooses his nation.

But the young man is not happy in his choice and struggles to accept the sacrifice of Rose, turning to other characters—first his brother and then his mother—to bolster his national commitment. Even though his mother instructs him to "bear [his] loss like [a man]" and not "mar [his] sacrifice to principle by any vain regrets," Robert cannot take her advice, and his eventual recovery of much of what he has lost is due to the efforts of other characters. That Alcott is trying to argue for a more communal understanding of duty is evident when Rose, inspired by Robert's losses, undertakes "the long quest which was to teach her a memorable lesson, and make a loyal woman of the rebel beauty" (238).[101] Using her Southern connections, Rose finds Richard in a Southern prison, not lost in battle, and arranges for his exchange, nursing him back from the brink of death as a testament of her love for his brother. Rose's conversion is like that of many heroines of postbellum reunion stories, in which Southern heroines embrace Northern values with Union men. Already attuned to the superior character of commitment to principle, not pleasure of passion, Rose's recognition of the *deficiency* of Southern sympathy, represented by the malice other Southern women displayed for captured and wounded Union soldiers, leads to her ultimate conversion to loyalty. For her conversion—and the rescue of Richard—Rose wins the respect of Mrs.

Stirling and the material "reward" of Robert Stirling himself, damaged as he is. Robert, in turn, is made as close to whole as he can be, getting back his beloved and his brother; as solicitous as they are, however, they cannot make up for the loss of his arms.

What is most striking about this tale, however, is Mrs. Stirling's final remarks to the long-suffering Richard, still in love with Rose: "Ah, my good son, the world will see Rob's sacrifice, and honor him for it, but yours is the greater one, for through many temptations you have been loyal, both to your country and yourself. God and your mother love and honor you for that, although to other eyes you seem to stand forgotten and alone" (255–256). There are multiple ways to suffer, Alcott explains, and the most painful are often the least spectacular. Richard's deepest wound—and the one for which he deserves both "love and honor"—is not received in combat; similarly, whereas the narrative lingers with the women searching for their lost men, it skims almost entirely over the experience of battle. Moral suffering is "greater" than physical suffering, and the story insists that both are integral to a full definition of loyalty.[102] Indeed, Alcott indicates that it is the "good" son's affective sacrifice that teaches Rose "a truer loyalty, a purer love" (253). Whereas Elizabeth Young argues that Richard's internalization of "the disciplinary mode of self-mastery" marks "the radical reworking of the relationship between men and women," Alcott's tale captures more than gender politics at work; Richard's sentimental sacrifice is necessary not just to individual moral growth but also to national security.[103] The soldier provides the model for the emotional renunciation required of all loyal citizens who do their duty—"the greater one"—by ignoring their own feelings. Loyalty assumes some feeling for others, but, as the characters in Alcott's tale learn, it demands that these feelings be disciplined in the name of the larger good, understood in terms that conflate the personal and the national. As will become clear in subsequent chapters, however, the paradoxical union of sentimental form and a (putatively) abstract content was not as stable as Union writers asserted and assumed. Indeed, as Eve Kosofsky Sedgwick shrewdly noted, "It would be hard to overestimate the importance of vicariousness in defining the sentimental."[104] The "vicariousness" of postbellum sentimentality yields a narrative of the Civil War structured by romantic tropes and assumptions, as loyalty shed the particular connotations it had acquired during the war years.

In "Love and Loyalty," however, loyalty's distinct features are consistently stressed, particularly the kind of behavior it required. Mrs. Stirling dismisses Rose, for example, demanding tangible proof of the young woman's changed allegiance. Most notably, Alcott is clear throughout the tale that the body offers a poor index to either personal or national affect; people might read the loss of Robert's arms as a sign of sacrifice, but private insight reveals that his was the more shallow commitment. Indeed, the end of the story suggests that the *most loyal* individuals may well be those who disguise their feelings in a performance that masks the truth of their affiliations. It is the performance of loyalty in renunciation that wins Mrs. Stirling's most ardent regard and is, she assures her son, most valued by God. If the truest loyalty is hidden, then "Love and Loyalty" ends with the gothic conclusion that patriotism, like romantic love, is indistinguishable from its absence.[105]

The suggestion that presence and absence might be impossible to differentiate was not one likely to meet with much approval during a bloody civil war. To the contrary, security for both populations could only be guaranteed if friend was systematically and reliably distinguished from foe, if the private self was seen as fully expressed in public performance. Put differently, war takes what has been argued is an element of the political as such, the opposition of friend and enemy, and, stripping away all potential nuance, demands the clear categorization of all persons and actions. As Barbara Johnson incisively observes, "all gaps in cognition" during war function not as "mere absences" but instead take "on the performative force of true acts." There is no *empty* meaning in war, and seeming absences are viewed as aggressively full of meaning. Silence, refraining *from* "patriotic utterances," the Peaceable Man of "Chiefly About War-Matters" suggested, could appear "a kind of treason" (43). "The *force* of what is not known is all the more effective for not being perceived as such," Johnson continues.[106] What is not known becomes, in other words, more potent, more dangerous, more forceful—which certainly seems to account accurately for the kind of anxiety that can mount during a time of genuine danger. How, then, can we correlate Johnson's keen observation with Mrs. Stirling's statement to Richard in which she suggests that the truest loyalty is that which can only be perceived by the keen observation of mother or God? The most forceful loyalty might be that which cannot be perceived, but by the same measure the most traitorous sympathy is also that which cannot be perceived: how is one to differentiate between these two kinds of absences? How is force for the Union distinguished from force for the Confederacy when *neither* is available to cognition? Indeed, Johnson's observation that absence can carry performative force, can itself behave *like* an action, points to a second, but by no means secondary, concern for Union partisans—articulating loyalty's formal components.

The problem that Alcott registers relative to the martial male body becomes even more acute when applied to the Union population as a whole. What did loyalty look like? How did, or should, a loyal person act? If loyalty were a rational emotion, how did the body manifest it (especially if, as Alcott seems to suggest, even dismemberment is not the clearest guide)? "The great work" of the nation called for everyone's loyalty, but what if a person were "too feeble to bear arms," without money to fund a regiment or sons to fill it?[107] If one wanted to fake loyalty—as one might fake sympathy in an antebellum novel—how could others distinguish the traitor in their midst? "The most corrupt may put on a fair and honorable exterior, and deceive," one patriotic sketch pointed out; how were the truly loyal to be differentiated from the false?

The loyal citizen had multiple "outward duties" that could demonstrate his or her national allegiance, one pamphleteer wrote, and, as they were disseminated from "every loyal pulpit and in every loyal print," there was no excuse for any confusion.[108] *The First Duty of the Citizen* (1863) suggested that citizens could post "pithy and emphatic sentences on a card" and affix them to their "front door." If repeated often enough, the pamphlet's author maintained, these "Mottoes for Loyal Men" would prove "one of the most expressive demonstrations of [an individual's] loyalty" that could be given.[109] Loyalty could, of course, be established at the ballot box by voting for the Republican ticket.[110] Women were told they could display their loyalty by encouraging men to enlist, participating in Sanitary fairs, nursing the wounded or dying, renouncing worldly goods and men who refused to fight, or demonstrating unwavering commitment to the nation.[111] John Greenleaf Whittier's "Barbara Frietchie" (1863) showed that even the very old ("fourscore years and ten") could "fight" heroically for the nation. In the poem, Frietchie fearlessly flies the Union flag, "show[ing] that one heart was loyal yet," and so moves Confederate general Stonewall Jackson that he orders his men to leave both untouched. Even as it lauds the recently deceased Confederate general, the poem predicts the North's eventual victory as "loyal winds" stir the "free flag" under which "the rebel host" march.[112]

Of equal importance was the need for the vigilant citizen to recognize the power of language to shape political and military conditions.[113] "Give yourself to patriotic utterances," a character in "What Can I Do?" suggested, and "put fire into the hearts of those who have both the strength and the will to bear arms."[114] Nathaniel Hawthorne also chimed in:

"insulating one's self from the universal fear and sorrow, and thinking one's idle thoughts in the dread time of civil war" were clearly inappropriate. "Fantasies" are no longer "harmless," he concluded, only partially joking (43). The following year, Lincoln likewise signaled the danger of silence: "he who dissuades one man from volunteering, or induces one soldier to desert, weakens the Union cause as much as he who kills a Union soldier in battle."[115] In an influential 1862 pamphlet, Charles J. Stillé asserted that verbal attacks on the government were a "hideous moral leprosy," evidence of the "base spirit of faction" unfortunately attendant upon "free peoples."[116] Summarizing the predominant attitude, Frederick Douglass asserted that "words are now useful only as they stimulate to blows."[117]

But if the right kind of words could "fire" the hearts of others, the wrong ones could seriously misfire. "Men seem to forget," W. G. Eliot wrote, "that talking, when it goes to a certain extent, *is acting*, and that, while we rightly claim liberty of speech, the abuse of this liberty becomes a crime."[118] The wrong kind of words—"indiscreet speech, bitter and angry works, denunciations, vindictive threats, imprecations of evil"—"encourag[e] the disloyal," for they suggest that the nation is neither "manly, nor brave, nor patriotic," and criticizing the administration demoralizes the nation without instituting any useful changes.[119] "We all feel here," a Pennsylvania man wrote in 1864, "that the Administration should become more stringent on *home traitors*, that is rebel sympathizers.... Every disloyal mouth should be shut, every treasonable sheet must be closed."[120] Even the wrong song could damage the nation: singing the "Marseillaise," especially popular in the Confederacy, led to the arrest of a troupe of French actors in New York, judged to be Southern sympathizers for their choice of song.[121] "It might be easy to overlook the potent criminality of speech during sunny days," Henry Bellows explained, but "when threatening and anxious times come upon us," what shines most brightly are the "great realities."[122]

In these "threatening and anxious times," any opposition to the war was easily conflated with disloyalty to the state, and its power was quickly mobilized to enforce proper allegiance.[123] The Potter Committee, created in July 1861 (and terminated in 1862) to investigate the loyalty of government employees, was just one manifestation of the pervasive sense that people should watch what they might say—and think—carefully; censorship of periodicals critical of the administration took this sense even farther.[124] Under such conditions, Henry Bellows explained, old attitudes toward speech, when "Oaths of office, and solemn compacts with man and God" were made "half-consciously" and taken too "lightly," must be abandoned in favor of a new seriousness. "Who can deny," he asked an 1861 audience, "that a certain laxity of conscience, a careless sense of obligation, a feeble respect for promises, a light view of oaths, has been growing among us?" "Our love of spicy exaggeration" debased the press, while "reckless talking" destroyed public faith in the messages from pulpits and congressional chambers alike, he opined.[125] "Gigantic dishonesties, meanwhile, stalk abroad almost without shame," Beecher worried.[126] A taste for "spicy exaggeration" had encouraged citizens to reject the bland fare of naked truth, which had led, in turn, to the gradual denigration of all verbal transactions. "Oaths, vows, promises, compacts—these are all sealed with the conscience and witness by God," Bellows reminded his readers, "and if the sight of them is dimmed, if the feeling of them is dulled—woe to the people, woe to the world."[127] In his first inaugural address, Abraham Lincoln assured his "dissatisfied fellow-countrymen" that he, for one, did not take his oath lightly, vowing, "The government will not assail *you*": "*You* have no oath registered in Heaven to destroy the government, while I shall have the most solemn one to 'preserve, protect, and defend' it."[128] For a nation formed by declaration and united by common consent, Bellows's position—that "woe" awaits those who ignore the bonds created by "oaths, vows, promises, compacts"—carried both political *and* moral implications.

At a meeting of the Loyal National League, a political association organized to instill loyal sentiments across the North, Francis Lieber asserted that even after two years of "sacrifices of wealth, of blood, and limb, and life," it remained important to pledge one's loyalty as a sign of national devotion:

> We profess ourselves to be loyal citizens of these United States; and by loyalty we mean a candid and loving devotion to the object to which a loyal man—a loyal husband, a loyal friend, a loyal citizen—devotes himself. We eschew the attenuated arguments derived by trifling scholars from meagre etymology. We take the core and substance of this weighty word, and pledge ourselves that we will loyally—not merely outwardly and formally, according to the letter, but frankly, fervently and according to the spirit—adhere to our country, to her institutions, to freedom, and her power, and to that great institution called the government of our country, founded by our fathers, and loved by their sons, and by all right-minded men who have become citizens of this land by choice and not by birth—who have wedded this country in the maturity of their age as verily

as their own. We pledge ourselves as national men devoted to the Nationality of this great people.... Loyalty is pre-eminently a civic virtue in a free country. It is patriotism cast in the graceful mould of candid devotion to the harmless government of an unshackled nation.

Subsequently published as one of the pamphlets issued by the Loyal Publication Society, of which Lieber was president, *No Party Now; but All for our Country* rejected all species of false divisions—like class or party affiliation—and maintained instead that "loyal men" should "stand by their country" and forget "what sentiments they may have uttered in the excitement of former discussions."[129] The Union must stand united against "the appalling confusion of ideas" embraced by treasonous Southerners, Lieber argued, and reject the comfort of compromise offered by various Democratic candidates in their campaign speeches. A professor of political philosophy at South Carolina College from 1835 to 1853, Lieber spoke from personal experience when describing Southern institutions and principles; in 1851, he argued against the rumblings of secession, claiming that the "federal compact was unbreakable," and shortly thereafter relocated to the North.[130] Loyalty, "graceful" and "candid," was that virtue best expressed through pledges of devotion, made to a "harmless" government.

When Lieber called for Northerners to pledge their loyalty, then, he was not speaking metaphorically. From the early months of the war, the Union relied, sometimes heavily, on loyalty oaths to police the allegiance of Union citizens. Although many objected to the practice, and some of the provisions for administering the oaths were ruled unconstitutional after the end of the war, there was ample historical precedent for using oaths to safeguard the nation and its values. Before embarking for their new home, the Puritans identified the necessity of evaluating the loyalties of potential settlers and, once there, instituted an oath in which the individual swore to be "true and faithfull" to the commonwealth, "by the great and dreadful Name of the Everliving God." When the English colonies established a printing press in 1639, the first item off the presses was the loyalty oath. Their descendants in the Revolutionary era similarly embraced the loyalty oath; in 1775, George Washington wrote, "it is high time a test act was prepared and every man called upon to declare himself; that we may distinguish friends from foes."[131] And Abraham Lincoln, in the "Address to the Young Men's Lyceum of Springfield, Illinois" (1838), argued that oaths would be an effective means of countering the "natural" "alienation of [citizens'] affections from the Government":

The question recurs "how shall we fortify against it?" The answer is simple. Let every American, every lover of liberty, every well wisher to his posterity, swear by the blood of the Revolution, never to violate in the least particular, the laws of the country; and never to tolerate their violation by others. As the patriots of seventy-six did to the support of the Declaration of Independence, so to the support of the Constitution and Laws, let every American pledge his life, his property, his sacred honor;—let every man remember that to violate the law, is to trample on the blood of his father, and to tear the character of his own, and his children's liberty.[132]

Little wonder, then, that Lincoln's wartime administration would ask citizens—repeatedly—to swear their loyalty as well as sacrifice their lives and property.

From 1861 through the end of Reconstruction, the verbal oath was seen to be a prime mechanism of stabilizing individual allegiance, providing a way to reconstitute the national community and re-people the South with citizens. The operative premise of the loyalty oath is that "the persons taking the oaths see their own self-identity to be derived from the community to which the oath is directed."[133] This is especially clear in the cases of those *unwilling* to swear. In early 1864, Senator James A. Bayard of Delaware resigned his seat in the Senate rather than take the Ironclad Oath, railing against oaths as "demoralizing acts of tyranny."[134] Arguing that the oath was unconstitutional, Bayard was willing to "cheerfully accept the imputation of disloyalty if loyalty mean ignoring the Constitution."[135] Particularly "odious" to Bayard, and others, was the Ironclad Oath, which sought to establish the juror's past, present, and future loyalty. By the middle of 1863, no wavering in allegiance was acceptable, and the Ironclad Oath's sweeping perspective became the federal standard for loyalty. In the words of one Southerner, the Ironclad Oath was "unprecedented, unjust, cruel, impolitic, unworthy of the age and of the American people" because of its requirement that men "swear to their past actions or past feelings."[136]

The Ironclad Oath drew particular ire for its requirement of loyalty, but Lincoln's 1838 Lyceum speech makes a similar point: a "pledge" fuses past ("the blood of his father"), present (an individual's liberty), and future ("his children's liberty"). Collapsing historical difference, the pledge or oath reconfigures national time into a series of repetitions, projecting the present into the future and replacing the changes of time with a consistency that seems to guarantee security. Indeed, as Paul De Man notes, "the mode of existence" of the performative is "temporal," or, more precisely, "time is the phenomenal category produced by the discrepancy" between the "theoretical statement" (the performative act of the promise or pledge) and its "manifestation."[137] What De Man is pointing to, in other words, is that the experience of time is created by waiting for either fulfillment or betrayal, the counterfactual possibility George Fletcher associates with the narrative structure generated by loyalty. Even as it manufactures a "present that is always past with regard to [the promise's] realization," the oath or pledge imagines, and radically forestalls, the future, flattening the nation's time into a single moment. According to Hannah Arendt, "Without being bound to the fulfillment of promises, we would never be able to keep our identities; we would be condemned to wander helplessly and without direction in the darkness of each man's lonely heart, caught in its contradictions and equivocalities—a darkness which only the light shed over the public realm through the presence of others, who confirm the identity between the one who promises and the one who fulfils, can dispel."[138]

The particular temporality of performative speech, and its signal importance to Civil War discourse, is on display in "The Man without a Country" (1863), a cautionary tale in which an impetuous young officer, Philip Nolan, learns "the spiritual cost of disloyalty."[139] In the story, Nolan makes two fatal errors. First, he allows himself to be seduced by Aaron Burr, who "enlist[s]" the young man, "body and soul," in a plot against the United States because the nation "had picked [him] out first as one of her own confidential men of honor."[140] Like a young woman in a seduction novel, betraying principle for flattering confidence, Nolan pays for this error with his life. While such a moral misstep is sufficient to secure his fate—few get a second chance in a seduction tale—Nolan's rash recalcitrance, his second mistake, turns his punishment into a protracted ordeal.[141] On trial for treason, Nolan is given the chance to repair his fidelity to the nation he has betrayed; "in a fit of frenzy," Nolan refuses, yelling, "Damn the United States! I wish I may never hear of the United States again!" (666–667). His judges are appalled at this "cavalier[]" behavior and sentence the prisoner "to have his wish fulfilled": he is to remain on American naval vessels for the rest of his life and "under no circumstances" may he "hear of his country" again (667, 668).[142] In so doing they enact what Philip Fisher has argued is the defining quality of rashness, namely its transfer of "the single present moment into the final moment of time" because the "relations between the passions and permanent conditions—ever, never, forever—lie at the heart of rashness as a temporal scheme."[143]

Not only does the tale thus consider the implications of breaking the bonds of national fidelity, it also takes seriously the idea that "words are also actions, and actions are a kind of words."[144] Nolan may laugh at the sentence, but he comes to experience the terrible pain associated with rebellion: the loss of home and nation. At the same time that Nolan learns this lesson, the reader is exposed to the tremendous power of the oath to protect the nation and script its future. It is a feature of "melodramatic structure," and thus of the general culture of war, that a promise or vow functions as absolute, "ineluctable," and unwavering. "We are not encouraged," Peter Brooks continues, "to investigate the psychology of the vow or the logic of the deadline but, rather, to submit to their dramaturgy, their functioning as mechanism."[145] This mechanism, "The Man without a Country" makes clear, is in part a time machine. When successful, the vow or pledge strips the future of contingency and change, installing unvarying sameness and repetition in their stead: the promise of national allegiance is, in other words, always melodramatic. What makes "The Man without a Country" so effective, finally, is that it finds two ways to restrict (and rescript) Nolan's future, first through the temporality associated with rashness and then with his subsequent submission to the promissory "mechanism." The story's great popularity suggests that Hale's moral—impetuous emotion is dangerous and the loss of one's country a horrible privation—found a ready audience among Northern readers eager for clarity about the value of national allegiance.[146]

The end of the story shifts focus, however, from loss to reconstruction. As a final warning to all "the young Nolans and Vallandighams and Tatnalls of to-day" who fail to understand "what it is to throw away a country," the narrator concludes with a letter from an officer on the *Levant* about the circumstances of Nolan's death (677). Asking if the narrator recalled their speculations about Nolan's room, Danforth goes on to provide a thorough description that lingers with the shrine Nolan has constructed to the United States:

> The stars and stripes were triced up above and around a picture of Washington, and he had painted a majestic eagle, with lightnings blazing from his beak and his foot just clasping the whole globe, which his wings overshadowed. The dear old boy saw my glance, and said, with a sad smile, "Here, you see, I have a country!" And then he pointed to the foot of his bed, where I had not seen before a great map of the United States, as he had drawn it from memory, and which he had there to look upon as he lay. (677)

As his dying wish, Nolan asks to be told the history of the nation, for, he vows, "there is not in America,—God bless her!—a more loyal man than I," thus replacing his youthful curse with a mature blessing (678). "How like a wretched night's dream a boy's idea of personal fame or of separate sovereignty seems, when one looks back on it after such a life as mine!" he exclaims (678). His visitor complies, telling Nolan all that "would show the grandeur of his country and its prosperity," remaining silent, however, on the subject of "this infernal Rebellion!" (679). Ending with a reference to the Civil War, Hale underscores the dreadful losses awaiting Southerners should they receive their wish and manage to leave the nation, as well as the dangers attendant upon the cavalier assumption that words do not matter.

As "The Man without a Country" makes clear, when temporality is disrupted by an oath, fantasy replaces history, making the latter "quaint" and "queer" (45). The distortions and narrative lacunae—first mandated by court order and then by emotional necessity—prevent Nolan from *ever* knowing his country: not learning about the Civil War, he dies with yet another false image of the nation in his heart. At the same time that he narrates a story on the value of national affiliation, that is, Hale also tells the story of its dependence on fantasy. In every representation of the nation, there are elements that must be redacted, ignored, or suppressed; devotion requires idealization. As we will see in chapter 2, popular reconstruction narratives also relied on the efficacy of memory and a disciplined love to reimagine the nation, although their visions will replace what is "queer" in Nolan's world with a relentless heteronormativity. "The Man without a Country" sets Nolan adrift in a sea of undifferentiated time, which he subsequently shapes in a manner consistent with loyalty.

The unvarying sameness created through the agency of Nolan's youthful assertion and the authority of the tribunal's sentence illustrates the allure of performative language: because they erase the difference between historical moments, promises, pledges, and oaths have the capacity to master uncertainty. Yet this certainty comes at the cost of specificity, fact, and freedom. "Freedom's possibility announces itself in anxiety," Søren Kierkegaard indicates, because uncertainty, the lack of concrete knowledge about the future (or, indeed, the present), is the condition of possibility for freedom's existence.[147] Kierkegaard's definition of anxiety—in which performative speech is the metaphor for freedom's introduction—captures the intimate relationship between the two that troubled Civil War–era Americans. Anxiety, which for Jacques Lacan is structured like "a twisted border," is generated by performative speech and potentially controlled by performative speech: "anxiety," he explains, "is only overcome where the Other names itself."[148] The important thing to note in these passages is the reiteration of a definitive correlation between performative speech, anxiety, and a particular future orientation.

Hale's story circumvents anxiety by replacing the vow or promise with the juridical sentence, but this substitution only serves to bring contemporary anxieties about language—and the future—into sharper relief. During the war, Union citizens were quick to identify how limited language might be in safeguarding the nation's security. One November 1861 commentator bitterly remarked that the oath of allegiance was a deadly "serious jok[e]": "Clearly a man who thinks that the Government of this country may be justly overthrown will have no compunction in taking the oath of allegiance to the Government in order that he may more effectually injure it." How could an oath provide "a defense against treason," for "how is the government ever to know whether a traitor is really converted or not"? "And yet, what other test can there be than an oath?"[149]

Pledging allegiance—taking a loyalty oath—involves the expression of individual will, which is why it seemed to many the best way to perform or demonstrate loyalty. Unlike the involuntary and embodied responses associated with sympathy, loyalty oaths *appeared* to rely on a rational understanding of duty and responsibility. As the reading of *Moby-Dick* with which this chapter began established, however, the belief that oaths were safe from the influence of overheated emotion was not necessarily well-founded, and a quick review of how two political philosophers—Hannah Arendt and Thomas Hobbes—have thought about promises and oaths only underscores the judiciousness of Melville's concerns. According to Arendt, promises master the "darkness of human affairs" by correcting the "unreliability" that arises from two sources: the fact that people cannot "guarantee today who they will be tomorrow" and that it is impossible to foretell "the consequences of an act within a community of equals where everybody has the same capacity to act" (244). Uncertainty is intrinsic to the human condition, and political communities, rather than containing this uncertainty, tend to exacerbate it. Promises provide "islands of certainty," moments of respite from the "darkness of human affairs," as they safeguard, albeit tenuously, the "space of appearances in which [people] gather and the power which keeps this public space in existence" (244–245). Arendt's spatial metaphor gestures to the ability of the promise to shape national locality as an interior as well as exterior state, a move that recapitulates the relationship between national belonging and individual morality associated with American identity.

It is hard to see, though, how the uncertainty Arendt celebrates can be correlated to the cultural conditions of civil war, when the fragile promise is as impotent as the spontaneous action it ensures is undesirable.[150] The political oath, which could be said to replace the promise, falls far short of the lofty standards Arendt identifies.[151] Whereas the promise heralds the unpredictability of action and agency, the oath is embraced because it replaces the possibility of action with something regular, what Arendt calls "behavior." Behavior encourages "conformism," she complains; its regularity may be necessary to a mass society (she admits it generates security) but is antithetical to a rich sense of possible human interaction (41). Indeed, Arendt suggests that "the moment promises lose their character as isolated islands of certainty in an ocean of uncertainty, that is when this faculty is misused to cover the whole ground of the future and to map out a path secured in all directions, they lose their binding power and the whole-enterprise becomes self-defeating" (244). Put differently, "misused" promises shape the future simplistically and monolithically, thus destroying the democratic contestation that, for Arendt, is key: there are no promises, as Arendt defines them, in "The Man without a Country," only a totalitarian impulse to map or script the future absolutely.

Like Arendt, Thomas Hobbes recognizes the political importance of oaths and promises, although he celebrates the very element that disturbs her: their utility in "map[ping] out a path secured in all directions." As he explains in *On the Citizen*,

> An *Oath* is an utterance attached to a promise; by it the promisor gives up his claim to God's mercy if he does not do as he promises. This definition follows from the actual words in which the essence of *swearing* is contained, namely, *So help me God*, or the equivalent, as, among the Romans, *O Jupiter, kill the oath-breaker as I kill this Sow*. It is no objection that sometimes an *Oath* may be said to be not promissory but declarative. For in strengthening an affirmation by means of an *oath*, he declares that he is giving a true reply.[152]

For Hobbes, however, the danger is that oaths might not be binding *enough*: "The force of Words," he writes, "being (as I have already noted) too weak to hold men to the performance of their Covenants; there are in mans nature, but two imaginable helps to strengthen it. And those are either a Feare of the consequence of breaking their word; or a Glory, or Pride in appearing not to need to break it."[153] Even as he notes the power of pride, however, Hobbes dismisses its ultimate efficacy, for it "is a Generosity too rarely found to be presumed on, especially in the pursuers of Wealth, Command, or sensuall Pleasure," in short among "the greatest part of Mankind" (200). What is needed to secure the verbal contract, on Hobbes's view, is more fear: "For *Swearing oaths* was introduced precisely in order to strike men with a greater fear of breaking faith than the fear we have of men (from whom our actions may be hidden) by consideration of God and by religious scruple." Because it includes the potential for punishment—the reality that it is not merely a moral transgression but a crime against divine law—the oath may be more likely to succeed, coercing swearers into conformity, although even here Hobbes is far from sanguine: "The only effect then of an *oath* (men being prone by nature to break the faith they have pledged) is to give those who have taken an oath more reason to be afraid to do so."[154]

Importantly, the Hobbesian view of politics is saturated with, indeed formed in response to, emotion. His stark assessment of human nature—in which people are driven to compete for power unless sheltered in political communities—led him to a definition of the political contract that involved the "mutuall transferring of Right" to a sovereign who would henceforth neutralize the possibility for discord (192). Harassed by fear and anxiety, people thus can only find emotional or political comfort if they are protected from worries and desires, their own and those of other people. On Hobbes's view, anxiety—"this perpetuall fear" about the future (169)—explains the evolution of religion and provides the impetus that leads to the initial formation of the social contract as well as the glue that holds it together once formed: "Feare and Liberty are consistent; as when a man throweth his goods into the Sea for *feare* the ship should sink, he doth it neverthelesse very willingly, and may refuse to doe it if he will" (262).[155] Not only do we fear events, but we also fear other people (who fear us in turn), creating a structure of fear within which we live.[156]

Leviathan articulates numerous reasons for the necessity of the monarch, and a circumscribed understanding of "Libertie," among them worries about the future and how it is produced or determined by events in the past. Predicting outcomes for actions can be "called *Foresight, and Prudence,* or *Providence*; and sometimes *Wisdome*," Hobbes asserts, but it is difficult to take "all circumstances" into account, so often these seemingly wise conjectures prove "very fallacious": "The *Present* only has a being in Nature; things *Past* have a being in the Memory onely, but things *to come* have no being at all; the *Future* being but a fiction of the mind, applying the sequels of actions Past, to the actions that are Present; which with most certainty is done by him that has most Experience;

but not with certainty enough" (97). The confusion of "fiction" with the "certainty" craved by people in a state of "perpetuall fear" about their future is reason enough, according to Hobbes, to account for the necessity of the sovereign to the commonwealth.

Returning to the American nineteenth century, it is now possible to see how the Hobbesian worldview clarifies the importance of oaths and promises in the definition of Union loyalty.[157] People turn to oaths (and other kinds of performatives) to solve problems of certainty: I don't know if I can trust your loyalty so I ask you to demonstrate it with an oath. The problem, which Hobbes makes clear, is that despite the frequency with which oaths are so used, performative speech is incapable of establishing the trustworthiness it must presuppose.[158] In this conclusion, in fact, Hobbes's ideas about language intersect with various subsequent considerations of the topic. According to David Hume, for example, a promise is "*naturally* something altogether unintelligible" that fails to generate, on its own, obligations among "naturally selfish" men.[159] What is required, then, is the mental resolution to fulfill the promise, but it is impossible to know if this resolution, this mental act, has been made or if it will be kept.[160] Similarly, J. L. Austin admits that promises are dependent on the honesty and integrity of the speaker.[161] There may be contextual conditions that augment the likelihood that the speech act will be authentic, but, he acknowledges, no such accessory can evacuate the problem presented by the speaker who chooses to take an oath under false pretenses. If I lack certainty about your trustworthiness, swearing an oath, which only works if I find you trustworthy, will not give me the certainty I seek. The problematic here articulated—that oaths fail to establish the security for which they are introduced—may be a generalized feature of *all* performative speech; the promise or oath is only ever verifiable, Austin explains, in retrospect—but such assertions would surely do little to dissipate worries about the political efficacy of the loyalty oath.

Despite the above limitations, oaths were deployed during the Civil War to clarify loyalty, which meant they provided a mechanism for surveilling an individual's will *and* affections, putatively extending the domain of certainty by mapping consistency and conformity both temporally and spatially.[162] Given the multiple loyalty tests introduced—and the generalized worries about the power of words, the performance of allegiance, and the nature of consent—it is little wonder that Union literature regularly incorporated scenes of swearing, promising, and pledging. For example, when the speaker in Fitz James O'Brien's "The Prisoner of War" (1862) "swear[s] an oath as sacred as a soldier ever can swear," he erases the distance between himself and his captured comrade, vowing that "I will be with you there, or you will be free!" The oath guarantees that the bond between the men remains unbroken despite their different circumstances; the poem mirrors this bridging of distance as the speaker moves from thinking about his friend to the assertion that he "feel[s] the shackles" and "see[s] the mocking faces" his friend must be enduring.[163] The community created by the bond of affiliation—here the military bond is complemented by a prior quasi-fraternal connection—is protected from change thanks to the power of the "sacred" oath he swears in and through the poem. In the contingent world of democracy, and the even more contingent world of civil war, bonds are always in need of defense. The relationship between affect and narrative, dependent in this instance on an impossible certainty, leads to an explosive proliferation of anxiety and dread, which in turn motivates a near-constant search for affective release in yet another oath. Were they to succeed, oaths would ensure a reliable future conformity, an unrelieved repetition of consistency from which freedom would be entirely removed.

Loyalty's use as an alternative to sympathy, damaged by a perceived Confederate bias, had moral as well as political implications. As J. T. Trowbridge's sensational novel *Cudjo's Cave* (1863) indicates, the two coalesced around the status of the promise and the oath. "A partisan book, frankly designed to fire the Northern heart," *Cudjo's Cave* thrilled readers with the dangers that men, women, and children faced from unscrupulous Confederates.[164] As in popular novels about the American West, Trowbridge's borderland setting locates the reader in a place of shifting allegiance to pursue unsettling questions about nation, race, and allegiance; at its conclusion, fixed and clear answers have been provided for all the questions.[165] Set in Tennessee, the novel follows the adventures of Penn Hapgood, a Quaker schoolmaster who must negotiate conflicting allegiances: his country and his religion. (He chooses the former.) Two secondary characters—Carl Minnevich, an adolescent of German descent, and Salina Sprowl, a minister's daughter with an unfortunate husband—enable Trowbridge's analysis of the role of the oath or promise during war, a project he forwards via the marriage vow and the political oath. Characters in *Cudjo's Cave* are attacked by bears and trapped in forest fires, yet the problems presented by promises are depicted as equally harrowing, as the struggle to escape the moral dangers of deceit, loss of honor, and faithlessness are likened to physical peril.

Early in the novel, young Carl, a Union supporter, enlists in the Confederate army to save Hapgood's life; through much of the novel, therefore, Carl struggles to reconcile his sense of what a word *should* mean with the reality that his interests might not allow him to behave according to his conscience. "I have made vun promise," the young boy muses. "It vas a pad promise, and a pad promise is petter proken as kept. But if I preak it, they vill preak my head. Vot shall I do?" (330). The answer here, as elsewhere in the novel, is to rely on the explicit meaning of words, and Carl repeatedly finds a way to keep his "pad promise" while remaining true to his ideals and his friends. Carl's literalness allows him to negotiate the most difficult moral situations, implying that the potency of words derives from *treating* them as powerful. For a person of character, Trowbridge argues, even a "pad promise" cannot be recklessly discarded.[166]

While Carl's verbal gymnastics are entertaining, the moral dilemmas Salina Sprowl faces are far more sinister. Salina's most significant trials derive from her poor choice of husband, a man she cannot fully repudiate: "Strange as it may seem, she loved this worthless Lysander. She hated him for the misery he had caused her; . . . but her heart was lonely, and it yearned for reconciliation" (306). The extremities to which Lysander's repeated lies drive her strike at the core of the domestic ideal she so poorly approximates. Enraged by his treatment of a beloved family servant, for example, Salina sets fire to her own home, swearing, "I don't care for the house any more than I care for my life, and that's precious little" (320). For Trowbridge's Northern readers, Salina's willingness to destroy the family home may have recalled the elision between Southern emotional excess and the politics of domestic recklessness. Even though Salina eventually corrects her affections, the earlier destruction of her home points to yet another potential danger of Confederate victory: what would prevent the transformation of the gentle domestic angel into "the angel roused to strife," armed with an ax and prepared to wreak havoc if crossed (458)?

Trowbridge raises this worry about the politics of gender, and the gendering of politics, but buries it, literally, with Salina's death. Despite her extensive experience with his perfidy and even after burning down her own home, Salina continues to expect Lysander will be true to his word and his marriage vow. After freeing him to join his Confederate comrades, she exclaims, "He swore to me that he would not take advantage of his escape to betray or injure any of you. He will keep his oath. If he does not—" (438). While his first betrayal leads her to destroy the home, his second results in even greater destruction. Sneering at his "pledge" of "sacred honor," Salina ominously intones, "You have broken your oath to me. But I have made an oath I shall not break!" (459). As Lysander advances toward her and her sister, Salina shoots him and is herself subsequently killed by a bayonet. Driven by a bad husband to abandon the domestic ideals for which she longs, Salina's marital revolt—and her decision to keep a vow more binding than the marital pledge of love, honor, and obedience—demonstrates the poverty of Southern defenses of revocable consent as well as the importance of recognizing when breaking a promise is precisely the right thing to do. Rather than rely on the standard example set by Hapgood, Trowbridge uses Carl and Salina to sensationalize the moral imperatives associated with verbal pledges, showing in the process that being able to trust an oath is critical to national—and domestic—character and security.

The harrowing exploits depicted in *Cudjo's Cave* complicate the novel's purported commitment to the Union conception of loyalty this chapter has traced, however. Not only is sensation fiction organized by a desire to strike the reader, and the more physically the better, it does so, as Luciano notes, by manipulating the experience of time. "'Sensation,'" she writes, "signals a mode of intensified embodiment in which all times but the present fall away—a condition simultaneously desired, in its recollection of the infantile state, and feared, in its negation of social agency."[167] By its very nature, then, sensation fiction would seem inconsistent with the Union ideals and their temporal orientation that Trowbridge is trying to establish. Salina's ability to make *and keep* a pledge seems intended to reestablish her agency, although shooting her still-cheating husband seems more consistent with uncontrolled passion than calm reflection. Here, as in "The Man without a Country," we might want to say, then, that the vow is better compared to a curse than a contract. "A curse," Fisher argues, "takes what is a momentary peak of vehemence and, instead of spilling it out at once in an equally momentary act like a blow, even a murderous blow, freezes it like a law into an abstract punishment. The morally central part played by promises and contracts in the life of reason, binding oneself in the future to the state of mind and understanding of the present moment, is played within the passions by the curse or vow."[168]

While Salina's rash rage represents one danger presented by oaths, namely that they do not index rationality, Lysander's perfidy presents another: how could people be prevented from lying, from swearing falsely? These issues are perhaps more easily approached by looking at arguments made by Confederate partisans, eager to prevent their friends and neighbors from swearing, falsely or not, loyalty to the Union. After the capture of New Orleans in 1862, General Benjamin Butler required extensive loyalty tests of the area population, and those who refused would "be treated as rebels and enemies." By August 1862, 11,732 civilians had sworn their loyalty to the Union, despite the considerable social penalties associated with so doing.[169] In response to these distressing facts, Benjamin Palmer wrote *The Oath of Allegiance to the United States, Discussed in Its Moral and Political Bearings* (1863). He lingers over General Butler's "tyranny," which included the establishment of a "system of espionage" to ferret out plots against the Union. As a result, Palmer observes, "the poison of suspicion" was "universally diffused," and Confederate citizens were "either bullied or cajoled" "into a form of submission denied by the heart as often as it was sworn by the lips." When coupled with Order 28 (which treated women who insulted Union soldiers as prostitutes), the effect was that "these nameless, formless horrors, presented by a morbid fancy" encouraged them to swear their allegiance to the United States.[170] "Human society cannot exist without mutual confidence," he worries, sounding like a character from Melville's *The Confidence-Man* (1857). "Choose the dungeon and the scaffold a thousand times," Palmer concludes, "rather than transmit the taint of this leprosy to your offspring."[171]

The issue of moral "leprosy" aside, the balance of conscience and necessity runs throughout Civil War–era reflections about the moral force of a coerced oath. From the parodic perspective of one Confederate prisoner,

> To swear or not to swear, that is the question.
> Whether 'tis nobler in a man to suffer
> Imprisonment, exile and poverty,
> Or take the oath amidst a sea of troubles,
> And by submission end them? To swear, to lie,
> Once more, and, by a lie, to say we end
> Starvation, nakedness, and all the ills
> That rebels are heir to—'tis a perjury
> Devoutly to be wished.[172]

There, in short, was the rub. As William H. Ruffner asserted from his Lexington, Virginia, pulpit in March 1864, this was "one of the great practical questions of the time."[173] Falsely swearing might create the expectation that the sufferer would then behave in accordance with the promise, implying, in short, that the "sea of troubles" would not end with the single act of perjury, as its implications threatened the character—both political and moral—of the nation.[174]

* * *

"Before the war," Ralph Waldo Emerson wrote in 1864, "our patriotism was a firework, a salute, a serenade, for holidays and summer evenings, but the reality was cotton thread and complaisance." "The deaths of thousands and the determination of millions of men and women" changed American patriotism from a holiday affair into something substantial and undeniably "real."[175] Emerson's view—that American nationalism was born in the Civil War—has been widely embraced, as many historians see the war as a definitive moment in the evolution of a coherent national identity. "Before the Civil War we had no history in the deepest and most inward sense," Robert Penn Warren observed nearly 100 years later, as the nation was gearing up to celebrate the war's centennial; this "great, single event" fired the "American imagination," and "we became a nation, only with the Civil War."[176] But was the war a "single event"? As Anthony Smith explains, the multiple materials that cultures create to narrate and celebrate their wars prove more enduring and more influential than the events themselves. The "bonding" that occurs through war, as nations justify the sacrifice of lives and the use of resources, he writes, is importantly served by "myth-making processes," as "set down in epics, dramas, ballads, or hymns" that "possess a long-term power to shape distant relations that far outweigh and surpass the episodes themselves."[177] I would add novels to Smith's list in accounting for the "myth-making" that goes on in the wake of the Civil War.

It little matters, in other words, if Emerson and Warren are right that our national identity was indeed initially shaped during these years of conflict since we have long since accepted the position's truth. This identity is itself crafted with reference to the ideal of loyalty and the promissory structures associated with its definition of allegiance. Equally important, however, are the counterfactual possibilities, the live possibilities that an individual might reason his or her way into swearing allegiance from prudential, rather than genuine, motivations; that a person might be coerced into pledging allegiance; or that someone might falsely promise other reasons undermined the kind of certainty in personal and political relations that oaths and loyalty were supposed to contain. Further, the emphasis on rationality associated with loyalty was hard to maintain, as many of the works surveyed in this chapter indicate. Not only does war tend, as Edmund Wilson reminds us, to prevent thought—"as soon as a war gets started, few people do any more thinking about anything except demolishing the enemy"—but it is easy to become confused about the relationship between particularity and abstraction in matters of opinion and belief.[178] Finally, adapting sentimental narrative for its dissemination, loyalty had as much of a genre problem as a body problem. All of which means that loyalty proved, in short, no more reliable than sympathy had been. And yet when we look at literature shaped by the war and its memory, we see the enduring influence of both loyalty and its oaths. The legacy of the Civil War includes, that is to say, the problem of promising, even though we have mainly studied this moral and political concern via its impact on legal traditions. Even after the cruel war was over, oaths and promises coupled the hope for national security with the realization that no test—verbal or embodied—could provide accurate insight into the minds or hearts of others. The ideal of loyalty offered a counternarrative to the sentimental public sphere, one that could withstand neither the passions associated with war nor the American affiliation to our own states of feeling.

2 / One Big Happy Family, Again?

> *We in this Union would be an unwilling bride, a Union where one party is tied and dragged, if can be well drubbed first!*
> —MARY CHESNUT, *DIARY FROM DIXIE*

"The country is weary of being cheated with plays upon words," observed James Russell Lowell at the start of the Civil War.[1] "We all declare for liberty," Abraham Lincoln told a presumably wearier Baltimore audience in 1864, "but in using the same *word* we do not all mean the *same thing*."[2] Three years later, Edward A. Pollard echoed these claims, arguing that "shallow" partisan accounts had fatally misrepresented Southern values and had thus played a more than nominal role in driving the nation to war: it was wrong to call the "system of negro servitude" slavery or the "war of 1861, brought on by Northern insurgents against the authority of the Constitution," a "*Southern rebellion*." "Names are apparently slight things," Pollard continued, "but they create the first impression; they solicit the sympathies of the vulgar; and they often create a cloud of prejudice which the greatest exertions of intelligence find it impossible wholly to dispel."[3] Particularly interesting here is how Pollard anatomizes nominal potency as an opposition between sympathy and mental effort: the problem with words is that they work too quickly on the emotions. No matter how powerful words might be or seem, it is "impossible" to bring the feelings they create "wholly" under control. Jefferson Davis likewise complained about the Union's "perversion of language," an "error" that led "straight to the subversion of all popular government," repeating a point he made in his inaugural address as Confederate president.[4] Hoping to rise above partisan sniping, John W. Draper's *History of the American Civil War* (1867) counseled "thoughtful men" to consider "whether it be in truth a democracy in which we are living, or whether we are only deluding ourselves with a name."⁵ These claims lack the grandeur of Walt Whitman's extravagant claim—the poet "is the most deadly force of the war"—but they endorse his idea that words, properly wielded, could "dr[aw] blood."⁶

Of the many issues that confronted the nation in the wake of the Civil War, two provide the basis for this chapter's intervention: What would reconcile the ideal that the nation had been "conceived in liberty" and the reality that force and compulsion had won its continued existence? How were words to be stabilized, trusted, and regulated? For many in the North, the ideal of loyalty offered one means to a solution, although it was not without limitations. Indeed, as one Union officer worried in 1865, "There is almost no such thing as loyalty [in Louisiana], as that word is understood in the North."⁷ "There may be the seed of loyalty," Sidney Andrews reported after visiting the South, "but woe to him who mistakes the germ for the ripened fruit! . . . How full of promise for the new national life is the Unionism which rests only on this foundation?"⁸

This chapter considers a pair of novels that proposed representative Northern answers to Andrews's question. The first, John De Forest's *Miss Ravenel's Conversion from Secession to Loyalty* (1867), is today the best-known example of the reunion romance; the second, *The Gates Ajar* (1868), by Elizabeth Stuart Phelps, was an international best seller, but until recently has been regularly ignored by critics. Both seek to disseminate loyalty on the national scale by demonstrating the domestic felicity of coerced consent and propose that companionate unions predicated on loyalty would stabilize rebellious tendencies and harmonize political families.

The image of a happy (monogamous, consent-based) nuclear family has long provided "an elementary sense of what the political community is like" by creating "units of feeling around which emotions of loyalty and assurance can cluster."⁹ In the case of the United States, with its foundational emphasis on consent, romantic love has been especially important; as Werner Sollors explains, American identity was forged from a mix of national and romantic language.¹⁰ The Civil War was, thus, love gone bad. "A husband and wife may be divorced," Abraham Lincoln reminded Congress in 1862, "and go out of the presence, and beyond the reach of each other; but the different parts of our country cannot do this. They cannot but remain face to face; and intercourse, either amicable or hostile, must continue between them."¹¹ Reading this passage, Priscilla Wald notes that political conditions "prompt[ed] Lincoln to reject the marriage contract as emblem of the bond of Union."¹² Indeed, during the years bracketing the Civil War, thinkers grappled repeatedly with how to characterize the consent institutionalized in the constitutional compact. They wondered, for example, how binding should the union be? Was it permanent, like a marriage, or open to renegotiation, like an economic contract? Was it the result of choice or a matter of necessity? In short, could its bonds be broken?[13]

These queries drew many different responses, including a literary genre: the reunion romance. In these stories, novels, and plays, a virile Union officer successfully woos a rebellious Southern belle: the resulting "heart-union" figures the happily reconstructed nation, implicitly endorsing the nuptial model of contract.[14] Although such stories were not postwar innovations—novels uniting the sections appeared consistently throughout the early nineteenth century—the harmonious future imagined in these increasingly popular tales not only united the sections but also put the gendered South in its proper (subordinate) place. As Karen Keely explains, reunion narratives posited that "what the United States needed was not military, legal, or financial Reconstruction, but rather a voluntary emotional reconciliation of Northerner and Southerner in a mutually forgiving relationship."[15] The close association of nation and family in definitions of loyalty, and the related belief, widely held, that lasting national affiliation should have an affective component, helps to account for the popularity of these idealized narratives of antipathy overcome. In short, "reunion romances operated in the confidence that passions—love, desire, and suffering—rule human emotions."[16]

What critics have neglected, however, is that "confidence" in the "passions" had been shaken to its core by several emotions not included in the above list—hatred, rage, and grief. Throughout the war, Northerners regularly claimed that being ruled by emotion engendered chaos, not moral and social peace. Given the tremendous costs that had been incurred by feelings out of control, one needed to be careful with whom one identified and what kind of emotional connection ensued. Failure to consider how emotion was (de)valued during the Civil War, and the related decline of its cultural role, has led critics to misunderstand the aims and anxieties of authors writing in the early years of Reconstruction.

Through a key revision to the reunion romance, De Forest and Phelps register both resistance to reunion and the means of overcoming it. The Southern heroine in *Miss Ravenel's Conversion* marries a Union officer—and is unhappy. Not until she marries again, this time choosing a Union man fully approved by her father, does she finds marital happiness and fidelity. In offering *remarriage* as a model for reunion, De Forest adapts the political analogy between nation and family to represent the prevailing conditions of Reconstruction more accurately. Engaging in her own generic innovations, Phelps likewise revises the reunion romance to include the dead. The heavenly reconstruction of perfected families will, Phelps posits, safeguard the future of family and nation, converting rebels into productive members of the community. Second marriages provide both authors with the conditions of possibility for reinstalling individuals in nurturing and stable (national) families.

Remarriage, as opposed to initial courtships, "show[s] how the miracle of change may be brought about," Stanley Cavell opines in his study of Hollywood remarriage comedies.[17] "A running quarrel is forcing apart a pair who recognize themselves as having known one another forever," Cavell explains, "that is from the beginning, not just in the past but in a period before there was a past, before history." What remarriage brings to the fore, in other words, is how couples might come to appreciate, and alter, their "known disposition[s]" and entrenched prejudices (like those worrying Pollard). In bringing Cavell's study to bear on the reunion romance, I am expanding his focus on narratives about couples that remarry one another to narratives about remarriage more generally. In so doing, however, I retain what is, for Cavell, a critical element of the remarriage comedy: developing the capacity for recognition. Characters in the films he studies must learn to see, hear, and understand one another, putting aside past differences and established biases. As they imagine what "acknowledgment" would mean and require, these movies are fantasies that "express the inner agenda of a nation": "the reconciliation of genuine forgiveness; a reconciliation so profound as to require the metamorphosis of death and revival."[18] The reunion remarriage also "express[es] the inner agenda of a nation," particularly in its ability to re-cognize the nation's founding principles. Remarriage presupposes the importance of both a shared history *and* a thorough rupture to recognition and reconstruction for family and, by analogy, nation. Finally, the remarriage plot translates the repetition basic to the loyalty oath into an important structural feature of the novel.

The national agenda on display in the remarriage romance is not predicated on forgiveness, however. The issue for De Forest and Phelps is a preventative one; their shared aim is to forestall the possibility of future misunderstanding by associating recognition (and freedom) with authoritative oversight. In coupling the remarriage plot to an argument for concentrated authority, the ideal of recognition on display in *Miss*

Ravenel's Conversion and *The Gates Ajar* eschews knowledge for comfort, personal development for conformity. In the early years of the war, James Russell Lowell had asserted that "the nation cries out for a master mind, and the people, eager for the discipline of a true ruler, are learning anew the worth of authority, and willing to render as never before a loyal obedience."[19] In the "expanded authority" and "new set of purposes" of the national state, these cries were answered; they were also echoed in novels that reiterated the ideal of loyal submission, of learning *not* to rebel.[20] The "war demanded that soldiers be loyal to a new patriarchal authority, the state," and discipline and obedience came to be hallmarks of loyalty, patriotism, and moral fiber, and even evidence of good breeding.[21] Glossing over tensions inherent in the contradictory subject positions these competing requirements presupposed—submission to authority and the principle of uncoerced consent—was critical to the evolving definition of loyalty.

It is fair to say, in other words, that Phelps and De Forest take a quasi-Hobbesian stance on consent and coercion, in which freedom is vouchsafed through the installation of an authoritative guide. Given Hobbes's explicit goal—the prevention of civil war—this is surely no surprise. It is not "Battell onely, or the act of fighting" that characterizes civil war, he explains in *Leviathan*, because the "nature of Warre," like that of "the Weather," must be measured according to inclination or "known disposition[s]." According to Hobbes, without "a common Power," men remain in the condition of war, even if they are not in combat (185–186). In implicit agreement, De Forest and Phelps couple the concept of loyalty with the seemingly paradoxical claim that freedom's fullest expression occurs under the watchful eye of authority. The representation of remarriage subtends this position for two reasons: it more accurately reflects the political situation, and it indicates why continued guidance is necessary to achieve a happier future the second time around. Both authors work through the idea that neither self-interest nor the unguided will yields the conditions of possibility for us to realize our best, our most enduring, constitutional happiness; the paradox of American consent, they imply, is that we only develop the abilities to make substantive choices by recognizing our own limitations and submitting to authoritative control.

By returning briefly to Hobbes, we can see further how this argument also addresses the concern about referential instability with which this chapter began. As Don Herzog observes, "Imposing an authoritative judgment isn't another approach to interpretation; it's an attempt to escape the messy business of interpretation altogether." On Herzog's view, Hobbes's project can be defined as an attempt to furnish "a political vocabulary within which insurrectionary arguments" would be "incoherent."[22] Hobbes sought to address the "problem of distrust in politics" without turning to the kinds of rhetorical solutions he believed had led to the lack of trust in the first place.[23] For these reasons, then, it is the Hobbesian model of contract, rather than Locke's or Rousseau's, that resonates in the political choices made during the early years of Reconstruction.[24] In this historical moment, we see "less than fully democratic or open procedures" introduced "in the hopes of making things more democratic and open."[25]

One additional premise about language underwrites the novels examined in this chapter, namely that fiction can play a decisive role in shaping the national community and writing its history.[26] A powerful instrument of "the national culture industry," the novel provides readers with images and narratives that "replac[e] and simplif[y] memories people actually have with image traces of political experience about which people can have political feelings that link them to other citizens and to patriotism."[27] For De Forest and Phelps alike, there was one novel—*Uncle Tom's Cabin*—that offered an example of how people's "political feelings" might be inspired. Phelps calls Stowe "the greatest of American women," but De Forest's praise is even more fulsome. "Is there," he asks, "a single tale which paints American life so broadly, truly, and sympathetically that every American of feeling and culture is forced to acknowledge the picture as a likeness of something which he knows? Throwing out 'Uncle Tom's Cabin' we must answer, Not one!"[28] "There were very noticeable faults in that story. . . . But there was also a national breadth to the picture, truthful outlining of character, natural speaking, and plenty of strong feeling. Though comeliness of form was lacking, the material of the work was in many respects admirable. . . . It was a picture of American life, drawn with a few strong and passionate strokes, not filled in thoroughly, but still a portrait."[29] The merely local could not speak so directly to "every American," a danger that surely seemed more frightening in 1868 than it does today.

Critics tend to locate American literary nationalism in the years before the Civil War, but Reconstruction witnessed a new permutation of its aims as novels were seen as providing a way "to create a vital national culture, to unify a heterogeneous society, to heal political divisions, and quiet political contentiousness."[30] As Marianne Noble reminds us, "the sentimental project is one of unification."[31] It is no surprise, then, that its conventions would have appeared ideally suited to the conversion of rebels into contented citizens. Ellen Warner's mother only has a cameo role in *The Wide Wide World* (1850), yet this is time enough to teach her daughter a critical lesson: "though we *must* sorrow, we must not rebel."[32] Taming the rebellious temper of a female child differs, of course, from tempering the rebellious desires of a region, even one regularly gendered feminine, but the analogy is underwritten by the intimacy asserted between moral affect and national allegiance. As the preceding chapter demonstrated, the generic mission of sentimental novels consisted in the defense of right feeling as a moral necessity; loyalty easily enough replaced sympathy in popular postbellum narratives. "The American female culture industry," Lauren Berlant explains, "developed a series of generic strategies—which might be called 'modes of constraint'—whose purpose was to testify to the heretofore 'private' trials of womanhood, to demystify patriarchal practices, and to consolidate female collective identity without necessarily abrogating 'woman's' loyalty to heterosexual culture."[33] By demonstrating that a like consolidation was forwarded by a different ideal in the romances of reunion under examination in this chapter, it will be possible to see how "'women's' loyalty to heterosexual culture" could be conflated directly with the nation. More attuned than their antebellum peers to how region, race, and gender might complicate the novelist's nationalizing ambitions, De Forest and Phelps not only believed that the novel of remarriage could accomplish these goals but, further, that through fiction "every American" would be "forced to acknowledge" his or her place in the nation.

One last observation before turning to the novels themselves: romance is not the only possibility for envisioning national reconciliation. Walt Whitman's "merge" sought to achieve national unification, without relying on the normative nuclear family as its exclusive vehicle. Using the new genre of the detective novel, Metta Victor argued that epistemological clarity was more likely to heal the damage done to the nation by violence and death than a convenient union. Finally, the Ohio Hegelians found in dialectic a potent vision of how opposing positions could result in a fruitful synthesis. In short, there were options available to writers interested in depicting national reconciliation besides the nuclear family; that authors, including De Forest and Phelps, chose to rely primarily on romantic heterosexual love speaks volumes about Americans' symbolic investment in a particular model of family as the repository of national legitimacy and personal morality.[34]

* * *

Miss Ravenel's Conversion from Secession to Loyalty follows the adventures of the Ravenel family, displaced from their New Orleans home before the start of the novel. Stalwart in his loyalty, Dr. Ravenel would have easily met the stringent requirements for loyalty established by the Reconstruction Act *after* the novel's publication: refusing all voluntary aid to the Confederacy, he abandons his home rather than be associated with convictions he cannot share. Now domiciled in New Boston, the doctor and his daughter Lillie, an ardent rebel, make the acquaintance first of Edward Colburne, a native of New England, and then of Virginian John Carter, both of whom become enamored of Lillie. Despite her father's preference for Colburne, Lillie marries Carter. The marriage ends badly, as Carter's infidelity more than justifies the doctor's early dislike, but Lillie is spared embarrassment and divorce by her husband's honorable and convenient death on the battlefield. With time, Lillie's heart conforms to her father's wishes, her political affiliations shift, and she chooses Colburne as her second husband. The novel moves between New Boston and New Orleans, to which the Ravenels return in the hopes of repairing their fortunes. Their southern sojourn is complicated by the schemes of Mrs. Larue, a relative by marriage; an attempt to mend their fortunes by employing freed slaves on a deserted Louisiana plantation; and various military campaigns. The close of *Miss Ravenel's Conversion* finds the extended family happily settled in a Northern cottage, contemplating the antics of Lillie's young son, Ravvie, and musing upon the fate of the nation.

Since its initial publication, critics have seen *Miss Ravenel's Conversion* as divided into two unequal parts, dismissing the trials of its "trifling" heroine while lauding the realism of the "light, strong" depiction of war.[35] But overlooking Lillie's conversion from local partisan to national patriot obscures important dimensions of De Forest's political program, fashioned from a combination of sentimental conversion and contemporary political philosophy.[36] De Forest's investment in "national breadth" is manifested in *Miss Ravenel's Conversion* by a constant concern for the cultivation of proper national affect necessary to transcend perilously narrow or local affiliations. Early in the novel, for example, Lillie is faulted for having "strictly local" and "narrowly geographical" "feelings and opinions."[37] "Born and nurtured among Louisianans," Lillie "held rather firm for Louisiana in spite of the arguments of the adored papa and the rather agreeable admirer" (58). Nor is this unique: sadly, the narrator explains, "all young people and almost all women" share Lillie's preferences (11). "It is worthy of passing remark," the narrator notes, "how loyal the young are to the prevailing ideas of the community in which they are nurtured. You will find adult republicans in England, but no infant ones; adult monarchists in our own country, but not in our schools and nurseries" (58). The "prevailing ideas" of a community so influence the young that their opinions are a matter of emotion or instinct, not careful reflection or volition. The feelings we have for our native soil—Lillie declares "that Louisiana was her country, and that to it she owed her allegiance"—should not be confused, De Forest cautions, with an obligation established by other means (58): it is all too easy to be seduced by "the prejudices and trammels of geographical morality" (51). "Geographical morality" should not be confused with proper loyalty, De Forest contends; the latter combats the tyranny of the local by introducing a critical perspective that helps us to balance personal and public, local and national interests. Even as the novel argues for this position, however, it is clear that such equilibrium is hard to maintain, for being partial to people and places near to us is integral to the human condition. Remaining vigilant is thus a critical dimension of the discipline required for proper allegiance.

By offering a detailed investigation of the different kinds of affective affiliations and their impact on the nation, De Forest takes seriously Stowe's charge to "See, then, to your sympathies in this matter!"[38] For De Forest, the man or woman who feels wrongly, rebelliously, and partially is a traitor, actual or potential; personal sympathies must be subordinated to and disciplined by loyalty. Thus Carter's decision to fight for the Union, not his home state Virginia, wins him the support of many of the Northern characters—but not the narrator. His opposition to secession notwithstanding, Carter is still "a true child of his class and State," for "it was only in political matters that he was false to his birth-place. In his strong passions, his capacity for domestic sympathies, his strange conscience (as sensitive on some points as callous on others), his spendthrift habits, his inclination to swearing and drinking, his mixture in short of gentility and barbarism, he was a *true child* of his class and State" (144). A "capacity for domestic sympathies" may appear out of place, yet in the wake of the war this seeming virtue was still a potential source of treason. In Carter's case, potential becomes actual when he betrays the U.S. government, just like his parent state.

The "capacity for domestic sympathies" is not only a problem for children, however, as De Forest is equally severe with mothers. Ruled by "the cry of [her] mother's heart," Mrs. Colburne's loyalty is compromised by her love for her son: "Earnestly as she sympathised with its loyal and humane objects, she was not logical enough or not firm enough to sympathise with the iron thing itself" (68). Included as a didactic impediment—her narrative role seems exclusively to *prevent* her son from enlisting in the Union army—Mrs. Colburne underscores for readers that properly disciplined affections are a *national* problem because potential rebellion is rooted in formerly prized sentiments.[39] "Other women's sons," the text continues, "yes, if there was no help for it—but not hers—might put on the panoply of strife, and disappear from anxiously following eyes into the smoke and flame of battle" (68). Captured in this overwrought sentence is a common theme of wartime literature, namely that a loyal mother would never prevent her son from enlisting. In "Mother, Can I Go?" a representative 1862 enlistment poem, a "Connecticut lad" exhaustively "flame[s]" the "ardor on [his] loyal mother's part" so she will agree that he is "old enough . . . to be loyal, proud and true."[40] Mrs. Colburne's inclusion recalls such enlistment propaganda and extends De Forest's engagement with the definition of loyalty to include its conflict with the familial affections at the core of antebellum arguments about sympathy's moral power. It was easy enough to argue with Horace Bushnell that loyalty was akin to "family love," but such a comparison should not be confused, De Forest contends, with the endorsement of a maternal love that hampers the nation's ability to fight.

In addition to differentiating loyalty from sympathy, De Forest distinguishes *between* kinds of sympathetic identification, some negative, like overly emotional sympathy for the Southern cause, and some positive, as in appropriately directed "patriotic sympathy" (6). Because he had been driven from New Orleans by his emotional neighbors, "[Dr. Ravenel's] story was worth telling," the narrator notes, especially as "it had to do with his sentiments and convictions" not "his interests." Why should he not relate it to a stranger who was evidently capable of sympathising with those sentiments and appreciating those convictions?" (11). The balance of "sentiments and convictions"—necessary to the choice of loyalty—is a story "worth telling," one in which Northern patriots would rightly have a sympathetic interest. That is to say, loyalty did not require the repudiation of *all* feeling but instead the combination of emotion with reason and duty—the regulation of emotion, not its eradication.

Associated with De Forest's anatomy of various modes of affective affiliation is a concern, shared with Pollard, about the limits of language to influence or change emotion. The narrator thus complains that "women, especially warm-hearted women... are so terribly illogical!" The only way to convert "Miss Ravenel from the doctrine of state sovereignty" is to attack—literally—someone she loves: "If Mr. Secretary Seward, with all his constitutional lore and persuasive eloquence, had argued with her for three weeks, he could not have converted her; but the moment a southern ruffian knocked her father on the head, she began to see that secession was indefensible, and that the American Union ought to be preserved" (139). That women's emotions resist rational argument, established political practices ("constitutional lore"), and "persuasive eloquence" presents a special challenge to anyone hoping to alter their convictions. After a conversation with a young woman disfigured at the Brown's Island munitions laboratory, recorded in *The South: A Tour of Its Battle-Fields and Ruined Cities* (1865), J. T. Trowbridge similarly concluded that women could not be converted by rational appeals:

> A man may be reasoned and beaten out of a false opinion, but a woman never. She will not yield to logic, not even to the logic of events. Thus it happens that, while the male secessionists at the South have frankly given up their cause, the female secessionists still cling to it with provoking tenacity. To appeal to their intelligence is idle; but they are vulnerable on the side of the sentiments; and many a one has been authentically converted from the heresy of state rights by some handsome Federal officer, who judiciously mingled love with loyalty in his speech, and pleaded for the union of hands as well as the union of States.[41]

Trowbridge gestures here at the facticity of the romance of reunion: on this view, the romances were not utopian fantasies but accurate reflections of authentic conversion. Separate from confusing the relationship between fiction and fact, Trowbridge's assertion troubles the neat boundary critics have tended to draw in *Miss Ravenel's Conversion* between the realistic battle scenes and the love plot. In 1867, discerning the difference was neither easy nor obvious.

If words have so little power to convert, why do De Forest and Trowbridge devote significant energy to deploring violent rhetoric? Turning again to *The South*, we see Trowbridge assuring his Northern readers that the seeming vehemence of Southern speech should be ignored as so much impotent frustration: "The mere utterance of disloyal sentiments need not alarm any one. It is often sincere; but it is sometimes mere cant, easily kept in vogue, by newspapers and politicians, among a people who delight in vehement and minatory talk, for the mere talk's sake."[42] The

South lacks the resources and will to turn again to armed rebellion, he observes, so these speech habits—"vehement and minatory"—are entirely empty. Yet Trowbridge's explanation fails to resolve the loyalty worries he hopes to combat: to assert that Southerners do not mean what they say reiterates the concern about unreliability that animated Northern anxiety about loyalty oaths. If Southern speech is not trustworthy, why should readers believe those former Confederates who declare their eagerness to rejoin the nation? Because, Trowbridge explains, for many Southerners, rejoining the union "was like going home." "You are glad [your state] is back in the Union again?" Trowbridge asks a Virginian he meets on his travels. "To tell you the truth, I am," the Virginian replies:

> "I think more of the Union, too, than I ever did before. It was a square, stand-up fight; we got beaten, and I suppose it is all for the best. The very hottest Secessionists are now the first to come back and offer support to the government." He tapped a little tin trunk he carried. "I have fifty pardons here, which I am carrying from Washington to Richmond, for men who, a year ago, you would have said would drown themselves sooner than take the oath of allegiance to the United States. It was a rich sight to see these very men crowding to take the oath. It was a bitter pill to some . . . ; but the rest were glad enough to get back into the old Union. It was like going home."[43]

Returning "home" to the nation is not only a figure: without taking the oath, Southern men could not regain their rights as U.S. citizens. The image included in *The South* to illustrate this homecoming strips the act of taking the oath of its monumental aspects, representing it instead as uneventful and even bureaucratic (fig. 2). Some men wait calmly in a line, others chat in pairs; no one carries a weapon, and, although some of the men wear Union uniforms, no national or political emblems are evident. Indeed, when compared to other visual representations of oath-taking, like Jacques-Louis David's famous *Oath of the Horatii* (1784–1785), for example, the most striking aspect of this drawing is that it is *dull*, utterly resistant to the kind of drama that David associated with the act of swearing an oath. If the French painter conveys the "physical moment of tension of founding the future in the exaltation of the moment," the anonymous illustrator of "Taking the Oath of Allegiance" works diligently to drain the event of anything approaching either tension or drama.[44] Although the men in the foreground could be said to frame the central action, the busy visual program makes it surprisingly difficult

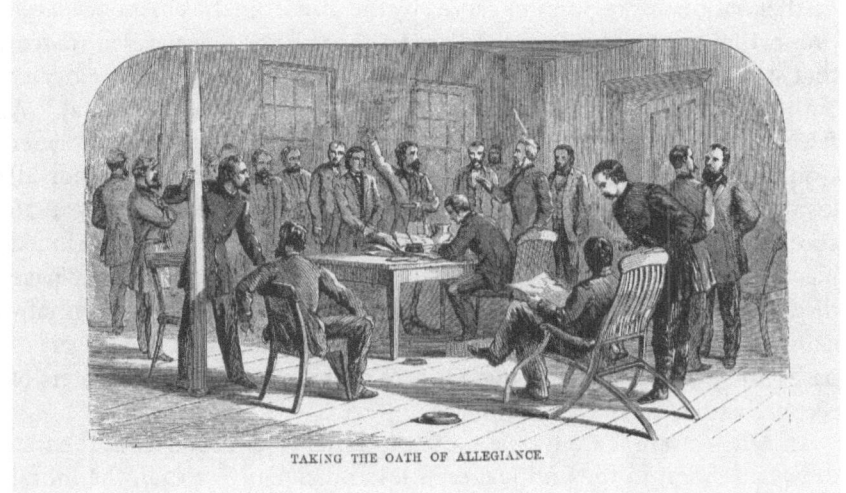

FIGURE 2. "Taking the Oath of Allegiance," from J. T. Trowbridge, *The South: A Tour of Its Battle—Fields and Ruined Cities*. The composition generally recalls John Trumbull's "Declaration of Independence," placed in the Capitol rotunda in 1826. Its visual program counters Southern complaints of Northern tyranny, while endorsing the idea that the Union victory meant a refounding of the nation according to the ideals of the framers.

to focus on the act of swearing, especially as a strong vertical line in the foreground, a white column, distracts the eye, without providing any substantial symbolic or narrative content.

While the illustration works hard to present the act of swearing as banal, Trowbridge admits that for some Southerners, the oath—a "bitter pill"—was precisely the opposite: "We would not vote for [men who had taken the test oath]," one Southerner tells him. "We had rather have no representatives at all. We want representatives to *represent* us, and no man *represents* us who can take your test oath."[45] In the "Supplement" to *Battle-Pieces*, Herman Melville summarizes the political problem facing the nation: "Not readily can one perceive how the political existence of the millions of late Secessionists can permanently be ignored by this Republic. The years of the war tried our devotion to the Union; this time of peace may test the sincerity of our faith in democracy."[46] These competing perspectives anticipate the changing political fortunes of Civil War loyalty oaths. For a time, such tests prevented former Confederates from political participation, but Washington soon determined that neither nation nor region was served by the disenfranchisement of a large proportion of the population. In 1867, the Supreme Court ruled (twice) that state and federal legislation requiring individuals to swear a loyalty oath in order to continue in their professions was unconstitutional.[47] A few years later, the General Amnesty Act (1872) allowed most former Confederates to hold national office, and by the end of Reconstruction all loyalty tests were revoked, their constitutionality in question. The 1876 compromise that seated Rutherford B. Hayes as president abandoned black Americans to decades of violent oppression. Politicians may have discarded the project of measuring loyalty through oaths as pragmatically impossible, but Americans retained a keen interest in the powers of oaths and promises, the proper affect of allegiance, or the parameters of reconciliation.

In *Miss Ravenel's Conversion*, the prominence of promises and oaths draws attention to the political realities and, equally crucial, the moral implications of verbal contracts, especially the role of individual honor in establishing their obligations. De Forest's project—articulating the new parameters of national allegiance—is thus conjoined to an articulation of new "ethical rules" associated with it, a move that parallels and completes his careful explication of sympathy's limits. His emphasis on the verbal pledge—characters repeatedly promise, swear, and pledge—is key, in part because the antebellum South had associated moral certainty with personal honor. "In societies of small communities," where "judgments of behavior are ratified by communal consensus," honor organizes a "cluster of ethical rules," Bertram Wyatt-Brown explains.[48] The new "ethical rules" De Forest posits in *Miss Ravenel's Conversion* replace individual honor with duty, defined in part by an external authority. In an early discussion of a Union officer of mixed blood, De Forest sketches the tension between honor and duty:

> "When this war broke out [Major Meurice] came home to see if he might be permitted to fight for his race, and for his and my country. He now wears the same uniform that I do, and he is my superior officer."
>
> "It is shameful," broke out Lillie.
>
> "It is the will of authority," answered Colburne,—"of authority that I have sworn to respect."
>
> "A southern gentleman would resign," said Mrs. Larue.
>
> "A northern gentleman keeps his oath and stands by his flag," retorted Colburne. (164)

The compelling claim, on Colburne's view, is the one vouchsafed by authority, military hierarchy, and the kind of honor associated with doing one's duty: characteristically these are best represented in the flag. Although De Forest softens the critique, by putting the Southern masculine ideal in women's mouths, the interchange nonetheless establishes the Northern model as the more binding.

These issues return with more narrative and theoretical emphasis when Carter schemes to defraud the Union government. As his partner in crime, Carter needs a man whose word he can trust: this man must also, of course, break his oath of allegiance to the nation:

> "Mr. Hollister," said Carter, "I hope I shall not offend you if I say that I know you have suffered heavily by the war."
>
> "I shall certainly not be offended. I am obliged to you for showing the slightest interest in my affairs."
>
> "You have taken the oath of allegiance—haven't you?"
>
> Mr. Hollister said "Yes," and bowed respectfully, as if saluting the United States Government.
>
> "It is only fair that you should obtain remuneration for your losses. . . . I know of a transaction—an investment," pursued Carter, "which will probably enable you to pocket—to realize—perhaps twenty thousand dollars."
>
> "I should be indebted to you for life. Whatever service I can render in return will be given with all my heart."
>
> "It requires secrecy. May I ask you to pledge your word?"
>
> "I pledge it, Colonel—my word of honor—as a Louisiana gentleman." (378)

Carter seeks certainty that his dishonorable behavior will remain secret, certainty he uses the performative pledge to deliver. The repetition of the demand, however, reveals again the theoretical problem we saw previously in using the oath to establish certainty: only in retrospect can a promise be judged to have been truthfully made. In this instance, Carter cannot know if Hollister is promising honestly, the very information the second pledge, the "word of honor," is intended to verify. Indeed, given Dr. Ravenel's prior claim—that anyone remaining in Louisiana after the start of the war could *not* be loyal to the government—it is likely that Mr. Hollister has already made an oath that is not genuine. If, as Brook Thomas argues, the nature of the contract presupposes "handing over their reputations as trustworthy people to one another" and allowing "themselves to be measured by the same standard of accountability," then it is hard to see how Northerners could trust traitorous Southerners.[49] That is to say, "one's reputation as a reliable person," crucial to any account of promising, is precisely what the Civil War rendered incoherent.[50] The above reiteration of pledges points beyond the economic agreement, which is successfully negotiated, to what remains uncertain—the reliability of the parties involved.[51]

There is one final element of this scene's representation of pledging relevant to its commentary on the state of contemporary politics and morals. The conversation opens as Mr. Hollister offers the colonel "a glass of brandy" from his well-stocked cellar. Carter quickly drinks "half a tumbler of pure brandy," while his host sips "a weak sling" "to keep his visitor in countenance" (378). Contemporary readers would surely have linked Carter's moral failings with this taste for liquor, but there is more at stake in De Forest's decision to frame this scene of shady business practices with social drinking. As Amanda Claybaugh argues, temperance narratives often relied on a technique of "doubled promising," in which a temperance pledge repeats and augments a marriage vow; typically this second promise would stress the necessity of submission.[52] De Forest's use of the temperance theme twists the critique of marriage Claybaugh finds operative in stories like "The Dangers of Dining Out" and "The Favourite Child," making it consonant with the political priorities of the romance of reunion.

The irrationality, loss of control, and potential violence affiliated with representations of alcohol abuse are correlated in *Miss Ravenel's Conversion* with the depiction of Southerners as savage. Throughout the novel, Southerners are likened to multiple savage others—the Ashantee (6), the Chinese (9), "the pirates of the Isle of Pines" (48), the Pawnee (190), and the Amazon (217)—continuing the American tradition of racializing enemy combatants.[53] When Lillie complains that Northerners are "so ferociously federal," Dr. Ravenel replies, "My dear, if one of these loyal ladies should say a word for her own lawful government in New Orleans, she would be worse than glared at. I doubt whether the wild-mannered cut-throats of your native city would let her off with plain hanging. Let us thank Heaven that we are among civilized people who only glare at us, and do not stick us under the fifth rib, when we differ with them in opinion" (50). As will be explored in chapter 3, such associations also drew upon events on the western frontier, most notably the Dakota conflict of 1862, for their rhetorical force. Compared to wartime representations, however, De Forest's characterization is tame; in "Bone Ornaments" (1862), a Virginia woman "forget[s] the loss of her slaves" by ornamenting herself with decorative items made from Union skeletons, including a "white and fine" brooch and a fan crafted from the "finger-bone of a Lincoln man."[54] An 1862 cartoon could serve as an illustration to the poem; the pseudo-civilization of "Secesh" culture is clearly depicted as vicious, complete with references to scalping (fig. 3).[55] Like Trowbridge, De Forest assigns the fiercest rhetoric to Southern woman, allowing him to express respect for Confederate soldiers while deploring the effects of Southern nationalism. Lingering regional antagonism is thus dismissed as a violent fit of feminine pique.

It is to De Forest's understanding of submission, to the constitution of appropriate control and guidance, that I now turn. In *Miss Ravenel's Conversion*, many of the problems associated with sympathy, as either a political or a moral mode of affiliation, can be cured through the careful tutelage of an authoritative figure, someone who has cultivated an abstract perspective. This person can be trusted to make judgments of benefit to the entire nation, not just a particular family, region, or state. Because self-interested people cannot be relied on to choose what is best for either themselves or their nation, the freedom in free consent is best achieved through control and coercion. In the failure of Lillie's first marriage, De Forest offers clear evidence of this position. Carter's careful self-presentation and a misplaced confidence in her own knowledge blind Lillie to the dangers of placing her trust in him.

> Her father hinted; but she thought him unreasonably prejudiced; she made what she considered the proper allowance for men who wore uniforms. She had very little idea of the stupendous discount which would have to be admitted before Colonel Carter could figure up as an angel of light, or even as a decently virtuous member of human society. She thought she stated the whole subject fairly when she admitted that he might be "fast;" but she had an innocently inadequate conception of the meaning which the masculine sex attaches to that epithet. (89)

Lillie's mistakes are depicted as innocent, but her faith in her own knowledge, coupled with an inability to recognize her limits, renders her obstinacy dangerous as well as naive.

Informed that Lillie has accepted Carter's offer of marriage, Ravenel must confront the challenge of consenting against his will, of resisting the urge to behave like a tyrant:

> "I can *not* consent. I will *not* consent. It is *not* my duty. Oh, Lillie!

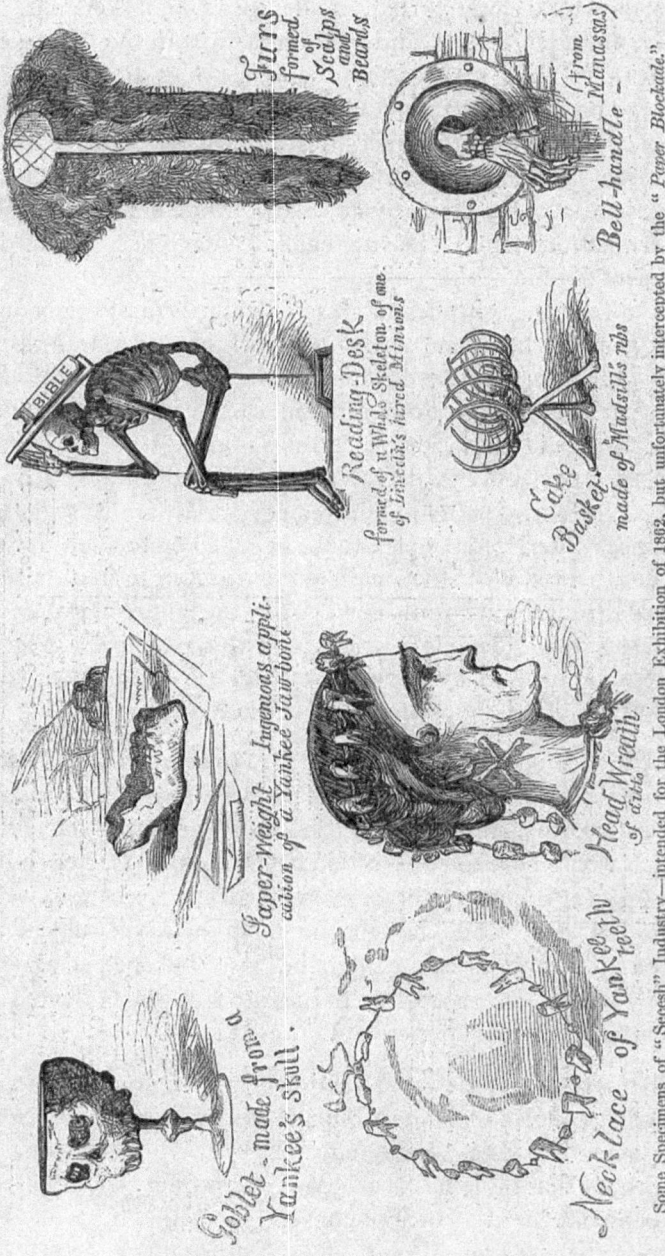

Some Specimens of "Secesh" Industry—intended for the London Exhibition of 1862, but unfortunately intercepted by the "Paper Blockade."

how could you choose the very man of all that—! I tell you this must not be. It must stop here. I have *no* confidence in him. He will *not* make you happy. He will make you miserable. I tell you that you will regret the day you marry him to the last moment of your life. My child," (persuasively) "you *must* believe me. You *must* trust my judgment. Will you not be persuaded? Will you not stop where you are?" (181)

The series of short, declarative sentences forcefully presents Ravenel's predicament: his experience with men like Carter anticipates the man's eventual career. Rather than deny his consent, however, he institutes a series of rules designed to provide his daughter with the time to reflect more carefully on her choice. The narrator justifies the apparent contradiction in his eventual assent—if an authoritative guide is necessary, why does he allow Lillie to make this mistake?—by associating too-narrow, too-directive behavior with scheming women (a gendering strategy pervasive throughout the novel). Because De Forest is reconstructing consent along with the nation, his characters *must choose* to follow the proper path, even if they stumble several times along the way.

The political stakes of De Forest's argument become clearer when the novel is compared to Martha Finely's *Elsie Dinsmore* (1868), which likewise explores a relationship between father and daughter. In Finely's Southern tale, however, the father's authority is far from beneficial to his child. Judging Elsie's rigid piety as rebellion, the father seeks to thwart what he deems her attempts to "conquer" him. The extended scene, which repeatedly returns to the question of how to negotiate between submission and personal belief, culminates in violence when Elsie falls from a stool and cuts her head. In response, members of the household opine that "a parent has no right to coerce a child into doing violence to its conscience."[56] Literally overturning the Northern position, Finely implies that strategies like the one De Forest recommends result in bloodshed because they value coercion over conviction, secular forms of authority over divine command. On Finely's alternate view, reminiscent of Confederate claims, resistance to the charges of an overreaching authority constitutes the moral mode of behavior.

But for De Forest, it is only a mature (and thus national) perspective, one that has subdued the rebellious potential of local partisanship, that can achieve the consent integral to the country's future. On his view, a

FIGURE 3 (opposite page). "Some Specimens of 'Secesh' Industry," *Harper's Weekly*, June 7, 1862. (Courtesy HarpWeek, LLC)

child—such as Lillie or Elsie—is too readily swept up by local enthusiasm to be reliable. Once Lillie has achieved the self-knowledge De Forest associates with maturity, she can "resig[n] herself" to "the man whom she ought always to have loved" (463). To demonstrate the completion of Lillie's conversion, De Forest includes a second suitor—the wealthy Mr. Whitewood—who proposes, and is refused. Recognizing that she loves Colburne more than her first husband, and that "[she is] right in loving him," Lillie asks her fiancé if the years of separation have diminished his affections for her. "You are all the dearer for it," he replies, "perhaps it ought not to be so; but so it is, my darling" (464). The second marriage replaces the first—the narrator is clear that the characters never speak of it again—demonstrating how romantic reconciliation can efface years of separation, hardship, and pain.

It is not in religion, or politics, or even "Authority" that De Forest finds the model for how this perfected knowledge is best formed, however: he turns instead to science and its seeming methodological objectivity (219). Not only is Ravenel professionally committed to medicine, he devotes his spare time to "a life-long scientific enthusiasm" for mineralogy (45).[57] For the nineteenth-century American, mineralogy, a branch of geology, presented a thrilling (or horrifying) new way of thinking about the world: Charles Lyell's *Principles of Geology* (1830) revealed the earth to be vastly older than the Bible proposed, replacing belief with seemingly impartial facts. While Charles Darwin's subsequent discoveries proved more unsettling over time, Lyell's geology permitted the conclusion that science, not God, might provide the final authority for human matters. According to Lyell, the geologist had to abandon the "merely local" for a broader—systemic or global—perspective.[58] Free of bias, superstition, belief, or prejudice, the kind of objectivity Ravenel refines through mineralogical research enables him to make equally evenhanded judgments in other areas. Using Ravenel's amateur endeavors to demonstrate the values of science, De Forest refigures the tension between the local and the systemic or national, coupling it to a new source and model of authority.

De Forest develops this argument across the early pages of the novel, as he melds domestic space, scientific experiment, and political theory. After the arrival of "a weighty box of specimens," Dr. Ravenel, suddenly "dowered with an embarrassment of riches," becomes wed to his work, although his attitude toward the specimens—he "domineered with a face wrinkled with happy anxiety" over the rocks spread across "his bed, sofa, table, wash-stand, chairs and floor"—could be read as equally parental as spousal (54). It is not just rocks he domineers, though, for Ravenel routinely demands—it was his "constant prattle"—that Lillie respect his efforts by keeping quiet (53). The balance between the father's tendency to raise "the standard of revolt" and the daughter's chatty rebellions notwithstanding, the pair are said to be on terms of near equality: "Ever since Lillie's earliest recollection they had been on these same terms of sociability, companionship, almost equality. The intimacy and democracy of the relation arose partly from the Doctor's extreme fondness for children and young people, and partly from the fact that he had lost his wife early, so that in his household he had for years depended for sympathy upon his daughter" (51, 53). References to "revolt," "equality," and "democracy" all associate the house with heated contemporary political debates. Despite the purported equality of the relationship between father and daughter, however, Lillie's constant interruptions ("twice or thrice each morning") meet with "velvety and harmless cuffing" to enforce the rule of silence and other means of "aveng[ing]" transgressions (53). What is most important about this early scene, though, is how De Forest uses the Ravenel family to envision democracy in a postwar context. Linking their domestic arrangements with political organization, De Forest argues that equality and democracy are consistent with authoritative oversight, figured in the passage as the response of "an affectionate old cat" to a playful kitten (53).[59] Naturalizing hierarchy, imbuing it with maternal instinct and associating it with the cute play of kittens, De Forest's comparison of nation and family presupposes that the careful control of unruly women (or feminized sections) is best accomplished by a parental figure with only the best of intentions.

The doctor's commitment to universal forms of knowledge is aligned in the novel with a form of democracy inflected with monarchical hierarchy; his is a gentle form of domination, saturated with "genial" and "sympathetic" qualities, and the reader is hastily assured that, unlike the severe parent of *Elsie Dinsmore*, there was not "the least intention of punishment" in his behavior (53). In *Miss Ravenel's Conversion*, De Forest presents a fictional reply to Charles Eliot Norton's question, "Is there any one who will assert that 'the people' in any country is so wise that it can know, or so calm that it can choose, what is best for itself? Does it not everywhere need counsel, restraint and education?"[60] Democracy and equality are best nurtured, De Forest contends in *Miss Ravenel's Conversion*, through disciplinary intimacy, to borrow Richard Brodhead's phrase.[61] Silencing his loquacious daughter and colonizing the domestic space with Brownites, Smithites, and Robinsonites, the doctor demonstrates how domestic affections could be disciplined, and thus perfected, by an interest in universal principles and laws, here represented by geology.[62]

De Forest was not alone in celebrating the values of scientific objectivity in stabilizing national affections and their expression. In the *Thoughts on the Future Civil Policy of America* (1865) and the *History of the American Civil War* (1867), John W. Draper joined other postwar thinkers—like Francis Lieber and Elisha Mulford—who sought to define the nation so as to prevent further confusions or disagreements. While some claimed that religion provided the theoretical basis for government, Draper argues that "a stern logic of events" gave each nation its particular "national life." Pointing to climate to explain regional (and racial) difference, and associating "the force of Ideas" with inevitability, Draper concludes that "there shall exist on this continent one Republic, great and indivisible, whose grandeur shall eclipse the grandeur of Rome in its brightest days."[63] Draper's analysis is informed by a thorough positivism, but the bright future he depicts requires that the newly reunited nation recognize that "centralization is an inevitable issue in the life of nations. Power ever tends to concentration."[64] Draper urges his readers to resist a quick rejection of this view by asking them to consider if "in our Legislatures, it is the public good or individual interest that compels attention and secures its ends," if "Individualism is not overweighing Patriotism." Individualism, he asserts, had caused the Civil War (when the South recognized that "the political influence [it had] so long enjoyed ... was about to be lost")—and could still "prove to be the ruin of the nation" unless checked "by some higher, some better motive." Rather than "lament the loss of that which, if we will only open our eyes, we may see that we never possessed," Draper maintains that "political influence and the guidance of affairs" should be transferred to "hands of established ability." To protect U.S. greatness from the decline its Roman ancestor had suffered, "centralization" would have to "rest on Intelligence, and not on brute force" through the education of all children, regardless of race.[65] Like De Forest, in other words, Draper places the future of the nation in the hands of educated men.

The significance of these ideas for *Miss Ravenel's Conversion* is demonstrated when Dr. Ravenel extends his experimentation beyond rocks. In the novel's extended consideration of race, Dr. Ravenel agrees to undertake the direction of an abandoned plantation. "These negroes *must* be induced to work," "Authority" maintains, and Ravenel, "honestly and intelligently delighted" by the plan, quickly accepts the challenge

(219–220). The phrase "*must* be induced" couples necessity and the illusion of freedom, while the diacritical emphasis points the reader to the more pressing of the two. Ravenel undertakes the project "for the sake of a long oppressed race" in the hopes of teaching principles of "industry and other social virtues" necessarily ignored under slavery (222). Because this is a novel structured according to the ideal of remarriage, the experiment is destined to fail before it even begins. Put differently, the experiment itself *cannot* succeed because of the novel's commitment to repetition as a condition of success: the workers' failure provides an alternate representation of the claims figured more fully by remarriage. Even through the scientific racism of the plantation experiment, one can discern De Forest's attempt to instill an attitude to racial politics that will acknowledge the necessity of both time and some failure to eventual success. Ravenel's response—establishing a series of strict rules, placing limitations on his workers' movements and sleeping arrangements, and outlining acceptable moral attitudes—leads to a marked increase in the plantation's efficiency and thus exemplifies the novel's contention that authoritarian practices can lead to "the love of individual liberty".[66] "'They have already acquired the love of individual liberty,' said [Dr. Ravenel]. 'The cognate love of liberty in the abstract, the liberty of all men, is not far ahead of them. How superior they already are to the white wretches who are fighting to send them back to slavery!'" (276). The plantation interlude is brief, and its message is complicated by a letter from Colburne decrying the abilities and characters of African Americans ("I am as much of an abolitionist as ever," the captain writes, but exposure to former slaves could cause him to "become an advocate of slavery" [242]). Nonetheless, it reiterates the novel's basic political intervention: that liberty, which must be taught *twice*, can be best facilitated by processes that are seemingly inimical to its fullest expression. What Ravenel learns from the scientific method he had perfected in his home, and exports to the Southern plantation, is that scientific discipline offers "the necessary tools of modern social solidarity and citizenship."[67]

The proper posture for this doubled lesson, regardless of race or gender, is "resignation and obedience" to the commands of a superior, and De Forest is clear that discipline is beneficial in cultivating the preconditions for loyalty:

> A soldier's life cultivates resignation and obedience. . . . You are roused at midnight, march twenty miles on end, halt three or four hours, perhaps in a pelting rain; then you are faced about, marched

back to your old quarters, and dismissed, and nobody ever tells you why or wherefore. You take it very hard at first, but at last you get used to it and do just as you are bid, without complaint or comment. You no more pretend to reason concerning your duties than a millstone troubles itself to understand the cause of its revolutions.... You may grumble at it, but you do it all the same. At last you forget to grumble and even to ask the reason why. You obey because you are ordered. (438)

Even though Colburne musters out of the army before the novel ends, the military discipline depicted above is translated to civilian life in the man of science. The soldier, here likened to a "millstone," can surely anticipate a good deal of solicitude from Ravenel the mineralogist. "War, civil war, with its dread punishments, is not without its uses," Draper opines in 1865. "In no other school than that of war can society learn subordination, in no other can it be made to appreciate order. It may be true, as has been affirmed, that men secretly love to obey those whom they feel to be their superiors intellectually. In military life they learn to practice this obedience openly."[68] De Forest and Draper would likely rejoin that "liberty ... is always, if such a paradox may be excused, liberty under restraint."[69] The introduction of science as an idealized mode of inquiry completes the conversion the novel narrates, demonstrating that individual passion and enthusiasm in service of abstract principles will lead to individual fulfillment *and* the future comfort of a society based on industry and knowledge. Most important, De Forest's social vision associates authority with a (putative) meritocracy easily correlated to American ideals.[70]

De Forest's subsequent novels continue to explore the structural necessity of repetition and authoritative guidance (although without the emphasis on science displayed in *Miss Ravenel's Conversion*). The elderly Colonel Kershaw in *Kate Beaumont* (1872) ends a bloody feud between two Southern families, enabling his granddaughter to marry one of the enemy; set before the Civil War, the novel nonetheless explicitly ponders how to convert feuding families into peaceful neighbors. The novel concludes with Kershaw's resurrection in the young woman's husband; twice repeating "He is Kershaw over again," De Forest suggests that Kershaw's authority is perfected in its repetition.[71] *The Bloody Chasm* (1881) is even more forceful in its claims that authoritative guidance makes possible a happy future through repetition. Again an elderly man orchestrates a union between antagonists, in this instance by promising a young woman, Virginia Beaufort, a fortune if she will accept Harry Underhill's hand. Although marriage to a Northern officer horrifies the Southern rebel, necessity drives Virginia to accept the lucrative proposal; indeed, the novel could be said to be a prolonged consideration of the implications of the phrase "*must* be induced." The plan seems destined to fail when Virginia arrives at the wedding fully veiled and decamps immediately after the exchange of vows. In Paris, a "wonderfully converting" place, Virginia falls in love with a Confederate officer (her husband in disguise), and the novel ends happily with the reconciliation of the estranged spouses. Although the emotional conquest belongs to Underhill, he receives significant assistance from a Confederate general who offers "loyal help," for, as he explains, "In this fight I am a Union man, heart and soul." De Forest shows that political affiliations can be subordinated to other affective claims and responsibilities, as happiness is found in a union that again results from a scene of recognition—the general likens the South to "a generous and impassioned woman," a belated realization—that remarriage uniquely enables.[72] Consistently merging free consent with coercion, De Forest suggests that a national recognition of the full implication of loyalty, when "every American" can say with the general, "I see it now," will result in the successful reconstruction of the nation's domestic space, revitalizing the political principles upon which American democracy relies.

* * *

No family remains intact at the end of *The Gates Ajar*; no one is married, nor, for that matter, are there any romances between living persons. So it may seem perverse to claim that *The Gates Ajar* should be read as a reunion romance with an expansive political agenda. Nonetheless, I will show that Phelps works as efficiently as De Forest to discipline affective relations—from antipathy to love, from rebellion to loyalty—by displacing time and history in her vision of the reconstructed family and nation. Where De Forest turns to science, Phelps relies on a reconstructed heaven and God's authority to subtend her claim that all can enjoy the peace and pleasure of sentimental reunion, thanks to the divine promise that bodies, affections, and families will be reunited in heaven. Reunion is not just for those lucky enough to have their loved ones return from war, but, thanks to her "metamorphosis of death," is available to *all* Americans. Whereas *Miss Ravenel's Conversion*, like most national romances, could gesture to children as evidence of a rosy future, *The*

Gates Ajar strives to narrate a future that is simultaneously immediate and eternal: Phelps slips into allegory to circumvent the dilemmas thus raised. Unlike young Ravvie, Faith, the child inherited by the narrator in *The Gates Ajar*, can grace any home.

Implicit in my claim about *The Gates Ajar* is the acknowledgment that a religious novel in the 1860s is indistinguishable from a political one, because of religion's prominent political role during the Civil War era.[73] Antebellum reform discourse had infused an idea of what politics should or could establish with a religious sensibility; during the war this tendency became institutionally important. The Union added "In God We Trust" to its currency, while the Confederacy drafted a constitution that explicitly solicited the favor and "guidance of Almighty God": its national seal included the motto "Deo Vindice."[74] Southern ministers urged their congregations to understand military defeat as an incentive to perfect their Christian responsibilities as slaveholders, while their Northern brethren told parishioners to interpret suffering as evidence of divine mercy, reverses as God's retribution for their sinful ways.[75] Lincoln put the presidential imprimatur on this reading of the war, which, as Michael Rogin explains, "gave redemptive meaning to [the nation's] suffering." After Lincoln's assassination, "the Union rose to the sublimity of religious mysticism," Confederate vice president Alexander Stephens noted.[76] The preexisting and intimate association of religious vision and American national mission heightened wartime rhetoric, as definitions of loyalty merged family, church, and state allegiance. Some Northern thinkers thus argued that loyalty was identical to religious obedience: the social contract was binding because it was sanctified by God in addition to, and even before, the people.

While many critics concentrate on Phelps's depiction of a bourgeois heaven, this chapter explores instead the balance she seeks between abstract ideas and their particular expression—another way of approaching the issues De Forest addressed via the tension between the local and the national—in the creation of companionate relations across "the gates" separating the living from the dead, the historical from the eternal. Even as she relies upon the evangelical Protestantism crucial to wartime justifications of (both) national mission(s), Phelps's text relocates the truth of religion—and the horror of violence—in an intimate family world dominated by women, offering an alternative to the militarized evangelism of Union propaganda and seminary theology. The novel intervenes in the debate about how to reconstruct the nation by rebalancing various warring pairs—reason and imagination, truth and fiction, freedom and submission, the literal and the metaphoric—in remarriages dependent on loyal submission to an inscrutable, but infallible, divine authority.

The Gates Ajar traces the struggles of Mary Cabot following the death of her beloved brother, Roy, a Union soldier.[77] Devastated by the loss of "a future probable or possible," Mary finds little comfort in the routines of domestic life or the teachings of religion.[78] Her bitter existence is interrupted by the arrival of her widowed aunt, Winifred Forceythe, who preaches a religion markedly different from the fare on offer at Rev. Bland's church. With her help, Mary converts her anger into first resigned acceptance and then eager, but calm, anticipation. Winifred dies near the end of the novel, yet before she does, she mends the spiritual health of the town of Homer and leaves Mary with Faith, literalized in the figure of her boisterous young daughter.

Much of Phelps's novel is devoted to correcting representations of heaven as too abstract to provide comfort to suffering individuals. Told that she should hope that Roy is worshipping "before the great White Throne" without "individuality" or "human joy," Mary complains bitterly that he has gone to "that dreadful Heaven," where he can have no thought of her because "the singing and the worshipping must take up all his time" (13). Railing against the notion of "heaven as worship," Mary protests that the "glittering generalities, cold commonplaces, vagueness, [and] unreality" of this vision of heaven "hurt" and "cut" (13, 42). Expanding upon the legacy of Emmanuel Swedenborg and works like William Bronks's *Heaven Our Home*, Winifred's alternative presents "heaven as community," full of flowers, mountains, pianos, homes, machinery, and even potato fields, what one critic has dubbed a "consumer dream-world."[79] While Phelps clearly borrows from an evolving consumer culture in which material objects increasingly defined the individual, this observation should not obscure the impact of the Civil War in the evolution of Phelps's vision.

As the author explains, the novel was her response to the "general grief" caused by the Civil War. The suffering "swell[ed] to a tide whose invisible flow cover[ed] all the little resistance of common, human joyousness," she explained decades later, as a nearly "occult force" pervaded the national atmosphere "like a material miasma."[80] "The regiments came home," and for the soldiers the war was over, but "the mourners went about the streets" with no end in view for their struggles or pain.[81] Pointing to the unequal sacrifices made by the soldiers and their loved ones at home, Phelps takes a basic premise of much Civil War literature—that the home front and the battlefield were comparable in their contribution to the total war effort—and extends its implications.[82] In "The Sources and Uses of Suffering" (1875), Henry Ward Beecher makes a comparable claim: "The sufferers in the great war were not those who bled on the battle-field. The drops of blood that fell on the hearthstone were more and bitterer than those that fell on the field of battle. Not he who haply was a martyr in the cause of his country, but they that lived to mourn, suffered most—by their social connection, not only, but by their civil relationship."[83] Eliding the difference between literal and figurative blood, Beecher argues that mourners, who have been made to suffer for the nation, should not also be made to suffer *by* a nation inappropriately indifferent to their significant sacrifices.

Even as *The Gates Ajar* reorients the hierarchy of sacrifice to include mourners, its logic relies on, and adapts, assumptions about sympathetic identification familiar to readers of antebellum sentimental fiction. A sharp distinction must be drawn, Phelps contends, between helpful consolation and empty formalism; because of the war's unprecedented devastation, few of those "trampled down, without a choice, or protest" could expect to enjoy "real" sympathy.[84] Equally important, Phelps's reading of the "condolence system" explores its implications for notions of personal "liberty." "Who originated that most exquisite of inquisitions, the condolence system?" Mary asks (5).

> I am sure I do not meant to be ungrateful for real sorrowful sympathy. . . . But it is not near friends who are apt to wound, nor real sympathy which sharpens the worst of the needles. It is the fact that all your chance acquaintances feel called upon to bring their curious eyes and jarring words right into the silence of your first astonishment; taking you in a round of morning calls with kid gloves, and parasol, and the liberty to turn your heart about and cut into it at pleasure. You may quiver at every touch, but there is no escape, because it is "the thing." (6)

Here consolation functions according to a set of normative behaviors that regulate emotional excess while encouraging rote, thoughtless repetition. This is the point of Mrs. Bland's advice to Mary: she should exert herself more, otherwise "people would talk" (9). When a matter of pleasure or fashion (like "kid gloves" or "parasol[s]"), the condolence system is coercive, even violent ("wound[ing]" its recipients). Indeed, the passage's emphasis on embodied pain anticipates Phelps's later statement that the suffering of mourners exceeded that of the soldiers.[85] Instead of "real sorrowful sympathy," the wrongly conceived "liberty" of such practices "sharpens" the heart's pain. Trapped by these conventions—"there is no escape"—the sufferer is reduced to a body, one that the representation of norms as "the thing" might link to the embodied existence of slavery.

Yet assuming that "liberty" is identical to indulgence is equally problematic in the novel, and Mary's belief that her loss is entirely unique is expressed as nascent rebellion. Mary's servant Phoebe makes this clear when she states, "Laws now Miss Mary, my dear! This won't never do,—a rebellin' agin Providence, and singein' your hair on the lamp chimney this way!" (5). I will turn to the converting power of "singein'" later in the chapter, but for now it is enough to underscore the multiple ways that Phelps articulates the dangers of "rebellin'" (and the frequency with which they are linked to fire). In addition to Phoebe's remark, Mary herself observes, "We are most selfishly blinded by our own griefs. No other form than ours seems to walk with us in the furnace" (30). Equally important are the more circumspect ways that Phelps engages with the topic, notably through reference to "Lenora," a poem by Gottfried August Bürger, which Mary copies into her diary. In this popular poem, a young woman anxiously awaits her lover's return from war. In distress at his continued failure to appear, she rails at God's cruel indifference:

> Oh mother! God does well for thee,
> But He has not done well for me.
> In vain are all my prayers—in vain,
> To calm my soul, or ease my pain.

To Lenora's delight, William finally arrives and spirits her away to his "quiet, narrow dwelling." During the journey, he displays a disturbing interest in corpses and funerals, causing Lenora to cry repeatedly, "Speak not of the dead!"; when they arrive at their destination, his clothes fall off to reveal "a grinning skeleton." Lenora dies of terror, and the poem concludes with an exhortation to find patient consolation in divine mercy.[86] Yet it is not the final lesson that attracts Mary, but Lenora's earlier assertion that heaven and hell are best defined in terms of earthly passion. Winifred discovers the poem in Mary's diary and rejects it as "wicked"—"I believe Satan wrote that," she says—endorsing the deacon's earlier claim that excessive grief indicates a "rebellious state of mind" (34, 10). Linking rebellion with excessive and self-interested emotionalism, Phelps's argument for the cultivation of appropriate affect reiterates Northern claims that the South's fatal decision to secede from the Union was the result of emotional indulgence.[87]

Against these various forms of excess, Winifred models the symmetry between head and heart necessary to moral behavior, communal responsibility, and national belonging. Without discipline, the "material miasma" of uncontrolled emotion could encourage further revolt, as Mary's story makes clear; without genuine emotion, however, the sterility of various ideals—as exemplified in the town's established theology or social norms—could erode the ties that should unite communities. Winifred starts the process of Mary's conversion from rebellion to loyalty by modeling what careful comfort for the bereaved should entail: the letter announcing her visit acknowledges that it might be burdensome; once in Homer, she waits for her niece to mention Roy; and she gently recalls her own experience of loss in the death of her husband, hinting that comfort can be found in the prospect of a sure reunion.

But it is from the claim that families will be reunited in heaven and that this reunion will be satisfying because our individuality, memories, and affections are an integral and eternal part of the soul that Winifred's comforting abilities primarily derive. Family ties persist beyond the grave, she maintains, so emotional mistakes made on earth can be rectified in the afterlife, a position Phelps articulates explicitly in *Beyond the Gates* (1883). Implicitly engaging a common concern about maimed bodies, Winifred acknowledges the complication but persists nonetheless to assert that everyone will be beautiful in heaven and that she "shall have [her] pretty brown hair again" (74). Especially interesting, however, is how Winifred's argument encourages flexibility in identification: on her view, we must recognize that family roles are far more fluid than their eternal persistence would seem to suggest. The reader learns, for instance, that Mary and Roy had perpetuated their childish terms of endearment well into maturity: "I wonder if all brothers and sisters keep up the baby-names as we did," Mary muses (4). At the same time, Mary and Roy often seem to be lovers rather than siblings; Winifred promises Mary that she will "clasp his hand again, and feel his kiss on [her] happy lips" (66). At another moment, Mary recalls "his strong arms that folded in and cared for [her]," and because they had "loved together so long, we two together . . . he had grown to me, heart of my heart, life of my life" (7). The slippage of roles—from fraternal to spousal or romantic—is familiar from antebellum sentimental novels—recall Ellen's dream in *The Wide Wide World* where her uncle, mentor, and "brother" become momentarily confused in a kiss—but takes on new implications in *The Gates Ajar*. The many different roles Mary occupies relative to Roy—child, sister, wife, lover—accent his importance to her, and, because

Mary's loss is articulated across a variety of different subject positions, her narrative can, by its own logic of emotional equivalence, offer comfort to a range of mourners. More important, however, is the theoretical function of the novel's definition of family. On Phelps's view, heaven will free us from the limitations of temporality, restoring the bonds we had assumed to be lost or broken over the course of our lives and allowing us to establish those we had perhaps not been able to enjoy during our time on earth. Because we retain our memories and affections into the afterlife, the remarriages and reconstructed families made possible in heaven will build upon, and perfect, their earthly antecedents. Having a lifetime of experience on which to draw, and an eternity to enjoy the new, better families, heavenly remarriages will provide the proper basis for the pursuit of total happiness. Recognition, as Cavell defines it, will be perfect in heaven.

Although this should mean, technically, that Mary does not *need* her family reconstructed in the present, the novel does systematically revise her seemingly undeniable assertion "I am not 'a family'" (57). Because families exist beyond the grave, a single person is always already a member of an extended family. The fluidity of family roles, and the emphasis on atemporality, means any one person can occupy a variety of different positions within a family; these different emotional experiences constitute the feeling of family—and of nation. Without challenging the era's emotional emphasis on the family as the basic unit of support and comfort, Phelps argues that family ties are multiple and changing; when we imagine that they are unique and unchangeable, we are indulging an obstinacy that hints of rebellion. It is in the context of these ideas that we can make sense of the further disruption to Mary's family caused by Winifred's death; the text has already guaranteed that the actual presence of other people is not necessary for either the fact or the feeling of family.

There is one further implication of Mary's many roles that bears noting. In the same entry where Mary learns that Winifred is dying, she demonstrates how a more flexible identification might make possible the unification of the sections and the races. Playing with Faith, Mary takes on a series of different identities: "I was her grandmother, I was her baby, I was a rabbit, I was a chestnut horse, I was a watch-dog, I was a mild-tempered giant, I was a bear 'warranted not to eat little girls,' I was a roaring hippopotamus and a canary bird, I was Jeff Davis and I was Moses in the bulrushes, and of what I was, the time faileth me to tell" (126). Over the course of the day Mary crosses generational ("baby" and "grandmother") and species boundaries; she becomes the

Confederate president and the biblical patriarch closely associated with African American liberation. Offering an argument that echoes Walt Whitman's *Leaves of Grass*, Phelps suggests that identification allows us to enter into the experiences of all members of the nation–even those that might seem fundamentally incompatible, like Jeff Davis and Moses—and that this prepares the way for our thorough reconciliation. Radical independence is impossible, for our ties and affiliations always exceed our daily experience of them.[88] Mining the possibilities of identification in a representative democracy, Phelps suggests that reconciliation will be mere child's play—if we harken to Faith's command.[89]

Phelps pushes the reader to accept this kind of identification and its rewriting of the sympathy encouraged by sentimental fiction by stressing the violent contingency of daily life. In the middle of *The Gates Ajar*, a gruesome scene interrupts the narrative, breaking an entry in midsentence. The next installment explains that "a child's voice shouting incoherently something about the doctor, and *mother's killed! O, mother's killed! mother's burnt to death!*" had caused the disruption (118). The "horrible scene" that Mary witnesses defies description ("I shall not write down a word of it"), but she does describe its cause:

> It seems that the little boy—the baby—crept into the kitchen by himself, and began to throw the contents of the match-box on the stove, "to make a bonfire," the poor little fellow said. In five minutes, his apron was ablaze. His mother was on the spot at his first cry, and smothered the little apron, and saved the child, but her dress was muslin, and everybody was too far off to hear her at first,—and by the time her husband came in from the garden it was too late. (118–119)

Although the novel shrouds the soldier's body in mystery, leading one critic to suggest that *The Gates Ajar* "studiously avoids the corpse," the burned maternal body is vividly invoked, if not described, taking the ambivalence and violence Shirley Samuels sees as being associated with mothers in domestic fiction to a horrifying new level.[90] The failed chiasmus—the mother hears the baby's cries but the husband does not hear his wife's—echoes previous hints about the inadequacy of his familial attentions, while the passage's shifting perspective moves the reader away from the horror just in time, and delays her return, in the ghastly silence of the final dash, until it is "too late." The terrible violence of the scene, and its articulation of maternal heroism, takes the comparison of the suffering of women and soldiers to its extreme conclusion. Not only does

Phelps here show that violence is not limited to the battlefield, that it is dangerous work caring for children, but she likewise establishes the ease with which a domestic heaven can become a hell, enacting in another manner the "wicked" Bürger poem.

Over the next few weeks, as the Reverend Bland grapples with the horror of his loss and the new family roles he must adopt, he comes to embrace the spiritual principles he had previously repudiated, admitting to Winifred, "It will be a peaceful day for me if I can ever quite agree with your methods of reasoning" (122). His doctrinal conversion is registered as well by the decision to destroy the "laboriously done" sermon describing an abstract heaven. "I shall never preach *this* again," Bland says as "he held up before her a mass of old blue manuscript, and threw it, as he spoke, upon the embers of the grate. It smoked and blazed up, and burned out. It was that sermon on heaven of which there is an abstract in this journal" (123). Captured in the redundancy of the verbs—"smoked," "blazed up," "burned out"—the scene reenacts the violence of the wife's death, establishing a ghastly parallel between spouse and sermon. The unpleasant implication is that the death of the wife is a means to the second fiery end: the minister's symbolic repudiation of a theology predicated upon rigorous doctrinal regularity and logical necessity. Without a properly affective religion, in other words, death cannot be suffused with the meaning that will transform it from waste into sacrifice. And without recognition, and the repetition that makes it possible, we cannot learn this lesson. That is to say, according to the logic upon which the novel is structured, the wife *must* die for the minister to see how little he knows about loss and suffering; this had been one of the points made in the novel's critique of consolation conventions—that only through genuine suffering can we learn to help others adequately—and is part of the episode's meaning.[91] After this trial by fire, the Blands are ready to be married again, this time happily, in heaven.

Thus, not only is poor Mrs. Bland a gothic symbol of the dangers of abstraction, she is also an indication of Winifred's perspicacity (she predicts that "intense pain . . . shall shake his cold smooth theorizing to the foundation" [62]).[92] In short, the startling episode establishes the sweeping implications of Phelps's argument about family and, by extension, the nation. For communities to endure, Phelps suggests in a manner that recalls De Forest, horrible sacrifices must sometimes be made—Mrs. Bland sacrificed herself to save her son in a manner that is comparable to the sacrifice soldiers made during the war: Henry Ward Beecher, for example, told his congregation in 1863 that "human life has been a grand march of suffering. The race is a vast army; they have tramped to their own music—a music of sighs, and sobs, and sorrows."[93] Not only must we learn to deal with the real costs of these sacrifices, we must also learn how to honor and memorialize them. Sacrifice is not in vain if it is translated into a symbolical reenactment. "Without words to supply meaning," Priscilla Wald observes, "the battlefield is just a place where men fought and died. Words turn it into a symbol."[94] This is why Abraham Lincoln's Gettysburg Address stresses dedication, she continues, and it is a principle at the core of *The Gates Ajar*.[95] As Horace Bushnell contends in "Reverses Needed," a sermon delivered after the Union's defeat at Bull Run, loyalty needed extreme conditions to "burn" away personal interests and assumptions: "It must get hold of our solid convictions and burn itself through into our moral nature itself in order to become reliable and sure. . . . Then it will stand, then it is loyalty complete."[96] For Bushnell, as for Phelps, the proper kind of affective affiliation is one in which discipline burns away excess, so that we are ready to recognize the people, values, and principles to have and to hold.

The symbolic logic of *The Gates Ajar* suggests that loyalty, and the nation itself, depends on death; the proper response of the national citizen to this realization is an increase of action. Succumbing to passivity betrays the dead.[97] "Our dead are not asking mere rhetoric of us," Horace Bushnell explained in 1865, "but duty. They call us to no whimpering over them, no sad weeping, or doling of soft sympathy, but to counsel and true action."[98] That such positions might well commit the nation to an endless series of violent sacrifices is a point that neither Phelps nor Bushnell pursues, even though the arguments for active (and repetitive) memorialization imply that the structure of violence is integral to the future of the community and the possibility of the nation's symbolic reconstruction. Drafted in the "army of sufferers," Mrs. Bland's death is relieved of senselessness, for she, like the soldiers who gave their lives during the war, makes the national family safe for those left behind.

The repetition operative in the episode—first one fire then another—and across the novel—first one mother dies and then another—establishes the fragility of domestic space; it may be the most extravagant example of Phelps's interest in repetition's fundamental importance to the form and content of both novel and life, but it is certainly not the only one. We see a similar interest in the novel's use of catechism. Bland's sermon uses a catechistic structure to explain the features and activities of the Christian afterlife; in offering her revision of his theory, Winifred repeats, but revises, Bland's method. Winifred likewise deploys a kind of catechism, but whereas the sermon is formal, logical, and abstract, her instruction is casual, colloquial, and regularly interrupted by quotidian demands: lessons run across numerous entries in *The Gates Ajar*. Although Winifred gestures to learned sources as the basis of her interpretation, these are less important to her than the feelings of her audience, a claim made apparent when she asserts that a representation should match the intellectual capabilities of the individual: "If I told [Faith] that her heavenly ginger-snaps would not be made of molasses and flour," Winifred explains, "she would have a cry for fear that she was not going to have any ginger-snaps at all; so, until she is older, I give her unqualified ginger-snaps" (105).[99] Winifred justifies her practice by explaining that she treats her daughter "just as the Bible treats us, by dealing in *pictures* of truth that she can understand" (104–105). We err, she continues, when we fail to recognize that "the Bible specifies very little about the minor arrangements of eternity" and that what little there is is couched in metaphor and analogy (46). "Mrs. Forceythe's method," Gail Smith clarifies, "is simply to update St. John's imagery, while stressing always—as [her grandfather] did—that it is imagery, not literal truths, she is proposing."[100]

And Phelps deals with her readers much the way Winifred deals with the residents of Homer: as Winifred gives Faith "pictures of truth that she can understand," so does Phelps offer images of salvation in terms that will make heaven familiar to readers. At the core of Winifred's contentions is the insistent claim that God and Christ would not be "cruel" to their human charges; their goal is to guide us to eternal happiness, and this will most normally require the experience of pain. When Mary recognizes the extent of God's authority, her conversion is complete: "He was an inexorable Mystery who took Roy from me to lose him in the glare of a more inexorable heaven. He is a Father who knew better than we that we should be parted for a while; but He only means it to be a little while. He is keeping him for me to find in the flush of some summer morning, on which I shall open my eyes no less naturally than I open them on June sunrises now" (110). The transfer of God from a "Mystery" to a "Father" completes the expansion of Mary's family and is accompanied by the change of verb describing what has happened to Roy: Mary had felt that he had been taken from her, but she concludes that God is "keeping" Roy for her "to find" and that their parting will be temporary, not permanent.

As it installs an interpretation that encourages readers to submit to God's will, Mary's diary teaches us to believe that the dead are with us in a substantive way; at several points in the novel, Mary imagines that Roy is guiding her actions, and Winifred's final words—"John . . . why,

John!"—suggest that, for her, the family reunion has come to a very satisfying conclusion (137). Unlike the gothic narratives of Edgar Allan Poe or George Lippard, Phelps deploys romance as a means of *forestalling* epistemological and moral dislocation, even as her view of paradise borrows substantially from the (sometimes) gothic idea that affections endure beyond the grave and can animate us long after we have expired. "It is almost as if [Winifred] had raised [Roy] from the grave," Mary observes (108). But, as Winifred explains it, we should be glad "the absent dead" are far from absent: "'I do not doubt,' she went on, speaking low,— 'I cannot doubt that our absent dead are very present with us. He said, "I am with you always," knowing the need we have of him, even to the end of the world. He must understand the need we have of them. I cannot doubt it'" (50–51). Unlike the dead who insist on remaining present in Poe's tales "Morella" or "Ligeia," the undead dead in Phelps's novel haunt the living gently, and their desires remain within conventional bounds.

For Phelps, containing the dead's gothic potential is critical to keeping the nation from being overwhelmed by the miasma of grief that spurred the novel's composition in the first place. Her hermeneutics, then, can be read not only as a theory and practice of biblical interpretation but likewise as a reflection on strategies for successful political reconciliation. Talking about the romance model as a strategy for narrating national ideals, political theorist Bonnie Honig notes that in it, "obstacles are met and overcome, [and] eventually the right match is made" between "a people and its law, a state and its institutions," and "the newly wed couple is sent on its way to try to live happily ever after." On Honig's view, however, the idealization of romance needs to be tempered by gothic overtones to assist readers in learning to cope with the "responsibilities and challenges of democratic citizenship," thereby accustoming readers to the strangeness of the law and the precarious nature of the democratic present.[101] As compelling as this model may be, however, Phelps is writing for a historical moment in which gothic uncertainty must be contained to stabilize the insecurities introduced by all too real horrors. Sentimental discipline—the conversion of rebellious emotions into loyal ones—is more likely to generate security than gothic inversion or instability.

Despite the good behavior of the dead, *The Gates Ajar* leads its readers to consider one pressing question: if human affections are to endure eternally, why should there be a time when we must live without them? The answer, Winifred argues, is that this is "the only test of loyalty to God" (54). As we must respect the laws of the land or the claims of others, even when we find them capricious or onerous, so too must we endure a period of separation from loved ones who predecease us. In drawing upon the concept of loyalty to define the individual's relationship with God, Phelps reverses the arguments used to explain the absolute requirements of national loyalty during the war. Definitions of political loyalty were blunt about the "very perceptible and very close relation between loyalty and religion," for, as Horace Bushnell noted, "what is religion but loyalty to God?" "And the two homages, in particular that which goes after the state and that which goes after God, are so clearly related that one may even speak of loyalty as the religion of our political nature.... The two fires will burn together and one kindle the other."[102] I do not mean to suggest that Phelps references Bushnell directly in the fire that consumes Mrs. Bland, but rather to underscore the extreme rhetoric associated with the articulation of loyalty, locating the jarring scene in this context. What loyalty requires is the repudiation of rebellion in all its many forms and the subordination of individual will to "a process of divine discipline": only in this way, Horace Bushnell contends, do persons, and the governments they form, "get their moral crowning of authority."[103] Early in *The Gates Ajar* Mary characterizes God as "dreadful," "snatch[ing]" Roy away and abandoning him "in the hideous wet and snow" (7). "God wants it all," she complains (14). Yet after her conversion, she revises this position, concluding that what had previously seemed the expression of divine selfishness is actually solicitude; from a "Mystery" shrouded in the "inexorable," God becomes a generous parent, saving a treat for her to enjoy "no less naturally" than "the flush of some summer morning," a delight for which she must wait just "a little while." Because we are under the benevolent care of "Father," it is possible to experience the kinds of identification that Phelps argues are so crucial to national healing and reunification, to a "national kind of happiness." No matter what our position in earthly society, we share, or should share, a basic experiential fact: we are all subordinate to God's absolute mastery and authority. Phelps's representation of this submission extends the Calvinist tradition, which likewise valued duty and submission, but adapts it to a domestic frame familiar to both sentimental and patriotic readers.[104]

Should the loyal nation achieve its goal of approximating "the celestial kingdom," it would be more like "a close Theocracy than a wild commune," the narrator explains in *Beyond the Gates*, the second of the three *Gates* novels. It turns out that heaven is rigidly hierarchical, organized according to a system "simple yet ... autocratic"; the reverent attention paid to heavenly "differences of rank or influence" far surpasses what the narrator had been accustomed to on earth (205). If, as

Castronovo succinctly argues, "a corporeal politics is an imperfect one," what we see in heaven is political perfection, where hierarchy is readily acknowledged, vouchsafed by the literalization of the relationship between monarchical justification and divine power.[105]

The last of the series, *The Gates Between* (1887), depicts one man's struggles in finding his way to faith, submission, and the happy reconstruction of a family he had not known how to value while alive. The tale of his life, death, and afterlife replaces his earthly values—including a rewritten Declaration of Independence ("life, liberty, and the pursuit of a vacation")—with ideals more fitting to a hierarchical society structured around spiritualized compliance (238). Heavenly happiness, Dr. Thorne eventually realizes, does not come from individualism but instead from submitting to the direction and purpose supplied by the Christian god. His acceptance of these principles is ultimately coerced, spurred by the arrival of his baby son for whom he is responsible. Slowly Thorne gains an "admission to citizenship" as he works to win the "national kind of happiness" for his child (319, 326). As the novel ends, the fully reconstructed family begins an eternity of this "national kind of happiness." Phelps's use of the language of national citizenship links the heavenly country with the American nation as she argues that a "great central purpose" has the ability to universalize love and affection, while effacing the factitious distinctions generated by individualism and the love of fame and fortune it nurtures (313).[106]

When it includes the dead, the romance of reunion thus makes it easy to abandon rebellious tendencies, converting mourning into a loyalty that dematerializes a pressing "miasma" of grief and materializes a heavenly home. What we get in both Phelps and De Forest is the *double* infantilization of the American citizen; not only do we need "unqualified ginger-snaps" to recognize what is in our best interest, but in making this choice we recognize that without the substantial guidance of an authoritative figure, we cannot be expected to make rational or mature decisions. There is no end to our submission or tutelage in these models; what we accept in the place of autonomy is pleasure, happiness, and security in a national family that attends to our emotions by protecting us from distress and choice.

In 1894, Phelps published "The Oath of Allegiance," a story that returns to topics she addresses at length in *The Gates Ajar*. The start of the Civil War interrupts the courtship of Miriam Thornell, the daughter of a professor, and one of her father's students. Afraid to commit to her given the dangers of war, the youth departs without asking for Miriam's hand in marriage and is shortly killed in battle. Even without a formal exchange of promises, Miriam mourns his death for fifteen years, at which time she receives an actual marriage proposal from another man who has loved her loyally since childhood. Just before she accepts his offer, a *long*-delayed letter arrives from her former lover, asking for her hand in marriage and including a ring as a token of his promise. When the living arrives at the door, the servant delivers the disappointing news, "There's a dead man got ahead of yez." Wearing the dress she had on when she bid her lover farewell, she "proudly" takes "the oath of allegiance which binds the living to the dead,—that ancient oath, so often taken, so often broken, and sometimes kept." Lifting "the solemn face of the happiest woman in the land," "Miriam put his mother's ring upon her marriage finger."[107] Miriam's commitment to her not-quite fiancé demonstrates one of the fundamental limitations of loyalty—the ease with which it can nurture fanaticism and unquestioning obedience, a worry that the next chapter explores at length. The "indefinite promise of devotion to the dead" is, for Phelps, a sign of rectitude, although George Eliot, from whom the phrase is taken, is less sure about our promissory obligations to the dead.[108]

When considered in the context of the pervasive marriage metaphor used to conceptualize reunion, the implications of this reading become even sharper. This is a future too thoroughly limited by the past to participate fully in the development of the nation. Lauren Berlant is entirely right, in other words, in her discussion of "infantile citizenship," which she argues is characterized by a "faith in the nation, which is based on a belief in the state's commitment to representing the best interests of ordinary people," a faith that in turn "vitalizes a person's patriotic and practical attachment to the nation and to other citizens."[109] Phelps and De Forest differently define faith—the former finds hers in religion, the latter chooses science—but they deploy their faith similarly to create infantile national affiliations, using loyalty as both the means and the end of citizens' relationship to the nation. By overlooking loyalty, which becomes the dominant mode of discussing national affective affiliation in the wake of the Civil War, Berlant and others fail to recognize how the institutionalization of submission as loyalty reified the posture of infantilization.

Appreciating the critical differences within the romance of reunion complicates our understanding of the kinds of political arguments nineteenth-century novels were able to make and suggests that we have missed something important about the construction of national myths and affiliations by accepting too easily our own propaganda about the nation and the war so often said to have defined it fully and finally. The dangers of believing our own myths, and the problems associated with rendering authoritative habits of mind palatable, form the basis of the next chapter.

3 / Pledging Allegiance in Henry James

In the 1880s, readers and theatergoers fell in love with the reunion romance.¹ Unlike the novels examined in the previous chapter, the stories that held American audiences captive were far from ambivalent about the promise of romantic love. Not only did they heartily embrace the idea of its healing potential, they were also openly nostalgic for the lost elegance of the Old South and explicitly committed to the redemptive power of masculine heroism. As *Shenandoah: A Military Comedy* (1889), the hit play by Northerner Bronson Howard, makes clear, later reunion romances dispensed with political theorizing.² In its opening act, two army officers, Kerchival West, a native of New York, and Virginian Robert Ellingham, gaze out on Fort Sumter. Despite having trained together at West Point, having served in the same regiment, and having shared a history of combat, the friends will declare opposing allegiances in the impending war:

KERCHIVAL. Our Southern friends assure us that General Beauregard is to open fire on Fort Sumter this morning.... Are you Southerners all mad, Robert?

ELLINGHAM. Are you Northerners all blind? We Virginians would prevent a war if we could. But your people in the North do not believe that one is coming. You do not understand the determined frenzy of my fellow-Southerners.... I tell you, Kerchival, a war between the North and South is inevitable!

KERCHIVAL. And if it does come, you Virginians will join the rest.

ELLINGHAM. Our State will be the battle-ground, I fear. But every loyal son of Virginia will follow her flag. It is our religion!

KERCHIVAL. My State is New York. If New York should go against the old flag, New York might go to the devil. That is my religion.

ELLINGHAM. So differently have we been taught what the word "patriotism" means! . . .

KERCHIVAL. Bob! I only hope that we shall never meet in battle!

ELLINGHAM. In battle? The idea is horrible!

KERCHIVAL. My dear old comrade, one of us will be wrong in this great fight, but we shall both be honest in it.[3]

This exchange deploys the most familiar elements of the popular reconciliation narratives: both men are "honest" and true to their values; wartime allegiance is akin to religion; the "right" side will win, but questions of "right" and wrong are trumped by issues of honor and personal integrity. The problem of meaning we saw in chapter 2 remains but is no longer fraught: by the 1880s, the war could be seen, at least by some, as "an interregional 'miscommunication'" rather than a profound political conflict.[4] The passive construction of Ellingham's observation ("So differently have we been taught") strips the men of responsibility for the political situation. Giving a line with echoes of Daniel Webster's famous 1830 quip ("Our notion of things is entirely different") to the Southern officer, Howard weakens the moment's already attenuated political content.[5]

True to its comic mode, *Shenandoah* quickly converts the brutal brothers' war into one fought by *sisters*, as Madeline Kerchival squares off against Gertrude Ellingham:

MADELINE. I *am* a Northern girl.

GERTRUDE. And I am a Southern girl.

KERCHIVAL. The war has begun.

GERTRUDE. General Beauregard is a patriot.

MADELINE. He is a Rebel.

GERTRUDE. So am I.

MADELINE. Gertrude!—You—you—

GERTRUDE. Madeline!—You—

MADELINE. I—I—

GERTRUDE. I—

BOTH. O—O-h! [Bursting into tears and rushing into each other's arms, sobbing, then suddenly kissing each other vigorously.]

KERCHIVAL. I say, Bob, if the North and South do fight, that will be the end of it.[6]

Using what Peter Brooks has called the "aesthetic of muteness" characteristic of melodrama, the "war" quickly concludes with a reconciliation that is tearful but painless.[7] The interlude ends as the Northern officer predicts the future, suggesting that the actual war will end in a comparable manner, effacing the fictional status of *Shenandoah* itself.

But most important for my argument is the Southerner's assertion that "every loyal son of Virginia will follow her flag!" Ellingham's association of loyalty and the flag mirrors wartime deployments of the term, but crucially replaces national with state allegiance. Here, as in *Miss Ravenel's Conversion*, it is the Southern officer who expresses the primacy of local affiliation, yet even though the Northerner counters his assertion, the talk turns to wonder ("How different have we been taught"), not acrimony. There is no other challenge to this "different" definition of loyalty. Given the energies put into the definition of loyalty during the Civil War, and its role in the cultivation of appropriate national affiliation, why would Howard's play resist (or ignore) these connotations?

The nationalization of loyalty stripped it of some of the specificity it had accrued during the war years, replacing it with a celebration of commitment as such. Loyalty to any flag thus supplanted loyalty to the U.S. flag. In this way, loyalty increasingly came to represent a form of absolute allegiance, rather than attachment to a set of defined principles and values. As a structure of allegiance, loyalty continued to provide a critical way of understanding how affiliation could be predicated on an abstract principle or ideal—but the emphasis increasingly fell, as Howard makes clear, on the heroic commitment of men who fought in both armies rather than the causes for which they fought. What this means, in short, is that loyalty's importance ceased to be a matter of content—what it meant to be loyal to the nation—to one of form—how might one be loyal to one's beliefs, no matter how "different" they might be. To understand loyalty's increasing formalism, one need look no further than the melodramatic oppositions around which the war's narrative had itself been structured: "The institution of slavery," Edmund Wilson observes in *Patriotic Gore*, "supplied the militant North with the rabble-rousing issue which is necessary in every modern war to make the conflict appear as a melodrama."⁸ That the conflict was more motivated by issues of power, not the "pseudo-moral" ones often trumpeted as justification, means that the combination of victory and time led to a consistent diminution of the importance of "rabble-rousing." Put differently, even though reliance on the content may have decreased, the *form* of commitment associated with melodrama remained, becoming more important in the process. Loyalty, in short, increasingly functioned like the melodramatic vow "which cannot be violated." Recall Peter Brooks's definition of the melodramatic promise: "vows and pacts are always absolutes; there is never a thought of violating them" for they "provide an iron and ineluctable structure of plotting, a version of ancient tragedy's *moira*. We are not encouraged to investigate the psychology of the vow or the logic of the deadline, but, rather, to submit to their dramaturgy, their functioning as mechanism." Given the ease with which the war accommodated melodrama's Manichaean oppositions of good and evil, loyalty's form became increasingly like melodrama's promise.⁹ Although an 1876 story, "In the Cotton Country," could still indicate the difference between conceptions of loyalty—a Southern woman observes to a Northern interlocutor that "love of our State seemed loyalty to us"—much greater flexibility in its use is evident as the century progresses.¹⁰

Conceived as "very national, very typical," *The Bostonians* examines the culture created in the wake of the Civil War, particularly its deep confusion about what commitment to the nation required or authorized.¹¹ Like *Shenandoah* and the reunion romances examined in the preceding chapter, *The Bostonians* envisions life in the reunited nation, but Henry James is substantially less sanguine than his predecessors or peers about the abstract ideals that justified the war, sustained the home front, and shaped the war's memory. Whereas De Forest and Phelps worked to establish loyalty's hegemony, James deplored the consequences of their success as his "American story" takes up the problems created by loyalty when it abandons its moderation. On James's pessimistic view, loyalty so defined is indistinguishable from fanaticism, a zealous and affect-saturated attachment that blocks and warps perception, installing in its stead a rigid core of dearly held but unreasoned assumptions. Unable to countenance critique or dissent, the inflexible characters in *The Bostonians* enact fully what seems to have been for James the most salient dimension of the Civil War's legacy—rigidity, intolerance, fanaticism. Despite its regional title, *The Bostonians* is best read as a "national" novel, for in it James demonstrates that these qualities do not pertain to any one section as they had increasingly come to define personal as well as political affiliations.

Critics have long speculated about James's relationship to the Civil War—how it influenced his family, his understanding of masculinity, and his development as a writer—reaching divergent conclusions.[12] This critical fray misses the basic point, however; it is not how important the war was to James that matters, but instead how James perceived the war's importance to the culture it created. This chapter will show that *The Bostonians* demonstrates a remarkable sensitivity to the political rhetoric of the Civil War, the continued (and often fierce) partisanship of its aftermath, its association with events in the West, and the (uneasy) embrace of cultural reconciliation. That the characters are fanatically devoted to political causes is explicit from the novel's earliest pages, but that this zealotry, remarked upon but unconsidered in the critical literature, is an important element of James's serious consideration of the reconstruction of allegiance—personal and national—has been generally misunderstood. In James's hands, this general theme leads to the assertion that even the highest-minded convictions can damage relations between people and the nation they inhabit by providing the conditions of possibility for fanaticism. Any truly zealous commitment presupposes and perpetuates coercion, he contends, for it implies the rigid imposition of one's personal viewpoint and experience on the world. Locating a crucial scene in Memorial Hall, a building on the Harvard University campus erected to honor students who died in the Civil War, James indicates that this tendency was nurtured in, and continues to be sustained by the memory of, the Civil War. In short, *The Bostonians* explores the abstractions, affections, and allegiances humans fight to protect, and the costs of such combat to humanity.[13]

An 1892 essay about James Russell Lowell demonstrates James's familiarity with the specifics of Union nationalism during the Civil War era, particularly its combination of abstract conception and strong emotion in the definition of loyalty. James's reminiscence begins with an 1877 visit with Lowell that provided "hours of repatriation" for the young expatriate: admitting his partial knowledge of the United States, James writes "it would have been pleasant indeed to know even less than I did, so that I might have learned the whole story from Mr. Lowell's lips" because "his America was a country worth hearing about, a magnificent conception, an admirably consistent and lovable object of allegiance." Stressing Lowell's love for this "magnificent conception," James notes that Lowell's allegiance was the "strongest form of piety": the Civil War was "the time that kindled his steadiest fire." "When [Lowell] felt at all he felt altogether—was always on the same side as his likings and loyalties. He had no experimental sympathies, and no part of him was traitor to the rest."[14] The "experimental" emotions associated with sympathy can lead one to internal (and external) division. Lowell suffers no such conflict, no part is in rebellion, and his "loyalties" and "likings" are always "on the same side." He did not "experiment" with his affiliations, remaining entirely true to his beloved (and equally "consistent") country.

Even as he demonstrates his knowledge of the political connotations sympathy and loyalty accrued during the Civil War, James begins the essay with a general worry about the nature of loyalty itself. Struggling to represent Lowell to readers, James complains that death makes us all "more typical and general"; although "the deposited image is insistently personal, the generalizing principle is that of loyalty."[15] In an essay that displays a clear knowledge of the specific implications of loyalty, James's use of the term here acquires a quietly critical dimension. To say that the "generalizing principle is that of loyalty" is to suggest that death's cognitive disruptions generate a basic inability to discern the particular, the "insistently personal." As a partial remedy, we turn to loyalty, to the "typical." In the difference between these two understandings is the crux of James's intervention in *The Bostonians*. When used as an ethical term, as a way of organizing relations between individuals, loyalty problematically undermines our ability to engage intimately with others. (Nor does sympathy fare better, although this point is not specifically germane to the Lowell essay.) James's command of concepts from the war years, particularly those concerning how sides and feelings were to be distinguished, structures *The Bostonians*' investigation of the grounds of allegiance, the piety of conviction, and the problem with taking sides. With its gloomy view of the future, its bleak reflections on the powers of speech and the crippling effects of heroic devotion on the American character, *The Bostonians* shows James exploring the Civil War's legacy, asking under what conditions allegiance should be granted to people, promises, and nations.

To be sure, James's interest in loyalty complicates the oft-remarked connection between *The Bostonians* and Nathaniel Hawthorne's *The Blithedale Romance* (1852). Even before *The Bostonians*, James's own national loyalty as measured by his 1879 *Hawthorne*, seen in "some quarters" as "high treason," was already in doubt.[16] A like question, without the rhetorical invocation of treason, returns with James's reworking of his predecessor's romance. If one dimension of Hawthorne's aims in *Blithedale* is the exploration of "the way the present alternately struggles against the past's weight and seeks to renew its embrace," *The Bostonians* revises this inquiry, asking what happens when the past dictates the future to the present.[17] James's use of Hawthorne reveals why, despite the importance of the Civil War to James's understanding of the nation and his thinking about allegiance, recent readings that correlate *The Bostonians* with popular reunion romances miss the scope of James's ambition in the novel, which he confided to his brother William would tackle a "big and important subject."[18] Like Albion Tourgée in *A Fool's Errand* (1879), James borrows from romance—as conceived by Hawthorne *and* popular writers of reunion narratives—to establish its generic poverty. "There is as yet no such Faery Land," Hawthorne had opined in the preface to *Blithedale*, "so like the real world, that, in a suitable remoteness, one cannot well tell the difference, but with an atmosphere of strange enchantment, beheld through which the inhabitants have a propriety of their own."[19] The Civil War had been no fantasy, but its memory, "so like the real world" and yet informed by a "strange enchantment," established its special proprieties. Its "remoteness" from everyday life had taken hold of the American imagination, James demonstrates, and *The Bostonians* records the result of taking romance literally. Put simply, in *The Bostonians* James expresses his deep skepticism about the terms being dictated in reconciliation fiction, the confusion between these fictions and historical fact, and the dependence of both fact and fiction on the melodramatic conventions of romance.[20] Ending with possibly the least propitious marriage in all of American literature, a marriage that I will show is figured along the generic lines of the captivity narrative, James underscores the "remoteness" of a happy future for any reunion so imagined.

Much of the existing scholarship on *The Bostonians* focuses on issues of privacy and gender: the propriety of public speech for women, changing cultural attitudes about intimacy and publicity, and the novel's representation of sexuality. Even as I approach these issues from a new angle, shifting focus from Verena's performances to the more general concern of what it means to use speech acts to establish and police allegiance, I will show that they contribute importantly to James's study of postbellum culture. James tackles the possibility that words might work to wound or heal by interlacing three related kinds of narrative allegiance: to people, to ideals or causes, and to the nation. Not only does James thus complicate the concerns raised by oaths discussed in previous chapters, but he also examines the moral, social, and political power of speech, especially the performative force it can be said to muster and how this performativity shapes the way we govern ourselves and others.[21] In a 1905 speech at Bryn Mawr College, James observes that "all life therefore comes back to the question of our speech, the medium through which we communicate with each other; for all life comes back to the question of our relations with each other. These relations are made possible, are registered, are verily constituted, by our speech, and are successful (to repeat my word) in proportion as our speech is worthy of its great human and social function; is developed, delicate, flexible, rich—an adequate accomplished fact." James develops his topic in the lecture by detailing the importance of tone for women, concluding that (feminine) care in this matter will be of national benefit, transforming women into "models," "missionaries," and "even martyrs" to "the good cause" of American national development.[22] Compelling connections have already been made between *The Bostonians* and "The Question of Our Speech," and I only cite the lecture here to indicate the ethical and political significance James identifies as fundamental to speech. That performativity cycles back to ways of conceptualizing and defining gender only complicates our appreciation of what James is after in *The Bostonians*.

* * *

Although William James's *The Varieties of Religious Experience* (1902) does not mention the Civil War—and appears more than a decade after *The Bostonians*—the brothers' shared interest in the peculiar psychology of fanatic allegiance makes it a fine introduction to the problems of fervent devotion and shrill partisanship that Henry carefully explores in his novel. In *Varieties*, William briefly outlines the features of religious zeal, including its possible transfer to other kinds of experience. "Fanaticism," he bluntly contends, "is only loyalty carried to a convulsive extreme."[23] We should not blame religion for "the basenesses so commonly charged to [its] account," for they more usually arise from its "wicked practical partner[s]"—"the spirit of corporate dominion" and "the spirit of dogmatic dominion." These evil spirits explain religion's sometimes intolerance, its occasional "passion for laying down the law in the form of an absolutely closed-in theoretic system" (337). Such "exclusive devotion" is common enough in religion, but war also inspires it, encouraging the individual to risk his or her life for the sake of chieftain, king, or nation (340). What "we now need," William opines, is "to discover in the social realm . . . the moral equivalent of war: something heroic that will speak to men as universally as war does," something that could replicate war's ability to make life seem "cast upon a higher plane of power" (367, 366). Given the popularity of works like *Shenandoah* proposing precisely the opposite, this is a need that seemed very likely to go unmet.[24]

Or so Henry James appears to have thought. In *The Bostonians*, social and political causes are consistently depicted as "absolutely closed-in theoretic system[s]," complete with conversion narratives and fantasies of violent martyrdom.[25] It is the "dominion" associated with such modes of thinking, and the fanatic allegiance they demand of adherents, that James explores. His analysis focuses on the blurred distinction, particularly evident in fanaticism, between reason and emotion, between the abstract ideal and the affective bond. For wartime partisans, especially those in the Union, this had been a crucial means of distinguishing between genuine and specious allegiance. That this distinction might always be more nominal than real is at the core of James's argument, although his emphasis in *The Bostonians* is on all-too-common instances of zealotry. Not only do such cases rely on melodrama for their narrative mode, but they also create habits of both mind and heart that make it impossible to escape the overwrought affect and polarizing rhetoric of popular romance. As Jennifer James has recently argued, "melodramatic sentiment" is indistinguishable from fanaticism, and thus the moral clarity it purports to offer is illusory.[26]

An incident from the novel's early pages—Olive Chancellor's response to a conversation with a famous women's rights activist—establishes the recurring features of James's representation of fanatic and "exclusive devotion." Feeling as if she has been "placed under a spell," Olive is "inspired" and intoxicated, delighted that "the great representative of the enfranchisement of their sex (from every form of bondage) had chosen for her."[27] That being "chosen for" is preferable to choosing for oneself indicates that this understanding of "inspired" transport is ethically troubling. Isn't one of the hallmarks of "bondage" the inability to choose for oneself? Nonetheless Olive is certain, to borrow a phrase from William James, that her life has been "cast upon a higher plane":

> The barren, gas-lighted room . . . seemed to expand, to open itself to the great life of humanity. The serious, tired people . . . began to glow like a company of heroes. Yes, she would do something, Olive Chancellor said to herself; she would do something to brighten the darkness of that dreadful image that was always before her, and against which it seemed to her at times that she had been born to lead a crusade—the image of the unhappiness of women. The un-

happiness of women! The voice of their silent suffering was always in her ears, the ocean of tears that they had shed from the beginning of time seemed to pour through her own eyes. Ages of oppression had rolled over them; uncounted millions had lived only to be tortured, to be crucified. They were her sisters, they were her own, and the day of their delivery had dawned. This was the only sacred cause; this was the great, the just revolution. (30–31)

Consuming passion overwhelms logic as Olive simultaneously imagines her sisters' "silent" suffering and its clearly speaking "voice," "always in her ears." Here James elegantly illustrates the link, traced by Albert Hirschman, between "episodes of passion" and "the state of war," particularly as the former suspends an individual's ability to engage in the present tense of everyday life.[28] The exorbitant rhetoric is heightened as the passage continues and Olive imagines herself as the triumphant vehicle of their salvation:

It must triumph, it must sweep everything before it; it must exact from the other, the brutal, blood-stained ravening race, the last particle of expiation! It would be the greatest change the world had seen; it would be a new era for the human family, and the names of those who had helped to show the way and lead the squadrons would be the brightest in the tables of fame. They would be names of women weak, insulted, persecuted, but devoted in very pulse of their being to the cause, and asking no better fate than to die for it. It was not clear to this interesting girl in what manner such a sacrifice (as this last) would be required of her, but she saw the matter through a kind of sunrise-mist of emotion which made danger as rosy as success. (31)

The necessity of the "revolution" is indicated by repetition of "must" in the first three clauses; although the subsequent sentences switch to the conditional, the mood of the passage seems, if anything, to become more extreme, until abruptly concluded by the narrator's sober judgment.

Olive's mission is motivated by past injustice and dreams of glory; her desire to shine "brightest in the tables of fame" anticipates James's description of the commemorative markers in Memorial Hall later in the novel. There, "white-ranged" memorial "tablets," each "inscribed with the name of a student-soldier" fallen during the Civil War, provide a focus for the reader's engagement with the war's memory (189). Yet neither in Memorial Hall nor here at the beginning of the novel are those who have fallen named or particularized, although both scenes assert the power of names to secure "fame." It is telling that the reader never learns the names of Olive's brothers killed during the Civil War. Olive's fantasy concludes with a brief celebration of a woman who is "already a martyr." Miss Birdseye's precarious legacy depends on her "grotesque, undistinguished, pathetic little name" as the relentless adjectives establish what is for James the deception of zealous devotion, especially in the wake of a civil war increasingly said to have been instigated by sectional fanaticism (31). Individuals who believe in causes hope by their sacrifice to change the world, yet even when successful, their actions are usually anonymous and "undistinguished." No change would be possible without such sacrifices, and people are encouraged to make them through the suggestion that they will linger in memory, but James proposes that these claims are merely manipulative fictions. As the romantic naïveté of Olive's hopes—her faith in the power of the name—converts bloody persecution into a "rosy" "sunrise-mist of emotion," James indicts the easy sentimentality of "sacred cause[s]."

Critics often assume that the novel's representation of the dangers of zealotry is either incidental or evidence of James's own stance on the issue of women's rights.[29] "The truth," Irving Howe offers as a notable corrective, "is that in his way Ransom is as deeply entangled with his ideology as Olive is with hers."[30] Howe's "truth" is too limited, however, for, with one important exception, all the major characters in the novel are "deeply entangled" with some ideology, indeed stridently so. The novel is most profitably read, in other words, as a critique of ideological investment *as such*: any attachment to an abstract cause or principle, loyalty to anything, can generate fanatics, people who sacrifice everything and everyone to what they perceive to be more important aims. The persistent reference to combat and war helps James to make this point, although the novel is more concerned with the implications of obsessive allegiance than it is with any of the particular positions its characters take.[31] Women's rights thus functions like a "spell" for Olive, and Basil Ransom suffers from various "addict[ions]," "to judging his age" and "the old forms of address and gallantry" (148, 151). *The Bostonians* asks, in a Nietzschean mode, if a culture comprised of antagonistic camps of intoxicated enthusiasts can ever *not* be at war since, when compared to various thrilling campaigns, normal life is "rather poor and pale" (122). Put differently, "Extreme positions are not succeeded by moderate ones but by extreme positions of the opposite kind."[32] What James, echoing Nietzsche, registers is that ideals simplify our engagement with the world, generating absolute narratives that are easy, predictable, and best countered by similarly "extreme positions." It is "the dark danger of Megalomania" that disturbs James, a concern he would express across his long career.[33] The lurking horror of "Megalomania" is that it closes one off from the fact that life is "all inclusion and confusion."[34] While the hope that social conditions might improve is a noble one, in the Jamesian reality those working for such changes too often suffer from "Megalomania," and therefore work more effectively for the destruction of the social realm than they do for its amelioration.

Olive and Basil are the most fully represented, but they are not alone in their excesses: Mrs. Luna is passionately committed to the ideals represented by an aristocracy; Mrs. Farrinder has long since devoted her life to the cause of women's rights; Mrs. Tarrant hails from a family of famous abolitionists; and her husband's attachment to publicity as an end in itself calls forth James's withering sarcasm. But the most notorious of James's fanatic characters, at least for contemporary readers of *The Bostonians*, is Miss Birdseye, "one of the earliest, one of the most passionate, of the old Abolitionists":

> She was a little old lady, with an enormous head; that was the first thing Ransom noticed—the vast, fair, protuberant, candid, ungarnished brow, surmounting a pair of weak, kind, tired-looking eyes, and ineffectually balanced in the rear by a cap which had the air of falling backward, and which Miss Birdseye suddenly felt for while she talked, with unsuccessful irrelevant movements. She had a sad, soft, pale face, which (and it was the effect of her whole head) looked as if it had been soaked, blurred, and made vague by exposure to some slow dissolvent. The long practice of philanthropy had not given accent to her features; it had rubbed out their transitions, their meanings. The waves of sympathy, of enthusiasm, had wrought upon them in the same way in which the waves of time finally modify the surface of old marble busts, gradually washing away their sharpness, their details. (22–23)[35]

A stinging repudiation of the "practice of philanthropy," James's description suggests that her unwavering sympathy had rendered Miss Birdseye's humanitarian actions as "unsuccessful" and "irrelevant" as the futile attempts to keep her cap on her head. Rather than a source of enrichment or moral authority, Miss Birdseye's "waves of sympathy" erase both her individuality and her knowledge of others. Presented as synonymous with enthusiasm, sympathy works as a "slow dissolvent" that "wash[es] away" both "sharpness" and "details," destroying, not fostering, complexity. "After fifty years of humanitarian zeal," Miss Birdseye is said to know "less about her fellow-creatures, if possible, than on the day she had gone into the field to testify against the iniquity of arrangements" (23).

Miss Birdseye is not the only target of this diatribe, however: equally under assault is the assumption that sympathy engenders nuanced moral relations between people. This was one of Phelps's complaints in *The Gates Ajar*; it surfaces forcefully in the diary of Henry's sister, Alice James; and it is an important part of the severe representation of Miss Birdseye. Here, in the name of sympathy, Miss Birdseye inserts her own desires in place of those she is purporting to assist. In short, sympathy is a form of attachment that seems always to make one part of a person a "traitor to the rest." It is in the context of this contention that James makes the bold suggestion that even in Miss Birdseye's case, "philanthropy" is not disinterested: "Since the Civil War much of her occupation was gone; for before that her best hours had been spent in fancying that she was helping some Southern slave to escape. It would have been a nice question whether, in her heart of hearts, for the sake of this excitement, she did not sometimes wish the blacks back in bondage" (23).[36] As with Olive's passionate desire to be martyred or Basil's hopes to "breathe forth [his] views in glowing messages to a palpitating Senate" (256), "excitement" motivates Miss Birdseye, at least in part. "They had been the happiest days," the narrator observes, "for when causes were embodied in foreigners (what else were the Africans?), they were certainly more appealing" (24). Even when we would like to be able to claim that causes win our approval because they are honest or just, the reality, James argues, is that we prefer them to be "appealing" and pleasurable. Underwriting this idea is the common practice of winning converts to abolition and women's rights by embodying their causes in an affective body.[37] One of the paradoxes of the novel, in other words, is that the young woman over whom Basil and Olive fight, Verena Tarrant, is useful to the women's rights movement precisely because of her physical appearance, her "talent for embodying a cause" (93). Projecting her protégé's eventual success, Olive notes that "Verena was not abstract; she seemed to have lived in imagination through all the ages," and for this reason she is preferable as a leader to the "too abstract" Mrs. Farrinder (67). I turn more fully to the relationship between bodies and abstractions in chapter 5, but it bears noting here that James makes clear that being too abstract is detrimental to the communication of abstract ideas. Verena's importance to the cause thus lies in her ability to rouse desire, "to take hold of the outsiders, ... of those who are prejudiced or thoughtless" and "wake up attention" (184). The larger point is that no matter how often characters in *The Bostonians* employ the language of principle, they are primarily motivated by desire, rooted in the passions. Reducing a person to a body that can personalize a set of ideas to others instrumentalizes individuals, on James's account, and thus corrodes the core of civil society.

The characters are lost in their causes, certainly, but James gives this realization an ironic twist as he demonstrates that the Lost Cause *should* refer to abolition, not the dream of a separate Southern nation. Although this statement might seem perverse, by the time depicted in the novel (the late 1870s) and even more during its composition (the mid 1880s), the rights vouchsafed in the Thirteenth, Fourteenth, and Fifteenth amendments had become increasingly nominal as Jim Crow laws prevented their full realization. By this time, many white Americans had concluded that the goals of abolition and emancipation had been shortsighted, premature, or just wrong: the abolitionists, on this view, were "the century's villains," fanatics who had "marched the nation to the brink of self-destruction in the name of an abstraction."[38] In *The Bostonians*, it is the Southerner who expresses this opinion—"And as for our four fearful years of slaughter," he observes to Verena, "the Abolitionists brought it on" (72)—but it would be wrong to conclude that only Southerners held it. For those committed to reconciling North and South, eager to minimize the importance of the moral and political principles that had led to the war, the memory of the abolition movement was an impediment to progress.[39] As I argue in the next chapter, nostalgic plantation fiction, which also attracted a vast readership in the 1870s and 1880s, relegated the "earnest, unremitting work" of these activists to the margins, as the slaves for whom abolitionists had labored sighed for their lost days of happy slavery (138). In returning repeatedly to Miss Birdseye's efforts, to the "glorious and brilliant, but obscure and wastefully heroic" battles she had devoted her life to fighting (138), James reminds us that even victorious causes can be lost to posterity if they prove inconvenient over time.

What, then, of the character who is *not* a fanatic? What of Verena Tarrant? A flip response to this query would suggest that, because she lacks substance, she could never form the kind of attachment that would allow her to become a fanatic. One might say, in this vein, that she struck James himself as a lost cause, for he abandoned his initial plan to structure the novel entirely around her.[40] At its start, she is a passive figure who delivers a "strange, sweet, crude, absurd, enchanting improvisation" on "the gentleness and goodness of women," but only after her father, a mesmeric healer, animates her performance (48). Over time, and with the encouragement of her parents, Miss Birdseye, Mrs. Farrinder, Olive, and others, Verena becomes increasingly interested in the rights of women, although much of the plot turns on the strength of her allegiance, the depth of her feeling, and what she is (and is not) willing to sacrifice in the name of the cause. The novel concludes with Verena's second conversion, from loyalty to secession, from the expansion of rights to their total repudiation. How is it that Verena comes to be someone from whom so many people anticipate so much, given that she is consistently said to lack continuity? This is the judgment Olive passes on her, and it is implicit in Basil's repeated assertions that she does not mean what she says. Although Verena may seem too slight a character to inspire serious inquiry, James nonetheless uses her to pose the novel's central question about commitment, precisely because of her apparent triviality.

It is Verena who routinely draws conclusions unavailable to the other characters: when she and Olive read history, for example, Verena observes that women "intrusted with power ... had not always used it amiably, who brought up the wicked queens, the profligate mistresses of kings" (136). Similarly, Verena resists Olive's sweeping tendency to "dislike men as a class," which Olive decides is Verena's "sole infirmity and subtle flaw" (223). Unlike and despite Olive, Verena insists on specific and individual conclusions, although, notably, these are no guarantee of happiness in *The Bostonians*. That is to say, among the Civil War casualties listed in *The Bostonians* are moderation and reflection, both necessary to ethical and political affiliations and both threatened by fanaticism's need for absolute certainty. How, James wonders, do these needs affect how we value and evaluate the experiences, goals, or opinions of others? The desire to change "want of continuity" into infinite certainty, especially through oaths and pledges, erases the promise of the future, making it a stale reenactment of outmoded conventions (114).

* * *

The Bostonians announces its own (possibly fanatic) commitment to the serious consideration of how speech works from its very first lines: "Olive will come down in about ten minutes; she told me to tell you that. About ten; that is exactly like Olive. Neither five nor fifteen, and yet not ten exactly, but either nine or eleven. She didn't tell me to say she was glad to see you, because she doesn't know whether she is or not, and she wouldn't for the world expose herself to telling a fib" (5). One way to read this passage, and the entire opening scene from which it is taken, is as a reflection on what it means to give one's word. While Olive's language is rigid in its precision, her sister, Mrs. Luna, mocks such exactitude, noting her own preference for banter in which compliments, selective rather than accurate, predominate. In reply, Ransom taunts, "I pretend not to prevaricate," simultaneously suggesting three ways of saying something that might not be true: through imagination or fiction, through dishonesty or lies, and through the trope of irony (5). James presents these multiple positions on the epistemological and ethical import of speech through a compact reflection on civility's requirements that, in turn, introduces the novel's most important theoretical topic: how words and actions intersect in promises, oaths, and pledges. Although James's interest has wide-ranging implications, my emphasis here will be with how his study of performative language builds from and contributes to his engagement with the Civil War and its legacies.[41] In considering how statements, intention, and veracity relate, James recasts the wartime anxiety about verifying allegiance as a social problem—how do we know whom to trust, or does Verena mean what she says? This would be an important question in any of James's novels, but in *The Bostonians* it is complicated further by Verena's projected career as a public speaker; two important scenes set her, literally, on stage, and Basil's arrival in the novel's final pages prevents her from speaking at a third, decidedly public, forum. Beyond explicit concerns about shifting boundaries between public and private life or speech, the characters engage an array of issues related to how one should speak, what words can do, and under what conditions words can be judged to have been successful.[42] If, as I argue in this chapter, the novel is fundamentally about words, actions, and allegiance, then we can see that *The Bostonians* explores the political and ethical possibilities of speech as such—confessions, contracts, promises, orders, excuses, even prayers—not just the more limited issue of particular instances of public speech.

This part of the chapter moves selectively through these concerns, focusing on how James uses speech in the novel to extend his examination of fanaticism. Monomaniacally devoted to their principles (and the propagation of them), Olive, Basil, and their peers interpret the world through a set of preconditions, whether reading a text or listening to a speech; these fixed interpretive paradigms are repeatedly said to lead the characters to the truth, "new truths" in Olive's case, medieval ones in Ransom's. At the same time, the characters work to extend the dominion of their theories into the future through the agency of promises and vows. As with the oaths examined in chapter 1, promises in *The Bostonians* are uttered in the hopes of containing anxieties about allegiance, temporality, and the power of language: throughout the novel, however, characters worry that promises might rather prove "a form of words that committed [the speaker] to nothing" (191). It might be fair, thus, to adopt Deborah Esch's claim about *The Princess Casamassima*—that it presents "a mise-en-scène of promising" as it "thematiz[es] the 'obsessions' remarked by [J. L.] Austin"—for *The Bostonians*.[43] By explicitly setting the novel in the shadow of the Civil War, James can show that its use of loyalty oaths to police affiliation may not have been able to ensure allegiance to specific ideas, but they did transmit to the future the anxieties that had motivated their introduction, guaranteeing the formal perpetuation of the Civil War.

The Bostonians is so obsessed with words and politics that even children are asked to swear: "Mrs. Luna . . . clutch[ed] the irrepressible Newton to her bosom . . . and demand[ed from] him a vow that he would live and die in the principles of his mother. . . . [He] took an infant oath that he would never be a destructive, impious radical" (125). This brief example offers a humorous introduction to the relationship between "destructive" politics and speech acts that try to delimit the future's potential contours and possibilities being outlined in the novel. When Newton swears to his mother that he will not grow up to be "a destructive, impious radical," he shapes the world in a particular way that can only be judged by its felicity or success; one day, if he has become a radical, we might be able to say that his oath was infelicitous, but at the moment he utters it such an assessment is impossible. J. Hillis Miller clarifies this point through a reading of Wallace Stevens's "Anecdote of the Jar," which he takes to be "an allegory of a happy speech act" when the poet says that the jar "took dominion everywhere."[44] In its ability to transform the surrounding environment, Miller explains, the jar's effect replicates, albeit in a different register, the kind of work enacted (or hoped for) in the felicitous speech act. In other words, the jar's "dominion" is no different from the two kinds of dominion William James identified as integral to fanaticism. Although seemingly a digression, Miller's example thus highlights one of James's central insights about speech in *The Bostonians*: oaths and promises, if they are felicitous and forceful, structure the world along the lines of a "closed-in theoretic system," extending the dominion of an individual or a cause. In turning to what we now call performative language, James examines how the desire for dominion shapes not just what we see or read but, more crucially, also what we say and how we imagine these words to work.⁴⁵

In the most prolonged discussion of speech in the novel—when Olive asks Verena directly to renounce men—James shows how language can be deployed as a weapon against uncertainty, fear, and the future. The setting for the women's interchange is telling: "the vague snow looked cruel," the air was "silent and sharp," and the carefully staged dialogue recalls the insistent repetition and stark surroundings of tragic drama (103).

> "I have asked you before—are you prepared to give up?"
> "Do you mean, to give *you* up?"
> "No, all our wretched sisters—all our hopes and purposes—all that we think sacred and worth living for!"
> "Oh, they don't want that, Olive." Verena's smile became more distinct, and she added: "They don't want so much as that!"
> "Well, then, go in and speak for them—and sing for them—and dance for them!"
> "Olive, you are cruel!"
> "Yes, I am. But promise me one thing, and I shall be—oh, so tender!"
> "What a strange place for promises," said Verena, with a shiver, looking about her into the night.
> "Yes, I am dreadful; I know it. But promise." And Olive drew the girl nearer to her, flinging over her with one hand the fold of a cloak that hung ample upon her own meagre person, and holding her there with the other, while she looked at her, suppliant but half hesitating. "Promise!" she repeated. (104)

Framing her desires as negative imperatives, Olive, "dreadful" and "cruel," asks her friend to perform an act that is the repudiation of action. Indeed, as Brook Thomas notes, "Olive seeks, as in a marriage contract, a promise that 'would bind them together for life.'"⁴⁶ Given the rhetorical shivers James includes, as the promise to renounce all other men is extended to *all* men, we are encouraged to experience this moment as a gothic horror "(think of *The Monk* or *Frankenstein*) where variant allusions to the marriage vow function as maledictions or curses."⁴⁷ The malevolence of Olive's imperative echoes in Verena's "startled mind," for it presents a future that is "rather awful": "But the idea, uttered as her friend had uttered it, had a new solemnity, and the effect of that quick, violent colloquy was to make her nervous and impatient, as if she had had a sudden glimpse of futurity. That was rather awful, even if it represented the fate one would like" (105). An agreement to perform one action among many, promises carry with them the negation of possibility, but this scene foregrounds that fact, drawing attention to how promises work to shape a world that is "absolutely closed-in." As he underscores the moment's violence, James points to how a promise can serve the desire for dominion, while presenting the illusion of individual choice and agency.

Although the promise Olive hopes for is a general one, Verena's subsequent reflection narrows the question substantially as she "remark[s] to herself that there could be no difficulty in promising Olive so far as [Matthias Pardon] was concerned." Extrapolating from her lack of interest in marrying this particular man, Verena concludes that "once she came to think of it, she didn't want to marry any one." The decisive factor—to give Olive the promise she desires—is pleasure: "So it would be easy, after all, to make Olive that promise, and it would give her so much pleasure!" (105). The conversion of "awful" to "easy" gestures to the ease with which the relationship between pleasure, desire, and renunciation can be skewed, as a request becomes a demand.

James's meditation on promises in this prolonged interchange lingers with how speech acts negotiate the relationship between present and future, touching as well on the necessary conditions for promising. As J. L. Austin makes clear, a promise given under duress is not a performative.[48] Both Newton's "infant oath" and Verena's promise not to marry occur under coercive conditions that render them suspect. The coerced promise is no promise at all. Olive comes to a like conclusion for, in the subsequent scene, she shifts from demanding a pledge from Verena to refusing it when offered. With this important shift, James brings to the fore the necessity of considering the impact of coercion when evaluating an oath or promise. "'Don't you want any promise at present?' Verena asks. 'Why, Olive, how you change.'" "I don't want your signature," Olive responds, "I only want your confidence—only what springs from that. I hope with all my soul that you won't marry; but if you don't it must not be because you have promised me" (106). Austin explains that performatives "are designed for use by people who hold certain beliefs or have certain feelings or intentions. And if you use one of these formulae when you do not have the requisite thoughts or feelings or intentions then there is an abuse of the procedure."[49] But knowing if we have the "requisite thoughts or feelings or intentions" is difficult, given the complexity of all three. As James makes clear, Verena is increasingly caught in the "fine web of authority, of dependence" that Olive creates around her (130). How then are we to understand, when Verena expresses a desire to please Olive and acts accordingly, whose thoughts and feelings she is articulating? James approaches this problem from a second direction when Olive stresses that what she truly wants from Verena is what "springs" from her feelings, "confidence," and loyalty.[50] During the Civil War, the desire for an impossible certainty—to know that the oath or promise is true—led to the proliferation of oaths. The fundamental problem turned on the fact that speech acts cannot provide certainty if what is being requested is already in doubt. Unlike a constative statement, there is no test to see if a performative is accurate. Thus the oaths could *never* accomplish the true goal—guaranteeing loyalty—since it was precisely loyalty that needed to be tested. Olive reasserts this basic problem when she indicates that what she truly wants—trust—cannot be created by any promise if it does not already exist; the doubt about this existence creates the desire for a promise that, not addressing the basic issue, does little to satisfy the desire. How are we to trust our associates or intimates if their allegiance may prove to be like Verena's? If only violence can give us the illusion of trust, what is the basis for civil (and civic) discourse?

In this conversation Olive moves from the ardent desire for a verbal guarantee of allegiance to the equally ardent rejection of the very same guarantee. "Don't promise, don't promise!" Olive cries, although she qualifies this new imperative with the threat that Verena's failure to prove trustworthy will have mortal consequence: "But don't fail me—don't fail me, or I shall die!": "she wished to extract a certainty at the same time that she wished to deprecate a pledge, and she would have been delighted to put Verena into the enjoyment of that freedom which was so important for her by preventing her exercising it in a particular direction" (108). The desire motivating Olive is for her friend to *feel* free, to have the "enjoyment" of freedom, while preventing her from acting on that freedom. What differentiates this moment from the melodramatic promises with which the chapter began, however, is that James's interest is precisely in "the psychology of the vow," the kind of "logic" that it presupposes. Although *The Bostonians*, in the end, is as wed to submission as is melodrama, it consciously explores how the mechanisms of coercion work. Thus we see here that the force of Olive's imperatives in the "violent colloquy" have already so severely limited Verena's freedom that it could be read as removing anything remotely resembling freedom. Her desire for certainty has structured Verena's options as stark binaries—she will choose either life or death for her friend—that offer only the mirage of choice.

Even though Olive does not accept Verena's general pledge, subsequent interactions between the women demonstrate that Olive assumes her friend has made a sweeping promise to devote her life to the movement, as later references to a "phase" preparatory to her eventual vow make clear (116). Before continuing, it is worth noting that Verena does make a promise to Olive during the prolonged discussion of marriage vows—and to this one she remains faithful throughout the novel: "In spite of her friend's dissuasion [Verena] declared that she should like to promise. 'I will promise, at any rate, not to marry any of those gentleman that were at the house,' she said" (108-109). This promise not to marry Messrs. Gracie, Burrage or Pardon is one that can be both made and kept over time. Like the novel's opening sentence, the promise has a specificity that makes its efficacy easy to evaluate; it has the disadvantage, however, of having almost no value. As Melissa Ganz has recently argued, "narrowly conceived promises can improve relationships by fostering accountability and limiting boundless desire."[51] What is clear in *The Bostonians*, however, is that narrow promises evacuate relations of content, replacing obligation with empty form while doing little to curb desire or ambition.

Near the novel's conclusion, as Olive endures the excruciating end of her two closest relationships, she concludes that, at best, Verena's allegiance has been a mere "hothouse loyalty," incapable of withstanding the elements (319). As part of these sad reflections, Olive recalls the pledge Verena had offered to make:

> She remembered the magnanimity with which she had declined (the winter before last) to receive the vow of eternal maidenhood which she had at first demanded and then put by as too crude a test, but which Verena, for a precious hour, for ever flown, would *then* have been willing to take. She repented of it with bitterness and rage; and then she asked herself, more desperately still, whether even if she held that pledge she should be brave enough to enforce it in the fact of actual complications. She believed that if it were in her power to say, "No, I won't let you off; I have your solemn work, and I won't!" Verena would bow to that decree and remain with her; but the magic would have passed forever out of their friendship, the efficacy out of their work. (296-297)

That no promise can assure allegiance into the future, that no test fully distinguishes between "hothouse" and genuine loyalty, except for an act of betrayal that ends such indeterminacy, illustrates how the national anxiety about allegiance is simultaneously an issue for personal relations. How are we to trust our associates if their allegiance may prove to be like Verena's? To whom does Verena owe allegiance, having possibly promised Olive that she will give her life to the cause? Does the recognition that this is a coerced promise exempt her from censure at breaking her word? What is the difference between a promise and a contract, like the one Verena breaks by leaving Music Hall at the end of the novel? And, most pointedly, are the only promises that we can safely and felicitously offer those that are empty?

Before turning to how James uses his thinking about promises to engage broadly with the Civil War's legacy, there are two additional points to consider. For James, an interest in the efficacy of promises and oaths dovetails with a concern for evaluating the kind of force language can muster. This is a topic to which I return at the end of the chapter, but it bears noting that in *The Bostonians* the issue is often framed through the rhetoric of conversion, and, despite the regularity with which it is mentioned, only one character—Verena—is actually swayed by the power of words:

> The change that had taken place in the object of Basil Ransom's merciless devotion since the episode in New York was, briefly, just this change—that the words he had spoken to her there about her genuine vocation, as distinguished from the hollow and factitious ideal with which her family and her association with Olive Chancellor had saddled her—these words, the most effective and penetrating he had uttered, had sunk into her soul and worked and fermented there. She had come at last to believe them, and that was the alteration, the transformation. (299)

At the same time that the narrative is clear that the words that work this change are the "most effective and penetrating" Basil has ever spoken, it also links their effect to his "merciless devotion." Nowhere else in the novel do words have the power to change a person's mind, no matter what the characters might assert. In selecting Verena as the character who undergoes a transfer of affection and allegiance, James inverts the convention of reunion novels in which Northern officers correct Southern women's misdirected attachments. While Verena's marriage to Basil may reflect James's view of proper gender relations, his manipulations of the standard reunion formula, which include the suggestion, not found in De Forest, that words have a role to play in converting women, bespeaks his discomfort with the conventions of sentimental reconciliation, especially if they include women learning to embrace ideas that make them feel "slightly sick" (260).

The second issue to underscore, albeit briefly, is the way in which promises raise questions about the role of truth. "It was simply that the truth had changed sides," Verena acknowledges in her shift of allegiance (299): Olive scorns her sister for ignoring "the new truths," Miss Birdseye happily contemplates her participation in "the way the new truths advanced" (139), and Verena speaks as if "only thing in life she cared for was to put the truth into a form that would render conviction irresistible" (206). The claims beg one crucial question, however: what is a "new truth"? How does something that might properly be called an opinion or a belief become a truth? Even if modern readers agree with Olive, nineteenth-century Americans were unlikely to accept her "truths" as such. If it is impossible to agree on what is true, if the shared ground of knowledge is unstable and undermined by conflicting ideologies that disrupt the purported objectivity promised by truths in the first place, how can a shared understanding ever arise? How, in other words, might the nation *end* the Civil War if varying senses of the truth perpetuate a world in which people can wonder about how "differently" they have been taught? James uses these epistemological and ethical inquiries to engage a number of pressing political questions: How can we ever decide what is true about a contentious national event like the Civil War? In a partisan world, where can we find common ground? Most important, how can we be sure that what we believe to be a place of "peaceful" consensus is not actually a site of coercion (189)?

* * *

Henry James began thinking about the relationship between the Civil War and memory even before the conflict ended, as one of his earliest published tales, "A Story of a Year" (1865), reveals. "If by chance I'm taken out of the world," says Lieutenant Ford to his fiancée, "I want you to beware of that tawdry sentiment which enjoins you to be 'constant to my memory.' My memory be hanged!" Aware that "tawdry sentiment" could strip a man of his "personality" and "rights," he urges his fiancée to refrain from "inflict[ing]" his memory on others; in turn, he promises to forget her equally promptly should the need arise:

> I expect to see a vast deal of shabbiness and baseness and turmoil,

and in the midst of it all I'm sure the inspiration of patriotism will sometimes fail. Then I'll think of you. I love you a thousand times better than my country,' Liz.—Wicked? So much the worse. It's the truth. But if I find your memory makes a milksop of me, I shall thrust you out of the way, without ceremony,—I shall clap you into my box or between the leaves of my Bible, and only look at you on Sunday.

Constancy, as Ford explains it, is a complicated matter, requiring the careful and prudential balance of allegiances. A false sense of what it means to be faithful, the assumption that one's affection should prevail regardless of the circumstances, carries the distinct possibility of generating a gruesome excess of corpses: the soldier runs the risk of becoming a corpse if too fully engaged with the memory of his beloved while "widows and bereaved sweethearts" turn into versions of "the peddler in that horrible murder-story, who carried a corpse in his pack."[52] As it turns out, Ford would have been better served had he *not* questioned the virtue of constancy so explicitly to the young woman who, comparably quickly, forgets both her promise and her fiancé.[53]

James's sensitivity to the complex connections between affection, allegiance, corpses, and memory made necessary by the Civil War grew in the years between "A Story of a Year" and *The Bostonians*, but not as much as did the "demands" placed on the soldiers, living and dead, who were asked to shoulder significant figurative burdens for the nation. While grief surely accounts for much of the rising interest in remaining "constant," Kirk Savage explains that, because the war damaged the "founding mythology of the American nation," postwar memorial activities had both personal and national work to do.[54] Monuments erected after the conflict were supposed in part to reconstruct this mythology by offering "a genuine testimonial of the people's memory, an eternal repository of what they held most dear."[55] Yet the desire to create something eternal was complicated by the fact that even national memory is partial. Civil War monuments presented a redacted version of the past, eliding the issues of allegiance to celebrate the transcendent nature of the soldier's individual commitment to his comrades. Veterans themselves in periodicals, speeches, and memoirs routinely forwarded the arguments presented in the opening act of *Shenandoah*, with which this chapter began. These works agreed with Oliver Wendell Holmes Jr., who famously claimed that "the soldiers of the war need no explanations; they can join in commemorating a soldier's death with feelings not different in kind, whether he fell toward them or by their side."⁵⁶ The experience of war was a "great good fortune," Holmes reminded Grand Army of the Republic (GAR) veterans in 1884, because it demonstrated that "life is action and passion." That "passion and heroism immunized from motive" was what should be remembered, he maintained. Annual Memorial Day celebrations "embod[y] in the most impressive form our belief that to act with enthusiasm and faith is the condition of acting greatly," he concluded.⁵⁷ "We are all, North and South, incalculably richer for [our war] memories," Theodore Roosevelt similarly asserted.⁵⁸

James was far less sanguine than Holmes or Roosevelt about what was being "shrined in the temple" of Civil War memory.⁵⁹ As Verena and Basil stroll through Memorial Hall, James shows how the culture of memory that sprang up around the Civil War relied upon habits of blindness similar to those revealed in his exploration of personal fanaticism; the nation, on his account (as on Benedict Anderson's), is as selective and inflexible in the narratives and ideals it endorses as are its citizens.⁶⁰ In Memorial Hall we experience the techniques of consensus and dominion deployed to make people—North and South—feel "national," the myths these techniques sustain, and the possibilities they forestall and enable. What is particularly intriguing about using Memorial Hall to examine such issues is the fact that, despite claims to the contrary, the memory institutionalized there is overtly partisan. Of the Harvard students and alumni who died during the Civil War, only 136 are commemorated in the building; those who fell while supporting the Confederacy were not included.⁶¹ Put differently, Memorial Hall was "to stand as a conspicuous and constant reminder of alumni who had fought and died in the Civil War," as long as they had chosen the right side.⁶² (It is worth noting that *The Bostonians* was first published in *Century Magazine* [February 1885–February 1886], at the same time as the popular *Century* War Series [1884–1887]. Elaborately illustrated, the *Century* War Series sought to explain the war from the perspective of its participants.⁶³ Readers who encountered the novel in *Century* would have had a decidedly enthusiastic version of Civil War memory with which to contrast James's sardonic critique.)

James's intervention builds directly from his interest in the power of language: in Memorial Hall we learn that a successful national narrative is formally akin to a performative, shaping history for each viewer in both the present and the future. Bypassing questions about truth in favor of proper feelings about national belonging, the monument transmits a specific interpretation of the past in a form that is utterly resistant to dissent. Monuments write over, or superscribe, the reality of violent death by offering an alternate story, one that creates a narrative of the nation and its citizens' sacrifices that make both seem necessary and timeless; although representation and memory are exclusive and partial, national symbols obscure these facts by providing the comforting illusion that they depict the right and natural order of things: history as destiny and necessity, not chance or luck. In his depiction of Memorial Hall, James flags this aspect of memorials when Basil includes "dedicated" and "superscribed" in the list of verbs describing the impressive building; indeed, as Verena Tarrant points out, Memorial Hall is a building "which you see from every point":

> the ornate, overtopping structure, which was the finest piece of architecture [Ransom] had ever seen, had moreover solicited his enlarged curiosity for the last half-hour. He thought there was rather too much brick about it, but it was buttressed, cloistered, turreted, dedicated, superscribed, as he had never seen anything; though it didn't look old, it looked significant; it covered a large area, and it sprang majestic into the winter air. It was detached from the rest of the collegiate group, and stood in a grassy triangle of its own. (188)

The building performs a significance that exceeds its history ("it didn't look old") and is altogether "too much" (fig. 4). Among the building's other claims to significance is the sense it conveys of being "dedicated," a feeling that "overwhelms" Basil's aesthetic qualms about the design's excesses much as the building's "majestic" presence had overwhelmed ("enlarged") his "curiosity." A veritable temple to the embattled "masculine character" Ransom has pledged himself to defend, Memorial Hall stirs the Southerner in a variety of ways.[64] Another means of considering what James is after in this passage is to imagine that people entering memorials to dead soldiers could partake of something akin to the religious or spiritual experience William James describes, solemnly encountering through their allegiance to the nation its values embodied by a "temple" to its martyrs. Surely Memorial Hall, with its explicit echoes of gothic cathedrals, erected as a monument to a war so often said to be holy, encourages such an association.[65]

James carefully prepares the reader to enter Memorial Hall by densely littering the pages leading up to this encounter with references to war, heroism, and bravery, taking the martial imagery that had suffused national discourse to new extremes.[66] Women are "slaughtered" by men, Basil is twice referred to as an "enemy," Verena expresses her adoration

FIGURE 4. Memorial Hall, Harvard University, Cambridge, Massachusetts. (Courtesy of the Frances Loeb Library, Harvard Graduate School of Design)

of "heroism," and the "bravest men" are said to quake with fear before their female combatants (176, 184). The most pointed moment in this concentrated invocation of the Civil War topoi comes, however, in a discussion of sacrifice. When Verena mentions that her mother "would make any sacrifice for affection," Ransom boldly asks, "And you? would you make any?" Verena gave him a bright natural stare. 'Any sacrifice for affection?' She thought a moment, and then she said: 'I don't think I have a right to say, because I have never been asked. I don't remember ever to have had to make a sacrifice—not an important one'" (181). That Verena cannot immediately recall the promise Olive has asked her to make and, when (or if) she does, discounts it as unimportant indicates how easy it is for people to forget, proleptically justifying the need for this elaborate reminder of wartime "sacrifice and example" (189).

As they enter Memorial Hall, Basil prepares himself for a return to battle. "I must be brave enough to face them," Ransom states, "it isn't the first time" (188). In this belated skirmish, however, the enemy combatants are replaced with "white, ranged tablets,"

> each of which, in its proud, sad clearness, is inscribed with the name

of a student-soldier. The effect of the place is singularly noble and solemn, and it is impossible to feel it without a lifting of the heart. It stands there for duty and honour, it speaks of sacrifice and example, seems a kind of temple to youth, manhood, generosity. Most of them were young, all were in their prime, and all of them had fallen; this simple idea hovers before the visitor and makes him read with tenderness each name and place—names often without other history, and forgotten Southern battles. For Ransom these things were not a challenge nor a taunt; they touched him with respect, with the sentiment of beauty. He was capable of being a generous foeman, and he forgot, now, the whole question of sides and parties; the simple emotion of the old fighting-time came back to him, and the monument around him seemed an embodiment of that memory; it arched over friends as well as enemies, the victims of defeat as well as the sons of triumph. (189)

In the symbolic economy depicted, the "student soldier[s]" are interchangeable with the men Ransom met in battle, men he now figures as his comrades, not the enemy, for the "whole question of sides and parties" evaporates.[67] We should bear in mind, Lynn Wardley reminds us, that "this is a scene of reading."[68] But, as with other examples of reading in the novel, it seems more apt to dub it a scene of *misreading*. The particularities of the soldiers' lives, including their actual names, are replaced with a "simple idea" and "the sentiment of beauty." The narrative follows the monument in indicating the value of the proper name, although the repetition of the impersonal pronoun "it," which refers simultaneously to the building *and* its effect on the visitor, undermines the specificity the names might inscribe.[69] The confusion of reference creates a relationship, depicted as necessary (one cannot help but feel it), between the visitor and the effect of the building, which is represented as resulting from two sources: the building's very presence ("It stands there") and its implicit speech ("it speaks of sacrifice and example"). In these sentences James universalizes the "effect" of the monument as all readers feel an identical "lifting of the heart." It is impossible, the passage implies, to feel differently, for the "simple idea" hovers before the visitor and makes him or her read with "tenderness each name and place."[70] Nearly a decade later for an actual Harvard audience, Oliver Wendell Holmes Jr. would similarly argue that Union soldiers "respected [the Confederates] as every man with a heart must respect those who give all for their belief."[71] Put differently, the language in both passages so aligns individual and mass or national identity that difference is erased as all citizens are assumed to share a single, simple response.

"National sorrows" "impose obligations," historian Ernst Renan observes in 1882, and for this reason a "heroic past, of great men, of glory" provides "the social principle on which the national idea rests."[72] Throughout James's description, emphasis falls on how this imposition works, on the involuntary nature of the viewer's response, the way in which the monument organizes itself around what Dana Luciano calls "its task," not the teaching of history but the instruction of how we should feel about history.[73] As he looks at the monument, the "old fighting-time" comes "back to [Basil]," and one might expect that the emotion of combat would be other than "simple." Yet this is precisely the role monuments are designed to have in the construction of national identity and identification. As "the real dead are simultaneously forgotten, replicated, sequestered, serialized, and unknown," Ransom and the reader are alike "embedded" in what Benedict Anderson calls "homogenous, empty time," a form of temporal effacing he likens to the forgetting of childhood.[74] Coordinating the purported timelessness of aesthetic response and the political temporality associated with both monuments and oaths, James indicates that being able to identify the nation through "the sentiment of beauty" is one way in which aesthetics might be deployed "to absorb and redeem a violent breach" on Wardley's view or sustain fanaticism's investment in its own perpetuation on my own.[75] Although the monument's list of names seems intended to remind future visitors of the unique individuals who died, the passage stresses instead the generalizing thrust of memory.[76] The further indication that the memory is singular—"that memory" instead of "those memories"—recalls the Lowell essay, demonstrating in an institutional frame what James had there indicated was a feature of all memory: its tendency to generalize. In Memorial Hall, collective or communal responses replace specific or personal ones, a process that subordinates individual preference to established ideology. Especially striking is the passage's emphasis on embodiment. Given the novel's recurrent interest in how to embody an abstract idea—Verena, escaped slaves, Miss Birdseye ("a battered, immemorial monument" of "the heroic age of New England life" [308])—the use of a building to continue that interest implies that official memories, the kind that "arch[] over friends as well as enemies," are like causes in that they too require embodiments; the irony of this gesture, however, is the fact that the bodies are precisely missing.

Despite its genuine solicitude for the lives lost during the war, the passage is as much engaged with forgetting as it is with remembering:

the names on the tablets are "without other history," the "Southern battles" have been "forgotten," as are "the sides and parties." According to Nietzsche, in *On the Advantage and Disadvantage of History for Life* (1874), this is precisely how monumental history works; because it presupposes that the utility of the past inheres in the example it provides for the future, it necessarily must overlook a good deal, "ruthlessly" forcing the past into "a general form" where "all its sharp edges and lines" are "broken for the sake of agreement." In the case of *The Bostonians*, what gets "broken," or lost, is the *content* of the causes leading up to the war: "monumental history will not find ... truthfulness to its advantage," Nietzsche continues, "it will always approximate, generalize and finally equate differences; it will always weaken the disparity of motives and occasions in order, at the expense of the *cause*, to present the *effect* monumentally, that is, as exemplary and worthy of imitation."[77] It is form, not cause, that generates this critical effect: to return to James, the effect of Memorial Hall "gradually wash[es] away ... sharpness [and] ... details."

Verena's assertion—"It is very beautiful—but I think it is very dreadful"—calls Ransom, and the reader, "back to the present" (189). "It's a real sin," she continues, "to put up such a building, just to glorify a lot of bloodshed. If it wasn't so majestic, I would have it pulled down" (189). Her objection to the celebration of this particular national narrative is predicated on a real objection (why do we glorify war?) and rooted in the views she expresses about women's rights (that women are less inclined to violence). By including this objection, James exposes what is forgotten or repressed in the drive for national unity—the ability to dissent.[78] Angrily dismissing Verena's statement, Basil insists that it is *irrational* to see the building in a manner than diverges from his own and, in so doing, refuses to recognize her challenge to the totalizing implications of national patriotism. This is Verena's most political moment in the novel, as James approaches the issue of national virtue directly. Ransom's refusal to acknowledge the logical possibility of alternate interpretations—he discounts Verena's deviant opinion as "feminine logic"[79]—speaks directly to the author's concern about the democratic future of a culture addicted to idealized views of its past and similarly narrow visions of its future.

At the same time, however, Verena's comment gestures to the prime justification *for* commemoration because she seems to know little about the war, despite her worshipful attitude about heroism. During the scene, Verena "wondered what could have happened to [Basil] to make him so perverse. Probably something had gone wrong in his life—he had had some misfortune that coloured his whole view of the world.... Of

Basil Ransom's personal history she knew only what Olive had told her, and that was but a general outline, which left plenty of room for private dramas, secret disappointments and sufferings" (254). The "general outline"—war, loss of home and property, financial ruin—should be enough to account for his cynicism, but Verena overlooks these potential sources of trauma, seeking instead something "private" or "secret." Here, what had previously seemed a potentially positive trait—her ability to see the individual—is shown to be a liability instead. Like her failure to recall her supposed sacrifice, Verena's inability to imagine the war's effect indicates why cultures feel the need for monuments in the first place. She concludes by acknowledging that Memorial Hall is "peaceful," an assertion that reflects the not inconsiderable pleasures vouchsafed by the kind of harmony the monument makes possible, coercive though it might be (189). Holding the viewer rhetorically captive to a particular interpretation of the Civil War, Memorial Hall makes clear that symbols or narratives that strive to create consensus do so, as Nietzsche explains, "ruthlessly," imposing a "general form" on past and future simultaneously.

* * *

The Bostonians' troubling final scene finds its central characters once again in an important Boston building—Music Hall—considering the supposedly opposed claims of causes and sentiments. Whereas violent conflict had been a memory in Memorial Hall, at the end of the novel it seems a present and live possibility. Basil and Mrs. Tarrant separately worry about the "mob" gathered to hear Verena speak, he catching a "glimpse of the ferocity that lurks in a disappointed mob," she shrieking, "Do you want us all to be murdered by the mob, then?" (335, 343). The state's authority to deploy violence in its name is likewise present, embodied in "a robust policeman" hired to protect Verena from Basil's intrusion (336). But neither the officer nor the mob can equal the threat that Basil imagines himself to represent. "He had never been in the Music Hall before, and its lofty vaults and rows of overhanging balconies made it to his imagination immense and impressive. There were two or three moments during which he felt as he could imagine a young man to feel who, waiting in a public place, has made up his mind, for reasons of his own, to discharge a pistol at the king or the president" (333). Ransom might not yell "Sic semper tyrannis," as did John Wilkes Booth after shooting Abraham Lincoln at Ford's Theatre, but there is no doubt as to the reference. The "immense and impressive" architecture of Music Hall, with "its lofty vaults," recalls the scene in the equally impressive Memorial Hall, further associating Ransom's planned assault on the symbolic leader of the women's movement with Booth's assassination of the U.S. president.[80] Given this fantasy, Ransom's favorite oath—"Murder"—belatedly becomes both an expletive and an imperative, while his early quip about carrying "a six-shooter and a bowie-knife" to dinner is stripped of the humor it had seemed to wield in the genteel Boston parlor of the novel's opening (6). To be sure, the continual violence of the closing scene troubles the idea that James intended this as a happy ending. While Verena's affections for Basil undeniably grow, in a novel that considers the power of speech so relentlessly, it is at the very least disturbing that what she actually says to her lover in this final episode is dismissed and discounted. The violent rebel Ransom, defying both law and public opinion, kidnaps the Union heroine, whisking her away from civilization and hiding her, possibly in the sixteenth-century world celebrated in his periodical essay.

But is this right? Are the "scared, haggard eyes" Ransom sees on the faces of Verena and Olive indicative of fear of him or fear of the audience, which, refusing to be "pacif[ied]," roars ever louder (345)? Is Verena correct that the gathered crowd is "fine," or is Ransom's view that they are "senseless brutes" who will "howl and thump according to their nature" more accurate (347)? James repeatedly returns to the suggestion that the "multitude" is on the verge of going wild with an "agitation" that waxes and wanes "in waves and surges" (348). If the crowd is so fierce, perhaps Basil is saving Verena after all, liberating her from the clutches of "senseless brutes" and returning her to safety.

It is impossible to distinguish between these opposed scenarios, impossible to specify if Basil's actions take the form of rescue from savagery or a savage abduction. Because of this uncertainty and the scene's constant invocation of savagery, I contend that the ending of this "very American" novel borrows productively from the rhetorical conventions of a "very American" genre, the captivity narrative. Although captivities first flourished during the earliest years of the nation's (pre)history, the nineteenth century witnessed a renewed interest in captivity tales of women snatched from "civilization" and forced to wander through the wilderness in the company of "savages," especially around the time of the Dakota conflict of 1862.[81] As Janet Dean has recently demonstrated, documents penned after this gruesome incident exposed tensions in prevailing definitions of savagery, civilization, and sexual violence. The decades leading up to the publication of *The Bostonians* were marked by a series of violent clashes between white settlers and Native Americans, including the Comanche, the Apache, and the Lakota, all of which culminated in the 1887 Dawes Severalty Act, legislation designed to replace communal reservation lands with individually owned property.[82] Put simply, the time represented in *The Bostonians*, as well as the period of its composition, witnessed ongoing and violent turmoil in the West, conflicts often associated with the Civil War.

While twenty-first-century readers might tend to see these events as separate, this was not the case in the nineteenth century.[83] As demonstrated in chapter 2, Union literature regularly paralleled Confederate partisans and Native peoples. An 1862 cartoon from *Harper's Weekly* attacked the Confederacy for the brutality of its allies (Native Americans fought on both sides in the Civil War, although more supported the South than the North) (fig. 5). Anecdotes, like the one recorded in an 1864 diary, where one Virginia soldier recounts finding a comrade "executing a species of Indian War Dance around a Poor Yankee," were common.[84] Popular dime novels throughout the 1860s consistently associated conflicts with Native Americans and the Civil War, representing both as "internal, domestic struggles." Edward Ellis's *Indian Jim* (1864) and *The Hunter's Escape* (1864) maintained that "secessionists, contrabands, and 'red-skins'" were "in some ways interchangeable"—and in each case it was the responsibility of respectable white men to bring the savages back under control.[85] In an 1867 address to the New York Young Men's Republican Union, Charles Sumner listed three examples of the "incalculable mischief of State rights": the "barbarous independence" of Native Americans ("Each chief is a representative of State Rights"); the republic of Mexico (whose twenty-three unruly states had led to "chaos"); and the Confederate States of America. All three represented the "deadly enemy lurking in State Rights," Sumner concluded, a principle he believed to be equivalent to "turn[ing] their backs upon civilization itself."[86] The rhetoric of these disparate genres established a tradition of thinking about the Civil War through the conflicts and conquest of the western portions of the North American continent.

Such connections made it easy for James to mine the tensions associated with Native savagery in closing his meditation on the legacy of the Civil War in U.S. culture.[87] *The Bostonians* is throughout engaged with captivity: this is Olive's constant theme, one she shares with Basil despite their differing opinions about how freedom or rights should be distributed. Desirous of saving the world from its captivity by a most "damnable feminisation," Basil consistently sees the women's movement as an

PLEDGING ALLEGIANCE IN HENRY JAMES / 133

FIGURE 5. Cartoon from *Harper's Weekly*, September 13, 1862. The caption cites a statement by Jefferson Davis associating the Confederate president with the violence of the Dakota conflict. It reads, "I am happy to inform you that, in spite both of blandishments and threats, used in profusion by the agents of the government of the United States, the Indian nations within the confederacy have remained firm in their loyalty and steadfast in the observance of their treaty arrangements with this government." As the caption seeks to make clear, neither "confederacy" conforms to standards of loyalty. (Courtesy HarpWeek, LLC)

attempt to destroy the civilized world (260). His dreams of "kidnapping" or "wresting [Verena] from the mighty multitude . . . that would fight for her" recall James Fenimore Cooper's romantic recasting of captivity narratives in *The Last of the Mohicans* (306, 333). If the 1884 election of Democrat Grover Cleveland allowed, in the words of one Southerner, the South to "escape from captivity and humiliation," then the rhetoric of captivity that James uses in this scene may extend his subtle commentary on the legacy of Civil War memory to include contemporary politics.[88]

What is especially salient about reading the ending of *The Bostonians* as informed by the captivity narrative is not just the thematic possibilities it presents but also how it concludes the text's structural concerns with speech. The ending of *The Bostonians* replaces Verena's speech about national "scripts of identity" with her silence.[89] Throughout the novel, Verena has quite literally held her listeners in thrall, which Basil, a former master, seems unable to abide: "Keep your soothing words for me—you will have need of them all, in our coming time" (347). Silencing her, he seizes power and returns himself to mastery. Basil's musings on his potential for violence recall, finally, that he has previously considered how to police Verena's speech; in his first thoughts about their union, he reflects that, were they to wed, "he should know a way to strike her dumb" (249).

The final scene thus weds an interest in rhetorical force to a continuation of the novel's engagement with performative language, particularly as it pertains to marriage. Although Ransom makes clear that he intends to marry Verena, he broaches the subject with an imperative (hidden inside the future perfect) rather than a question:

> [Ransom] perceived, tossed upon a chair, a long, furred cloak, which he caught up, and, before she could resist, threw over her. She even let him arrange it and, standing here, draped from head to foot in it, contented herself with saying, after a moment:
> "I don't understand—where shall we go? Where will you take me?"
> "We shall catch the night-train for New York, and the first thing in the morning we shall be married." (347)

Nowhere in the scene does Verena state her consent to marrying Ransom; to the contrary, she begs her lover to "let [her] off," asks him "to go away," turning to him with "a supreme appeal" to let her speak to the crowd (343, 346, 347). No matter what she says, however, Basil's position predominates the scene and narrative. Note that it is from his perspective that we are offered this interpretation, including the justification of the use of force in removing her:

> She had evidently given everything up now—every pretence of a different conviction and of loyalty to her cause; all this had fallen from her as soon as she felt him near, and she asked him to go away just as any plighted maiden might have asked any favour of her lover. But it was the poor girl's misfortune that, whatever she did or said, or left unsaid, only had the effect of making her dearer to him and making the people who were clamouring for her seem more and more a raving rabble. (346)

The non-assent Verena provides here replays the discussion she has with Olive about the need to give one's word, but with one crucial difference.

Whereas Olive had refused Verena's pledge, hoping to trust in her actions, Basil dispenses with Verena's words and actions altogether. Yet for consent to be meaningful, it must be "voluntary, "distinguishable from captivity," a condition hard to measure in the above passage.[90] "The virtue of '*consent*' depends," Frederick Douglass pointedly observes, "much upon the mode of gaining it. If a highway-robber should at the *pistol's mouth* demand my purse, it is possible that I should '*consent*' to give it up."[91] In this closing scene, James demonstrates that in reality consent is all too often dependent on assumptions that resist both argument and action: in these cases, consent is operative in name only. Given that all of Verena's possible responses ("whatever she did or said, or left unsaid") lend support to Basil's argument, it is clear that his belief in her consent obviates her need to express or endorse it. Acquiescence alone is sufficient, yet without some form of expression, how is consent to be differentiated *from* captivity? Being able to make such a distinction is, Gregg Crane observes, an "ethical imperative," perhaps most especially, one might add, when a rhetoric of heroic martyrdom renders it even harder to identify.[92] Recalling the political arena James invokes throughout the text, the question at the end of *The Bostonians* could thus be rephrased as follows: how much coercion can be tolerated before its effect overwhelms and negates consent? The rhetoric of captivity comments directly, in other words, on the politics of postwar reconciliation and, in a typically Jamesian twist, ethical bonds of attachment. Much like a promise, perhaps we can only make determinations about the relationship between consent and coercion *after* the fact.

There is one further dimension of the novel clarified by this association with captivity narratives. *The Bostonians* talks about the cause of abolition but argues for its contemporary irrelevance, the ambiguity of its presumed moral authority; the only black characters are in silent positions of service. Basil's views about the rights of women and minorities, coupled with the fact that he had owned slaves before the war, justifies the conclusion that Verena is again entering a kind of slavery, refiguring the financial transaction between Olive and Verena's father and echoing the contemporary claims of women's rights activists equating marriage and slavery.[93] In sum, the novel's final pages offer a careful indictment, hard to hear over the din of the crowd, of reconciliationist schemes that would erase centuries of chattel slavery from national memory and that would make emancipation—for African Americans and women—a farce. In *The Bostonians*, we see Verena move from one kind of captivity to another, a claim enabled by the Anglo-American legal tradition that held that marriage and slavery were both domestic relations.[94] Bringing together multiple forms of promissory obligation and associating them subtly with captivity, James offers a bleak assessment of a future in which passion would trump law and its forms. That women's rights activists turned to contract as a way of forwarding their claims for equality further underscores the penetrating force of James's analysis—and the grim dimension of his conclusions.

In *The Bostonians*, James carefully demonstrates the dangers and limitations of Manichaean oppositions; on his view, the world seldom devolves to the stark poles of good or evil, friend or foe, black or white. These binaries might be necessary during war, when issues can be matters of life or death, but the extension of wartime requirements into civilian life troubles human interactions at every level. Olive and Basil were created by the Civil War, and their continued belief in the values, priorities, and structures it necessitated guarantees that peace will be hard to declare, for in *The Bostonians*, as powerful as speech may be, it is always trumped by both physical violence and violent belief. Why would James write a work that deplores the culture created by stark oppositions and then ends in a way that encourages further opposition? The answer, such as it is, is found in the novel's famous final sentence: "It is to be feared that with the union, so far from brilliant, into which she was about to enter, these were not the last tears she was destined to shed" (350). In Verena's silence, the reader must give voice to her future, imagining and creating the eventual outcome of this "very national, very typical" captivity. Forcing the reader to pick sides, the novel forcibly shows that our civil wars are far from over.

4 / Loyalty's Slaves

A cartoon published in the *Chicago Inter-Ocean* on May 30, 1898, shows two soldiers on a pedestal engraved in bold black letters with the word "loyalty" (fig. 6). The man on the left carries a U.S.A. '61 canteen, identifying him as a Union veteran; his companion, mounting the pedestal, has a C.S.A. '61 canteen and wears the Confederate's slouch hat. Both men are draped in the national flag as they stare off at a distant fire, Cuba in flames. "One decoration will do for both this year," its caption asserts, underscoring the cartoon's message that the Spanish-American War finalized the reconciliation of North and South. Southern newspapers, like the *Atlanta Constitution*, proudly proclaimed that former Confederates soldiers, now "profoundly loyal to the stars and stripes," "are eager to exhibit their fidelity upon the field of battle."[1] "The forces of fraternity have culminated in the Spanish-American war," Southern reformer Belle Kearny enthused in her 1900 memoir.[2] Northerners celebrated as well, flocking to revivals of plays like *Shenandoah*, which lauded the martial prowess of the *American* soldier.[3]

To the contemporary viewer, the cartoon soldiers might summon no specific connotations. Fin-de-siècle Americans, however, would have quickly recognized them as modeled on a common type of Civil War monument. A testament to the valor of the enlisted man, sculptures of average soldiers celebrated "the American citizen-soldier as a superior native, white 'type' of manhood," Kirk Savage explains. While people across the nation celebrated this "white 'type'" of loyalty, a handful of

FIGURE 6. Memorial Day, 1898, from *Cartoons of the War of 1898 with Spain from Leading Foreign and American Papers* (Chicago: Belford, Middlebrook, 1898).

organizations were working to memorialize another kind of loyalty, also associated with the Civil War. In 1896, Confederate veteran Samuel White provided the money to erect a simple monument—a small obelisk with two relief panels—in Fort Mill, South Carolina. It sought "to teach generations yet unborn that though black in skin, and servile in station, there existed between the negro and the master a bond of love broken only by death." An inscription on the monument explains that it was "dedicated to the faithful slaves who, loyal to a sacred trust, toiled for the support of the army, with matchless devotion, and with sterling fidelity guarded our defenseless homes, women, and children, during the struggle for the principles of our 'Confederate States of America.'" Rather than national allegiance, the loyalty lauded by the Fort Mill monument is domestic, a "bond of love" located on the plantation. Whereas standing soldier monuments were common in the late nineteenth century, memorials to loyal slaves were not—although not for lack of planning. Prohibitive costs prevented the realization of most of the projects, and, because these memorials were "really about sentiment not slavery," it was easy enough for planners to indulge their nostalgic sentimentality about the peculiar institution in other, less expensive ways.[4] A popular outlet for these feelings was provided by the plantation narrative, which recalled the gentility of the Old South, often through the fond memories of an ex-slave who recalled the "bond[s] of love" that had inspired his or her ceaseless fidelity to his or her former owner.⁵

These two monuments—one imaginary, one actual—concisely indicate the complicated and sometimes contradictory assumptions about memory and loyalty operative at the end of the nineteenth century. If it is difficult at the close of *The Bostonians* to determine whether Basil Ransom is taking Verena Tarrant captive or rescuing her from a dangerous captivity, it is equally difficult to understand how to correlate the meanings of loyalty—one an affiliation purportedly predicated on commitment to a set of political ideals, the other a premodern attachment to an individual person—represented by the two monuments. But as George Fletcher points out, "inequality reigns" in the "realm of loyalty."⁶ The next two chapters examine the problems generated by these divergent and unequal understandings of loyalty, revisit the relationship between sympathy and loyalty, and explore the implications of the correlated reconstruction of these important concepts at the end of the nineteenth century.

The questions that motivate this chapter are derived from thinking about the Fort Mill monument. Why did the loyal slave become a nationally important figure thirty years after emancipation? In 1866, J. T. Trowbridge dismissed concerns about the instinctive loyalty of former slaves, arguing that even though "strong instinct" might replace "actual knowledge" among former slaves, this was no cause for concern because

> that instinct inspires them with loyalty to the government, and it will never permit them to vote so unwisely and mischievously as the white people of the South voted in the days of secession. Moreover, there are among them men of fine intelligence and leading influence, by whom, and not by their old masters, as has been claimed, they will be instructed in their duty at the polls. And this fact is most certain,—that they are far better prepared to have a hand in making the laws by which they are to be governed, than the whites are to make those laws for them.⁷

Trowbridge's argument for the extension of the franchise depends, in other words, on the supposed docility and tractability of Southern blacks, not on their capacity for self-reliance or the ideal of consent; for ex-slaves, loyalty is the product of "instinct" rather than reason, an "instinct" one can trust to protect personal—and national—interests.

Distasteful as Trowbridge's argument may be, he was intervening in an active debate about the political future of former slaves, the Southern states, and the nation as a whole. What, then, was at stake in the resurgence of narratives about instinctive black loyalty in the later years of the nineteenth century? What were the implications of loyal slaves, attached once again to "their old masters," for the cultural, political, and ethical understandings of loyalty in particular and allegiance more broadly? In partial response to these questions, this chapter argues that in its return to a sentimentalized, prestate idea of loyalty, the loyal slave as trope enacts at the level of culture and narrative the assumptions underwriting late-nineteenth-century defenses of the contract, the rise of Jim Crow legislation, and the conservative judicial philosophy that enfeebled the citizenship rights supposedly guaranteed by the Fourteenth and Fifteenth amendments. What these disparate examples share is a fundamental commitment to an organization of power—individual and state alike—predicated on racial hierarchies and principles. To locate these changes within the terms that have been the primary focus of this book, the figure of the loyal slave brings to view how new inflections in the use of sympathy changed the meaning of loyalty, minimizing the already fluid distinctions between the terms. In its consideration of fanaticism, the preceding chapter began the work of unraveling this distinction so important during the Civil War, demonstrating how we can be blinded by a passionate commitment that only *appears* to be abstract or rational. The next two chapters engage that line of argument as it structured the political reality for African Americans, considering the difficulty of either postulating or maintaining differences between abstract and particular engagements with the world.

The specific focus of this chapter is on the figure of the loyal slave, its evolution in plantation fiction and the rebuttals by African American authors that it inspired. After a brief overview of the cultural conditions influencing the rising popularity of the loyal slave figure, as well as efforts by black writers and thinkers to reject its cultural and political authority, the chapter turns to the counternarratives of two writers—Charles Chesnutt and Paul Laurence Dunbar—who grapple critically with the pervasive trope, seeking to instill nuance and complexity into its homogeneity. As they reappropriate the meanings and limits of a national and racial model for allegiance, Chesnutt and Dunbar provide related explanations of what a full sense of responsibility—for Chesnutt, ethical; for Dunbar, civic—entails in a nation that tends to reduce issues to simplistic black and white oppositions. The loyal slave is an expression of white desire, and the political structures that sustain it, and the works of Dunbar and Chesnutt expose the ease with which racialized desire finds its fulfillment. That their efforts are constrained by the terrain demarcated by the very tales they seek to revise suggests the comparatively narrow possibility of such projects.[8]

David Blight argues that loyal slave stories are "at the heart of Civil War memory" and thus provide a potent example of "history giv[ing] way completely to mythology."[9] Yet despite their importance to how Americans understood their recent past, it is Reconstruction, not the Civil War itself, that provides the important historical context for understanding their appeal. In the chaotic years after the war, it was far from clear what shape the nation's future would take. One "utopian vision," sketched by congressional radicals, pictured "a nation whose citizens enjoyed equality of civil and political rights, secured by a powerful and beneficent national state"; according to Republicans like Senator Charles Sumner and Representative Thaddeus Stevens, "there was no room for a legally and politically submerged class in the 'perfect republic' that must emerge from the Civil War."[10] For a few years, such ideas seemed ascendant, even if most Americans disagreed with the premise—equality for all—on which they relied. Before long, however, the majority view reasserted itself, and one can measure the change by comparing the universalist ambition of the Fourteenth Amendment with the more narrow aims of the Fifteenth.[11] Through the compromises and cynical revisions necessary to secure passage of the amendments, as well as "the desire to retain other inequalities, affecting whites" that "produced the Fifteenth Amendment," this "utopian vision" was efficiently dismantled.[12]

Americans did not abandon all "utopian" visions, however. Rather than looking forward to a society without distinctions based on race, they looked back with nostalgic affection to a time when racial hierarchies were the institutional and national norm. As Jim Crow separated the races in public, hundreds of narratives—fiction and nonfiction alike—depicted a fantastic intimacy between blacks and whites, recalling a time when sentiment rendered the intrusion of law unnecessary. The result, as Saidiya Hartman explains, was the transformation of slavery into a "utopian figure."[13] Such fantasies reconstructed the plantation as a site of consent, replacing iron shackles with bonds of love, fusing racial and national fantasies. In short, the loyal slave, familiar during the antebellum years but nearly omnipresent in postbellum culture, carried much of the ideological burden of reconstructing the American state as racialized in its very constitution, permitting white authors to assert their rights to both the privilege of abstraction *and* access to, as well as aid and comfort from, normative feeling.[14]

The emergence of the loyal slave trope as a common postemancipation figure is thus critical for two reasons. First, it responded to white anxieties about loyalty and submission by establishing that the obedience national loyalty required could be discriminated along racial lines. White loyalty, even when submissive, was not servile because it was predicated on an attachment to an abstraction, like a cause or an ideal, not a person.[15] Second, white authors and readers found in plantation stories ideals and principles that ratified the idea that the nation, whose past and future were seamlessly merged, continued to be organized by clear racial hierarchy. Regardless of the fact of emancipation, the Civil War thus enabled the articulation of a politics that, for many, quite literally reconstructed the racial assumptions upon which the nation had been founded. The loyal slave thus metonymically situated black Americans within the nation, figuring black equality as continued servility.[16] Narrating a past that justified the future thus imagined, loyal slave stories suggested that the changes undertaken in Reconstruction had been nominal or, better, had freed whites from slavery's burdens but left blacks enmeshed in the bonds of love that they cherished.

As I argued in chapter 1, Union ideology during the Civil War had proffered loyalty as the preferred model of affiliation, defining the concept as dependent on rationality and duty. These were better guides to conduct than either the emotions or sympathetic identification, Union partisans widely proclaimed. The loyal citizen subordinated his or her personal inclinations and followed authoritative directives; such discipline, with its clear republican echoes, made it possible for each citizen to do his or her duty for the nation. Given the standard interpretation of Southerners as unruly and passionate, self-control and emotional restraint were easily saturated with political content. Questions arose around the performance of loyalty and its temporal dimension, but the central tenets of national loyalty—that the loyal citizen was committed above all to the abstract nation and never distracted by competing sympathies or sentiments—were clear enough. The end of the war complicated this picture as questions arose about the nationalization of loyalty and the process of conversion it would require. As we saw in chapter 2, loyalty persisted as the rational affect of allegiance to the United States, even as questions about what constituted its successful performance became more vexed. Indeed, as critics like Henry James pointed out, abstract commitment was often, even usually, indistinguishable from a passion, preventing rather than nurturing rational thought or reasoned choice.

Even before the war was over, submission to the will of an external authority struck some as a kind of slavery. "We are just like Negroes," an Ohio soldier complained in 1861, while a Massachusetts man wrote, "I like a soldiers [sic] duty well enough, but I do not like to have a master [and] to be drove like a niggar [sic]."[17] Complaints about army discipline notwithstanding, the idea that the soldier was "an intelligent unity" who "permitted himself, for duty and for love, to be made into the cog of a wheel" seemed to many critical to the war effort.[18] A successful nurse needed to "put away all feelings," Katherine Wormeley explained, "and be a machine—that's the way to act, the only way." These wartime ideals found their way into fictional representations of the war as well. A Union colonel in Sherwood Bonner's *Like Unto Like* (1878) asserts, "Soldiers can't have votes. We've got to move like automaton chess-players, with somebody behind to do the thinking." Twenty years later, in Stephen Crane's *The Red Badge of Courage* (1895), Henry Fleming makes the crucial shift from "man" to "member" as when "something of which he was a part—a regiment, an army, a cause, or a country—was in a crisis. He was welded into a common personality which was dominated by a single desire."[19] What unites these disparate passages is the contention that being a part of a larger whole, to which one relinquishes thought and will, is integral to the full expression of "duty," "love," and loyalty.

The idea that being "the cog of a wheel" was central to a soldier's life likewise facilitated reconciliation between the sections, for it encouraged an emphasis on commitment rather than its content or motivation. In Howard's *Shenandoah*, Northerner Kerchival West underscores that he and his Southern friend will both be "honest" in the performance of their respective duties, ignoring the fact that these duties could include trying to kill one another. The Civil War is thus reinterpreted as nonideological, and the differences in beliefs are rendered inconsequential; what matters is the experiences the two men have had and can be said to have shared.[20] Veteran Oliver Wendell Holmes Jr. presents a fuller expression of this critical idea in the 1895 address "The Soldier's Faith": "In the midst of doubt, in the collapse of creeds, there is one thing I do not doubt, and that is that the faith is true and adorable which sends a soldier to throw away his life in obedience to a blindly accepted duty, in a cause which he little understands, in a plan of campaign of which he has no notion, under tactics of which he does not see the use."[21] In short, war's horrors are redeemed as soldiers learn the signal importance of attachment.[22]

Replacing the idea of loyalty with "faith," Holmes contends that reason plays no part in a soldier's allegiance, a point people in both sections embraced. Being attached, regardless of motivation, was thus the most important dimension of a patriotism increasingly dependent on "vague and unspecified causes" or "abstract and noble principles."[23] According to Holmes, it is utterly beside the point to comprehend the reason for which one is fighting, an idea driven home in the redundant clauses that conclude the passage. Stripped of content, national allegiance here requires little but the willingness to accept "blindly" a position of servile submission to the will of another. Whereas loyalty had originally been presented as a rational check on the emotionalism of uncontrolled sympathy, Holmes presupposes something quite different: comfort with a necessary *uncertainty* is the fundamental feature of the idea of national allegiance he articulates.[24] The shifting importance of certainty in the discussion of loyalty measures the conceptual move away from the rationality that putatively distinguished Union loyalty during the war. In its place, Americans celebrated a passionate affiliation that renounced the importance of agency or will. As Fletcher reminds us, "Loyalties generally lead people to suspend judgment about right and wrong."[25]

Although seemingly digressive, a brief glance at Mark Twain's *A Connecticut Yankee in King Arthur's Court* (1889) clarifies the larger importance of Holmes's claims.[26] That the novel broadly satirizes late-nineteenth-century culture is no insight, but that part of this attack concerns contemporary arguments about the nature of allegiance is easy to overlook in the midst of Hank Morgan's pyrotechnics and the pageantry of sixth-century England. Yet some of Twain's most explicit vitriol is reserved for confusions about the meaning of loyalty. "You see my kind of loyalty was loyalty to one's country," Hank Morgan explains,

> not to its institutions or its office-holders. The country is the real thing, the substantial thing, the eternal thing; it is the thing to watch over, and care for, and be loyal to; institutions are extraneous, they are its mere clothing, and clothing can wear out, become ragged, cease to be comfortable, cease to protect the body from winter, disease, and death. To be loyal to rags, to shout for rags, to worship rags, to die for rags—that is a loyalty of unreason, it is pure animal; it belongs to monarchy, was invented by monarchy; let monarchy keep it.

Predicated on persons ("office-holders"), a "loyalty of unreason" can be neither "substantial" nor "eternal." Revising the idea central to Ernst

Kantorowicz's argument for the two bodies of divinely constituted monarchies, Twain suggests that it is just to the idea, not its embodiment, that one owes allegiance, for in this way it is possible to resist the changing whims (or fashions) of the moment. The full passage outlines the duties of the citizen and rails against the idea that only the ruling minority has the right to determine the actions of government. At issue for Twain is the problem of partiality. One must keep the broader aims of the "country" in view, resisting the tyranny of partiality and personality. Even as Twain's extended clothing metaphor frays his argument, the passage nonetheless forcefully associates personal loyalty with the feudal past, notably stripped of the romantic trappings often associated with the medieval period during the later nineteenth century. To be loyal without thought is "pure animal," inconsistent with the practices and presumptions of democracy: "the citizen who thinks he sees that the commonwealth's political clothes are worn out, and yet holds his peace and does not agitate for a new suit, is disloyal; he is a traitor. That he may be the only one who thinks he sees this decay, does not excuse him; it is his duty to agitate any way, and it is the duty of the others to vote him down if they do not see the matter as he does."[27] The meaning of disloyalty and treason here is not rebellion, but instead failure to understand and don the responsibilities of citizenship, which importantly includes resisting "peace" in the name of political duty. Ideas, beliefs, and principles are important and, furthermore, worth fighting for. To the time-traveling Hank Morgan, these competing conceptions of loyalty can exist simultaneously even though they pertain, according to the historical logic of the novel, to different moments, the sixth and nineteenth centuries, respectively. The temporal displacement that sustains Twain's humor also fuels his political message: the "loyalty of unreason" belongs in the past. To bring a personal model of allegiance into the present, the novel suggests, one must deploy temporal and political displacements.

It is in the context of the above arguments about loyalty and citizenship that the loyal slave becomes important as an integral component of the postbellum "national fantasy." For people North *and* South, the evacuation of content from loyalty enabled the resurgence of a race-based model of affiliation and, with it, the reconstruction of slavery as a moment of childish innocence, an imagined preindustrial national utopia before the violence of war and the corruption of peace, sanitizing both past and future.[28] Exiled from a utopia of perfectly balanced affect and racial harmony, the loyal slave's purported dislocation and melancholy for the lazy days of plantation ease reoriented the claim that genuine allegiance required patriarchal guidance and structure, allowing white citizens to feel national again. Inverting the position for which Lincoln argued before the Civil War, the loyal slave trope metonymically represents the nation's reconstruction, including its return to the idea that sentiment provides the best basis for affiliation, even as it deploys Civil War rhetoric of Northern ideals of equality and freedom.[29]

Just as the loyal slave is at the "heart of Civil War memory," a revitalized—and racialized—understanding of sympathy is at the heart of the revised concept of loyalty that made the loyal slave both popular and pervasive. Throughout this book, loyalty's connotations have been charted in relationship with sympathy because the concepts were used in competing and overlapping ways to designate both individual and state affiliation. The opposition so evident to Civil War partisans between the concepts was, as the previous chapters have established, often more imagined than real, although that loyalty was meant to identify a resistance to a certain understanding of affective priorities in ethical and political allegiance remained unchanged. Indeed, what interest in loyalty indexes most clearly is uneasiness about the assumptions underwriting sympathetic identification, many of which have been incisively explored by scholars. What has received less consideration—and yet is crucial to the evolution and appeal of the loyal slave—is the deeply conservative dimension of sympathy's operation. Much critical attention has been lavished on the potentially transformative power of sympathetic identification, particularly Adam Smith's influential contention that "by the imagination we place ourselves in his situation, we conceive ourselves enduring all the same torments, we enter as it were into his body, and become in some measure the same person with him, and thence form some of idea of his sensations, and even feel something which, though weaker in degree, is not altogether unlike them."[30] The moral authority associated with the affections and imagination orients much antebellum American literature, as is well known. Yet that Smith goes on to suggest that our natural feelings are naturally hierarchical is much less widely considered. No matter what "whining and melancholy moralists" might maintain about our obligations to the unfortunate among us, we more readily sympathize with the rich, Smith argues, for we are "eager to assist them in completing a system of happiness that approaches so near to perfection." Smith's sympathy is part, it bears noting, of a larger philosophic vision that includes the necessary inequities of *The Wealth of Nations*. For this reason, poverty and other misfortunes often inspire our contempt, not our compassion. Although humans are "naturally sympathetic," they nonetheless "feel so little" for those "with whom they have no particular connexion"—those who are far from us in various ways—that a minor personal annoyance is more likely to be moving than a stranger's tragedy.[31] In those instances when we are confronted with a dilemma where it is unclear to whom we should direct our sympathies, Smith is clear that the sufferer will *not* automatically receive them if we are inclined to agree with the person causing his or her pain. "We cannot at all sympathize with the resentment of one man against another," he writes, "merely because this other has been the cause of his misfortune, unless he has been the cause of it from motives which we cannot enter into."[32] In sum, sympathy's efficacy is hampered, on Smith's account, by the very barriers its operations are routinely said to overcome.

Worse, differences between people often render them "intolerable to one another." Divergent "matters of speculation" and "taste" do not interrupt the "entertainment" we might find with others, but if our interlocutors lack "fellow-feeling" for our "misfortunes," we become unable to "converse upon these subjects. We become intolerable to one another. I can neither support your company, nor you mine. You are confounded at my violence and passion, and I am enraged at your cold insensibility and want of feeling."[33] What is clear, in other words, is that Smith's account of sympathy depends substantially on preexisting agreements of various kinds, including class, morality, nationality, and even affective states. It is not hard to see how race could become one of the important modes of agreement upon which sympathy could depend. Although this is not explicit in the text, and indeed Smith stresses the importance of entering into the "body" of another person, as Christopher Castiglia has recently made clear, *actual* bodies disrupt sympathy.[34]

Nineteenth-century writers and thinkers who turned to sympathy as a moral norm or political ideal may not have consulted *The Theory of Moral Sentiments* when crafting their appeals, but Smith's qualifications, honest about the ways in which personal prejudices complicate what we can feel for others, provide an important context for understanding how sympathy came to be used at the end of the nineteenth century to justify racial discrimination and violence. Despite the claims made for the power of sympathy to establish bonds of affection and allegiance between the races, cross-racial identification seemed to many unnatural and dangerous. Consider, for example, the use of contamination as a figure for the dangers of sympathy, the threats of unregulated imitation and contact between persons. While Benedict Anderson suggests that nationalism and racism have different trajectories and timelines—"The fact of the matter," he writes, "is that nationalism thinks in terms of historical destinies, while racism dreams of eternal contaminations"—sympathy conflates the two, guaranteeing that the American national imaginary is consistently plagued by the idea that its destiny is in the process of being polluted.[35] The important point here is neither to praise nor to condemn sympathy, but rather to demonstrate the extent to which its definition and use depended on other terms and ideas.

This hierarchical model of sympathy—conservative, favorable to the rich, and familiar—provides an important foil to definitions of loyalty faltering about the meaning of principle, certainty, and will. Although, as we have seen, loyalty continued to organize national allegiance, sympathy and loyalty were no longer opposed in their specific political connotations. To the contrary, changing ideas about the structure of commitment, ideas that seem to have accelerated reconciliation between whites, collapsed the differences between the terms, rendering both consistent with hierarchical and racist assumptions and practices. In short, both sympathy and loyalty could be deployed against African Americans.

One potent example of these claims is evident in the widespread use of *Uncle Tom's Cabin* in conservative plantation fiction. If Stowe's novel had established the moral value of right feeling in the years leading up to the war, it was equally effective at a new iteration of this task in the Civil War's wake.[36] In works like James Lane Allen's "'Uncle Tom' at Home in Kentucky" (1887) or Walter Hill's "Uncle Tom without a Cabin" (1884), authors deployed Stowe to realign sympathies and redefine loyalties, asserting the truth of the "poetic legend" her novel sought to repudiate.[37] "'Uncle Tom' at Home in Kentucky" provides a representative example of how the loyal slave trope was deployed to undermine black claims to equality by identifying a "historical" loyalty distinct from U.S. national allegiance. The essay is thus explicit that it aims to correct the historical record by capturing the "great moral landmarks" of the antebellum South before "mists of forgetfulness" obscure their important national lessons, a task Allen associates with discriminating between kinds of allegiance: "As citizens of the American Republic, these old negroes . . . have not done a great deal. The bud of liberty was ingrafted too late on the ancient slave-stock to bear much fruit. But they are unspeakably interesting, as contemporaries of a type of Kentucky negro whose virtues and whose sorrows, dramatically embodied in literature, have become a by-word throughout the civilized world."[38] Although, on Allen's account, black characters are incapable of forming abstract bonds, like those necessary for citizenship, they are nonetheless useful to "the civilized world" in fiction as examples *for whites* of the redemptive (and racialized) qualities associated with personal bonds of allegiance. This is especially evident in Kentucky, where "the kind, even affectionate, relations of the races under the old régime" have persisted after emancipation with just a "little interruption." "The blacks" in Kentucky "remain content with their inferiority," Allen asserts. For this reason, he concludes that agitation for equal rights, and the racial turmoil it engenders, only results from harsh treatment; given affection, ex-slaves will "lazily drift through life." The assertion of the "hopelessly inferior[ity]" of African Americans is made, he assures the reader, "as a fact, not as an argument" (867).[39] According to Allen's logic, this is a topic on which argument is wasted: fiction is the only way of conveying the truths about a race that is only distinguished by its ability to form emotional ties.[40]

Much of Allen's essay is devoted to explaining how slavery molded the character of white Kentuckians: the childhood affections it fostered; the adult responsibilities it imposed; and the "very noble types of character" it instilled in white men and women (861). Doggedly persistent in his defense of Stowe's fictional Kentucky family, the Shelbys, Allen ironically turns to fiction to establish the fact of his claim that Tom would have been better loved than any other slave on the plantation:

> Many a time [the young boy] slips out of the house to take his dinner or supper in the cabin with Uncle Tom; and during long winter evenings he loves to sit before those great roaring cabin fireplaces that throw their red and yellow lights over the half circle of black faces and on the mysteries of broom-making, chair-bottoming, and the cobbling of shoes. Like the child who listens to "Uncle Remus," he too hears songs and stories, and creeps back to the house with a wondering look in his eyes and a vague hush of spirit. (858)

The present tense of the passage erases the passage of time, as does the comparison of the postbellum child ("who listens to 'Uncle Remus'") with the young George Shelby. That one cannot determine if the child is listening to Uncle Remus the character or to an "Uncle Remus" story establishes Allen's position that the distinction between fact and fiction, as well as the passage of time, is unimportant when talking about slavery.

Allen's essay is accompanied by a series of drawings by E. W. Kemble, best known today for his illustrations of Mark Twain's *Adventures of Huckleberry Finn*. Kemble's images strip any subtlety from the personal relationships depicted in the text, replacing them with static icons that bolster Allen's claims to accuracy: as with the text they illustrate, these

THE MASTER.

phase which is to be distinguished as domestic; and it was this mode that had prevailed at the North and made emancipation easy.

Furthermore, in all history the condition of an enslaved race under the enslaving one has been partly determined by the degree of moral justification with which the latter has regarded the subject of human bondage; and the life of the Kentucky negro, say in the days of Uncle Tom, was further modified by the body of laws which had crystallized as the sentiment of the people, slaveholders themselves. But even these laws were only a partial exponent of what that sentiment was; for some of the severest were practically a dead letter, and the clemency of the negro's treatment by the prevailing type of master made amends for the hard provisions of others.

It would be a most difficult thing to write the history of slavery in Kentucky. It is impossible to write a single page of it here. But it may be said that the conscience of the great body of the people was always sensitive touch-

FIGURE 7. E. W. Kemble, "The Master." (Courtesy of Cornell University Library, Making of America Digital Collection)

tuckians often used it on serenading bravuras. The old fiddler, most of all, was held in reverent esteem and met with the gracious treatment of the ancient minstrel in feudal halls. At parties and weddings, at picnics in the summer woods, he was the soul of melody, and with an eye to the high demands upon his art, he widened his range of selections and perfected according to native standards his inimitable technique. The deep, tender, pure feeling in the song "Old Kentucky Home" is a true historic interpretation.

It is wide of the mark to suppose that on such a farm as that of the Shelbys the negroes were in a perpetual frenzy of discontent or felt any burning desire for freedom. It is difficult to reach a true general conclusion on this delicate subject. But it must go for something that even the Kentucky abolitionists of those days will tell you that well-treated negroes cared not a snap for liberty. Negroes themselves, and very intelligent ones, will give you to-day the same assurance. Nay, it is an awkward discovery to make, that some of them still cherish resentment toward agitators who came secretly among them, fomented discontent, and led them away from homes to which they afterwards returned. And I want to state here, for no other reason than that of making an historic contribution to the study of the human mind and passions, that a man's views of slavery in those days did not always determine his treatment of his slaves. The only case of mutiny and stampede that I have been able to discover in a certain part of Kentucky, took place among the negroes of a man who was known as an outspoken emancipationist. He pleaded for the freedom of the negro, but in the mean time worked him at home with the chain round his neck and the ball resting on his plow.

Christmas was, of course, the time of holiday merrymaking, and the "Ketchin' marster an' mistiss Christmus gif'" was a great feature. One morning an aged couple presented themselves.

"Well, what do you want for your Christmas gift?"

"Freedom! Mistiss."

"Freedom! Haven't you been as good as free for the last ten years?"

"Yaas, mistiss; but — freedom mighty sweet!"

"Then take your freedom!"

The only method of celebrating the boon was the moving in to a cabin on the neighboring farm of their mistress's aunt and being freely supported there as they had been freely supported at home!

Mrs. Stowe has said, "There is nothing picturesque or beautiful in the family attachment of old servants, which is not to be found in countries where these servants are legally free." On the contrary, a volume of incidents might readily be gathered, the picturesqueness and beauty of which are due so largely, if not wholly, to the fact that the negroes were not free servants, but slaves. Indeed, many could never have happened at all but in this relationship. I cite the case of an old negro who was

SAVING HIS MASTER.

FIGURE 8. E. W. Kemble, "Saving His Master." (Courtesy of Cornell University Library, Making of America Digital Collection)

images efface the differences between fact and fiction, past and present. Kemble's "The Master" (fig. 7), "The Mistress," "The Cook," and "The Mammy" are drawings clearly intended to speak with "authority" in their resistance to the established exaggerations of caricature, a move that conveys their "seriousness" and accuracy.[41] This is particularly evident in the series' culminating image, "Saving His Master" (fig. 8). Like "The Master," the sketch relies on sharp contrasts to frame the action; in the final drawing, however, the master is no longer the benign image of robust patriarchal power. Head thrown back, an unconscious white man is carried out of a river by a larger black man. The visual program contrasts strong horizontal lines—the river and horizon, emphasized by a break in the clouds over the white man's head—with equally strong vertical ones—the redundantly white arm dangling in the water and the erect posture of the black man, stressed by his impressive musculature. The white man's recumbent and effeminate body, a series of 45-degree angles, disrupts the carefully ordered scene. Despite the seeming reversal of power relations, the men's clothing communicates that social rank has not been affected; the slave wears rags while his master's clothes are well-tailored and, even in this crisis, neatly arranged. As in Thomas Nelson Page's "Marse Chan" (1884), or Allen's own "Two Gentlemen of Kentucky" (1899), the inversion of power reiterates the assertion that the bonds linking slave and master are based on affect, not domination or coercion. Nonetheless, the image's presentation on the page strongly suggests that this is a loving relationship that needs narrative boundaries to stabilize it: unlike the other large illustrations in the series, "Saving His Master" is bordered on three sides by text.

"Saving His Master" compels our attention for several reasons, not least of which is the fact that the picture does not illustrate anything in Allen's essay. Although he lauds the efforts of a slave who "followed his master to the battle-field" and, after the man's death, returned to his Kentucky mistress, Allen chooses not to discuss the loyalty of slaves, asserting that it "comprises a whole vast field of its own," which, if "ever written," would demand a Southern perspective to capture fully "the knowledge and *the love*" (867). The compensatory function of the loyal slave—a depiction of "impossible and uninhabitable positions"—is captured here by the excess it inspires: Allen's italic emphasis and Kemble's representation of "a whole vast field" with an illustration that has no narrative correlative.[42] The drawing provides, however, a vivid imagining of Allen's contention that black character is at its heroic best when acting selflessly on behalf of white others; as he carries white burdens, the former slave comes closest to embracing (literally) his civic responsibilities.[43] That such sacrifice could be reshaped to accommodate the ideals of civic republicanism is clearly beyond the scope of Allen's imagination, although, as we will see later in this chapter, it provides Paul Laurence Dunbar with the means of repudiating the loyal slave trope.

In sum, the consciously elegiac quality of the plantation narrative only partially disguises the polemic at its core. Rather than consent or contract, slavery defenders before the war and romancers in its wake maintained that emotion was far more likely to generate a just, equal, and secure world.[44] Varying in degrees of sentiment and violence—from paternalism to intense phobia—postbellum schemes for denying the just claims of African Americans sought to reestablish the putatively clear hierarchies of antebellum social organization, said to be in the best interest of all involved. Such a practice resolved the tensions, already evident in Civil War materials, that absolute devotion to the nation evacuated the possibility for consent and choice, worries that spread throughout the nation as it struggled through both reunification and the memory of the devastating war. Disseminated at all levels of culture—from advertising campaigns to elite literary magazines to history textbooks—the figure of the loyal slave, metonymically depicting the reconstruction of white privilege, collapses distinctions of past and present, fact and fiction, as it carries the burdens of national sentiments, again out of control.

* * *

After surveying representations of African American characters in American literature, Anna Julia Cooper sadly concludes "that an authentic portrait, at once aesthetic and true to life, presenting the black man as a free American citizen, not the humble slave of *Uncle Tom's Cabin*—but the *man*, divinely struggling and aspiring yet tragically warped and distorted by the adverse winds of circumstance, has not yet been painted. It is my opinion that the canvas awaits the brush of the colored man himself."[45] Calling for resistance to the predominance of loyal slaves, Cooper urges her peers to free themselves from traditions authorized by antebellum sentimental narrative. In novels, plays, autobiographies, and histories, black writers answered this call. Novels, like James Howard's *Bond and Free* (1886), replaced claims about the carefree existence slaves had enjoyed before the war with depictions of their (nearly) universal desire for freedom. Histories such as William Wells Brown's *The Negro in the American Rebellion: His Heroism and Fidelity* (1867), George

Washington Williams's *History of the Negro Race in America, 1619–1880* (1883), or William T. Alexander's *History of the Colored Race in America* (1887) corrected the nation's seeming amnesia about the realities of slavery and the contributions of African Americans to the nation's development: in his introduction, Williams stressed that slavery had created "antagonisms," not ties of affection, which prevented the proper development of American citizenship by dividing the nation both by region and by race.[46] Pauline Hopkins's "A Dash for Liberty" (1901), a narrative of the 1841 Creole revolt, reminded readers that freedom was something slaves had been willing to risk their lives to win.

Even autobiographical writings, the 1882 version of Frederick Douglass's *Life and Times*, for example, challenged the fictions structuring the conventional plantation narrative. The new materials contained in "Time Makes All Things Even"—the story of his own reunion with Captain Auld—would, he explains, excite the reader's "imagination with peculiar and poetic force."[47] Despite his printed denunciations of Captain Auld, Douglass describes the reunion with his former master, during which the men sit hand in hand and share "friendly conversation" about "past differences." "Now that slavery was destroyed," Douglass observes, "and the slave and the master stood upon equal ground, I was not only willing to meet him, but was very glad to do so. The conditions were favorable for remembrance of all his good deeds, and generous extenuation of all his evil ones" (875). The pleasant reunion employs several of the characteristic features of the plantation tale: it is a moment of sentimental reconciliation; it provides an opportunity to stress the white man's good qualities and deeds; and it hints that there had been mutual respect in their former relationship. Yet rather than wrenching the men from a pastoral idyll of loving care, Douglass stresses that emancipation saved both "victims" of slavery: "Our courses had been determined for us, not by us. We had both been flung, by powers that did not ask our consent, upon a mighty current of life, which we could neither resist nor control" (875–876). Not only does he explicitly deny that slavery was consistent with consent, Douglass quotes Auld as saying, "had I been in your place, I should have done as you did" (877). In the 1870s, Douglass had warned that "the South has a past not to be contemplated with pleasure, but with a shudder," but in the 1882 autobiography he seems to acknowledge the mass appeal of scenes of reconciliation—he opines his encounter with Auld could "well enough be dramatized for the stage" (874)—while seeking nonetheless to set the record straight about slavery's injustices.[48]

Douglass's recognition of the sentimental power reconciliation narratives could wield anticipates a general shift embraced by African American activists, rightly demoralized by a series of Supreme Court decisions that narrowed radically the meaning of the Fourteenth Amendment and the power of the federal government to intervene in state affairs.[49] The Slaughterhouse Cases (1873), the Civil Rights Cases (1883), and *Plessy v. Ferguson* (1896) defined black modes of allegiance as different from, and subservient to, those formed (and policed) by whites and, in the process, legally institutionalized the loyal slave. In response, many African American activists reoriented their efforts from political equality to economic independence. Associated with this change in tactics was a related move in uplift ideology, from the rights and guarantees of citizenship to the demonstration of a culture of self-improvement, bourgeois morality, and patriarchal authority, all intended to convey the worth of African Americans to hostile whites.[50] Whereas this focus on quiet morality proposed to protect blacks from white aggression by underscoring the moral qualities of black Americans, it had the unintended consequence of ratifying the racist presuppositions of the loyal slave trope, unchallenged in a seeming acquiescence to the premise that African American forms of allegiance were best defined as domestic, personal, or local. In his famous address at the 1895 Atlanta Cotton States and International Exposition, for example, Booker T. Washington described a future as comfortably familiar as the pastoral plantation past:

> in the future, as in the past, . . . you and your families will be surrounded by the most patient, faithful, law-abiding, and unresentful people that the world has seen. As we have proved our loyalty to you in the past, in nursing your children, watching by the sick-bed of your mothers and fathers, and often following them with tear-dimmed eyes to their graves, so in the future, in our humble way, we shall stand by you with a devotion that no foreigner can approach, ready to lay down our lives, if need be, in defense of yours, interlacing our industrial, commercial, civil, and religious life with yours in a way that shall make the interests of both races one.[51]

Washington draws an explicit parallel between a past peopled with loyal mammies tending to the needs of children and a future of equally "humble" partners, "ready to lay down" their lives for white families. Although the "interests" of the "races" merge, power remains unchanged as African Americans can easily enough be construed, to use Allen's phrase, as "content with their inferiority." Stressing the importance of local affections, Washington spoke to national fears about black migration and social status even as his program of industrial education validated the naturalness of plantation hierarchies.[52] It is hard not to recognize the pragmatism of this approach, the ways in which it calmed tensions that were increasingly manifested in horrible acts of racially motivated violence; nonetheless, it is also not hard to see how Washington's position lent credence to those claiming that loyal slave stories were factually accurate.

Washington's erasure of the difference between past and present points to the signal challenge presented by loyalty for African Americans at the end of the nineteenth century. Its Civil War echoes associated the concept with emancipation and the successful struggle for freedom, but its resignification as a figure for a national future reconstructed as a repetition of established racial hierarchies meant that the Civil War legacy was experienced by many as closer to fiction than fact. At the same time, interpretations of the importance—and extent—of "loyalty ... in the past" between the races led, in the waning years of the nineteenth century, to uncertainty about race loyalty for *both* whites and blacks. What did race loyalty entail, demand, or preclude? White supremacists were explicit in their statements about the simple and pressing need for white solidarity, principles they disseminated widely.[53] For African Americans seeking to counter the prejudices thus inflamed, the issues were more complex. Did an ideal of individual self-reliance accommodate the pressure to work for the race, particularly given the reality that expressions of this ideal tended to underscore class differences within African American communities? What was the relationship between loyalty to the race and to the nation, given legislative and legal moves to bar black access to the rights supposedly guaranteed in the Constitution?

With these questions in mind, the remainder of this chapter narrows its focus to consider more thoroughly the efforts of two authors—Charles Chesnutt and Paul Laurence Dunbar—to expose the distortions of the loyal slave trope and all that it entailed. I have selected these authors from the many who sought to rebut the powerful figure for several reasons. First, as W. E. B. Du Bois points out, they "spoke to the whole nation."[54] Both Chesnutt and Dunbar published in widely circulated and prestigious periodicals, earning critical notice from influential editors and reviewers: their arguments reached a national audience. Focusing on the problems of memory, allegiance, and recognition, both reject the nostalgic loyal slave and, in the process, recuperate loyalty as an important indicator of exemplary citizenship. In so doing, they do not simply respond to the racist fiction popularized by the plantation school, although that is surely one of their goals, but simultaneously engage with the ongoing debate about national affect and the parameters of both sympathy and loyalty. Although they approach the problem variously, both conclude by articulating the importance of an ethical, as opposed to a conventional, relationship between persons; what I mean to convey with this distinction is that they actively resist the stereotyped responses to too-familiar problems, introducing instead a more nuanced sense of what it means to be committed to an ideal or a value. Chesnutt and Dunbar underscore how the homogenization engendered by the loyal slave reduces moral complexity by replacing individuals with a metonymic construction of white desire and anxiety. The proper response to this convention is to step outside of the norms, assumptions, and conventions to find a specific reason to be consciously and thoughtfully loyal. Without rejecting the importance of the local, each author engages with the question of place by asking what it means to find it, in Chesnutt's case, or, in Dunbar's, to belong to it.

Building from their uneasiness with an unreflective embrace of the sentimental figure, Dunbar and Chesnutt manifest a basic concern about the unintended consequences of using the family as a model for the nation, distancing themselves from the political agenda of many African American writers of the period. Claudia Tate has compellingly explained how late-nineteenth-century African American women authors used representations of the middle-class black family to demonstrate the political worthiness of African Americans, a position Dunbar and Chesnutt resist.[55] As their stories make clear, accepting the family as the national model includes accepting the discriminatory affective structures associated with it, as well as the ways in which the plantation school had conflated loyalty and emotion in its powerful reframing of the terms of national belonging. Instead, Dunbar and Chesnutt alike emphasize the close connection between loyalty and moral reasoning. In the place of an entirely subservient model of loyalty, Chesnutt and Dunbar offer a version of loyalty that stresses choice and reason as the basic qualities of the American citizen; what emerges from this repudiation of servile loyalty as an embodied and instinctual trait specific to African Americans is a clear articulation of the moral dimension of loyal allegiance and the relationship between national affiliation and moral behavior and attitudes.

* * *

In a journal entry of May 1880, a young Charles Chesnutt expressed the hope that his writings would spark a "moral revolution" by breaking down the "unjust spirit of caste," a significant "barrier to the moral progress of the American people."[56] Musing over the obstacles he faced, Chesnutt conceded that the average black American needed preparation for "social recognition and equality"; it was the "special province" of literature "to open the way for him to get it—to accustom the public mind to the idea; and while amusing them to lead them on, imperceptibly, unconsciously, step by step, to the desired state of feeling." African Americans had been given "the rights of citizenship," but their full exercise was impeded by "the subtle almost indefinable feeling of repulsion toward the negro, which is common to most Americans." "Easily enough accounted for," this feeling could also be easily enough dismissed if writers would recognize that "the elevation of whites" was the first step in the "elevation of the colored people," an argument for uplift that reframes the importance of race by extending the scale of the problem.[57]

To accomplish this "high, holy purpose," however, Chesnutt had to confront the significant impediments introduced by plantation fiction.[58] Writing to George Washington Cable in 1890, Chesnutt complained that fictional African American characters tended to have only one trait, a "dog-like fidelity": "The many Negroes (excepting your own) whose virtues have been given to the world in the magazine press recently, have been blacks, full-blooded, and their chief virtues have been their dog-like fidelity to their old master, for whom they have been willing to sacrifice almost life itself. Such characters exist. . . . But I can't write about those people, or rather I won't write about them."[59] Although the popularity of Southern tales enabled the success of Chesnutt's dialect tales, they also shaped his desire "to write a different sort" of fiction, one that replaced stereotypes with individuals, moral simplicity with complexity.[60] Limning the fallacies associated with conflating seeming submission or acceptance of racist hierarchies, Chesnutt's "different" fiction distinguishes between *motivations* for what might appear to be "dog-like" loyalty. In place of a monolithic stereotype, Chesnutt offers individuals who face the "adverse winds of circumstance," and relates these circumstances to their character, aspirations, and moral sense. Importantly, Chesnutt's narratives resist the depiction of simple heroic overcoming and unambiguously right and wrong conclusions. Railing against all homogenizing narratives, including those that might seem to celebrate African American achievement, Chesnutt suggests that the most common and pervasive ethical dilemma in the postbellum United States is the inability to appreciate the nuanced implications of differences between people. This is an argument that Chesnutt deploys against the loyal slave figure, but it carries sweeping implications of the kind that should establish Chesnutt, with the late Henry James, as an important ethical writer.

Committed to the families of their former masters, characters like Sandy Delamere in *The Marrow of Tradition* (1901) or Peter French in *The Colonel's Dream* (1905) maintain affective ties with whites that counter the effects of slavery, war, and New South economics. Interrupted as he tidies the graves of the French family, Peter explains, "Well, suh, I b'longed ter de fambly, an' I ain' got no chick ner chile er my own, livin', an' dese hyuh dead folks 'pears mo' closer ter me dan anybody e'se."[61] Peter's interlocutor, Colonel Henry French, is "touched" by this surprising expression of loyalty:

> This meeting touched a tender chord in the colonel's nature, already tuned to sympathy with the dead past of which Peter seemed the only survival. The old man's unfeigned delight at their meeting; his retention of the family name, a living witness of its former standing; his respect for the dead; his "family pride," which to the unsympathetic outsider might have seemed grotesque; were proofs of loyalty that moved the colonel deeply. (25)

In describing this reunion of former master and slave, Chesnutt provides both the colonel's assumption about Peter's loyalty *and* Peter's explanation for his behavior. Rejected by contemporary black and white society—the former "don' was'e much time wid a ole man w'at ain' got nothin,'" and the latter "ain' got no use fer niggers"—Peter explains that, for him, tending a graveyard "whar I knows ev'ybody and ev'ybody knows me" is comforting (24). The dislocation associated with industrialization and economic change so regularly invoked in fin-de-siècle fiction finds expression here, fusing exigency, loneliness, and nostalgia.

But the narrative emphasis is on the white man's interpretation, not Peter's attempts at personal comfort. Despite having lived in the North, the colonel easily adopts the (insider's) position that makes it possible to understand what otherwise might seem "grotesque," even as the fact that he is "already tuned to sympathy with the dead past" prevents him from transcending it. The past has "two sides" (16), the colonel reflects, whether it is stories from youth or the history of emancipation:

> The old man's talk rambled on, like a sluggish stream, while the colonel's more active mind busied itself with the problem suggested by

> this unforeseen meeting. Peter and he had both gone out into the world, and they had both returned. He had come back rich and independent. What good had freedom done for Peter? In the colonel's childhood his father's butler, old Madison, had lived a life which, compared to that of Peter at the same age, was one of ease and luxury. How easy the conclusion that the slave's lot had been more fortunate. But no, Peter had been better free. There were plenty of poor white men, and no one had suggested slavery as an improvement of their condition. (29)

Rejecting the "easy" conclusion that slavery was preferable to freedom because it provided care for elderly slaves, an argument dear to both antebellum proslavery advocacy and postbellum slavery nostalgia, the colonel recognizes freedom's value. But his understanding has limits. The "sluggish stream" of Peter's narrative brings forcefully home to the colonel all that he himself gained through emancipation:

> Had Peter remained a slave, then the colonel would have remained a master, which was only another form of slavery. The colonel had been emancipated by the same token that had made Peter free. Peter had returned home poor and broken, not because he had been free, but because nature first and society next, in distributing their gifts, had been niggardly with old Peter. Had he been better equipped, or had a better chance, he might have made a better showing. The colonel had prospered because, having no Peters to work for him, he had been compelled to work for himself. He would set his own success against Peter's failure; and he would take off his hat to the memory of the immortal statesman, who in freeing one race had emancipated another and struck the shackles from a Nation's mind. (29–30)

The soaring rhetoric of the final sentence belies the colonel's comfortable coordination of nature and society. Although both had been, as he says, "niggardly with old Peter," the colonel still measures his "success against Peter's failure," a move made possible by emancipation. That is to say, even though the colonel is more progressive on race issues than other characters in the novel, Chesnutt flags the limits of his thinking as he points to the man's inability to measure society's responsibility *for* Peter's "failure" or consider the relationship *between* success and failure. Forgetting Peter entirely when he meets another old friend, the colonel again abandons his former companion to the chance he seemingly associates with the relation of success and failure; that the man is immediately victimized by a government agent indicts the colonel's moral calculus.⁶²

A basic human need for affective ties is not the only explanation Chesnutt offers for the fidelity of former slaves, however. In "Mars Jeems's Nightmare" (1899), the narrator, Julius, is said to have "a peculiar personal attitude, that may be called predial rather than proprietary" toward land recently purchased by a Northern couple. "[Julius] had been accustomed," the Northern man surmises, "until long after middle life, to look upon himself as the property of another. When this relation was no longer possible, owing to the war, and to his master's death and the dispersion of the family, he had been unable to break off entirely the mental habits of a lifetime, but had attached himself to the old plantation, of which he seemed to consider himself an appurtenance."⁶³ His are "a sort of squatter right[s]" Chesnutt elsewhere observes of Julius.⁶⁴ While Julius's success at manipulating his white employer casts doubt on this confident interpretation, the passage's emphasis on habit provides a plausible explanation of a fact too often read as evidence of enduring devotion. As William James contends in the 1892 *Psychology, Briefer Course*, "Habit is . . . the enormous fly-wheel of society, its most precious conservative agent. It alone is what keeps us all within the bounds of ordinance, and saves the children of fortune from the envious uprisings of the poor."⁶⁵ In Jamesian psychology, habit allows us to perform countless daily activities and is necessary to the function of the human mind; it is, however, of equal importance to our moral and social lives. Over time, habit hardens, and "the character," once soft and pliant, "set[s] like plaster."⁶⁶ Put differently, Julius's inability "to break off entirely the mental habits of a lifetime" is a limitation to which *all* people are liable, not the particular attribute of one race. Habit renders us all slaves to the past, to how we have learned to negotiate the world; this argument universalizes the behavior associated with the loyal slave trope and collapses the racial distinctions plantation fiction maintained. The anxieties about routinization and monotony the loyal slave figure neutralized had to be recognized, Chesnutt posits, as intrinsic to the human condition. "Human character," he writes in "The Web of Circumstance," "is a compound of tendencies inherited and habits acquired" (261).

Yet another, and less appealing, depiction of a loyal ex-slave is included in *The Marrow of Tradition*, Chesnutt's fictional account of the 1898 race riots in Wilmington, North Carolina.⁶⁷ The novel opens with the premature birth of a son to a prominent white couple, Major and Olivia Carteret; during a brief respite in Olivia's labor, the attending doctor chastises an elderly servant for inattention to her mistress. Replying in "an unctuous whisper," Jane Letlow defends her service to Olivia's family: "Mis' 'Livy is my ole mist'ess's daughter, an' my ole mist'ess wuz good ter me, an' dey ain' none er her folks gwine ter suffer ef ole Jane kin he'p it" (468–469). "Your loyalty does you credit, Jane," the doctor approvingly replies (469). Jane later opines that her mistress had taught her more as a slave than freed blacks could learn in a thousand years and that black residents of Wellington should be careful to "not crowd de w'ite folks," a strategy that will guarantee they have "ernuff ter eat" and the chance to "live out deir days in peace an' comfo't" (499). Again, a white interlocutor praises her principles heartily: "You have friends upon whom, in time of need, you can rely implicitly for protection and succor. You served your mistress faithfully before the war, you remained by her when the other negroes were running hither and thither like sheep without a shepherd; and you have transferred your allegiance to my wife and her child" (499).[68] Like Peter, Jane is attached to the family she served, and as with Julius, entrenched habits have set her in her ways and in her place. Her excessive solicitude for her mistress's family would seem to endorse Smith's contention that our moral sentiments are often characterized by "obsequiousness to our superiors," a tendency that "arises from the advantages of their situation" rather "than from any private expectations of benefit from their good-will."[69] "Even when the order of society seems to require that we should oppose them," Smith continues, "we can hardly bring ourselves to do it." Our inclination to be obsequious to "our superiors" is as natural, on Smith's analysis, as are our sympathetic sentiments, so that no matter how much reason tells us to resent oppression, it is easy to "forget all past provocations" as our "principles of loyalty revive," we "run to re-establish the ruined authority of [our] old masters."[70] What Smith is suggesting, in other words, is that our feelings for others can often depend on knowing with Jane Letlow what our place in society is. While this is not an attractive claim, Chesnutt acknowledges the accuracy, if not the justice, of Smith's position as he demonstrates that some former slaves derive comfort from knowing where they belong, an idea that he refracts both racially and spatially.

This is not Chesnutt's last word on the subject. Jane may consent explicitly to her "place," but her grandson, raised "ter be 'umble, an' keep in 'is place," is less committed to the situation to which he has seemingly been consigned. Unwilling to defy the supremacy of the whites directly, Jerry's attempts to change his place by altering his skin color with a topical cream explicitly rebut the contention that he "knows his place," and is "content with the face and place assigned to him by nature" (533). In this brief but telling incident, Chesnutt simultaneously challenges two ways of thinking about place: the class hierarchy of moral sentiment and the assumption that remaining in one's place is equivalent to consenting to it. "After the state is instituted," Elaine Scarry explains, "residence implies consent."[71] But if it is impossible to move from place to place, how can the "consent" that results be anything but nominal? Indeed, in the episode's cynical conclusion, as Jerry chooses to follow his grandmother's example by "keep[ing] [his] mouf shet an' stan[ding] in wid de Angry-Saxon race," Chesnutt depicts the impoverished nature of consent so understood (536).[72]

That loyalty to the "Angry-Saxon race" kills both members of the Letlow family thus measures the depth of Chesnutt's discomfort with the familiar conflation of moral and political principles with a restrictive sense of place. Mortally wounded as she hurries toward the major's home, Jane's dying words—"Comin,' missis, comin'!"—literally re-place her as she "join[s] the old mistress upon whose memory her heart was fixed" (694–695). Her grandson is less fortunate. Swept up in the riot, Jerry frantically tries again to change where circumstance has placed him. Calling to Major Carteret, he cries "It's me, suh, Jerry, suh! I did n' go in dere myse'f, suh,—I wuz drag' in dere! I would n' do nothin' 'g'inst de w'ite folks, suh,—no" (702). Unfortunately for Jerry, the major cannot hear his cries and turns away as Jerry is murdered by some very "Angry-Saxon[s]."

Jerry and Jane are not the only vehicles through which Chesnutt explores the relationship between place, consent, and morality in the construction of affiliation. If the refusal of consent could be articulated by movement, then limiting the ability of African Americans to relocate undermined the very possibility that they could have a consensual relationship with the state. This is, in fact, the problem with which *The Marrow of Tradition* opens, as a young black doctor is harassed while traveling from North to South. Forced to ride in a segregated car, Dr. Miller's thoughts turn to questions about democracy, inspired by "a party of farm laborers, fresh from their daily toil," who join him in the car. He feels "an expansive warmth" for the noisy group, even as he calls them "an affliction" (511). Recognizing that "the democratic ideal . . . meant so much to his race," he nonetheless can "easily imagine" why those "with the power in their hands" might prefer to "strain" the "ideal" to avoid being grouped with these fellow travelers. "Surely," he concludes, "if a classification of passengers on trains was at all desirable, it might be made upon some more logical and considerate basis than a mere arbitrary, tactless, and, by the very nature of things, brutal drawing of a color line." The color line's brutality is echoed in Miller's concluding thought on the standards it sets: "Those who grew above it must have their heads cut off, figuratively speaking,—must be forced back to the level assigned to their race; those who fell beneath the standard had their necks stretched, literally enough, as the ghastly record in the daily papers gave conclusive evidence" (512). The choice between beheading and lynching violently inscribes on the body, already the default measure of "classification," the twinned pressures of white supremacy and middle-class respectability. The yearning for logic is paired with the reflection that the fate of the "democratic ideal," alternately embraced and "strain[ed]," is precarious in a world determined by "power," "force," and feeling.

It is, however, in Chesnutt's collection of short stories, *The Wife of His Youth and Tales of the Color Line* (1899), that he most relentlessly addresses questions about race, loyalty, abstract ideals, and affective affiliation. To date, critical consensus has seemingly coalesced around the idea that Chesnutt's mind was decided on racial issues and that these stories forward a clear moral imperative—an appealing position, but one that significantly downplays the sophistication and complexity of Chesnutt's representation of moral dilemmas.[73] Upon closer inspection, what becomes evident is a pervasive concern for what it might mean to find one's place, an issue substantially complicated by the difficulty of bracketing individual assumption, premises, and desire. Although each story explores an issue related to principle, duty, or allegiance, sometimes comically, more often tragically, I will linger with the ways in which the title story engages with the loyal slave trope. "The Wife of His Youth" offers a searching indictment of how sentiment, particularly self-regarding sentiment, structures the kinds of judgments we can make about what it might mean to be loyal to others and to ourselves.[74]

The tale opens on the eve of a ball, at which Mr. Ryder has planned to propose marriage to a young, educated widow, who will grace his home and improve his social standing. His plans are interrupted by a poor elderly woman searching for her husband, a common mission "right after the war" but comparatively novel by the time of the story (106). The woman, Liza Jane, explains that her lost husband, Sam Taylor, had narrowly avoided being sold into slavery by her intervention; in return, he had promised to buy her freedom. Had the Civil War not intervened, Liza Jane assures Ryder that Sam surely would have done so, for "he sot a heap er sto by me, Sam did" (107). After the war, she began the search for her husband—and had continued it through the intervening twenty-five years: "'I know he's be'n huntin' fer me all dese years,—'less'n he's be'n sick er sump'n, so he could n' work, er out'n his head, so he could n' 'member his promise.... Fer I knows I 'll fin' 'im some er dese days,' she added softly, 'er he 'll fin' me, an' den we'll bofe be as happy in freedom as we wuz in de ole days befo' de wah'" (107). But Liza Jane is wrong. Ryder is Sam Taylor and, all protests to the contrary ("I'd know 'im 'mongs' a hund'ed men . . . an' I could n' be mistook" [108]), she does not recognize her husband in this affluent man. Quizzed about her search—the possibility of Sam's death, remarriage, or significant change of character—Liza Jane remains adamant that signs have indicated Sam is alive and increasingly near. No argument shakes her conviction in her husband's unfaltering fidelity to his promise. Notably, reason might betray Liza Jane, but conjure does not; "de signs an' de tokens" she consults assure her that Sam is close, confirming a fact she cannot recognize (108). At the end of the story, Liza Jane is reunited with her husband, who acknowledges his former wife at the ball he had planned for another woman.

As this brief summary makes clear, "The Wife of His Youth" relies upon, but substantially revises, the loyal slave trope. Liza Jane is devoted to a past she recalls as an ideal of harmonious relationship: her understanding of obligation and loyalty is absolute, and her bond is based on affect, rather than another form of affiliative obligation, like a legal contract. (My assumption that Chesnutt's concern here is not primarily a legal one is ratified by the gesture toward the legality of slave marriages in Ryder's speech, as well as its central importance in one of the volume's later stories, "Uncle Wellington's Wives."[75]) Liza Jane differs importantly from the loyal slaves of plantation narrative, however, as her lasting attachment is to her spouse, not her former master; nor does she spend her life patiently awaiting his return. Replacing a master with a husband, then, Chesnutt's tale echoes, albeit unsatisfactorily, the many postbellum narratives positing that romance and companionate marriage would provide the answer to political and social ills.[76] In the place of the happy nuclear family—neither Ryder nor Liza Jane gets a dream-mate—"The Wife of His Youth" offers a racial loyalty that ignores the differences of class and skin color. Given Liza Jane's single-minded devotion to her husband, we are right to wonder if she, like Jane Letlow, will be able to "transfe[r] [her] allegiance" from one person to another (499). Finally, like the post-Reconstruction novels of African American women writers, Chesnutt's tale reunites a family disrupted by slavery and war.

That the story is critical of the intraracial prejudice practiced by groups like the Blue Vein Society to which Mr. Ryder belongs is evident from its opening paragraphs. It begins with Ryder's endorsement of exclusive racial principles and closes with their seeming rejection, a position that seems to have surprised a number of contemporary readers who wonder what sort of "consideration" Liza Jane might warrant.[77] In a letter to *Atlantic* editor Walter Hines Page, Chesnutt reports the judgment of another editor, Mr. Gilder of *Century*, who wonders if Ryder might not merit "a compromise of some sort":

> "I read the *Atlantic* story that you asked me to read. It is certainly very striking, but somehow it seems as though that poor fellow was entitled to a compromise of some sort. I don't know just what it would be, but the precise outcome hardly seems humanly right." It is surprising what a number of people who have done me the honor to read that story, do not seem to imagine that the old woman was entitled to any consideration whatever, and yet I don't know that it is so astonishing either, in the light of history.[78]

Although asserting that Liza Jane merits more sympathy than Gilder would seem to grant her, Chesnutt does not elaborate what appropriate consideration for Liza Jane would or should look like, quickly qualifying his criticism of the important editor. But the letter raises several provocative questions: What would it mean to consider Liza Jane? How might focusing on her desires, hopes, or ideals (particularly those concerning promissory obligations) complicate the problems of history, memory, and loyalty Chesnutt explores in "The Wife of His Youth"?

At the end of the tale, Liza Jane stands "startled and trembling" before a dazzling display of "brilliant gayety," "neatly dressed in gray" with "the white cap of an elderly woman" on her head (112). The confident person of the afternoon, sure of her mission, her husband, and her future, is gone, replaced by a silent and scared old woman. Eric Sundquist reads this scene as indicative of Chesnutt's embrace of his "own cultural obligations," including "the popular conceptions of 'the old plantation life' ... being generated by racist commentary."[79] The transformation of loafing Sam Taylor into the industrious and successful Mr. Ryder would seem to support Sundquist's claim about countering stereotypes, but the treatment of Liza Jane reveals the negative implications of such a reading. She becomes a mere symbol of the past—not a person with desires, motivations, or needs—that should be carefully edited, a process effectively represented by her change of clothes. When she first approaches Ryder, she is dressed in "a blue calico gown of ancient cut, a little red shawl fastened around her shoulders with an old-fashioned brass brooch, and a large bonnet profusely ornamented with faded red and yellow artificial flowers" (105). This head-turning outfit—"As she walked down the street with mincing step, he saw several persons whom she passed turn and look back at her with a smile of kindly amusement" (109)—is replaced with the entirely proper, and deeply bland, neat gray dress. "Tak[ing] control" of the past means, in this instance, replacing its individuality with conformity. Critics have noted, of course, that Liza Jane is as much a caricature as a character. "Her withered black form is constructed out of the same visual clichés that constituted black identity on the 'coon show' stage," Henry Wonham observes, while Werner Sollers draws attention to her resemblance to a character from Abraham Cahan's 1896 *Yekl: A Tale of the New York Ghetto*.[80] What troubles these otherwise fine readings, however, is that Liza Jane's first appearance is not just visual: her history and desire complicate her figuration of "the old plantation life" (105). Chesnutt's complex tale thus captures how intraracial assumptions replicate the strategies of white racism, reducing Liza Jane to "a vehicle for the exploration of [another's] anxieties."[81]

The cost of the "democratic ideal" in "The Wife of His Youth" is silence, as Liza Jane is marginalized as the price of admission into the bourgeois world of material comfort. For clarification, it is instructive to compare the relationship of Ryder and Liza Jane to the household created by reunion in *Iola Leroy* (1892). In Frances Harper's novel, the heroine's uncle Robert attends intellectual gatherings with his educated and cultured niece, commenting afterward on the progress of his race since slavery. Yet as Russ Castronovo observes, he "does not participate; his ideas do not find a larger democratic forum" than private conversations with his family as "incorporation tokens neither privilege nor responsibility but 'marginalization and silence.'"[82] The newly reconstituted family in "The Wife of His Youth" will surely be marked by similar dynamics.[83] The happy future Liza Jane had envisioned, as the head of a household supported by her industry, will hardly be realized with the independent and diligent man Sam has become or in the patriarchal family elite views of uplift prescribed. This is, for her, "too little, too late" despite "the formal closure" of the plot.[84]

When Ryder presents the dilemma at the ball—should the man reveal his identity?—he presupposes that it is necessarily a boon to bring Liza Jane's search to an end, a conclusion that seems far from obvious if we actually consider what she had been searching for over the past twenty-five years. "He wuz good ter me, Sam wuz," Liza Jane explains, "but he wuz n' much good ter nobody e'se, fer he wuz one er de triflin'es' han's on de plantation. I 'spec's ter haf ter suppo't 'im w'in I fin' 'im, fer he nebber would work 'less'n he had ter. But den he wuz free, an' he did n' git no pay fer his work, an' I don' blame 'im much. Mebbe he's done better sence he run erway, but I ain' 'spectin' much" (108). Liza Jane's belief that she would find a man who would value and need her, complicates the dilemma in "The Wife of His Youth" in ways critics have failed to recognize. Because the story is told from Ryder's perspective, the reader's access to Liza Jane is limited in a way that anticipates the colonel's interpretation of Peter's behavior in *The Colonel's Dream*. Indeed, as Ryder tells the story, Liza Jane's expectations are replaced by a narrative structured around the stark binary of "dutiolatry," to borrow a term from Howells's 1892 *An Imperative Duty*.[85] According to Howells, an overactive sense of duty often fuels smug self-satisfaction, replacing the ethical consideration of another with a self-regarding concern for personal honor or the communal endorsement of right behavior; on this view, honor and duty can disrupt justice as readily as serve it. Considering the dilemma so starkly—recognition or deception—Ryder and his Blue Vein audience ignore the possibility that their society might not be desirable and that the satisfaction they might feel at doing the right thing could obscure its more ambivalent character.

It is thus crucial that the story presents the public performance of Ryder's choice, complete with costumes and fine soliloquies. We never see Lisa Jane's response to the news that the man she loves has long since disappeared; in its place we hear Ryder's tribute to female devotion, a speech that moves his auditors to tears: as they listen "attentively and sympathetically," a "responsive thrill" awakens "in many hearts" (110). Admitting that he knows their "hearts"—perhaps because the "thrill" that unites the Blue Vein members is anticipated by Ryder's own "appreciative thrill" when reading a verse celebration of Queen Guinevere—Ryder gets "the answer [he] expected" from a group that prefers its slave legacy in sentimental garb; this is an inclination the narrator establishes early, noting that some members of the society "had come up from the South and from slavery" but, because "their history presented enough romantic circumstances to rob their servile origin of its grosser aspects," they could join the Blue Veins (105, 112).[86] In the final scene, the traces of Liza Jane's "servile" career are similarly erased. On Chesnutt's view, the fervent celebration of duty, of sacrifice, and of a certain kind of heroism is itself a form of emotional excess that delivers expected narratives and sentiments. Chesnutt's concern in "The Wife of His Youth," and throughout the collection it opens, is to articulate that such thinking about moral choice—surely necessitated in no small measure by the uncompromising demands of an enveloping white racism—impoverishes the very possibility for ethical interaction *because* particular claims, like Liza Jane's, must be subsumed or ignored.

Acknowledging Liza Jane's sacrifice, and her claim to have a claim on Sam, Ryder's narrative, the product of a "fancy" set free, skims over her years of struggle to linger with his reasons for *not* struggling, presented via an imaginary dialogue between a moral self-made man and his "wise" counselor and friend, Polonius (111–112). The doubling in Ryder's speech mirrors the bifurcated identity that has generated the story's moral dilemma, as the multiple iterations of Ryder indicate that recognition is integral to narratives about allegiance and loyalty. Polonius's advice—"to thine own self be true"—begs the question of whether it is possible for Ryder (or the reader) to discern which of the many selves presented is properly Ryder's "own": Sam, Ryder, the self-made man, the wise friend of the hypothetical scenario. At the same time that the story-within-the-story complicates the question of Ryder's identity, it also establishes the central importance of honor to the tale's resolution. Ryder states unequivocally that his friend is someone "who loved honor" (111). What are we to make of this love of honor, however? Is this a virtue that Chesnutt's tale endorses? In his study of honor in Southern culture, Bertram Wyatt-Brown asserts that honor is "self-regarding in character" for "one's neighbors serve as mirrors that return the image of oneself."[87] On this view, the narrative refracts Ryder's identity even more radically, as the reflection of his sacrifice changes the crowd into a group of reflected Ryders.

As Liza Jane's individuality disappears under the mask of respectability, there is one person who may not share the "thrill" at Ryder's behavior. The replacement of his actual struggle with a sanitized and sentimentalized parable of honorable sacrifice undermines what is laudable about his decision, as it becomes another means of improving his social standing. Of course it is a boon to be recognized by Mr. Ryder, even if you love Sam, the group unanimously assumes, because status is associated with bourgeois normativity, not emotional satisfaction. Rather than moral outrage that Ryder had broken his promise to his wife, the group delights in the shift of tragedy into romance or melodrama, *Hamlet* into *All's Well That Ends Well*. In this story, and throughout the volume, Chesnutt dissects the institutional practices that create and perpetuate dysfunctional communities, using the "highly ordered structure of melodrama" to "mak[e] legible" the era's "conflicting racial, regional, and political loyalties."[88] In questioning the value of acceptance and progress as defined by the Blue Vein Society, I seek to register Chesnutt's *ambivalence* about the social and political implications of the conformity proposed by uplift ideology.[89] Rigidly gendered, this ethos "idealized black men" as it "threatened to limit the place of black women," Jacqueline Goldsby reminds us.[90] Part of what we see in "The Wife of His Youth," then, is a critique of this moral economy, as it substitutes group compliance for personal satisfaction.

There is, finally, an even more troubling set of implications associated with the story's conclusion when it is considered in the context of questions about consent and place. Saidiya Hartman's analysis of the "burdened individuality" articulated for African Americans after emancipation reveals some of the ways in which the (partial) conferral of rights resulted in experiences that obscured the difference between freedom and slavery. Reading the conduct manuals written for freedmen, with the aim of rendering their behavior less offensive to whites, Hartman notes the ways in which arguments against idleness attempted to forestall not only the freedom of movement of ex-slaves but also their ability to enact models of freedom inconsistent with American assumptions about property and individuality. Were we to consider Liza Jane's itinerant and active pursuit of happiness in tandem with Hartman's analysis, it is possible to see how Ryder's actions reinstall her in a place not so very different from the slavery she had long ago left. Indeed, not only is her expression of identity erased with the change of clothing, but her name is equally obscured: by way of introduction, Ryder says, "Ladies and gentlemen, . . . this is the woman, and I am the man, whose story I have told you. Permit me to introduce to you the wife of my youth" (112).[91] The social death she is destined to suffer at the hands of the exclusive Blue Veins suggests that Liza Jane is no longer a "symbol of the plantation past" but, as the wife of Ryder's youth, is now a figure of the sanitized constriction of postbellum liberty.

As I have been reading it, "The Wife of His Youth" enacts a thorough revision of the loyal slave trope, associating its implications with intra- and well as interracial loyalty. That Chesnutt is working through the lingering implications of Civil War models of allegiance is equally evident in the tale's sustained consideration of the nature of promissory obligations: How long are we bound by a promise? How much should change in circumstance or character influence the bonds we create when we make a promise? Similar questions intrigued eighteenth- and nineteenth-century moral theorists, who worried that an overly strenuous notion of promissory obligations would reduce personal freedom *and* that a loose sense of what the promise required would undermine the social fabric generally, also reducing personal freedom. As David Hume notes, "we are not surely bound to keep our word because we have given our word to keep it."[92] Liza Jane clearly rejects this view; her uncompromising commitment to the pledge structures the melodramatic ending that erases her future. Yet the idea that context would have no influence on promissory obligation is equally problematic. For some rigorists, the expectations and assumptions created by the promise were critical to assessing its ongoing power to bind people to a particular sense of the future and their place in it. On this more strenuous account of promissory obligation, the desires of others impose significant limits on our own choices and possibilities. Indeed, for some, "the pleasurable anticipation of the promise being performed" itself should factor into the obligation.[93] With this sense of the promise in mind, one that values reliance rather than pleasure, we might assert that Liza Jane's *search* imposes an obligation on Ryder; no one is the "sole judge of what duties he owes to his fellow men," P. S. Atiyah maintains.[94] Ryder's decision to recognize his former wife, compromised by sentiment and performance, enacts the rigorous view of promissory obligation, while revealing its limitations.

Chesnutt's interest in how bonds between people are created is evident across his fiction as characters regularly reflect on which promises they are obliged to keep, which obligations should be paramount.[95] When allegiances collide, when responsibility to the future conflicts with ties to the past or present, how are we to decide on an appropriate course of action? In Chesnutt's world, these questions resist easy answers. In "Her Virginia Mammy," for example, a second character is asked to choose between recognition and deception. Many years after their separation during a steamboat accident, a black woman stumbles upon her lost daughter, unknowingly passing as white. This young woman is torn between her love for a young man who wants to marry her and uncertainty about her own past, fearful that she might bring some unknown disgrace upon his family. The story thus offers a different iteration of the dilemma examined in "The Wife of His Youth," yet comes to the opposite conclusion when the mother decides *not* to acknowledge her child. It is likely that the Blue Vein Society would have felt a "thrill" at hearing this story too, which returns us to Chesnutt's concerns about the relationship between sentimental narrative and ethical reasoning. As "Her Virginia Mammy" succeeds "The Wife of His Youth" in the collection, it is hard to avoid the conclusion that Chesnutt is contending that circumstance and perspective critically shape the ways in which bonds of obligation are assessed; when we forget that this is true, we run the distinct risk of being loyal not to persons but to figures and fantasies as damaging as the loyal slave.

One thing is certain. Falling for a romance of honor and duty ends poorly in Chesnutt's world. Sentimental homogenization, dictated by bourgeois norms and complicit with the goals of white supremacy, cannot right the wrongs done by the romantic plantation past. The "democratic ideal" underwrites the progressive moments that the stories and novels celebrate, but often what would seem to be an ideal, like a moral norm or a peculiar social institution, provides instead the opportunity for the installation of a convention that replaces justice or democracy with popularity and oligarchy. That these ideas are sentiments in disguise exposes the genuine difficulty for anyone attempting to understand how abstractions shape the social world. Easily overtaken by passions, abstract values, like the "democratic ideal," fall short, sometimes violently so. Nonetheless, the alternatives lead to nothing short of social death, sustained by comforting fictions and familiar figures. Perhaps the best conclusion to be drawn is that the "moral revolution" Chesnutt hoped to cause with his writings is one that would lead to a more perfect union of American values and their expression.

* * *

In "A Plea for the American Negro" (1900), Chesnutt opined that "there will undoubtedly be a race problem in the United States, with all its attendant evils, until we cease to regard our colored population as Negroes and consider them simply as citizens."[96] As a conclusion to this chapter, I briefly explore how Paul Laurence Dunbar deploys citizenship to frame his engagement with the loyal slave, particularly the way in which the figure embodied a specific idea of loyalty. Possibly the most popular American poet of the period, and easily the most famous black poet, Dunbar's dialect poems satisfied even readers and writers of the plantation tradition with their quaint representations and picturesque vignettes of Southern black life. Contemporary white critics and readers enthused over Dunbar's ability to "exult[] in his material" despite its "commonness," and expressed particular appreciation for how he brought white readers "nearer to the heart of primitive human nature in his race," although this same quality led subsequent generations of black writers to distance themselves from what they took to be Dunbar's betrayal.[97] Distracted by the question of Dunbar's potential capitulation to racist stereotypes, however, critics, both past and present, have failed to register Dunbar's direct engagement with the Civil War heritage, especially as it informed how people understood the requirements of allegiance and loyalty. Indeed, one of Dunbar's four novels—*The Fanatics* (1901)—engages the problem of allegiance during the war directly, as its characters regularly consider how to adjudicate between competing and conflicting attachments. In one of the many passages considering the question, the narrator asks, "Is the love of country, which we call patriotism, a more commendable trait than filial affection and obedience, and can one deficient in the latter be fully capable of comprehending the former?" The narrator quickly dubs questions of this sort as "sophistries," but the novel recurs to their ilk obsessively as characters weigh the comparative importance of national loyalty, or loyalty to "an idea of a larger allegiance," and personal bonds of affection and family, concluding with the sardonic assertion that, North and South, "they were all fanatics."[98]

Rather than engage with Dunbar's representation of white characters' obsessive national affiliation, however, I will consider his rendition of the familiar story of a chance encounter between former master and slave in "Nelse Hatton's Vengeance" (1898), which explores the close relationship between the figure of the loyal slave and definitions of citizenship. When the vengeance of the title becomes an act of potentially problematic generosity, the story forces a reflection on the relationship between the heart, the body, the duty of the citizen, and the dictates of Christian morality. While its ending might have continued to satisfy readers whose tastes ran to plantation school stereotypes, it also reveals the emancipatory possibilities still available through the concept of loyalty at the end of the nineteenth century.

The tale opens into the twilight of a summer day in a little Ohio town we are told to call Dexter. Peopled with small town folk engaged in typical after dinner behaviors—smoking on the porch, reading the evening paper, washing the dishes—the narrative resists specific details as it balances the familiarity of these generalized tasks with the particulars of individual experience: "To one who knew the generous and unprejudiced spirit of the Dexterites, it was no matter of wonder that one of their soundest and most highly respected citizens was a coloured man, and that his home should nestle unrebuked among the homes of his white neighbors."[99] The generalizations of the opening description elide racial difference, indicating that, in Dexter at least, citizenship is defined by other qualities. As he quickly repeats both "respect" and "citizen"—the reader learns that the title character had "won the love and respect of his fellow-citizens by the straightforward honesty of his conduct and the warmth of his heart"—Dunbar establishes the tale's national pretensions despite its local colors (186). Nelse Hatton has attained, to borrow the language of Justice Bradley's opinion from the Civil Rights Cases, "the rank of a mere citizen."[100] But, as Dunbar is quick to indicate, Hatton is still different from his neighbors; throughout the tale, Dunbar stresses Hatton's "sympathetic heart," which not only provides the means of his acceptance as a "fellow-citizen" but further distinguishes his moral excellence (187). Yet even when Hatton's "heart throb[s] with pity" at the sight of a white straggler who begs for food, the explanation he offers his wife for feeding the man relies on impersonal standards. "I believe in every person doin' their own duty," Hatton explains, a sentence that shifts from the language of emotion that dominates the beginning of the story—"I feel badly"—to one oriented around abstract moral obligation (188).

Hatton's sense of duty is quickly distinguished, at least by the recipient of his food, from that of other Northern citizens. When asked why he approached a black household instead of a white one, the straggler responds, "Go to them up here? . . . never. They would give me supper with their hypocritical patronage and put it down to charity. You give me something to eat as a favour. Your gift proceeds from disinterested kindness; they would throw me a bone because they thought it would weigh something in the balance against their sins" (189–190). It turns out this opposition—between "disinterested kindness" and a calculating moral economy—is associated with what it means to belong to nation and race. Whereas Hatton suggests that the straggler's people should properly be white regardless of region, the white man disagrees, exclaiming that his "are the people of the South,—the people who have in their veins the warm, generous blood of Dixie!" (283). On his way back to Kentucky, "where people have hearts and sympathies," the man implies that black people share the "blood of Dixie" and, as such, are more properly "his people" than Northern whites. "Five years of fruitless struggle in different places out of Dixie have shown me that [the North] isn't the place for a man with blood in his veins," the man continues, "I thought that I was reconstructed; but I'm not" (190). That "blood," "hearts[,] and sympathies" are determined by region rather than race, a familiar plantation feint for installing racial hierarchies, allows Dunbar to question the structure of identification; while advocates of white supremacy and paternalism contended that there existed among members of any race an instinctive preference and sympathy for one another, a topic I explore in the next chapter, Dunbar counters that blood and region are *both* metaphors for kinship. At the same time, the white man rails against the connection between sympathy and class, preferring a model of affiliation that reconstitutes the sympathetic family of plantation narrative.

That blood is more than a mere rhetorical flourish becomes clear when the reader learns that Hatton had once literally belonged to the white man. More crucial than the familiar invocation of a plantation family, however, is the stress Dunbar places on the body once blood is introduced as a dimension of belonging, of being part of a people. For example, as the story progresses, scars provide the means of verifying the identity of both master and slave, although they instigate widely different responses. When the white man reveals his scar, the two "[rush] joyously into each other's arms," and all trace of "distinction of colour or condition" is ignored: "They were simply two loving friends who had been long parted and had met again," the narrator contends—although one friend calls the other master, "t'ain't nobody else but Mas' Tom" (193). A few moments later, when Hatton's scar is mentioned, the effect is radically different. "Ain't he the one that lef' that scar there?" his wife asks. "'Yes,' said Nelse, very quietly; but he put his hand up and felt the long, cruel scar that the lash of a whip had left, and a hard light came into his eyes" (197). Rather than an outpouring of affection, this scar recalls murderous rage: "'What did you tell me?' [the wife] asked. 'Didn't you say that if you ever met him again in this world you'd—' 'Kill him!' burst forth the man; and all the old, gentle look had gone out of his face" (197–198).

The tale reaches its conclusion by reversing the dynamic that had transferred the citizen into the loyal slave, one of Mas' Tom's people, by diffusing Hatton's anger at his former master. Rather than murdering the man, as both the interchange with his wife and the title of the story would seem to anticipate, Hatton provides him with money and a new suit of clothes for his return south; this act of generosity, which could suggest that Hatton embraces his former role with his former master, nonetheless shifts the focus of the narrative from an injured black body to a dissected and dead white one. "I'll take it Nelse," Tom Hatton says, accepting the monetary gift, "but you shall have every cent back, even if I have to sell my body to a medical college and use a gun to deliver the goods!" (201). Dunbar's emphasis on the white body anticipates the resolution of "The Lynching of Jube Benson," in which part of a white body, a piece of skin, reveals the displaced justice enacted in lynching. The rhetorical inversion of associating Southern tradition with the restrictive embodied qualities usually reserved for black characters, also evident in Chesnutt, viscerally establishes the problems generated by conflating race and nation. Even as it reenacts the relationship Kemble sketches in "Saving His Master," Dunbar provides a narrative explanation for Hatton's action, suggesting that replacing vengeance with forgiveness saves all involved, not just the white man.

Hatton's shift from rage to generosity is effected, the reader learns, by his idea of civic duty. Explaining to his wife what he has done, Hatton apologizes for giving away their money by noting, "He's goin' back home among my people, an' I sent 'em my love" (202). Here we see that the tension that had been the basis of the discussion between Hatton and his former master, the question of what constitutes belonging or place, is likewise operative at the end of the tale as the white man is reduced to a figure for Hatton's expression of support and solidarity with his "people" "back home." Not only does his generosity offer a means of spiritual renewal (he feels like a "young convert" at the end of the story), it also enacts a subtle vengeance as he strips the agency from his former master, who is now bound, body and soul, to the ex-slave (202). Whereas earlier in the story Hatton had struggled with the implications of making "the poor wreck of former glory conscious of his changed estate," by its end he leaves the white man—ironically named Tom—in a position of necessary dependence and hopeless gratitude, the position that the loyal slave should have adopted (194). But this vengeance is indistinguishable from the behavior of a respected citizen doing his or her duty. Indeed, if plantation school authors used a utopian setting to demonstrate that "African Americans can only form a part of a functioning culture so long as they have white masters," Dunbar's tale rejects this claim by suggesting, to the contrary, that membership in a "functioning culture" depends on actions, not material or biological possessions.[101]

I would be remiss were I not to note that I can read the tale far less hopefully. With its emphasis on religion and Hatton's unwillingness to force the man to confront his past behavior, his actions recall both the most famous loyal slave in literature, Stowe's Uncle Tom, and some of Dunbar's own dialect poetry, like "Chrismus on the Plantation." When Dunbar points to the "tender sympathy" that "is natural to the real Negro," such a comparison seems unavoidable (194); note as well that Hatton's wife points to the slave remaining in Nelse when he first reveals the straggler's identity to her. Dunbar's frequent use of the name Tom, particularly to characterize abject white men, has suggested to Elizabeth

Young that we should read these stories as enacting "a covert critique" of "the tradition of racial representation created by Stowe."[102] While the civic emphasis of "Nelse Hatton's Vengeance" more closely parallels the republicanism of Stowe's *Dred* than the passive world of moral suasion depicted in *Uncle Tom's Cabin*, it nonetheless indicates "the political limits of strategies of appropriation"; Dunbar's engagement with how to perform a civic, as well as personal, duty locates the story fully in a postbellum world concerned with defining national belonging, particularly when skin color colors the ensuing definitions.[103]

Yet the crux of Dunbar's tale is, simply, the political power of forgiveness. Dunbar anticipates Hannah Arendt's proposition that promising and forgiving are intimately and integrally affiliated. "Forgiveness," she writes, "is the only reaction which does not merely re-act but acts anew and unexpectedly, unconditioned by the act which provoked it and therefore freeing from its consequences both the one who forgives and the one who is forgiven" (241). Together with the promise, the act of forgiving stabilizes the political—and human—condition, which Arendt otherwise views as contingent and uncertain. One might easily complain that her account is too hopeful, but her understanding of the necessary relationship between a functioning political realm and forgiveness helps to clarify what might otherwise seem troubling about the ending of "Nelse Hatton's Vengeance." Forgiveness, she explains, is "the exact opposite of vengeance," for while vengeance perpetuates an original transgression, creating a situation in which "everybody remains bound" to the original act, forgiveness disrupts cycles of harmful and violent repetition (240).[104] Surprisingly, forgiveness enables a kind of freedom that allows for a break from the past. Hatton forgives Tom for what he had once done and for the sake of loved ones in Kentucky, adapting the formula Arendt lays out, in which an individual is forgiven for who he or she is, while still demonstrating that forgiveness is an "eminently personal (though not necessarily individual or private) affair" (241). Dunbar's ironic title captures this relationship between vengeance and forgiveness, suggesting that the functioning political community requires the repudiation of the former and the performance of the latter.

For Dunbar, things are still "natural" to African Americans, but more important is how one earns communal respect; on his view, belonging to a people is not merely a bodily concern. One of the benefits of citizenship is that it permits an abstraction of person and body, as in the positive interchangeability of the Dexterites at the beginning of the tale, that makes the body matter less; that is to say, for a person who had once been little more than a body, abstract citizenship is equivalent to another form of freedom, in this case freedom from the requirement that what is written on the body determines who one is or how one must react in a given situation.[105] Put differently, Dunbar's citizenship begins *from* the body—the recognition that bodies make meaning—but resists the white supremacist claim that meaning is circumscribed *by* the body.[106] At the same time, however, Dunbar suggests that citizenship *necessarily* entails sacrifices that are unequally distributed; the relations created through these sacrifices, explains Danielle Allen via the writings of Ralph Ellison, *constitute* democratic citizenship.[107] But democratic citizenship, to be fully and fairly enacted, also requires understanding the political, social, and emotional implications of those sacrifices. "The nation blest above all nations," William James asserts at an 1897 ceremony honoring Colonel Robert Gould Shaw and the veterans of the Fifty-fourth Massachusetts, "is she in whom the civic genius of the people does the saving day by day, by acts without external picturesqueness, by speaking, writing, voting reasonably; by smiting corruption swiftly; by good temper between parties; by the people knowing true men when they see them, and preferring them as leaders to rabid partisans or empty quacks. Such nations have no need of wars to save them."[108] As the next chapter demonstrates, however, for a nation dependent on race, learning how to identify "rabid partisans or empty quacks" from "true men" may itself depend on an entirely new thinking about how to identify what we see.

5 / Philosophies of Loyalty

In 1905, Josiah Royce, professor of philosophy at Harvard University, urged members of the Chicago and the New York Ethical societies to reflect on a perennial and intractable social problem—the problem of race. "Is it a 'yellow peril,' a 'black peril,' or perhaps, after all, is it rather some form of a 'white peril,'" he challengingly asked, "which most threatens the future of humanity in this day of great struggles and of complex issues?"[1] Royce was certainly not alone in considering the question of race and its role in American life at the beginning of the twentieth century; in addition to the countless plantation stories, pamphlets, and newspaper articles, academics from a variety of disciplines—including ethnology, sociology, and anthropology—also focused their research on the insistent issue of race relations. In 1908, for instance, Franz Boas spoke to the American Association for the Advancement of Science meeting in Baltimore on the subject of "Race Problems in America." As had Royce before him, Boas admitted that his goal in choosing this subject was to confront the "grave issues [arising from] the presence of distinct types of man in our country."[2] Despite differing disciplines, presuppositions, and methodologies, both scholars endorsed the conclusion W. E. B. Du Bois announces in the early pages of *The Souls of Black Folk* (1903)—"The problem of the twentieth century is the problem of the color-line."[3]

For Royce, however, racial prejudice was not only a sociological, political, cultural, or historical problem but also a philosophical one. If people are regularly rendered uncomfortable by superficial differences, Royce asked his auditors, how can we negotiate in a world where we are increasingly thrown up against strangers? How are we to deal with "men who seem to us somehow very widely different from ourselves, in physical constitution, in temperament, in all their deeper nature, so that we are tempted to think of them as natural strangers to our souls, while nevertheless we find that they are stubbornly there in our world, and that they are men as much determined to live as we are, and are men who, in turn, find us as incomprehensible as we find them?" (5). In other words, how can we manage both our experience and our ideals to avoid finding others "incomprehensible"? What measures can guarantee that we approach people who seem naturally to be strange "fairly and humanely" (6)? If ethics helps us to understand relations between people, can it assist us in negotiating with difference that seems "incomprehensible"? For Royce, the answer to these complex questions is clear: we must learn to see beyond the body and the tropological manipulation it appears both to authorize and require. In opposition to thinkers like James Cutler, who notes in *Lynch-Law* (1905) that "abstractions still control where racial characteristics, circumstances, and conditions should be the determining factors," Royce contends that only when we recognize the constructed nature of what appears to us to be natural—both in terms of "physical constitution" and "deeper nature"—can we begin to change responses that seem to be necessary and normal.[4] Racial violence based on embodied prejudices can only be countered, Royce explains, by considering the assumptions underlying moral practices, particularly those that rigidly prioritize emotions over reason. Royce's argument in "Race Questions and Prejudices" engages directly with the questions of bodies, figures, and emotions explored in the previous chapter, concluding that abstraction could assist in countering the reality of persistent and violent racial hate.

Josiah Royce no longer enjoys widespread recognition and is usually remembered for whom he knew—T. S. Eliot, George Santayana, and William James—rather than for what he thought.[5] Scholars emphasize his prolonged philosophical exchange with William James or his attempts to adapt idealism to American traditions of thought; his popular philosophy, such as the lecture delivered to the Ethical societies, is routinely disregarded as uninteresting or trivial.[6] Complaining that his social interventions are deficient—"There [is] no analysis of the roots of concrete social problems, no examination of the distribution of power that determine[s] the structure of the economy, no concern with the patterns of the interest represented by politics, and no grasp of the American political economy"—Bruce Kuklick concludes that "Royce appears to have derived his knowledge [of social issues] from what he picked up in the press and popular literature."[7] Demanding that Royce observe scholarly norms more appropriate to the early years of the twenty-first than the twentieth century, Kuklick dismisses Royce's contribution to the consideration of racial issues, despite the fact that Alain Locke lists Royce's *Race Questions and Other Matters* as a book worthy of note for its contribution to the American discussion of race in his important 1925 anthology *The New Negro*.[8]

Re-placing Royce in the context of late-nineteenth- and early-twentieth-century moral, epistemological, political, and social concerns and considering more fully the implications of the social responsibilities the philosopher was expected to negotiate, however, transform him from a late-Victorian curiosity into an insightful critic of the influential tradition of prioritizing emotion in moral matters.[9] Arguing for a reconsideration of the role of abstraction, and thus engaging from a different angle the concerns that occupied Northern thinkers during the Civil War era, Royce persuasively challenges assumptions about the efficacy and individuality of emotional engagement in ethical issues, especially the limitations inherent in a reenergized and racialized conception of sympathy. Indeed, Royce's claims about the limitations of certain kinds of moral reasoning, which he demonstrates both theoretically and rhetorically in *The Philosophy of Loyalty* and "Race Problems in America," reveal a compelling justification for the use of disembodied abstractions in ethics. Not only does Royce provide a way to parry the complaints that nineteenth-century novelists launched against "anaesthetizing abstractions," as well as those that recent cultural critics have registered against abstract language as an instrument of political coercion, he also enacts a set of rhetorical strategies to counteract racial hatred and violence.[10] While abstractions can certainly provide a mechanism for political and social oppression—as literary critics such as Lauren Berlant, Elaine Scarry, Hortense Spillers, and Michael Warner have compellingly argued—Royce demonstrates that they also provide a useful method for evading, and potentially refashioning, prejudice based on bodily identity.[11]

The three crucial elements of Royce's attack on affect-based moral reasoning—the theory of loyalty, his emphasis on interpretation, and his explicit repudiation of embodied prejudice, like that reified in the black body—unite to suggest that his public philosophy merits far more of our attention than the passing mention it has received. In this chapter, I situate Royce's popular philosophy within a literary and social context to clarify how abstraction can respond to, and participate in, broad postbellum cultural concerns; in so doing, this chapter provides a complement to the argument against homogenizing figures forwarded in chapter 4. Rooting abstraction in the local community, rather than the national public sphere, Royce's moral theory negotiates the embodied limitations of a commercialized and conservative sentimentality by redefining the relationship between the mind and the heart.

* * *

The preface, "To the Reader," of the inaugural issue of the *Journal of Speculative Philosophy* (1867) announced the journal's dedication to the reconstruction of the Union through philosophy's power to shape social "consciousness": "The national consciousness has moved forward on to a new platform during the last few years. The idea underlying our form of government had hitherto developed only one of its essential phases—that of brittle individualism—in which national unity seemed an external mechanism, soon to be entirely dispensed with, and the enterprise of the private man or of the corporation substituted for it."[12] If anything had been learned from the recent bloody conflict, in other words, it was that the individual substantially depended on the "State as such." The emphasis on individualism characteristic of antebellum culture had rendered both the individual and, as it turned out, the nation "brittle." Although it still needed "to be digested and comprehended," the new phase of American existence offered an ideal opportunity for philosophy, "the Speculative" in the jargon of the Ohio Hegelians who started the journal, to establish its footing as an intrinsic component of everyday experience. If one accepts their triumphalist rhetoric, they took Hegel's claim—"America is therefore the land of the future"—literally, as an indication that spirit would reveal itself in the United States.[13] Philosophical abstraction would foster a more enduring way of thinking about "national unity" than the overly individualized model that had recently proved so liable to fracture. The *Journal of Speculative Philosophy* provided an important platform for late-nineteenth-century thinkers, such as William James, C. S. Peirce, and John Dewey, but its issues sought to engage with readers on essays on music, art, and literature as well as philosophy. Despite its grounding in German idealism, many of the most famous contributors to the *Journal* shared a conviction that knowledge was, at its core, social, committed to a trajectory of intellectual inquiry that would result in the development of pragmatism.

Echoing many of the basic notions outlined in the *Journal of Specula-

tive Philosophy's mission statement, without the thorough emphasis on a popularized (and Americanized) Hegelianism, John Mackenzie noted in the 1890 primer *An Introduction to Social Philosophy*:

> Many of the ideas and principles of conduct by which men were formerly guided in dealing with the great questions of the life and welfare of human beings in societies have been discredited or swept away. We are now engaged in groping our way to something new; and whether the new light is to be better than the old, will depend mainly on the thoroughness with which we set ourselves to discover what is ultimately true and what is ultimately desirable with reference to social affairs.[14]

In the postbellum United States, as in England, the "ultimately true" and "desirable" was a reintroduction of abstraction as central to moral reasoning. Thanks to challenges posed by scientific advances, religion no longer held the central position for adjudicating moral behavior it had previously enjoyed; the relative insecurity of religious certainty, however, provided a prime opportunity for other disciplines, the chief of which was philosophy (although the budding social sciences also benefited), to argue that they could more than adequately replace the comforts faith had provided. "The common intellectual language of the shared myths were gone," D. H. Meyer explains. "But this loss . . . was counterbalanced by the persistence of the civil religion in which all Americans participated, the continued growth of organized religion as churches competed like businesses to reach new members, and the rise of a pseudo-intellectual religiousness in which sentimentalism and popular philosophy combined to produce an inspirational literature designed for a middle-brow culture."[15] In the 1880s and 1890s, for example, altruism, a "carryall for a wide assortment of notions on improving man's lot," reigned supreme as a source of social comfort. For those individuals eager for more structure, the Ethical movement, a loose international association of local societies organized for the popularization of moral philosophy, also worked to slake secularly unquenched spiritual desires, substituting reasoning for feeling, as a means of negotiating the world.[16]

In the introduction to *Ethics and Religion*, a collection of essays on the efficacy of popular moral instruction, the editors from the Society of Ethical Propagandists observed that "the criticism most frequently brought against Ethical Societies is that they do not rest upon any philosophical bases. The implication is that they have therefore no foundation in thought at all." Such a criticism errs, the Ethical Propagandists noted, in confusing an emphasis on actual behavior with a rejection of theoretical thinking. Were these scoffers to scrutinize the positions of Ethical societies more closely, the editors observed, they would recognize that being "uncommitted to any [one] theory of the universe" does not preclude the "investigation and construction" of moral ideas.[17] Although they rejected complex theoretical models as both unwieldy and unwelcoming, the leaders of Ethical societies endorsed an emphasis on abstract reasoning as the best means of inculcating "philosophic discipline and habit." Throughout their history, Ethical societies sought a balance between theory and practice, with the trained philosophers who addressed audiences emphasizing practical concerns and Ethical enthusiasts pushing for more abstract presentations.[18] Even if a mean was hard to maintain, Ethical societies still satisfied various social needs; when philosophy's desire to impact the lives of average citizens was coupled with the hopes of individuals to find philosophical answers to spiritual questions, the result was a brand of popular philosophy that attempted to replace the affect-based appeals to sympathy characteristic of antebellum America with abstraction and the claims of reason.

While Josiah Royce was skeptical about the Ethical movement itself, his consistent concern for popular philosophical exposition; his acquaintance with Felix Adler, a prominent figure in the movement; and his aid in forming the Ethical Culture Society in the United States all indicate that the cultural context of popular philosophy is critical to appreciate the range of Royce's intellectual projects and ambitions.[19] Even if Royce questions these groups in his private correspondence, he accepted speaking engagements as early as 1889 on topics congenial to the explicitly stated goals of the Ethical movement. In presenting what he hoped would be a practical contribution to moral reasoning through his philosophy of loyalty, Royce engaged (critically) with the trajectory of philosophy and contemporary debates concerning moral norms and racial assumptions. Because of the cultural connotations clustered around loyalty and the contested sense of allegiance it connoted, Royce's use of this term situates his argument historically, even as his claims for the value of abstraction resist a complete immersion in the contingency of historical specificity. Rather than merely situating his idealism on the margins of American philosophy, Royce is profitably read as participating in the larger discussions about American cultural practices and values that both Ethical societies and the loyalty debates before them took to be of central importance.

In his 1905 address to the Ethical Society, Royce blames improper social training for many of our narrow-minded ideas. Allowing us to elevate "cruder and more childish social reactions" into "a sort of sacred revelation of truth, sacred merely because it is felt, a revelation merely because it has won a name and a social standing," we are taught from an early age that our feelings importantly register social norms (50, 52). Returning to this concern in the *Philosophy of Loyalty*, Royce observes, "Our young people [have] grown up with a great deal of their attention fixed upon personal success, and also with a great deal of training in sympathetic sentiments; but they get far too little knowledge, either practical or theoretical, of what loyalty means" (103). Effective social preparation should instead be predicated on rational reflection and should teach individuals how to discipline their immature, and potentially brutal, responses to others.[20] Given both claim and context, it is perhaps surprising that Royce only mentions lynching, the most violent manifestation of "crude" responses, once in "Race Questions and Prejudices." While he refers repeatedly to the problem of evil—asking "Is, however, the irritation which seems to be the accompaniment of some of the recent Southern methods of teaching the negro his place an inevitable evil, a wholly necessary accompaniment of the present transition period in the South?"—Royce elides most specifics about "Southern methods of teaching the negro his place" (17). Considering the energy Royce devotes to deploring the human capacity for barbarism, the near total omission of this brutal aspect of American culture is explained neither by assuming his ignorance of prevailing cultural conditions nor by imputing to him a degree of squeamishness in confronting social evil. Why does Royce avoid the discussion of lynching in a paper explicitly intended to correct improper social training by helping his auditors and readers "to look at race questions fairly and humanely" (266)?

While many intellectual historians have dismissed Royce's contributions to social philosophy, particularly on the issue of race, I maintain that the strength of his argument is to be found in the answer to this question, which reveals his perceptive understanding of the structure and justification of existing American racial stereotypes. To embrace the subject of lynching in any way, either defensively or critically, was, for Royce, to engage the visceral emotional responses upon which racial prejudices were predicated. Lynching, as Robyn Wiegman has persuasively argued, enacted "a system of corporeal inscription that [linked] the body to cultural hierarchies of power": "lynching figures its victims as the culturally abject—monstrosities of excess whose limp and hanging bodies function as the specular assurance that the racial threat has not simply been averted, but rendered incapable of return."[21] What lynching enabled, in other words, was precisely the situation Royce was attempting to change—a violence both literal and figurative against the black body. In avoiding the subject of lynching, Royce circumvents feelings, imagined to be true, as well as the bodily morality they could be manipulated to justify, clearing conceptual and rhetorical space for a new mode of ethical figuration.

Arguing that our seemingly instinctive reactions are the product of cultural conditioning, Royce follows his Civil War predecessors by replacing sympathy with loyalty, material bodies with disembodied superindividual causes, a process he forwards via the deferral of direct confrontation with racial violence. Throughout his late ethical writings in popular philosophy, Royce consistently stresses both the constructed nature of belief and the ability of interpretation and abstraction to unsettle rigidly held opinions. Basing moral reasoning on a combination of abstraction and commitment rather than personal experience or familial connection, Royce tries to model a way of seeing difference "fairly and humanely." Devaluing empirical evidence in ethical evaluation, Royce replaces embodied prejudices with the social formula "Be loyal to loyalty."[22] With the redundancy of this phrase Royce identifies what is crucial about an abstract method of understanding moral dilemmas—the necessary erasure of the empirical, and with it a potentially coercive set of epistemological presuppositions, from interpersonal affairs.

* * *

Royce notes in a 1902 lecture, "Provincialism," that the distinction between sympathy and loyalty has fundamental implications for American social, political, and moral organization. Challenging sentimentality's presupposition that emotions are personal and individual, Royce argues that affective responses lead inevitably to "mob-spirit."[23] Despite the variety of "noble names" that can be, and indeed have been, applied to it, sympathy encourages the elision of individuality, a practice that generalized emotional appeals both presuppose and manipulate. "Psychologically it is the mob-spirit whenever it is the spirit of a large company of people who are no longer either taking calm counsel together in small groups, or obeying an already established law or custom, but who are *merely sympathizing* with one another, listening to the words of leaders, and believing the large print headings of their newspapers." The ease with which even a well-meaning sympathy could be misdirected into "mob-spirit" forms the basis of Royce's attack on its dominion. "Every such company of people," he continues, "is a mob," "degraded" and untrustworthy, even "though they spoke with the tongues of men and of angels" (86-87). On his account, sympathy "is not necessarily even a kindly tendency," "for one may sympathize with any emotion,—for instance, with the emotions of a cruelly ferocious mob." "The basest absurdities may, upon occasion, seem to be justified," Royce concludes, "because an undiscriminating sympathy makes them plausible" (93). While Royce acknowledges the positive effects of sympathy tempered by rationality and intelligence, the "tendency to emotional excitability" that comes of "sharing the emotions of the crowd" dissolves for him the possibility of establishing nurturing social environments or effective political systems based on that aspect of human response that is *least* individuated and most easily manipulated. His philosophy is specifically intended to counter the "disastrous hypnotic slumber so characteristic of excited masses of mankind" (96).

"Provincialism," as Royce uses the term, serves to mediate between "narrowness," associated with a restrictive local perspective, and the nation as a whole, which presents the "danger of becoming an incomprehensible monster" (98). "Wholeseome" in its influence, Royce hopes that an increase in provincial importance will be matched by "more and not less patriotism, closer and not looser national ties, less and not more mutual sectional misunderstanding" (62, 66). Provincialism negotiates the binary, so important to De Forest and his peers, between the local and the national as objects of allegiance, allowing Royce to articulate, as Werner Sollors notes, an ethical "golden mean, the *juste milieu*," and linking his thought to that of his student, W. E. B. Du Bois.[24]

Loyalty functions, for Royce, in tandem with provincialism, defined as integral to human flourishing; his concept of loyalty contends that the moral individual is both rationally and passionately committed to a cause beneficial for humankind locally and universally. Abstract and embodied only provisionally, loyalty allowed Royce to circumvent the problems with (and of) sympathy, without absolutely rejecting the claims of emotion. Translating abstruse Kantian imperatives into a more accessible and more socially grounded formula in the 1908 *Philosophy of Loyalty*, Royce argues that "a cause is good, not only for me, but for mankind, in so far as it is essentially a *loyalty to loyalty*, that is, is an aid and a furtherance of loyalty in my fellows" (56). An individual's affiliations, the causes to which he or she is devoted, should promote personal and communal well-being. This is not to suggest, however, that the individual is required to adopt *any* set of beliefs perceived to be good for the community; on the contrary, Royce is clear that despite our imitative natures, "We never merely imitate. Conformity attracts, but also wearies us" (17). Loyalty is, for Royce, both personal and communal. "You can love an individual," he posits,

> but you can be loyal only to a tie that binds you and others into some sort of unity, and loyal to individuals only through the tie. The cause to which loyalty devotes itself has always this union of the personal and the seemingly superindividual about it.... Loyal lovers, for instance, are loyal not merely to one another as separate individuals, but to their love, to their union, which is something more than either of them, or even than both of them viewed as distinct individuals. (11)

Neither "mere emotion" nor "barren abstraction[]", loyalty permits the evaluation of competing claims, weighing both individual priorities and universal duties (10, 62).

In the race problem, then, Royce was presented with not only a social and political evil that a practical moral philosophy would need to consider but also a signal challenge in the evolution of loyalty as a philosophical concept that could make an impact on the world. When antipathies become naturalized in a body of tradition, how can even a rational abstraction like "Be loyal to loyalty" ever hope to counter their influence? What would prevent the man with the rope in his hand from maintaining that, in lynching his victim, he was faithfully following Royce's tenet and displaying his loyalty to his race?[25] Supplanting the unchecked emotionality of supposedly natural sympathies, Royce grounds his idea of loyalty within a network of communal ties and personal choice. What, however, if the ideals of a community, region, or nation led, instead of to social cohesion, to division and racial violence? Could his philosophy offer practical solutions to this seemingly intractable, and altogether explicable given his premises, dilemma?

In "Race Questions and Prejudices," Royce responds to the challenges of American racial tensions, placing his confidence in the power of interpretation to influence the world. Locating our moral lives in local communities, *Philosophy of Loyalty* envisions a moral system where social life is based on a constant and reasoned process of revision and reinterpretation consistent with the demands of loyalty: "As you train the social being, you make use of his natural submissiveness. But as a result of your training he forms plans; he interprets these plans with reference to his own personal interests, and he may end by becoming, if not original, then at least obstreperous" (17–18). In other words, Royce's fully formed individual naturally challenges the social order, questioning how his culture's laws and customs interpret the world. And this is good. "Revision," Royce notes, "does not mean mere destruction." "Let us bury the natural body of tradition," he enthusiastically urges his readers. "What we want is its glorified body and its immortal soul" (7).

The interpretive strategies in "Race Questions and Prejudices" reveal a variety of ways racial "truths" are figured. Beginning with the constructed nature of facts, Royce narrows the terms of the discussion to exclude appeals to science. "Why speculate and moralize," Royce imagines someone asking him, if "the races of men" have been studied recently by the sciences of anthropology and ethnology "with elaborate care?" (7). Rejecting the purported facticity of empirical evidence, and taking a potshot at competing disciplines in the social sciences, Royce admits to finding most race theories to be at best baffling examples of scientific objectivity, at worst racist fictions: "Much of our modern race-theory," Royce sniffs, "reminds me, in its spirit, altogether too much of some of the conversations in the 'Jungle-Book'" (9). In changing the subject of race from one appropriately approached not by "specialists" but by philosophers, Royce challenges both the tyranny of empiricism and the assumptions underwriting the installation of direct experience as the best guarantee of truth. When we consider the language of science carefully, he hints, we see that the presuppositions of the pseudo-scientific argument are prejudices disguised as concrete facts, rather than concrete facts in the service of abstractions. Throughout his lecture, Royce consistently reuses a rhetorical gambit based on this notion: take a fact, reveal it to be based on bias not evidence, and attempt to correct the basis of the bias by offering new ways of conceptualizing it. When you reveal the flaws in a person's interpretive model, Royce repeatedly posits, you provide the conditions of possibility for that person to change his or her moral perspective. Although the lecture's topic is race, the strategy Royce outlines has broader implications for American cultural organization at the beginning of the twentieth century; outmoded standards of behavior, which he suggests contributed to the outbreak of civil war, fail to provide the necessary basis for future success.

Royce's second rhetorical strategy draws attention to how the racialized body had become not a figure but a fact. Throughout his address, Royce converses with a host of imaginary interlocutors, assigning them particular, and particularly narrow, beliefs as well as bodies to house their intellectual and moral precepts. The Southern racist, the intellectual, the "enthusiastic lady in an American University town," the Northern liberal—all of these "types" briefly share the podium with Royce (13). Nonetheless, although he refers broadly to people degraded through years of systematic abuse, neither the slave nor the freed American black is introduced directly in the lecture. This is not to suggest, however, that Royce excludes all persons of color from his conversation; on the contrary, the funniest moment in the talk is provided by the witty remarks of an ironic "Japanese visitor." When the "enthusiastic lady" presses him to acknowledge Japan's debt to Christian missionaries, the visitor quips, "You are right; the missionaries in introducing Christianity, have indeed brought us a good deal. They have completed the variety of religions in Japan" (13). Encouraging his audience to chuckle with the Japanese visitor and at the lady enthusiast, Royce exposes the degree to which our assumptions, of the body and of the spirit, contribute to the formation of our scientific explanations and moral interpretations.[26] The unappealing and narrow positions of Royce's interlocutors push the reader and auditor to form new identificatory relations, redefining what is, or might be, unsightly. With this practice, Royce inverses the identification upon which the sentimental response had been normally based, revealing simultaneously the limitation of sympathetic reasoning and the corrective power of aptly deployed conceptual fictions.

Royce uses several test cases to demonstrate the limitations of bodies in both gathering and responding to information about race. Although Japan's recent defeat of Russia had augmented the military threat the Japanese presented, Royce launches his examination of race relations with this culturally and geographically remote people. "I remember well the Japan of the geography text-books of my childhood," Royce recollects, books that depicted a nation where "things were as perverse as possible" and "foreigners were excluded." Indeed, what could be more "perverse" than "exclud[ing]" the white man? Such a fact alone, the textbooks surmised, was enough to indicate that the Japanese were "plainly men of the wrong race." As their island was increasingly opened to the gaze of European and American visitors, however, the Japanese "became in our eyes a plastic race of wonderful little children, small of stature, quick of wit, light-minded" (11). Whereas their features had previously authorized judgments of unacceptable physical deviance—they were members of the "wrong race"—more information and exposure forces a revision of this stereotype. "Small of stature," the Japanese are represented as deserving the Western protection they all along had been assumed to need.

Because they are "light-minded" and "plastic" like the children to whom they are compared, these islanders clearly required the guiding hand of mature Western minds to guarantee that their instincts—particularly their martial instincts—would not lead them astray.

The experience Royce presents as his own differs significantly enough from each preceding characterization that he is driven, as his theory maintains he should be, to create his own interpretation. Through personal encounters with Japanese students, Royce explains that he realizes that even the revised stereotype is based on empirical misperception and colonialist logic. Even if they display a somewhat "obstinate" reserve, "facts" such as this, Royce contends, do not justify conclusions of racial inferiority. Building from this assertion, Royce postulates that the empirical observation upon which many racial assumptions are based is almost entirely useless when it comes to understanding other people both individually and communally. Because customs are not fixed, we must recognize that science, when predicated on assumptions about the past, present, or future, cannot make accurate predictions about the behavior or capacities of people of different races, Royce pointedly maintains. Indeed, when we believe we must verify a hypothesis from finite information, so-called objective science enacts perceptual error: "the true lesson which Japan teaches us today is, that it is somewhat hard to find out by looking at the features of a man's face, or at the color of his skin, or even the reports of travelers who visit this land, what it is of which his race is really capable" (14). Thanks to a range of culturally derived perceptual restrictions—the influence of fashion, of custom, and of familiarity—eyewitness reports are necessarily unreliable and should not be assumed to provide irrefutable evidence; in short, the "truth" Americans acquire in considering judgments about the Japanese is properly a truth about ourselves, our epistemological constraints, our moral standards, and our flawed interpretive paradigms.

Moving his analysis gradually closer to the continental United States, Royce briefly considers the examples of Jamaica and Trinidad. The important lesson to be learned from the history of Jamaica, he notes, is that black people behave in ways that are, or seem to be, the same as white people. Implicit to this discussion of Jamaicans is Royce's response to a central question of nineteenth-century racial speculation: which was more important, what someone *did* or who that person *was*? Overtly prioritizing doing over being, Royce maintains that personal possibilities and achievements are more likely to be a product of historical circumstance than of innate racialized abilities. What seems to be the result of hereditary traits and social degeneracy are instead the result of circumstances and of environment, and where such degeneracy has already gone so far that we have before us highly diseased human types, such as can no longer be reclaimed. *But such types are not racial types.* They are results of alcohol, of infection, or in some instances, of the long-continued pressure of physical environment. In such cases we can sometimes say, Here is a hopelessly degraded stock of men. But, then, civilization can create such stocks, out of any race of men, by means of a sufficient amount of oppression and of other causes of degradation, if continued through generations. (46, emphasis added)

"Environment," "oppression," and "degradation" provide, Royce posits, a more satisfying and thorough explanation of social degeneracy than does recourse to partial and inexact scientific hypotheses. Because Jamaicans are not reminded daily of their supposed inferiority, all people, black and white, can feel secure moving around the island. Although Royce admits that "life in Jamaica is not ideal"—the island is still segregated by race—the institution of civil and health services has accustomed both black and white Jamaicans to respect the law, their neighbors, and themselves, promising better social conditions in the near future (21). In short, the general population has learned "loyalty and order," a process necessary as an initial step "on the long road 'up from slavery'" (24).

Having presented a society characterized by racial harmony, Royce turns to the American race problem. Certain of our fears, he observes, like those people who differ from us inspire, seem "elemental, widespread," and "momentous." They are also, he notes, "extremely capricious" (47). If we can manage to circumvent them, we see that the problem that had seemed to loom menacingly before our eyes was real in our imagination only.

> Our so-called race-problems are merely the problems caused by our antipathies. . . . Let an individual man alone, and he will feel antipathies for certain other human beings very much as any young child does—namely quite capricious—just as he will also feel all sorts of capricious likings, for people. But train a man first to give names to his antipathies, and then to regard the antipathies thus named as sacred merely because they have a name, and you get the phenomena of racial hatred, of religious hatred, of class hatred, and so on indefinitely. (47-48)

While they are "peculiarly pathetic and peculiarly deceitful," like children in need of discipline and instruction, our emotional responses are manipulable when we resist the urge to assign them "names" or human forms (48). Once we have done so, Royce makes clear, antipathies become "sacred" precisely because they have been named, a formulation that captures the inflexibility that language can seem to introduce. Rejecting the truth value of childish innocence and spontaneity, and with it the turn-of-the-century enthusiasm for childlike traits and behavior, Royce notes that although we cannot control the fact that we have emotional, hence irrational, responses to difference, we can maturely control our interpretation of these responses. What might be to one person "an object of fascinated curiosity" can strike "another, slightly less stable, observer" with "terror" or "violent antipathy" (51). Consequently, fears sanctified by the garb of science and ceded empirical integrity undermine precisely the sort of color-blind objectivity that science and morality purport to introduce into the world. We can only escape the tyranny of what seems to be factual, particularly information provided by our eyes, when we realize the extent to which communal narratives and norms create the "facts" we are capable of seeing. Put simply, when we put our fears into words or embodied forms, we lose the capacity to recognize their contingent and constructed character. This argument explains why Royce avoids the black American body; his claims presuppose that its figuration has consistently and conveniently served as the repository for a range of violent emotions and fears.

With this elision, Royce engages in two processes of resistance and reform simultaneously. First, he opposes the spectacular dimensions of narratives and social practices constructed to contain fear by locating it in the dead bodies of African Americans. Exposing white assumptions about the black body, Royce then works to empower a colorless abstraction to reveal the chimerical, and constructed, aspect of existing race theories and beliefs. For Royce, this two-pronged solution to the race problem gained its potential strength from the power of interpretation and the intervention of abstraction. Recognizing the contingent nature of our perceptions, the ways history, society, and chance unite to mold our values, we gain, Royce suggests, the critical awareness to challenge our assumptions and remedy moral and scientific errors.

While Royce places significant weight on the ability of interpretation to shape the world, he is not blind to the obstacles impeding such an endeavor. "Modern conditions," Royce explains in "Provincialism," tend "to crush the individual" (75). Many factors combined to alienate and "crush" the individual, including "an excess of wandering strangers and unassimilated newcomers, an increasing tendency toward uniformity and mediocrity, and an increase of mob spirit."[27] Identifying metropolitan newspapers as one particularly pernicious aspect of this dimension of modern life, Royce notes that "when read by vast multitudes, they tend to produce a certain monotonously uniform triviality of mind in a large proportion of our city and suburban population" (77). Cosseted by a uniformity coloring much of American culture, the individual loses his or her "independence of spirit" that enables both thought and feeling (78). Independence, then, grants each person the authority to resist the "mob-spirit" of sympathy and the integrity to read the world "fairly and humanely."

Although Royce does not use the example of American race relations in this essay, the lethal potential of such "uniform triviality" is especially evident when considering the role of newspapers in late-nineteenth-century American racial violence. Postbellum newspapers and periodicals devoted significant space to reporting on American racial problems, although the tenor of such reports was often far from impartial and tended to reflect entrenched regional biases, as Southern papers reported crimes by African Americans and Northern ones documented vigilante violence.[28] In the midst of this media confusion, the *Chicago Tribune* began in 1882 to gather detailed statistics about the causes, locations, and numbers of lynchings throughout the United States, which it presented every January until 1918. Despite being a Northern paper, the *Tribune*'s statistics were considered so accurate that proponents on both sides of the debate, antilynching activists as well as apologists for vigilantism, used them to verify their claims.

Such statistical information was overshadowed, however, by local narratives about racial violence, often reported in the same newspapers that provided more factual accounts. "Fueled" by plantation tales, stories of "black urban pathology and immorality" were common in the decades after Reconstruction and became more frantic as Southern violence encouraged the mass migration of African Americans to the North.[29] Consider, for instance, the following example reported on April 2, 1905, in the *Tribune* itself concerning the attempted abduction of Mary Crimmins by Elijah Harris. "GIRL SEIZED; NEGRO CHASED," "THREATS OF LYNCHING MADE" the headlines scream. According to the story, "hundreds of pedestrians" "screaming for ropes" pursued "Elijah Harris" after he tried to "kidnap" Mary Crimmins, an eleven-year-old orphan on an errand for a nun. Although one cannot disregard the girl's trauma—the second paragraph of the article claims the girl is "seriously ill" for "in her struggles to escape from the attentions of Harris she suffered severe bruises to her arms"—the article quickly moves from the child to the crowd of people attracted by her screams and their subsequent pursuit of her would-be abductor. "While the scores of pedestrians were chasing Harris," the newspaper melodramatically details, "Mary slowly picked up the letter that had been hurled from her hand in the struggle, and carried it to the nearest mail box." Having established the familiar story of conjoined racial and sexual transgression, the rest of the narrative focuses on the detectives' attempts to prevent the mob from lynching Harris.

It is against common narratives like this one that Royce's interpretive strategy must be assessed. Not only was he countering firmly established assumptions about the depravity and deviancy of the average African American, but he also had to contend with entrenched conventions from countless sentimental authors about the value of emotion and the power of words. In the context of such conventions, however, the abandonment of Mary Crimmins seems odd. Why would the narrative shift to the crowd of onlookers eager to witness the lynching of a black man? The ease with which spectacular thrill overpowers sympathetic concern in this narrative of "mob-spirit" exposes the susceptibility of sympathy to be overwhelmed by other emotions, and to be undermined by the very narrative conventions its logic helped establish. In the Crimmins abduction narrative, there is little to have inspired actual fear in readers; Elijah Harris fails in his attempted misdeed and is apprehended by the appropriate authorities, protecting the community from this individual even if the larger menace remains unchecked. Entirely marginalized—both as an African American and because of the mental disability he is passingly said to display—the narrative concretizes in Harris the supposed physical and mental inferiority of other races. Were the crowd to have succeeded in lynching him, their act would, on one level, have unified the spectators, circularly verifying the truth of their beliefs in the inert body of the transgressor. What becomes clear in the Harris narrative, if one accepts Royce's argument, is that when confronted with well-established myths, sympathy fails to protect any of its victims—the child, Harris, or the reader.

* * *

In "Race Questions and Prejudices," Josiah Royce departs once from his strategy of addressing imaginary interlocutors when he refers directly to the popular Southern writer Thomas Nelson Page.[30]

> When ... I hear ... from my brethren of certain regions of our Union, I see how easily we can all mistake for a permanent race-problem a difficulty that is essentially a problem of another sort. Mr. Thomas Nelson Page in his recent book on the "Southerners' Problems" speaks, in one notable passage of the possibility which he calls Utopian, that perhaps some day the negro in the South may be made to coöperate in the keeping of order by the organization under State control of a police of their own race, who shall deal with blacks. (276)

In the collection of essays to which Royce refers, Page identifies the central problem facing the South as "the ever-present, ever-menacing, ever-growing Negro Question."[31] While Royce manipulates various rhetorical conventions to expose the ways figures are read literally in the construction of American racial prejudices, Page relies on precisely the organic, embodied language Royce eschews to forward his contention that not only do bodies make meaning, but that bodies of different racial types mean differently. Page serves in Royce's text as a metonym for the racial violence so carefully excluded, but his widely read justifications of lynching, and the rhetorical strategies they employ, are critical for appreciating Royce's answer to the American race question.

First in the prestigious *North American Review*, and then later in *The Negro: The Southerner's Problem* (1904), Page blames the intervention of inaccurate and inappropriate Northern "teachings" for the disruption of peaceful race relations in the South. As the Northern ideal of "equality" introduced during the war and Reconstruction took shape in the minds of blacks, it revealed a basic and contradictory presupposition: equality leads not to harmony but to enmity. "The teaching that the Negro was the equal of the white," he writes, led the freed slave to the conclusion "that the white was his enemy, and that he must assert his equality. The growth of the idea was a gradual one in the negro's mind."[32] Page's tendentious rendition of postbellum history elides the reality of white practices of intimidation and domination, emphasizing instead what he contends is an innate inability displayed by African Americans to grasp appropriately or fully abstract ideas like "equality." When African Americans finally reach what will function for them as comprehension, Page concludes, equality will necessarily find its manifestation in the body; the inevitable corollary to this "equality" is, for Page, the frequent demonstration of sexual aggression against white women and girls, acts heinous enough to justify even the most violent of responses.[33]

Although he explains that such horrors are "unnamable," Page nonetheless lists enough juicy detail to rouse the passions of his readers: "Indeed, an instance occurred not a great while ago in the District of Columbia, within a hundred yards of a fashionable drive, when, about three o'clock of a bright June day, a young girl was attacked within sight and sound of her house, and when she screamed her throat was cut. So near to her home was the spot that her mother and an officer, hearing her cries, reached her before life was extinct."[34] Never described, the perpetrator is assumed to be black. As the narrative interest for Page lies with the destruction of purity, represented both by the "young girl" and the "bright June day," the actual naming of the perpetrator is entirely beside the point; the reader's emotions are as much under attack as the "young girl." Because the crime occurs in the nation's capital, Page can imply that this is a crime against American moral, political, and economic values; even the "fashionable drive" fails to protect the young girl.

Having stirred the emotions of his readers, most of whom were likely to be white and middle class, Page complains that little can be done within the bounds of the law to protect white women from the sexual assaults of black rapists, a figure as firmly fixed in the U.S. imagination as the loyal slave.[35] Not even the death penalty, he laments, can prevent the "ravishing of women," which "instead of diminishing, steadily increased." "The criminal, under the ministrations of his preachers, usually professed to have 'gotten religion,' and from the shadow of the gallows called on his friends to follow him to glory. So that the punishment lost to these emotional people much of its deterrent force, *especially where the real sympathy of the race was mainly with the criminal rather than with his victim.*"[36] The dichotomy of true and false sympathy, here deployed in service of a conservative social agenda, establishes the point that black Americans cannot be trusted to understand how to think *or* how to feel. Only through the correction of black emotions and the white ideas spurring them forward, Page concludes, can the security of white bodies be guaranteed. Put differently, "these emotional people" need to be returned to the care of kindly masters and mistresses to be sure that the right kinds of sympathy and loyalty would prevail.

Despite his anxiety with the threats presented to female bodies, Page is almost equally agitated about the overthrow of white male rationality stemming from the contemplation and confrontation of such horrors:

> The death of the victim of the ravisher was generally the least of the attendant horrors. In Texas, in Mississippi, in Georgia, in

Kentucky, in Colorado, as later in Delaware, the facts in the case were so unspeakable that they have never been put in print. They could not be put in print. It is these unnamable horrors which have outraged the minds of those who live in regions where they have occurred, and where they may at any time occur again, and, upsetting reason, have swept from their bearings cool men and changed them into madmen, drunk with the lust of revenge.[37]

Their shared concern about the power of the press may well be the only substantive point of agreement between Royce and Page.[38] Although he finds their behavior entirely explicable, Page worries that otherwise reasonable men are "swept from their bearing" and changed into "madmen" by the sexual violence threatening white women, a scenario that duplicates the structure of "lust" and "revenge" that Page suggests causes the crimes in the first place. In short, black sexual violence is a contagion that must be carefully controlled. Keeping such information out of print is one way to limit the lust freed with the slaves, although as we have seen Page does not hesitate to incorporate inflammatory materials into his text. Normally characterized by reason and cool reflection, the white male experiences this loss of control because his sympathies are so thoroughly engaged with the sufferings of white female victims. Even if the details of the crimes remain hidden, available only through rumor and hearsay because their horrifying specifics could not be "put in print," the likelihood of repeat offenses occurring "at any time" justifies vigilante violence. What Page here suggests is that because the races have differing capacities for emotion as well as reason, one errs in applying the standards of sympathetic response without reference to such innate deviations. The best way to remedy this situation is to recognize that the default victim in any racial situation is the individual with the white body. Indeed, Page implies that it is impossible for white individuals fully to lose control of their faculties, for even the temporary loss of control previously described results from reasonable provocation. Consequently, even when he acts outside the law, Page's white male can still be trusted to remain within the limits of natural justice. Because "the rage of a mob is not directed against the innocent, but against the guilty; and its fury would not be satisfied with any other sacrifices than the death of the real criminal," Page justifies his own rhetorical manipulation of the readers' emotions by indicating that any anger he might arouse is best understood as righteous and fair.[39] Other commentators were less confident than Page, suggesting that lynching could be habit forming, addictive like a drug or contagious like a "fever."[40] Such counterclaims notwithstanding, Page's skewed argument maintained that the white body is always under control, even when "drunk with the lust of revenge"; the black body, however, is at the mercy of extreme emotion even when it appears to be under control.

Page's definition of sympathy as importantly organized by race has its antecedents in antebellum arguments about both identification and slavery. As we saw in the previous chapter, Adam Smith's *The Theory of Moral Sentiments* lists multiple limiting conditions for the development of sympathy, stressing the importance of shared social and cultural hierarchies and values in the formation of identifications. Explaining the "inequality of our sentiments," Smith proposes that were "the great empire of China, with all its myriads of inhabitants, . . . suddenly swallowed up by an earthquake," "a man of humanity in Europe" would of course express the properly "humane" sentiments but then quickly return to "his business or his pleasure" with "ease and tranquility."[41] Although he does not dwell on race in this example, pointing instead to the lack of connection between the populations of Europe and Asia, Smith's choice of China demonstrates the ease with which these ideas could be made to accommodate racialized sentiments as an explanation for the necessary inequality.[42] In his 1834 *Letters to a Gentleman in Germany*, for example, Francis Lieber, who describes slavery as "nasty, dirty, selfish," nonetheless opines that regardless of the "meaning attached" to "love of country," "the love of race has a weightier meaning still." "I am a white man, and I for one love my race; that race which,—however many misdeeds and crimes it may have forced history to enter on her records . . . —is, nevertheless, the favored one from which the Europeans have descended." One way to understand why "love of race" would have "a weightier meaning" than "love of country" is through Smith's argument about connection, a claim Lieber articulates indirectly through an argument about white "intellectual superiority."[43]

Slavery apologists likewise asserted the importance of race in determining sympathetic identification.[44] Caroline Lee Hentz's *The Planter's Northern Bride*, a rebuttal to *Uncle Tom's Cabin*, is explicit that white people suffer most profoundly because they are endowed with the qualities that make suffering keen and the responsibilities that make life difficult. And this is merely a softer version of a consistent element of proslavery writing—that sympathy should be racially motivated. As in the plantation writings examined in the preceding chapter, intraracial sympathy is posited as the moral norm. Understanding the true object of sympathy allows us to appreciate the anger and disappointment any white man would reasonably feel when his efforts at fairness and responsibility are not properly valued.

> As they approached the plantation, Moreland became silent and abstracted. The dependencies which hung upon him were heavier than the chains of slavery, and more galling. . . . He had fulfilled the duties of a master so faithfully and conscientiously, bearing them not only on his mind, but on his heart; had laboured so assiduously for his slaves, and felt towards them so tenderly and affectionately, that he could not think of their disaffection without bitterness and sorrow.[45]

Inverting the figures and effects of slavery, it is the master in *The Planter's Northern Bride* who labors without recompense, extends affection with no hope of its return, and is abused thoughtlessly. Such inversions were so prevalent in plantation fiction that Albion Tourgée complained in 1888 that the Confederate veteran had become the nation's most "popular hero," as U.S. literature had "become not only Southern in type, but distinctly Confederate in sympathy."[46] In short, the suffering white plantation owner became the literary figure most likely to move readers to tears, a move easy to enact once slaves were refigured as happy and loyal: Henry Ward Beecher and Thomas Wentworth Higginson were both said to have wept at the death of the young master in Thomas Nelson Page's "Marse Chan" (1884), for example.[47] Further, readers admitted to finding stories where ex-slaves narrate their master's death most affecting; an anonymous "Southern Matron," likewise moved to tears by "Marse Chan," admitted that the story's power arose from the fact that it came "from the faithful negro's heart."[48] A corollary to the reunion romance, plantation narratives, especially those written in dialect, provided the domestic context for stories of martial valor, like *Century*'s 1884–1887 series "Battles and Leaders of the Civil War." Nineteenth-century racial hierarchies maintained that it was the Anglo-Saxon male alone who could consistently negotiate both the abstractions and emotions of responsibility; because of his greater burden, he warrants the reader's sympathy. This false dichotomy is deployed across the nineteenth century as a means of defending slavery and justifying lynching, segregation, and other institutional forms of prejudice: indeed, it is implicit in all racialized arguments that rely on sympathy. No matter the agenda, the politics of sympathy repeatedly fails to challenge the "pseudo-natural differences" of the dominant hierarchy of nineteenth-century American culture—the idea of white racial superiority. Writing for the majority in *Plessy v. Ferguson* (1896), Justice Henry Billings Brown concluded that it was fallacious to believe that "social prejudices may be overcome by legislation." "If the two races are to meet upon terms of social equality," Brown continued, "it must be the result of natural affinities, a mutual appreciation of each other's merits and a voluntary consent of individuals."[49]

Throughout "The Lynching of Negroes," Page shares with Hentz the assumption that threats to white bodies and minds inspire sympathy and, more important, justify retributive violence, a belief that likewise colors his fiction. While most of his plantation tales memorialize antebellum society, Page turns in *Red Rock* (1898) to the Reconstruction era and the racial violence that he takes to be the inevitable result of the inadequate knowledge, misdirected sympathy, and imperial greed governing Northern policies during the period.[50] "The people of [the South] were the product of a system of which it is the fashion nowadays to have only words of condemnation," Page claims in the novel's preface. "Every ass that passes by kicks at the dead lion. It was an Oligarchy, they say, which ruled and lorded it over all but those favored ones who belonged to it. But has one ever known the members of a Democracy to rule so justly?"[51] As the novel opens, the justice lauded in the preface is immediately revealed to be predicated on interracial violence. Not only does a white man have the inalienable right to slaughter a man of color who injures his wife, but, in this part of the world, such an act guarantees his installation as a founding father.[52]

"The old Gray plantation, 'Red Rock,'" Page begins, "lay at the highest part of the rich rolling country, before it rose too abruptly in the wooded foothills of the blue mountains away to the westward." Quickly shifting narrative registers, Page turns from natural description to local history: "As everybody in the country knew, who knew anything, it took its name from the great red stain ... which appeared on the huge bowlder [sic] in the grove, beside the family graveyard.... And as was equally well known, or equally well believed, which amounted almost to the same thing, that stain was the blood of the Indian chief who had slain the wife of the first Jacquelin Gray." Knowledge here is a function not of verifiable fact but of established and inherited assumption. Signs, like the bloodstain on the rock that stands "as a perpetual memorial of the swift vengeance of the Jacquelin Grays," are best read according to the customs and values of the society they created; indeed, failing to read such signs in their customary manner exposes the ill-informed individual to significant personal and moral peril. As if to assure that his interpretation of signs and values will continue to rule into the future, the first Jacquelin hangs his "portrait, with its piercing eyes and fierce look, . . . in a black frame over the mantel, . . . [which] used to come down as a warning when any peril impended above the house" (1). Throughout the novel, Gray men are confused with the painting, inheriting not only the spoils of racial violence but its countenance as well. In *Red Rock*, the portrait offers a potent counternarrative to the pro–Civil War story. As in *The House of Seven Gables* or *Pierre*, the portrait establishes the genealogical authority of the white family in relation to the natives it has displaced.[53] But whereas the antebellum novels trouble the relationship between portrait, genealogy, and race, the legitimating agency of the Gray portrait endures beyond the family's ownership of the house, even acting to return it to its proper white owners. Swindled by Hiram Still, a crooked overseer, out of their home, the Gray family's claim is perpetuated by the portrait for "anything related to the 'Indian-killer' always discomposed him." Still's ultimate defeat is accomplished as much by the legend of the "Indian-killer" as by his heir (240). Originating *in* and authenticated *by* racial violence, *Red Rock* overtly thematizes the appropriate scope of and responsibility for revenge as justice. So while the South might technically lose the war, in Page's Reconstruction, its residents prove ultimately triumphant in reestablishing their values as normative for the region, a point underscored when they win a number of influential Northern abolitionists and politicians to their side.

Unlike Royce, Page does not hesitate to incorporate hosts of often marauding black individuals into his narrative, but he does resist directly narrating any lynching episodes. In the novel's concluding chapter, where ironically "some of the threads are tied," Moses, a freed slave from the region, is "hanged by a mob" after confessing to a "terrible crime" (581, 584). As this "crime" is never named in the newspaper account that reports Moses' death, the punishment meted out extranarratively is easily linked in the mind of the sympathetic reader to an earlier unpunished instance of sexual aggression. Luring Ruth Welch, a young white Northern woman, into a secluded part of the woods by preying on her sympathy, Moses emerges from the bushes with an intent no contemporary reader could have mistaken: "After regarding her a moment silently, the negro began to move slowly forward, bowing and halting with that peculiar limp which always reminded Ruth of a species of worm. She would have fled; but she saw in an instant that there was no way of escape. . . . The same idea must have passed through the man's mind. A curious smirk was on his evil face" (358–359). When Ruth attempts to escape, Moses "gave a snarl of rage and sprang at her like a wild beast" (360). Providentially rescued by a stereotypically dashing Southern gentleman, the attempted rape remains figural (her skirt is torn); in the logic of *Red Rock*, however, the figural nature of interracial sexual violence is literally immaterial, as truth and assumption amount "almost to the same thing." As with most nineteenth-century writing about race, the invented anxiety over rape did not need to distinguish between fact and fiction.[54]

It is for his figural crime, which places all white women at risk, that Moses must die. To stress the impact of improperly understood ideals and principles, Page incorporates two accounts of the execution, neatly recapitulating the differences between Northern and Southern racial attitudes that the novel lengthily depicts:

> The press of one side stated that he confessed not only the terrible crime for which he was hanged, but, in addition, several others sufficiently heinous to entitle him to be classed as one of the greatest scoundrels in the world. The other side asserted that he was a physician of standing, who had at one time enjoyed a large practice in another State, from which he had been run out by the bands of masked desperadoes who had terrorized that section. In proof, it declared that "he died calling on all present to meet him in heaven." As both sides, however, concurred in giving his name as Moses—, and his former domicile as Red Rock, we have some ground for supposing that "Dr. Moses," as Andy Stamper said, at last came to the end of the rope. (584)

Although "newspapers were culturally positioned ... as the arbiter of meaning in daily life," Page resists this understanding of their role, insisting instead on their persistent ideological bias: no "consensus of meaning" can be generated from these accounts beyond a mere nominal accuracy, which is itself unreliable.[55] The combination of social and political tension, reportorial narrative, black male sexuality, and the unavenged attack on Ruth Welch requires for Page the inclusion of what might otherwise seem like inappropriate violence in the closing nuptial chapter of a sentimental novel. Moses' continued existence would threaten not only the future bliss of the newlyweds but also the sanctity of the marital bed and the sanity of the region's white men. While Moses lives, no one can live happily ever after. The narratives of racial violence bracketing *Red Rock* reiterate Page's basic contention—traditional or local knowledge about race relations yields more accurate information than do abstract, or national, standards. Having provided justification within the novel to warrant the execution, the inclusion of the two newspaper accounts both validates Southern treatment of African Americans and stresses the inaccuracy of Northern narratives that claim to be truthful.

In Page's analysis, the Southerner's problem is located in the black body, a scenario that warrants the physical measures whites take to protect their bodies, female and male, from attack. Lynching, as Michael Hatt has argued, provides

> a concrete argument that cuts the Gordian knot of legal, moral, and political debate, and asserts a unified constituency of whiteness, providing no space for any objection or expression of disapproval or outrage.... Discontent, hatred and dissatisfaction could be projected on the black body, which would then be dismembered, and the reification of the black endorsed a sense of self for the white crowd, as if whiteness and subjecthood were synonymous.

A "refusal of black subjectivity," lynching also offers the necessary context for appreciating Royce's strategy of countering prejudice and sympathy with loyalty.[56] In Hatt's analysis, the "literally objectified black" is evident only at lynching spectacles and in other manifestations of hatred; in other contexts, like antilynching tracts, for example, he reads the black body as making meaning differently. Presupposing a simple opposition of responses—sympathy or fear—Hatt assumes that an image of a mutilated black body would generate disgust, motivating the reader to action. Yet if Josiah Royce is correct, even the most progressive depictions of the black body—narrative or graphic—perpetuate the system of assumptions and stereotypes that permitted its mutilation in the first place.[57] As Barbara Johnson reminds us, the stereotype is "an already-read text," resistant to attempts to rewrite its associations or implications.[58]

Because American slaves suffered horrible physical abuses, abolitionist narratives regularly incorporated affecting depictions of the black body exposed as helpless and vulnerable through the violence of slavery.[59] Yet even as they attempted to establish the humanity of African Americans enduring unspeakable torments, these narratives relied upon and perpetuated the logic of essentialism crucial to the very structure of American slavery itself, deadening readers' sensibilities through regular repetition. Antebellum reformers, fearful that they were exposing themselves to charges of perversion, "filled their writings with close descriptions of their own immediate emotional response to the spectacle of suffering, to demonstrate that their sensibilities remained undamaged."[60] To the extent that they were successful in moving white readers, then, these writers partially undermined their own long-term goals, perpetuating the idea of the black body as a site marked for physical response. Indeed, the restrictive embodiment of the black individual hampered nineteenth-century attempts to construct an image of African Americans as anything more than a physical presence, alternately menacing and abject. Rather than liberating their bodies, in other words, the pornographic dimension of these narrative strategies reified African Americans—either as subject or object—enabling the continuation of racial prejudices and impacting even individuals direly opposed to the practice of slavery. As Elizabeth Clark has made clear, "the expectations set up by formulaic or didactic storytelling" "enhanced the 'stability' (or, fixed the meaning) of the representations of slaves in pain." Dependent on a specific cultural context, these static representations were vulnerable to "unsympathetic emotions like sadistic pleasure or contempt."[61] "How does one give expression to these outrages," Saidiya Hartman rightly wonders, "without exacerbating the indifference to suffering that is the consequence of the benumbing spectacle or contend with the narcissistic identification that obliterates the other or the prurience that too often is the response to such displays?"[62] It is certainly hard to imagine what other strategies might have been available to abolitionists and other antebellum authors, but part of the legacy these moving images bequeathed to postbellum reformers was the perpetuation of a narrative dimension of slave culture into the language of a purportedly free United States.

What makes Royce's intervention so valuable is the deft and thoughtful manner in which he circumvents these images, figures whose culturally overdetermined status thwarted the very changes he hoped to encourage.[63] Although necessary to moral behavior, our instincts to benevolence go entirely astray when not kept in careful check by the plans of reason, Royce explains in 1893. "Do not be merely suggestible, imitative, sympathetic, plastic," Royce enjoins, "you cannot please everybody. Mere kindliness and plasticity accomplish nothing."[64] Installing an abstract concept between the imitative and reasoning faculties facilitates more thoughtful, indeed more ethical, behavior. In thus circumscribing the meaning of plasticity, Royce is likely responding to the work of his Harvard colleague William James, who had recently argued for the organic importance of plasticity in the development of habit. As opposed to James's association of "plasticity" with the physical body (its "nervous tissue" and other organic materials), Royce uses the term as a function of character. The different models of thinking about human behavior overlap, particularly in the ways in which they suggest that plasticity diminishes the individual's ability to attend to the world, but Royce's use of "plasticity" resists the embodiment that characterizes James's use of the word.[65] When sympathy is understood as mere suggestibility or plasticity, he asserts, it lacks the rigor to function as an effective moral guide. Linking benevolence, altruism, and sympathy in the *Philosophy of Loyalty*, Royce notes that, while important, these are "mere fragments of goodness, mere aspects of the dutiful life" (102). Nonetheless, despite its virtues, abstraction is repeatedly, and perhaps inevitably, discounted because it seems to disregard the specifics of the human condition. What it is important to remember, philosopher Onora O'Neill posits, is that "abstraction . . . is a matter of selective omission, of leaving out some predicates from descriptions and theories. . . . It is unavoidable . . . [and] needed if we are to reason in ways that can be taken seriously by others who disagree with us. By abstracting we may succeed in reasoning in ways that are detachable from commitment to the full detail of our own beliefs."[66] Without abstraction, in other words, we cannot reason outside our beliefs—good and bad. What is strange, O'Neill concludes, is that abstraction has been so frequently criticized given what is for her, and for Royce before her, its evident contribution. Indeed, were we not able to omit things, our lives would be intolerable, James asserts from a different place on the philosophical spectrum. The important issue, then, is not *that* we omit or ignore things, but how we understand or theorize these omissions. Put differently, just as the distinction between sympathy and loyalty (or between kinds of sympathy) depends more on matters of emphasis than on fundamentally different structures, so too is the purported dichotomy between the general or abstract and the particular often less fixed than our critical assumptions and paradigms contend.

Concentrating his intellectual energies on the "theoretical aspects of the problem," on refiguring "body" and "race," Royce elides *bodies* in his discussion of race prejudice (286). As members of the human race, we share common responses, instinctive emotions; the only race that matters in this construct, Royce concludes, is the one that unites us in our petty differences as well as our sublime similarities. Resisting the tendency to turn events, particularly those for which we have socially endorsed narratives, into spectacles, Royce's lecture avoids the trope of the black body, circumventing any material impediments to the acceptance of his perspective, in the hopes of reestablishing its presence without the deformation of social assumption. Manipulating emotion, or the lack thereof, as masterfully as the rabble-rousing Page, Royce provides the conditions of possibility for installing loyalty and its narratives in the place of sympathy's familiar sob stories.

Rebutting Thomas Nelson Page, Royce observes that responsibility, not degradation, breeds respect for the law, providing a practical rather than a "Utopian" solution. "When now I hear the complaint of the Southerner," he notes, "I now feel disposed to say: 'The problem that endangers the sanctity of your homes and that is said sometimes to make lynching a necessity, is not a race-problem. It is an administrative problem'" (276). Royce might sound dismissive here of the scale of the dilemma, but his emphasis on administration is meant to indicate that Southern whites have put in place institutions, broadly understood, that define lynching as an appropriate response to a problem those very institutions create. Changes to the organization, and articulation, of institutional power would reduce the need for such a violent response. Yet for Royce, as for members of the Supreme Court, political intervention would not resolve the situation, as he explains in his extended dismissal of the white Southerner. "Hence when various social conditions, amongst which is the habit of irritating public speech about race-questions is indeed one, though only one condition, have tended to the producing, and to the arousing of extremely dangerous criminals in your communities, you have no adequate means of guarding against the danger" (276). Although it is "only one condition" among a host of purposefully exacerbated problems, Royce singles out the material consequences and implications of speech. Not only does the content of Royce's talk underscore the possibility that language creates the world we inhabit, his address to an imagined white interlocutor shifts the problem from the black to the white body. In a rhetorical gesture that includes his own white body, Royce observes that it is easy to locate a justification for an untenably essentializing position in the superficial or accidental details of an individual's appearance: "In estimating, in dealing with races, in defining what their supposedly unchangeable characteristics are, in planning what to do with them, we are all prone to confuse the accidental with the essential. We are likely to take for an essential race-characteristic what is a transient incident, or a product of special social conditions" (277).[67]

Only in "pass[ing] to a somewhat wider view," dealing with the problem "a little more generally," can the way to a solution be found (277). Royce's final answer to the American race problem is located in appreciating the vast difference between race and "Race." Because we use these terms so vaguely, "almost any national or political or religious barrier, if it is old enough, may lead to a consciousness of difference of race" (278). With this point, Royce identifies the core of the problem: nationality is too easily conflated with race. What we need, then, is something less contingent about humanity upon which to base the evaluations and comparisons that seem intrinsic to our engagements with the world. Although it would certainly be hard to argue that as terms they are more specific than "Race," for Royce the concepts of mind and soul offer this enduring foundation. The very immateriality of mind and soul, in marked contrast to the materiality of the nineteenth-century brain and body, creates for Royce the potential for substantive change in the ethical world. Having established a "Race" without a body, akin to the corporate entity Walter Benn Michaels examines in *The Gold Standard and the Logic of Naturalism*, Royce can conceive of a social world consisting of loyalty, dignity, and respect.

Unless it is generalized, recognized in its fully figural dimensions, Royce concludes the figure of the body interrupts ethical human interaction. Extracting the "souls of men" from "the influences of culture," we discover that people are more difficult to classify than variations in hair or skin color lead us to believe (281). Although he does not make the connection in "Race Questions and Prejudices," Royce will eventually link his thought to the Pauline metaphor of the communal body in *The Problem of Christianity* (1913). In its preface, Royce notes that "since 1908, [his] 'philosophy of loyalty' [had] been growing."[68] Examining contemporary social ills, in other words, inspired Royce fully to rethink the implications of the body and its relationship to the notion of community. What results from his engagement with social problems, then, is "a consistent body of ethical as well as religious opinion and teaching" that he contends "concern[s] the central life-problems of all of us."[69]

"Royce's commitment to the priority of the social to the 'community of interpretation' as a 'corporate entity' 'more concrete' than 'any individual,' was virtually lifelong," Walter Benn Michaels observes.[70] Through local communities predicated on shared yet flexible structures of interpretation, we can generate intimacy and social cohesion. When interpretation becomes dogmatic and rigid and communities degenerate into sections, its power can also mar what for Royce is most valuable about being human. Sadly, the true lesson to be learned from racial prejudice is the extent to which our abilities to interpret are derailed by overdetermined figures.

Dead men not only tell no tales; they also, strange to say, attend no schools, and learn no lessons. And hereby they prove themselves in the eyes of certain students of race-questions to have been always of a much lower mental type than the cultivated men who killed them. Their surviving descendants, if sufficiently provided with the means of corruption, and if sufficiently down-trodden, may remain thenceforth models of degradation. For man, whatever his race, is an animal that you unquestionably can debase to whatever level you please, if you only have power, and if you then begin early enough, and devote yourself persistently enough to the noble and civilized task of proving him to be debased. (43)[71]

With thick irony and second-person pronoun, Royce assigns responsibility for the race problem to each of his white auditors and readers. Every day we organize our world in various ways, through the "tales" we "tell" and the "lessons" we both learn and teach. Through these processes, many of which we construct as objective, we disseminate our opinions and beliefs; when we commit ourselves to the imperative "Be loyal to loyalty," seemingly intractable social problems become easier to negotiate.

* * *

At the beginning of the chapter I cited W. E. B. Du Bois's famous line from *The Souls of Black Folk*—"The problem of the twentieth century is the problem of the color-line"; as its conclusion, I turn briefly to Du Bois, juxtaposing his interest in *Souls* with the one Royce pursues via loyalty. Rather than look at Du Bois's famous work however, I consider the 1909 biography *John Brown*. Not only does this work contribute substantially to the investigation of personal and national loyalty undertaken throughout this study, it also represents an alternate means of engaging with a disembodied understanding of loyalty. Indeed, as Du Bois's interest in history establishes, some dead men can tell tales, but only if the conditions of possibility for reading their lives are put in place.

Scholars have traditionally pointed to William James as Du Bois's mentor, and rightly so, but Royce was also crucial to his intellectual development at Harvard. "I reveled in the keen analysis of William James, Josiah Royce and young George Santayana," Du Bois writes in his autobiography, "but it was James with his pragmatism and Albert Bushnell Hart with his research method, that turned me back from the lovely but sterile land of philosophic speculation, to the social sciences."[72] Du Bois mentions Royce several times in the pages on his time at Harvard, although it is the time when he does *not* mention the philosopher that is most interesting for understanding *John Brown*, as well as Royce's "Race Questions and Prejudices." As a first-year student, Du Bois was required to take a course in composition. "I was at the point in my intellectual development when the content rather than the form of my writing was to me of prime importance," Du Bois explains:

> Words and ideas surged in my mind and spilled out with disregard of exact accuracy in grammar, taste in word or restraint in style. I knew the Negro problem and this was more important to me than literary form. I knew grammar fairly well, and I had a pretty wide vocabulary; but I was bitter, angry and intemperate in my first thesis. Naturally my English instructors had no idea of nor interest in the way in which Southern attacks on the Negro were scratching me on the raw flesh.

The essay Du Bois produced was judged "'E'—not passed" by his instructors and it was, he notes, "the first time in [his] scholastic career that [he] had encountered such a failure." This episode is important because the professor for Du Bois's course was Josiah Royce, aided by Ernest L. Conant and George P. Baker Jr. (any one of whom could have been responsible for grading Du Bois's work). As the *Autobiography* makes clear, however, Du Bois took away from this experience a critical lesson: "I realized that while style is subordinate to content, and that no real literature can be composed simply of meticulous and fastidious phrases, nevertheless that solid content with literary style carries a message further than poor grammar and muddled syntax."[73] The emphasis on style anticipates, although in a markedly different register, Royce's eventual argument about the formal problems of embodiment in the discussion of race in the United States. Given that Du Bois would have been Royce's student *before* the composition of "Race Questions and Prejudices," it does not seem a huge leap to consider that the philosopher's experience with this brilliant student might have influenced the development of the argument in that essay.

Like Dunbar and Chesnutt, Du Bois is carefully attuned to the implications of the Civil War for black Americans, a topic to which he returns repeatedly throughout his career, from *The Philadelphia Negro: A Social Study* (1899) to *Black Reconstruction in America* (1935). What is interesting about *John Brown*, however, is Du Bois's decision to focus on a white rather than a black man. Defending this choice in the preface, he explains that Brown is "the man who of all Americans has perhaps come nearest to touching the real souls of black folk" (xxv).[74] Although, as he alerts the reader, his biography of John Brown will not offer any new information or "special material" on his subject's life, Du Bois explains that it is his interpretation—his "view-point"—that distinguishes his work from the numerous other volumes available.[75] What emerges from his perspective, he explains, is a deep sense of the "great broad truths" of the impact of Brown's life on the "development of the Negro American" (xxv). The clear reference back to his own *The Souls of Black Folk*, especially as modified by the adjective "real," suggests that *John Brown*, like Du Bois's previous work, will continue the project of "foregrounding . . . history and mediated subjectivity against the grain of American ahistoricisms of various kinds."[76] That is to say, *John Brown* joins *Souls* in posing questions concerning historical necessity, ethical possibility, and heroic vitalism; it diverges from his earlier masterpiece, however, in confronting the role of violence more directly. Neither as positivistic as *The Philadelphia Negro* nor as lyrical as *The Souls of Black Folk*, *John Brown* offers a meditation on the ways in which the individual engages with his or her historical moment. As he tells the tale of Brown's life, Du Bois does even more than offer this new "view-point," for he also shows the ease with which seemingly good people can become complicit with immoral goals, and the dangers to moral philosophy and the rule of law that ensue.[77] As Du Bois meditates on the value of danger, attempting to distinguish between the ongoing costs of complicity and the economic and moral benefits of integrity, he argues for the philosophical value of history as a means of clarifying ethical ambiguities, once that history has been stripped from the romance and prejudice that obscure its lessons.[78] Here we have, in other words, a vision of history that resists, with Royce, the lure of embodied assumption or prejudice.

A brief glance forward to the fiftieth-anniversary celebrations of the Civil War confirms the importance of new "view-point" Du Bois brings to the life of John Brown and that would also inform his masterful *Black Reconstruction in America* (1935). The memorial activities between 1911 and 1914 confirmed that the history and memory of the Civil War had been wholly captured by romance and myth. White valor had effectively and efficiently sanitized battle, converting its horrors into a glorious narrative of noble action. This packaging "provided the crucial link between the antebellum plantation ideal and the postbellum era" as it shifted the "tragedy for both southern and northern whites from the war itself and their sectional animosity to Reconstruction and the setting of blacks over southern whites."[79] Disrupting the natural order of things (as it had existed on the plantation) had been the cause of all subsequent troubles and justified the institution of legal guarantees that such mistakes could not be reenacted—although no harm could come from reenacting moments of great battles, like Pickett's charge, in 1913. This is the broader cultural context for *John Brown*. Not only does Du Bois join Dunbar in rejecting the regular assertion that cross-racial identification was unnatural, but his economic focus returns the plantation past to history by reminding readers of its economic realities. What is most important, however, is Du Bois's argument about allegiance and causes. Loyalty is important, he maintains, but only in its critical aspect. Without actually quoting Emerson, Du Bois concludes that, when it comes to allegiance, "a foolish consistency is the hobgoblin of little minds, adored by little statesmen and philosophers and divines."[80] As had Emerson before him, Du Bois urges his readers to eschew conformity and question fixed wisdom about the content and requirements of personal morality and national commitment.[81]

John Brown effectively demonstrates Du Bois's sense that history needed to take ethical standards into consideration, rather than hiding behind a false sense of moral objectivity. In the closing chapter of *Black Reconstruction in America*, entitled "The Propaganda of History," Du Bois writes, "If history is going to be scientific, if the record of human action is going to be set down with the accuracy and faithfulness of detail which will allow its use as a measuring rod and guidepost for the future of nations, there must be set some standards of ethics in research and interpretation."[82] The example to which he points is American slavery. "It was morally wrong and economically retrogressive to build human slavery," he observes, and yet "our histories tend to discuss American slavery so impartially, that in the end nobody seems to have done wrong and everybody was right" (714). Attempts to identify moral responsibility—as when Du Bois insists that an entry in the *Encyclopedia Britannica* read "White historians have ascribed the faults and failures of Reconstruction to Negro ignorance and corruption. But the Negro insists that it was Negro loyalty and the Negro vote alone that restored the South to the Union; established the new democracy, both for white and black, and instituted the public schools"—are met with polite, but absolute, resistance (713). On Du Bois's view, it is first necessary to "make clear the facts" separate from any individual "wish and desire and belief" and only after they have been established is interpretation either possible or desirable. "We have spoiled and misconceived the position of the historian," Du Bois concludes, drawing a basic distinction between chronicling events and interpreting the past, an act he links with philosophy, prophesy, and science. "One is astonished in the study of history at the recurrence of the idea that evil must be forgotten, distorted, skimmed over.... The difficulty, of course, with this philosophy is that history loses its value as an incentive and example; it paints perfect men and noble nations, but it does not tell the truth" (722). This "paradoxical combination of objectivity and activism, detachment and engagement" helps to explain how Du Bois could claim that, without offering any new materials, his biography could nonetheless provide a new "view-point" on the subject.[83]

The early pages of the biography chart Brown's economic life story, presenting him as a man who could have fulfilled the stereotypical narrative of the self-made man but becomes, instead, the more illusive and important American: the moral man. After a very brief discussion of Brown's solitary childhood, Du Bois quickly moves to Brown's early life as husband, father, and worker, a period he admits "puzzles the casual onlooker with its seemingly aimless changing character, its wandering restlessness, its planless wavering." Brown worked variously as a surveyor, tanner, lumber dealer, postmaster, wool grower, shepherd, and farmer in equally various places; Du Bois nonetheless finds in this array "certain great currents of growth, purpose, and action" (14). Not only are these "currents" manifested in Brown's many children, they seem also to be demonstrated in his eventual prosperity—and his eventual ruin. Insisting upon fair practices, on determining the price of wool according to its value rather than the market, Brown refused, according to a fellow merchant, to play by the rules of the game. "Why? The ordinary answer of current business ethics would be that John Brown was unable to 'corner' the wool market against the manufacturers. But this he never tried to do. Such a policy of financial free-booting never occurred to him, and he would have repelled it indignantly if it had." This refusal, Du Bois explains, drove Brown out of the business because he was confronted with "one of those strange economic paradoxes which bring great moral questions into the economic realm." These are "questions which we evaded yesterday and are trying to evade to-day, but which we must answer to-morrow" (32).

As he conjoins "great moral questions" and economic practice, Du Bois suggests that one solution available would be to form an organization, "like the Middle-Age Hanse." Yet even as Du Bois locates Brown in his specific historical context, he gestures toward an explanation that transcends specific nineteenth-century practice in his reference to a "battle" between "two industrial armies" (33). It is easy to find in this passage evidence of the Hegelian influence on Du Bois's philosophy of history, but Hegel only gives a limited explanation of Du Bois's aims in

John Brown. As interested as Du Bois is in the philosophy of history, the biography of John Brown is focused on understanding how material conditions correlate to moral action. Consequently, many of the anecdotes included in these early chapters of the biography illustrate how the kind of ambition measured by money or things, the valued associated with the American self-made man, *impedes* moral action, a failing to which even the best of men are liable, as Du Bois demonstrates by including a lengthy passage from Frederick Douglass's 1892 *Life and Times*. Douglass recalls that Brown was, at the time, "a respectable merchant in a populous and thriving city." Their first meeting took place at his store, "a substantial brick building on a prominent, busy street" that "gave [Douglass] the impression that the owner must be a man of considerable wealth" (56). About Brown's home, however, Douglass finds less to praise: "I was, however, a little disappointed with the appearance of the house and its location. After seeing the fine store I was prepared to see a fine residence in an eligible locality, but this conclusion was completely dispelled by actual observation. In fact, the house was neither commodious nor elegant, nor its situation desirable" (56–57). In the context of Du Bois's narrative, Douglass moves slowly to the realization that the appearance of wealth is less important than the reality of principle. He eventually concludes that "everything implied stern truth, solid purpose, and rigid economy," but not before noting the simple, even rough, fare on offer in Brown's inelegant home (57). Perhaps because Douglass is praised early in the text for his extraordinary efforts, he is useful in this instance as an example of the kinds of moral positions with which we all too easily become complicit. The passage Du Bois includes underscores the superficiality of Douglass's values when compared to Brown's moral commitment. What this Douglass interlude establishes, in short, is Du Bois's belief that our priorities are truly impoverished when we assume that accounting for character is a matter of money.[84]

Having established Brown's financial profile, then, Du Bois begins the narrative anew, shifting focus. "There was hell in Haiti," he writes, "in the red waning of the eighteenth century, in the days when John Brown was born." "John Brown was born just as the shudder of Haiti was running through all the Americas, and from his earliest boyhood he saw and felt the price of repression—the fearful cost that the western world was paying for slavery" (40). As he urges his readers to consider what actually counts as a cost, and what economizing should mean in moral terms, Du Bois continues to link the moral problem of slavery to financial issues, even as he moves away from the generic parameters of the story of the self-made man. In Brown's case, as Du Bois has already demonstrated, the story of self-making exceeds monetary concerns, as becoming who he needs to be is a matter of weaning himself (and his family) from material comfort. The work's structure, thus, consistently relies on repetition, retelling, and reexamining issues. This redundancy serves not only to complicate the story but also demonstrates a claim Du Bois makes about how purpose and commitment evolve: "Human purposes grow slowly and in curious ways; thought by thought they build themselves until in their full panoplied vigor and definite outline not even the thinker can tell the exact process of the growing, or say that here was the beginning or there the ending. Nor does this slow growth and fathering make the end less wonderful or the motive less praiseworthy" (51). This passage is strange, especially its suggestion that "human purposes" "build themselves" in a seemingly impersonal and directionless way, but even more so in the context of one of Du Bois's goals in the biography—the exposition of a theory of agency, personal responsibility, and individual integrity. This is a work that places the potential for extraordinary action with the very ordinary individual; it is not birth or fortune or talent that makes a person a force for change in *John Brown*, it is rather careful economy, serious reflection, and ever-growing commitment to a simple moral principle. The combination of many different individual thoughts and choices will lead, eventually, to a "wonderful" and "praiseworthy" end, a message that locates the power for change and action quite specifically in the everyday (even as it mystifies its formation).

In writing the life of John Brown, Du Bois was writing as much about a symbol as an individual, allowing him to consider, more broadly, the use, and abuse, of national icons and historical narratives. Too often when we look to the past, Du Bois suggests, we see former ideals and achievements as no longer within our grasp: the past seems to have been a time without price, while the present is cheap and debased. By reshaping the moral economy of Brown's development, Du Bois opens the possibility of individual excellence to readers who might lack the commitment to literally strike a blow for justice but who can surely save a penny.

Du Bois adapts the standard celebration of martial heroism to recall rather than repress the causes of the Civil War. Agreeing with Theodore Roosevelt, Du Bois acknowledges the war's "material results," but whereas Roosevelt would claim that "we [American citizens] are all, North and South, incalculably richer for its memories," Du Bois asks his readers to consider carefully what they do with the riches of tradition and memory. According to the elaborate rituals and memorial practices that had evolved to honor the veterans of the Civil War, which regularly observed that theirs was a generation apart, men had fought and died for their ideals and principles in a time not debased by the vulgar materialism of the late nineteenth century. Du Bois's *John Brown* comments variously on this tradition. First, Du Bois unsettles the clear black and white binary of racial difference that had increasingly taken hold of American cultural assumptions and practices. Not only does the text begin with the close association of Africa and America (its opening sentence reads, "The mystic spell of Africa is and ever was over all America" [3]), but it repeatedly indicates Brown's respect for the situation and character of African Americans. Further, Du Bois manipulates the normative cues associated with skin color, as when he stresses that Brown blanches in horror and anger at moral wrongs or that the color of his ideas tinge Douglass's own. These little destabilizing moments make the visual markers of race more fluid and less reliable throughout the text. In *John Brown*, heroism is not exclusively a white trait, since black and white flow into one another across the story of Brown's life.

Du Bois's biography thus works to correct the historical narrative Dunbar ironizes in *The Fanatics*, offering a different interpretation of the nation's ongoing interest in the relationship between past and future. Unlike Chesnutt and Dunbar, Du Bois studiously avoids all sentimentalized nostalgia about the Old South. Instead of an ironic view on these romantic fictions and the easy amnesia they encouraged, Du Bois offers economics. "The decade 1830 to 1840 was one of the severest seasons of trial through which the black American ever passed," he argues, because "the great economic change which made the slavery the corner-stone of the cotton kingdom was definitely finished and all the subtle moral adjustments which follow were in full action" (139). In the place of plantations, or even representations of rural farm life, Du Bois details the rise of restrictive Black Laws (including the fines imposed on offenders) and the attempts by various activists (again including their financial arrangements) to counter such measures. As in the early chapters, this emphasis on the profits and costs of the slave system points to the close association between money and morals in American attitudes toward race and slavery. Whereas plantation fiction worked to disguise the economics of slavery under romance and references to a lost, chivalric age, Du Bois's emphasis exposes the moral poverty of this brand of sentimentality, as well as its real costs to the nation, by defining heroism as resistance to fiction and fantasy.

In its 1909 form, *John Brown* ended with a chapter entitled "The Riddle of the Sphinx." Beginning with a series of questions, this chapter lengthily argues for a relatively simple claim: "John Brown was right." Nonetheless, Du Bois's questions encourage his readers to interrogate their own principles and commitments, asking them to consider the dilemmas that confronted residents of the United States in the 1850s: "When a prophet like John Brown appears, how must we of the world receive him? Must we follow out the drear, dread logic of surrounding facts, as did the South, even if they crucify a clean and pure soul, simply because consistent allegiance to our cherished, chosen ideal demands it? . . . If we are human, we must thus hesitate until we know the right" (202). Here again we find the real dilemma of "consistent allegiance"; which events, facts, or "cherished ideals" warrant our allegiance and which do not? For Du Bois, this is the question the moral human being must "hesitate" over until "the right" becomes clear. "How shall we know it?" he asks (202).

The provisional answer to this question has to do with the problematic temporality of agency. It is easy enough to point to the past and show that someone has acted well (or not so well)—although as Du Bois shows throughout *John Brown*, this easy enough task is still very hard. But it is harder to motivate action in the future, unless one flattens complexity into a simple formula, removing doubt and thought and choice from the issue. This is clearly not a desirable model for the kind of agency that Du Bois wants to encourage. In short, agency shares structural similarities to performative speech in its deferral of evaluation and certainty. For Du Bois, it is clear that certainty about "the right" is possible, although difficult to reach. On the way to this ideal, however, we can tell and retell stories that force us to "hesitate," we can wander (seemingly aimlessly) and refine our beliefs, and we can continue to challenge them until the time when we can know for certain what is right and what is wrong. That we should pick a "cherished, chosen ideal" seems to be one of the points of *John Brown*, but our ongoing human responsibility is the consideration of whether it warrants our "consistent allegiance." What we learn from *John Brown*, finally, is that the extraordinary is not so very different from the ordinary; that commitment to principles and ideals is available to us all if, and this is where things become more difficult, we resist the lure of money and things and, sounding much like Whitman, the comfort of consistency. Du Bois shows his readers how the Brown family weaned itself from such distractions, a process that is neither easy nor instantaneous, in order to adopt an ethical posture in the world. In the end, the "broad truths" that Du Bois finds in the life of John Brown are not particular to any particular subset of Americans; they are, instead, applicable to us all.

Afterword

There is no denying that the Civil War was a pivotal moment in American history. Emancipation and national consolidation, important discoveries in medicine and technology, the reorganization of economic practices, and the institution of the income tax, to name only a few, all date from the war. As a literary scholar, I might add to this list the rise of realism as the dominant literary genre in the later nineteenth century. As Henry James notes in *Hawthorne* (1879): "The subsidence of that great convulsion has left a different tone from the tone it found and one may say that the Civil War marks an era in the history of the American mind. It introduced into the national consciousness a certain sense of proportion and relation, of the world being a more complicated place than it had hitherto seemed, the future more treacherous, success more difficult." Having "eaten from the tree of knowledge," the "good American" will henceforth be, James concludes, "an observer."[1]

That it is James's own writings that will satisfy the needs of the "good American" troubles his assertion, however, as does the fact that it is articulated in a volume in which he wrestles with the legacy of his important predecessor, Nathaniel Hawthorne. Were we to generalize the above skepticism, we might ask, as well, what other needs are served by drawing sharp distinctions between the "tone" of pre- and postwar America? What is at stake in our fascination, as potent now as it was on the eve of its centennial when Frank Sullivan wondered about the implications of "America's most popular war"?[2]

As I hope this book has demonstrated, the idea that the Civil War fundamentally altered "the national consciousness" justified, at least in part, the incredible sacrifices made by men and women in both sections. Lives were not lost or ruined without purpose but were instead integral to the perfection of the nation, itself worthy of such extraordinary offerings. Associated with the reading of the war as a sublime purification of the United States (which becomes, in its wake, a singular, rather than a plural, noun) is the idea that the Civil War resists representation, that its period was one in which literature did not flourish, to paraphrase Edmund Wilson.[3] On this view, because many of the authors who have risen to importance—Henry James, William Dean Howells, Mark Twain, Henry Adams—did not experience combat (or, in the case of Twain, did not experience combat for long), there was little worth studying from the period. Even as changing scholarly priorities and paradigms have reorganized the ways in which scholars engage with literary materials, however, the assumptions that excluded texts written by people of color or by women, no longer operative, seem to obtain. As Alice Fahs has convincingly demonstrated across *The Imagined Civil War*, the war bequeathed a legacy of literary production that has yet to generate sustained interest among literary scholars.

Institutional organization also explains why the Civil War is regularly overlooked by nineteenth-century literary critics. Dividing the century at 1865, as we usually do, has had the unintended consequence of removing the Civil War almost entirely from view for scholars and students alike. While recent critical efforts, upon which this study has most profitably drawn, have focused a new light on the war's effects, it remains the case that the 1860s, perhaps like the 1930s, function as a lost decade, neither here nor there, not yet realism but no longer romance, to draw on one of the distinctions associated with the narrative of rupture. This structural practice has had the effect, further, of exacerbating our understanding of the break introduced by the war, which did not end as quickly or as cleanly as is often assumed.

Nonetheless, given the willingness of scholars to recognize the ways in which American literature is constituted by alternate configurations of spatial influence—represented by interest in, for example, the Atlantic world, transnational, multinational, or hemispheric interventions—lingering resistance to rethinking the ways in which historical models shape what we think we know about the nation and its culture are somewhat surprising. The funny thing about the Civil War is that, at the same time that it has provided an object of elaborate fetishized historical scrutiny, it is also treated as somewhat mythical, a time that resists the realities of historical fact, a strange claim to make about the event that is said to have created the conditions of possibility for realism.

This devotional attitude toward the war is, of course, a mode of interpretation, dependent in part on determined civic hagiography that brought about the apotheosis of Lincoln, Lee, and Jackson (to name only the most obvious); Lost Cause ideology, nationalized far more effectively than loyalty; and the persistent racism reconstructed with the nation. Committed to the rise of realism, the ways in which these cultural forces fueled an ongoing affective relationship to the nation have been overlooked. If the end of the Cold War marked the end of history, in Francis Fukuyama's provocative phrase, the Civil War has been situated, inadvertently or not, as *before* history, as the mythic origin of the modern American nation. Unable to duplicate, or even adequately narrate, the reality of the Civil War (not to mention the fact that at the time of its centennial, there was not consensus about the war's name), we have chosen instead to accept its fables of unparalleled heroism. This is not to suggest that the soldiers who fought in the war were not heroic, of course, but rather that we ratify the racist assumptions that motivate the narratives of reunion, detailed in chapters 2 and 3, when we refuse to recognize that there are nontrivial differences in the motivations of our actions.

What would American literary history look like if we were to assume that the Civil War is woven into the fabric of the nation's narrative, rather than an absolute rupture of it? That the war is linked importantly, but not inevitably, to events in the 1830s, 1840s, and 1850s? Or that Reconstruction, despite its radical potential and transformative ideas, was, for many, a period of deep longing for structures and assumptions dating from the prewar decades? How would our understanding of the narrative of revolution change were we to align the American Civil War, as Michael Rogin does, with the European upheavals clustered around 1848? Returning the Civil War to the story of the American literary experience, locating it in a continuum of events from the nullification crisis in 1832 to the "end" of Reconstruction in 1877 would generate a different narrative of the war, as well as a different sense of the narrative changes it did, or did not, introduce. So considered, we would be able to see the Civil War era as involving not just the North and South but the West as well. We also might be able to see how this brief interlude influenced both a jump toward the future and a yearning, sometimes fierce, for continuity with the past.

The Civil War has tended, in other words, to authorize a "new birth" of American exceptionalism as well as freedom; were we to strip the Civil War of this rhetoric of exceptionalism, still so central to our national self-conception, not only would a very different picture of the nineteenth century emerge, so too would a new understanding of how to correlate the conventions variously associated with realism and sentimentality.

Notes

Introduction: Pledging Allegiance

1. For estimated participation figures, see Richard J. Ellis, *To the Flag: The Unlikely History of the Pledge of Allegiance* (Lawrence: University of Kansas Press, 2005), 21–23, 229n.51. See also Robert Rydell, *All the World's a Fair: Visions of Empire at American International Expositions, 1876–1916* (Chicago: University of Chicago Press, 1984); David Burg, *Chicago's White City of 1893* (Lexington: University of Kentucky Press, 1976); Reid Badger, *The Great American Fair: The World's Columbian Exposition and American Culture* (n.p.: N. Hall, 1979); on the legacy of Columbus in American culture, see Thomas Schlereth, "Columbia, Columbus, and Columbianism," *Journal of American History* 79 (December 1992): 937–968.

2. Clara Kirk, *W. D. Howells, Traveler from Altruria, 1889–1894* (New Brunswick, N.J.: Rutgers University Press, 1962), 104.

3. Ellis, *To the Flag*, 19, 210.

4. "National School Celebration of Columbus Day: The Official Programme," *Youth's Companion* 65 (September 8, 1892), 446.

5. Julia Stern, *The Plight of Feeling: Sympathy and Dissent in the Early American Novel* (Chicago: University of Chicago Press, 1997), 7.

6. George B. Forgie, *Patricide in the House Divided: A Psychological Interpretation of Lincoln and His Age* (New York: Norton, 1981), 4.

7. Cited in Shirley Samuels, *Romances of the Republic: Women, the Family, and Violence in the Literature of the Early American Nation* (New York: Oxford University Press, 1996), 16.

8. Elizabeth Barnes, *States of Sympathy: Seduction and Democracy in the American Novel* (New York: Columbia University Press, 1997), 3; Stern, *Plight of Feeling*, 1–29.

9. Francis Bellamy, "The Tyranny of All the People," *Arena* 20 (July 1891): 181–182. Borrowing from European philosophy and influenced by homegrown beliefs in American exceptionalism and millennialism, Francis Lieber, Elisha Mulford, John

William Draper, and Orestes Brownson had all argued for an organic nation, spinning different conclusions about its destiny, possibilities, and limitations from this first principle. These ideas were, in part, precipitated by the rumblings in anticipation of the secession crisis, in response to which American thinkers displayed an increased "self-consciousness about nationhood," seeking to stave off Southern withdrawal from the constitutional compact (Dorothy Ross, "'Are We a Nation?': The Conjuncture of Nationhood and Race in the United States, 1850–1876," *Modern Intellectual History* [2005]: 327). While these thinkers vary as to the influence of Hegel, the depths of their Christian conviction, or their commitment to positivism, all four urged readers to recognize that the organic nation could not be dismembered without significant damage to the moral life and freedom of the individuals living inside its borders, because a "necessary inter-relation" abided between them (Elisha Mulford, *The Nation: The Foundations of Civil Order and Political Life in the United States* [New York: Hurd and Houghton, 1871], 61).

10. Bellamy, "Tyranny of All the People," 182. Bellamy, a Christian socialist, explicitly opposes his views to "the military type of socialism," preferring to focus on "democratic socialism," social and economic justice, and U.S. nationalism ("Tyranny of All the People," 181). Like his cousin Edward Bellamy, author of *Looking Backward* (1888), Bellamy's political philosophy identifies corporate identity as the key to personal satisfaction.

11. Ellis, *To the Flag*, 210.

12. Philip Fisher, *The Vehement Passions* (Cambridge, Mass.: Harvard University Press, 2002), 45.

13. Nor do I mean to suggest that sympathy and loyalty are the only ideals of affiliation available in the nineteenth century. Critics have begun the important work of identifying the multiple ways that Americans understood what it meant to form connections to one another; for one example, see Ivy Schweitzer, *Perfecting Friendship: Politics and Affiliation in Early American Literature* (Chapel Hill: University of North Carolina Press, 2006).

14. Laura Wexler makes a related point when she observes that postbellum photographs "reshaped [the] reservoir of literary sentiment into a conservative—indeed, aggressively imperialistic—idea of war as peace" (*Tender Violence: Domestic Visions in an Age of U.S. Imperialism* [Chapel Hill: University of North Carolina Press, 2000], 34).

15. Among the exceptions are Wexler, *Tender Violence*; Kristin Boudreau, *Sympathy in American Literature: American Sentiment from Jefferson to the Jameses* (Gainesville: University Press of Florida, 2002).

16. Lauren Berlant, *The Female Complaint: The Unfinished Business of Sentimentality in American Culture* (Durham, N.C.: Duke University Press, 2008).

17. Walt Whitman, *Complete Poetry and Collected Prose* (New York: Library of America, 1982), 778. For a reading of the Civil War that stresses its resistance to representation, see Daniel Aaron, *The Unwritten War: American Writers and the Civil War* (Madison: University of Wisconsin Press, 1987); Edmund Wilson, *Patriotic Gore: Studies in the Literature of the American Civil War* (New York: Norton, 1964).

18. In addition to Berlant, see Priscilla Wald, *Constituting Americans: Cultural Anxiety and Narrative Form* (Durham, N.C.: Duke University Press, 1995); Franny Nudelman, *John Brown's Body: Slavery, Violence, and the Culture of War* (Chapel Hill: University of North Carolina Press, 2004); Elizabeth Young, *Disarming the Nation:*

Women's Writing and the American Civil War (Chicago: University of Chicago Press, 1999); Gregory Eiselein, *Literature and Humanitarian Reform in the Civil War Era* (Bloomington: Indiana University Press, 1996).

19. Glenn Hendler, *Public Sentiments: Structures of Feeling in Nineteenth-Century American Literature* (Chapel Hill: University of North Carolina Press, 2001), 35.

20. The definition of loyalty developed during the Civil War differs substantially from recent understandings of the term, like the one Wendy Brown offers in "Political Idealization and Its Discontents" (in *Dissent in Dangerous Times*, ed. Austin Sarat [Ann Arbor: University of Michigan Press, 2005], 23–45). Drawing from Plato and Freud, Brown details a theory of loyalty dependent on "the extreme idealization of the state" that, like love, resists critique and dissent (ibid., 33). Because of the particular historical conditions operating for Union thinkers during the Civil War, loyalty for them had a different set of connotations and associations, although, as I explain below, they struggled on occasion with how to understand the affective dimension of loyalty.

21. George Fredrickson, *The Inner Civil War: Northern Intellectuals and the Crisis of the Union* (Urbana: University of Illinois Press, 1993), 1, 50, 132.

22. Alice Fahs, *The Imagined Civil War: Popular Literature of the North and South, 1861–1865* (Chapel Hill: University of North Carolina Press, 2001).

23. Melinda Lawson, *Patriot Fires: Forging a New American Nationalism in the Civil War* (Lawrence: University of Kansas Press, 2002), and David Blight, *Race and Reunion: The Civil War in American Memory* (Cambridge, Mass.: Belknap Press of Harvard University Press, 2001), are invaluable historical resources on this topic. As I was in the process of finishing this book, T. J. Jackson Lears's *The Rebirth of America: The Making of Modern America, 1877–1920* (New York: HarperCollins, 2009) appeared; although its argument complements mine in interesting ways, I have not been able to address Lears's claims adequately here.

24. "Columbus Day," *Youth's Companion* 65 (November 17, 1892), 608.

25. Rogers M. Smith, *Civic Ideals: Conflicting Visions of Citizenship in U.S. History* (New Haven, Conn.: Yale University Press, 1997), 274.

26. Margaret Mitchell, *Gone with the Wind* (New York: Pan Books, 1991), 583.

27. There is an abundant literature on the development of an American idiom and its contribution to the evolution of early U.S. national identity; on the role of a national language in the Confederacy, see Drew Gilpin Faust, *The Creation of Confederate Nationalism: Ideology and Identity in the Civil War South* (Baton Rouge: Louisiana State University Press, 1988), 11–13.

28. Rydell, *All the World's a Fair*, 9.

29. "Official Programme," 446.

30. My interest in anxiety manifested by pledges during the Civil War builds from Paul De Man's exploration of performative speech, particularly the indeterminacy they enact. See Paul De Man, *Allegories of Reading: Figural Language in Rousseau, Nietzsche, Rilke, and Proust* (New Haven, Conn.: Yale University Press, 1979); J. Hillis Miller, *Speech Acts in Literature* (Stanford, Calif.: Stanford University Press, 2001), 140–154. In developing my argument, I have chosen not to chart the multiple nuances associated with performative language, focusing more narrowly on the materials that are directly applicable to the historical problems this study engages.

31. Abraham Lincoln, *Speeches and Writings, 1859–1865* (New York: Library of America, 1989), 536.

32. Dana Luciano, *Arranging Grief: Sacred Time and the Body in Nineteenth-Century America* (New York: New York University Press, 2007), 21.

33. The definition of loyalty I detail in the coming pages differs significantly from the one George Fletcher articulates, as do the moral norms against which it was measured. Fletcher's argument depends on a model of morality that takes as its central principle the idea of impartiality, less important to nineteenth-century Americans than it was to their twentieth-century descendants. It is against this impartiality, central to the moral theory of John Rawls, for example, that Fletcher defines loyalty as "recogniz[ing] who we are in our friendships, loves, family bonds, national ties, and religious devotion" (*Loyalty: An Essay on the Morality of Relationships* [New York: Oxford University Press, 1993], 175, 8–9). Other noteworthy treatments of loyalty include R. E. Ewin, "Loyalty and Virtues," *Philosophical Quarterly* 42 (1992): 403-419; Judith N. Shklar, "Obligation, Loyalty, Exile," *Political Theory* 21:2 (1993): 181-197; and Anna Stilz, *Liberal Loyalty: Freedom, Obligation, and the State* (Princeton, N.J.: Princeton University Press, 2009).

34. Although Fletcher suggests that "loyalty is better suited for the theater than for subtle and intricate psychological novels," pointing to *Antigone* and *King Lear* as examples (*Loyalty*, 26), I will show that the conflicts created by competing loyalties provide the basis for a number of carefully argued investigations of individual ethical life and the communities that nourish or impede it.

35. Brook Thomas, *American Literary Realism and the Failed Promise of Contract* (Berkeley: University of California Press, 1997), 1; Amy Dru Stanley, *From Bondage to Contract: Wage Labor, Marriage, and the Market in the Age of Emancipation* (Cambridge: Cambridge University Press, 1998).

36. Thomas, *American Literary Realism*, 8; Gregg Crane, *Race, Citizenship, and Law in American Literature* (New York: Cambridge University Press, 2002), 185.

37. Crane, *Race, Citizenship, and Law*, 190.

38. Theodore Woolsey, *Political Science; or, The State Theoretically and Practically Considered* (New York: Scribner, Armstrong, 1878), 72–73, 74, 75, 77. Woolsey extrapolates from his definition to determine that both immoral and illegal contracts, like those associated with false swearing, cannot be legally binding, although the latter may carry moral obligations (ibid., 76).

39. Oliver Wendell Holmes Jr., "The Path of the Law," *Harvard Law Review* 10 (March 1897): 463–464.

40. Melissa Ganz, "Binding the Will: George Eliot and the Practice of Promising," *ELH* 75 (2008): 569.

41. Thomas, *American Literary Realism*, 10.

42. Harold Hyman, *The Era of the Oath: Northern Loyalty Tests during the Civil War and Reconstruction* (Philadelphia: University of Pennsylvania Press, 1954), 13.

1 / Loyalty, Oaths, and the Nation

1. Herman Melville, *Moby-Dick* (New York: Norton, 2002), 152; all subsequent references will be to this edition and indicated parenthetically in the text.

2. The two enactments of consent presuppose different motivations—economic profit or personal revenge—and potentially incompatible configurations of authority and will; see Peter Coviello, *Intimacy in America: Dreams of Affiliation in Antebellum Literature* (Minneapolis: University of Minnesota Press, 2005), 121–123.

3. On *Moby-Dick* and consent theory, see Elizabeth Samet, *Willing Obedience: Citizens, Soldiers, and the Progress of Consent in America, 1776–1898* (Stanford, Calif.: Stanford University Press, 2004).

4. In making this claim, I am taking a position opposed to the one for which Samet argues. On her view, Ahab generates "a false communal feeling" among the crew, which he then cements through "blood and ritual." Whereas she maintains that Ahab's oath "exposes the crew as a collection of abject slaves," I contend that Melville's interest is more with the problems of consent than of obedience, especially as Pip does not join the crew in swearing (ibid., 76, 71).

5. As a prominent Ohio lawyer observed in 1862, "men in both sections" were driven to "examine for the first time . . . the vessel which has borne them, to understand the great timbers and braces that hold it together" (Rogan Kersh, *Dreams of a More Perfect Union: A Study of American Political Thought* [Ithaca, N.Y.: Cornell University Press, 2001], 191).

6. John Locke, *An Essay Concerning Human Understanding*, (New York: Dover, 1959), 2:3; Aristotle, *Politics*, trans. C. D. C. Reeve (Indianapolis: Hackett, 1998), 4; see Christopher Looby, *Voicing America: Language, Literary Form, and the Origins of the United States* (Chicago: University of Chicago Press, 1998), 13–98.

7. John Locke, *Two Treatises of Government* (Cambridge: Cambridge University Press, 1988), 296, 295.

8. Nancy Armstrong, *How Novels Think: The Limits of Individualism from 1719–1900* (New York: Columbia University Press, 2005), 149.

9. The text reads: "Section 3. No person shall be a Senator or Representative in Congress, or elector of President and Vice-President, or hold any office, civil or military, under the United States or under any state, who, having previously taken an oath as a member of Congress, or as an officer of the United States, or as a member of any state legislature, or as an executive or judicial officer of any state, to support the Constitution of the United States, shall have engaged in insurrection or rebellion against the same, or given aid or comfort to the enemies thereof. But Congress may, by a vote of two-thirds of each House, remove such disability." See Sanford Levinson, *Constitutional Faith* (Princeton, N.J.: Princeton University Press, 1988), 55–57, 92.

10. Friedrich Nietzsche, *On the Genealogy of Morals*, trans. Douglas Smith (New York: Oxford University Press, 1996), 36, 58. Similarly, David Hume opines that promises are "not intelligible naturally, not antecedent to human conventions" (*A Treatise of Human Nature* [London: Oxford University Press, 1967], 516). Philip Fisher provides germane contextual information on the nature of time (*Vehement Passions*, 80).

11. James Madison, Alexander Hamilton, and John Jay, *The Federalist Papers* (New York: Penguin, 1987), 184.

12. Locke, *Two Treatises*, 349.

13. Elaine Scarry, "Consent and the Body: Injury, Departure, and Desire," *New Literary History* 21 (Autumn 1990): 874.

14. Locke, *Two Treatises*, 290.

15. Lawson, *Patriot Fires*, 6.

16. Jay Fliegelman, *Declaring Independence: Jefferson, Natural Language, and the Culture of Performance* (Stanford, Calif.: Stanford University Press, 1993), 40.

17. Barnes, *States of Sympathy*, 3. Similarly, see Stern, *Plight of Feeling*, 1–29.

18. U.S. Constitution, Article III, Section 3, defines treason as consisting in "levy-

ing war against [the United States], or in adhering to their enemies, giving them aid and comfort." No one could be tried for having sympathetic feelings, but that did not mean that sympathy did not accrue newly negative connotations nonetheless. Barnes observes that the fear that feelings could not be controlled already exists in the early national period; this could well be part of the reason that the sworn testimony of two individuals is constitutionally required to convict a person of treason (*States of Sympathy*, 2).

19. Anthony Smith, *The Ethnic Origins of Nations* (London: Wiley-Blackwell, 1987), 149.

20. For the sake of argument, I have presented only a rough sketch of Confederate state building; John McCardell, *The Idea of a Southern Nation: Southern Nationalists and Southern Nationalism, 1830–1660* (New York: Norton, 1979); Emory Thomas *The Confederate Nation: 1861–1865* (New York: Harper Torchbooks, 1979); and Faust, *Creation of Confederate Nationalism*, treat the issue more extensively.

21. Cited in Harry Jaffa, *A New Birth of Freedom: Abraham Lincoln and the Coming of the Civil War* (New York: Rowman and Littlefield, 2004), 235–236.

22. Cited in Fredrickson, *Inner Civil War*, 132. O'Sullivan is most widely known for coining the phrase "manifest destiny," and his intellectual reputation—as editor of the *Democratic Review* and ardent supporter of Andrew Jackson—was firmly established.

23. Lawson, *Patriot Fires*, 10.

24. Hyman, *Era of the Oath*, 13.

25. Levinson, *Constitutional Faith*, 99.

26. Hannah Arendt, *Between Past and Future* (New York: Penguin, 1993), 164.

27. Levinson, *Constitutional Faith*, 94.

28. Sianne Ngai associates anxiety, characterized by "future-orientedness," with spatial and temporal displacements (*Ugly Feelings* [Cambridge, Mass.: Harvard University Press, 2005], 209).

29. Lawson, *Patriot Fires*, 35.

30. As Albert Hirschman makes clear, this is crucial when "countries resemble each other a good deal because they share a common history, language, and culture" (*Exit, Voice, and Loyalty: Responses to Decline in Firms, Organizations, and States* [Cambridge, Mass.: Harvard University Press, 1970], 81).

31. Nathaniel Hawthorne, "Chiefly about War-Matters," *Atlantic Monthly*, July 1862, 48; all subsequent references will be indicated parenthetically in the text.

32. Given the subtlety of the essay and the prevailing political climate, it is no wonder than many readers failed to appreciate the joke. Recalling the episode, Julian Hawthorne writes: "Intentionally absurd though these 'comments' were, they seem to have possessed verisimilitude enough to deceive most readers; and I remember one person, who felt the indignation which they pretended to express, declared, when apprised of their true authorship, 'Then I have no respect for a man who runs with the hare, and hunts with the hounds!' But our sense of humor in New England was, at this period, not seldom exanimated by our insatiable political conscientiousness" (*Hawthorne and His Wife: A Biography* [Boston: Houghton, Mifflin, 1884], 2:311–312).

33. Contemporary readers might have recognized the phrase "as the Lion wooes his bride" from Walter Scott's *Ivanhoe* (1819), where it introduces a chapter that lingers with the relative values of ambition, sacrifice, and rights. The source from which Scott

takes the passage—John Home's 1756 tragedy *Douglas*—also finds its subject in the correlation of necessity, choice, and tragedy.

34. James Bense explains the active role played by *Atlantic* editor James T. Fields, including how Hawthorne's text was altered as a result of the prevailing political climate ("Nathaniel Hawthorne's Intention in 'Chiefly about War Matters,'" *American Literature* 61 [1989]: 200–214).

35. That there may have been a Southern nationalism antedating the start of the Civil War has been the subject of some scholarly debate. See Susan-Mary Grant, *North Over South: Northern Nationalism and American Identity in the Antebellum Era* (Lawrence: University of Kansas Press, 2000); McCardell, *Idea of a Southern Nation*; Faust, *Creation of Confederate Nationalism*; Eric Foner, *Reconstruction: America's Unfinished Revolution 1863–1877* (New York: Harper and Row, 1988); Linda Frost, *Never One Nation: Freaks, Savages, and Whiteness in U.S. Popular Culture* (Minneapolis: University of Minnesota Press, 2005).

36. Benjamin Morgan Palmer, *The Oath of Allegiance to the United States, Discussed in Its Moral and Political Bearings* (Richmond: MacFarlane and Fergusson, 1863), 19–20.

37. George Fitzhugh, *Cannibals All! or Slaves without Masters* (Cambridge, Mass.: Belknap Press of Harvard University Press, 1988), 204; Wilson, *Patriotic Gore*, 341–364.

38. Faust, *Creation of Confederate Nationalism*, 7. Even before the war, Southerners had the reputation for being more local in their affiliations than their neighbors to the north; writing in the *New York Times* in 1854, Frederick Law Olmstead maintained that a Southerner's patriotic sentiment "centers between a man's heels," which he contrasted disparagingly with the "broad and generous" feelings characteristic of Northerners (Grant, *North Over South*, 81). "The Southern States are an aggregate, in fact, of communities, not of individuals," John C. Calhoun opined in 1833, and as such they were models of "harmony" and "stability" in comparison to the dislocation evident to the north (Thomas, *Confederate Nation*, 31). Even if most Americans experienced allegiance as local in the decades before the Civil War, as Alice Fahs has demonstrated, the use of an idiom familiar to *all* antebellum Americans built on established beliefs about the sections and, further, developed the idea that Southern regionalism, which found its political analog in the doctrine of states' rights, was the better means of protecting the ideal family (*Imagined Civil War*, 11).

39. Thomas, *Confederate Nation*, 85. On Southerners who remained loyal to the Union, see Foner, *Reconstruction*, 17.

40. James M. McPherson, *For Cause and Comrade: Why Men Fought in the Civil War* (New York: Oxford University Press, 1997), 21, 22.

41. Thomas, *Confederate Nation*, 19.

42. Faust, *Creation of Confederate Nationalism*, 7.

43. Coviello, *Intimacy in America*, 87.

44. Horace Bushnell, "The Doctrine of Loyalty," *New Englander* 22 (July 1863): 568. Although he was once "widely recognized as one of America's most important religious thinkers and philosophers of language," Horace Bushnell has not received much sustained critical attention in recent years (Cindy Weinstein, *The Literature of Labor and the Labors of Literature* [Cambridge: Cambridge University Press, 1995], 41).

45. Adam Gurowski, *Diary from March 4, 1861 to November 12, 1862* (Boston: Lee

and Shepard, 1862), 124. Thomas, a West Point graduate, was a Virginian who decided to remain in the Union army during the Civil War.

46. Although eighteenth-century philosophers and politicians were alert to the possibilities that sympathy could destabilize, as well as sustain, communities, the embrace of affect that characterized much of antebellum culture obscured these earlier concerns. See Armstrong, *How Novels Think*, 20; Cathy Davidson, *Revolution and the Word: The Rise of the Novel in America* (New York: Oxford University Press, 1986), 109; Stern, *Plight of Feeling*; Barnes, *States of Sympathy*; John Mullan, *Sentiment and Sociability: The Language of Feeling in the Eighteenth Century* (New York: Oxford University Press, 1988), 27; Jason Frank, "Sympathy and Separation: Benjamin Rush and the Contagious Public," *Modern Intellectual History* 6 (2009): 29.

47. Dana Nelson, "'No Cold or Empty Heart': Polygenesis, Scientific Professionalization, and the Unfinished Business of Male Sentimentalism," *Differences* 11 (1999/2000): 39.

48. Elizabeth Keckley, *Behind the Scenes: Thirty Years a Slave and Four Years in the White House* (Urbana: University of Illinois Press, 2001), 47. As the next chapter discusses, the sympathetic cast to Southern national identity was also useful in the postwar years to gender the relationship between the sections and model their reconciliation with a marital paradigm.

49. N. G. Upham, *Rebellion, Slavery, and Peace: Pamphlet 52* (New York: Loyal League Publication Society, 1864), 5.

50. James K. Hosmer, *The Thinking Bayonet* (Boston: Walker, Fuller, 1865), 97, 153.

51. Henry Ward Beecher, "Peace, Be Still," in *American Sermons: The Pilgrims to Martin Luther King Jr.*, ed. Michael Warner (New York: Library of America, 1999), 657.

52. John William Draper, *Thoughts on the Future Civil Policy of America* (New York: Harper and Brothers, 1865), 84–85.

53. Horace Bushnell, "Popular Government by Divine Right," in *Building Eras in Religion* (New York: Charles Scribner's Sons, 1881), 302. It bears noting that the fact that loyalty was not based on home sentiment did not preclude the regular comparison between the two. The relationship was one of analogy and not causality, however, which is a crucial measure of the distinction between the two nationalisms.

54. "Our Country," in *Lyrics of Loyalty*, ed. Frank Moore (New York: George P. Putnam, 1864), 283–284.

55. William Taylor, *Cavalier and Yankee: The Old South and American National Character* (New York: Oxford University Press, 1957); Thomas, *Confederate Nation*, 23–24, 28.

56. McPherson, *For Cause and Comrade*, 21.

57. Beecher, "Peace, Be Still," 659.

58. See Grant, *North Over South*, 162. For many in the North, Fredrickson observes, "revolutionary ideology had no further application to American society" (*Inner Civil War*, 135). As Catherine Holland explains, public rituals surrounding the body, often involving forms of public exposure, were sometimes used by members of the Revolutionary generation to reveal, at least figuratively, political loyalties (*The Body Politic: Foundings, Citizenship, and Difference in the American Political Imagination* [New York: Routledge, 2001], 63–64).

59. Ralph Waldo Emerson, "Self-Reliance," in *Ralph Waldo Emerson: The Oxford Authors*, ed. Richard Poirer (New York: Oxford University Press, 1990), 38.

60. Bushnell, "Doctrine of Loyalty," 560.

61. Fredrickson links James's oration to a millennialist interpretation of events (*Inner Civil War*, 68–69). James's idiosyncratic religious views (he was deeply opposed to concepts of selfhood) may have predisposed him to loyalty's tenets. On his beliefs, see Louis Menand, *The Metaphysical Club: A Story of Ideas in America* (New York: Farrar, Straus, Giroux, 2001), 84–85.

62. Henry James Sr., *The Social Significance of Our Institutions: An Oration Delivered by Request of the Citizens at Newport, R.I.* (Philadelphia: Rozov, 1966), 7.

63. Ibid., 9; Gordon Wood, *The Radicalism of the American Revolution* (New York: Vintage, 1991), 176. Wood notes that many of the loyalists during the Revolution left the colonies; after the Civil War, therefore, the situation facing the nation would have been far more complicated.

64. James, *Social Significance*, 9.

65. Ibid., 32, 37, 38, 40.

66. Lawson stresses the difference party affiliation made in defining loyalty, as well as the importance of party affiliation itself, in the construction of American identity (*Patriot Fires*, 9, passim). See also Adam I. P. Smith, *No Party Now: Politics in the Civil War North* (New York: Oxford University Press, 2006).

67. "What Is Loyalty?" *Harper's Weekly*, April 18, 1863, 243. Fernando Wood, a corrupt New York politician, one-time Grand Sachem of Tammany Hall, and mayor of New York City during the early years of the war, was a known Copperhead who suggests in January 1861 that the city also secede from the Union. G. Ticknor Curtis was also a New York resident.

68. Ibid.

69. For a representative example, see *Harper's Weekly* January 4, 1862; Elizabeth Young, *Black Frankenstein: The Making of an American Metaphor* (New York: New York University Press, 2008), 48–52.

70. Samuel Osgood, "Institutions and Men," *Harper's Monthly* 24 (February 1862), 275.

71. Smith, *Ethnic Origins of Nations*, 148.

72. Danielle Allen, *Talking to Strangers: Anxieties of Citizenship since Brown v. Board of Education* (Chicago: University of Chicago Press, 2004), 14.

73. Bushnell, "Doctrine of Loyalty," 567. According to Robert Mullin, earlier in his life Bushnell had denounced English loyalty, boasting that the United States did not need such old-fashioned forms of attachment because Americans' commitment to law was sufficient. The Civil War led Bushnell to reevaluate these positions and to conclude that his earlier views on loyalty had been mistaken (Robert Mullin, *The Puritan as Yankee: A Life of Horace Bushnell* [Grand Rapids, Mich.: William B. Erdmans, 2002], 222).

74. Harry S. Stout, *Upon the Altar of the Nation: A Moral History of the Civil War* (New York: Viking, 2006), 29.

75. Luciano, *Arranging Grief*, 222.

76. This point diverges from the one forwarded in *Imagined Civil War*. Fahs argues that national interest in "abstract nationhood" diminished as the war proceeds (12). My position differs in two specific ways: first, I am arguing for a differentiation between Union and Confederate nationalisms, rather than a split sense of American nationalism; second, I maintain that it is possible to articulate "abstract nationhood"

without recurring specifically to an obviously abstract symbol, that it is possible, in other words, for a personal account to have abstract implications, especially when its generic features strip away what might seem to be personal. On this latter point, see Nudelman, *John Brown's Body*, 2–13.

77. Henry W. Bellows, *The Advantage of Testing Our Principles, Compensatory of the Evils of Serious Times: A Discourse February 17, 1861* (Philadelphia: C. Sherman and Sons, 1861), 7.

78. Charles Eliot Norton, *Considerations of Some Recent Social Theories* (Boston: Little, Brown, 1853), 143–144.

79. "Review of *Dred*, by Harriet Beecher Stowe," *Blackwood's Edinburgh Magazine* (1856), 695. For a fuller reading of Stowe's critique, see Elizabeth Duquette, "The Republican Mammy? Imagining Civil Engagement in *Dred*," *American Literature* 81 (2008): 1–28.

80. Thomas, *American Literary Realism*, 116.

81. Deak Nabers, *Victory of Law: The Fourteenth Amendment, the Civil War, and American Literature, 1852–1867* (Baltimore: Johns Hopkins University Press, 2006), 173–174.

82. Contemporary treatments of the topic do the same. See Fletcher, *Loyalty*.

83. Bushnell, "Doctrine of Loyalty," 574.

84. Ibid., 572.

85. See Samuels, *Romances of the Republic*, 14–22.

86. Bushnell's association of loyalty with "family love" suggested that it was a natural form of affective affiliation and anticipates the heteronormativity of the reconstruction romance as he asserts that "complete men" crave its "equipment." One could likewise point to Bushnell's child-rearing principles, especially those predicated on natural relations between members of the family.

87. Cited in Frederickson, *Inner Civil War*, 140–141.

88. "Loyalty," *North American Review* 94 (January 1862): 162.

89. W. G. Eliot, *Loyalty and Religion: A Discourse for the Times* (St Louis: George Knapp, 1861), 8.

90. "'Loyal' versus 'Disloyal,'" *Old Guard* 1 (July 1863): 152. Founded in 1863 to express Copperhead opinions, the *Old Guard* was a New York periodical opposed to abolition, well enough known to appear in Mark Twain's *Roughing It* (1872) as the preferred reading material of the pro-Confederate admiral. The suspension of habeas corpus demonstrated, on the view espoused by the *Old Guard*, that neither side had a defensible claim to legality, having equally abandoned the principles upon which the nation was founded.

91. Bushnell, "Doctrine of Loyalty," 562, 565.

92. David Blight, *Frederick Douglass' Civil War: Keeping Faith in Jubilee* (Baton Rouge: Louisiana State University Press, 1989), 155. See, also, Lawson, *Patriot Fires*, 143-148.

93. Charles Sumner, *The Works of Charles Sumner* (Boston: Lee and Shepard, 1873), 7:83.

94. Blight, *Frederick Douglass' Civil War*, 155.

95. Lawson, *Patriot Fires*, 2.

96. Fahs, *Imagined Civil War*, 25.

97. Sentimental narrative was likewise important to Confederate nationalism. Be-

cause this use did not require as much revision, thanks to the Confederacy's dependence on sympathy in its articulation of a national identity, I do not treat the Southern materials here.

98. Lucy Larcom, "A Loyal Woman's No," *Atlantic Monthly*, December 1863, 726–727.

99. Nancy Bentley, "Marriage as Treason: Polygamy, Nation, and the Novel," in *The Futures of American Studies*, ed. Donald Pease and Robyn Weigman (Durham, N.C.: Duke University Press, 2002), 362.

100. Louisa Alcott, *Hospital Sketches and Camp and Fireside Stories* (Boston: Roberts Brothers, 1869), 198; all subsequent references will be indicated parenthetically in the text. The story was first published in *United States Service Magazine* 2 (1864).

101. Rose's conversion is similar to what many Southern women experience in reunion romances, like John De Forest's *Miss Ravenel's Conversion from Secession to Loyalty* (New York: Penguin, 2000), which I discuss in chapter 2.

102. Lawson, *Patriot Fires*, 32.

103. Young, *Disarming the Nation*, 105.

104. Eve Kosofsky Sedgwick, *Epistemology of the Closet* (Berkeley: University of California Press, 2008), 150.

105. Teresa Goddu, *Gothic America: Narrative, History, and Nation* (New York: Columbia University Press, 1997), 125.

106. Barbara Johnson, *The Critical Difference: Essays in the Contemporary Rhetoric of Reading* (Baltimore: Johns Hopkins University Press, 1980), 100.

107. "What Can I Do?" *Harper's Monthly* 24 (February 1862), 376.

108. J. T. Trowbridge, "We Are a Nation," *Atlantic Monthly*, December 1864, 773.

109. *The First Duty of the Citizen; The Grandeur of the Struggle and its Responsibilities; Southern Principles* (Philadelphia: n.p., 1863), 13.

110. Richard Franklin Bensel, *American Ballot Box in the Mid-Nineteenth Century* (Cambridge: Cambridge University Press, 2004), 217–285.

111. Lawson, *Patriot Fires*, 14–39. As the war progressed, other options than the ones mentioned in "What Can I Do?" emerged for individuals to perform their allegiance, including the purchase of war bonds and involvement with Sanitary fairs; on changes in women's roles during the Civil War, see Shirley Samuels, *Facing America: Iconography and the Civil War* (New York: Oxford University Press, 2004), 81–98.

112. John Greenleaf Whittier, "Barbara Frietchie," *Atlantic Monthly*, September 1863, 496.

113. In so doing, he or she would be following the example of the Lincoln administration, which silenced opposition newspapers in precarious border states. Mark E. Neely Jr. discusses the partisanship of Civil War–era newspapers and the role of censorship in *The Union Divided: Party Conflict in the Civil War North* (Cambridge, Mass.: Harvard University Press, 2002), 89–117.

114. "What Can I Do?" 376.

115. Lincoln, *Speeches and Writings, 1859–1865*, 457.

116. Cited in Fredrickson, *Inner Civil War*, 141.

117. James Dawes, *The Language of War* (Cambridge, Mass.: Harvard University Press, 2002), 20.

118. Eliot, *Loyalty and Religion*, 11. According to Eliot, women are even more susceptible to this "crime" than their male counterparts.

119. Ibid.; "What Can I Do," 378.

120. Neely, *Union Divided*, 105.

121. Faust, *Creation of Confederate Nationalism*, 13. Faust stresses the importance of music to Confederate nationalism, linking it to low literacy rates, limited access to publishing or printing resources, and severe disruptions in communications systems (ibid., 17–19). See "In Charleston, December, 1860" for a fictional depiction of which "tunes" would be most apt "for [Southern] people now" (*Harper's Weekly*, December 14, 1861, 798).

122. Bellows, *Advantage of Testing*, 4. By 1863, a military edict criminalized statements critical of the government, equating them to treason. Clement Vallandigham, an outspoken Copperhead leader, urged his followers to defy "such restrictions upon their liberties," for which he was arrested, convicted, and exiled to the Confederacy. Ohio Democrats stuck by Vallandigham, picking the exiled leader as their 1863 gubernatorial candidate (Lawson, *Patriot Fires*, 67, 74).

123. Smith, *No Party Now*, 85–100.

124. Hyman, *Era of the Oath*, 1–9. As Hyman makes clear, loyalty investigations persisted throughout the war.

125. Bellows, *Advantage of Testing*, 4, 15, 17, 16. Eighteenth- and nineteenth-century legal definitions of conspiracy, which held that the mere fact of having talked about a given act could be criminal, whether or not that act was ever realized, meant Bellows's worries were not mere empty words.

126. Beecher, "Peace, Be Still," 648.

127. Bellows, *Advantage of Testing*, 15.

128. Lincoln, *Speeches and Writings, 1859–1865*, 223–224.

129. Francis Lieber, *No Party Now; but All for our Country*, Loyal Publication Society No. 16 (New York: C. S. Wescott, 1863), 1–2. Publication societies sprang up in cities across the North to disseminate tracts designed to instill proper sentiments in the population. Like the Loyal Publication Society of New York, they printed a wide variety of tracts, many aimed at soldiers themselves. On Loyal leagues, see Lawson, *Patriot Fires*, chapter 4. Fredrickson observes that several of Lieber's pamphlets were written in response to O'Sullivan's attacks (*Inner Civil War*, 133–134).

130. Ross, "'Are We a Nation?'" 337. The Loyal Publication Society published Lieber's *An Address on Secession. Delivered in South Carolina in the Year 1851* in its pamphlet series.

131. Harold Hyman, *To Try Men's Souls: Loyalty Tests in American History* (Berkeley: University of California Press, 1959), 14–15, 74. That compelling oaths was ideologically problematic for the colonials and that they tended to establish allegiance at the state level were both important facts, Rogers Smith explains (*Civic Ideals: Conflicting Visions of Citizenship in U.S. History* [New Haven, Conn.: Yale University Press, 1997], 93). See, as well, Levinson, *Constitutional Faith*, 90–121.

132. Abraham Lincoln, *Speeches and Writings, 1832–1858* (New York: Library of America, 1989), 32.

133. Sanford Levinson, "Constituting Communities through Words That Bind: Reflections on Loyalty Oaths," *Michigan Law Review* 84 (June 1986): 1447. Levinson notes, however, that there are instances in which oaths do not challenge self-identity.

134. Smith, *No Party Now*, 99.

135. Hyman, *Era of the Oath*, 24.

136. C. Gayarre, "Oaths, Amnesties, and Rebellion," *DeBow's Review* 1 (March 1866): 283–303.

137. De Man, *Allegories of Reading*, 273; Homi Bhabha, ed., *Nation and Narration* (New York: Taylor and Francis, 1990), 14.

138. Hannah Arendt, *The Human Condition* (Chicago: University of Chicago Press, 1998), 237; all subsequent references will be indicated parenthetically in the text. Thomas likewise draws on Arendt in defining the "realists' sense of action" (*American Literary Realism*, 271).

139. Lawson, *Patriot Fires*, 125.

140. Edward E. Hale, "The Man without a Country," *Atlantic Monthly*, December 1863, 666–667; all subsequent references will be to this edition and indicated parenthetically in the text.

141. On language in seduction novels, see Barnes, *States of Sympathy*, 64.

142. Contemporary readers would not have missed the association between Nolan's Southern heritage and the invocation of the cavalier.

143. Fisher, *Vehement Passions*, 96–97.

144. Ralph Waldo Emerson, "The Poet," in *Ralph Waldo Emerson*, 199.

145. Peter Brooks, *Melodramatic Imagination: Balzac, Henry James, Melodrama, and the Mode of Excess* (New Haven, Conn.: Yale University Press, 1976), 30–31.

146. According to Lawson, the story was quickly reprinted and sold 500,000 copies. Hale later recalled that he had written the story in response to a statement made by Ohio Democrat Clement Vallandigham that he "did not want to belong to a nation which would compel by arms the loyalty of any of its citizens; he did not want to belong to the United States" (Lawson, *Patriot Fires*, 2, 125, 128).

147. Søren Kierkegaard, *The Concept of Anxiety*, trans. Reidar Thomte and Albert Anderson (Princeton, N.J.: Princeton University Press, 1981), 43.

148. Samuel Weber, *Return to Freud: Jacques Lacan's Dislocation of Psychoanalysis* (Cambridge: Cambridge University Press, 1991), 158, 164.

149. "That Oath," *Harper's Weekly*, November 9, 1861, 706.

150. Arendt's "blindness to structural violence," her emphasis on unpredictability, fails to reach the level of practicality that some have argued is the hallmark of her political philosophy (Beatrice Hanssen, "On the Politics of Pure Means: Benjamin, Arendt, Foucault," in *Violence, Identity, and Self-Determination*, ed. Hent de Vries and Samuel Weber [Stanford, Calif.: Stanford University Press, 1997], 249).

151. Arendt does not discuss political oaths explicitly in her writings, but it not difficult to deduce her likely stance. Her position on totalitarianism, for example, identifies its structure with the verification of everything that is possible, exemplified in the concentration camp. See Hannah Arendt, *The Origins of Totalitarianism* (New York: Harvest, 1968); Avital Ronell, *The Test Drive* (Urbana: University of Illinois Press, 2005), 327. Stanley Cavell argues that the difference between the promise and oath inheres in the "special procedure[s] for entering" the latter requires (*The Claim of Reason: Wittgenstein, Skepticism, Morality, and Tragedy* [New York: Oxford University Press, 1979], 297).

152. Thomas Hobbes, *On the Citizen* (New York: Cambridge Press, 1998), 40–41.

153. Thomas Hobbes, *Leviathan* (New York: Penguin, 1968), 200; all subsequent references will be to this edition and indicated parenthetically in the text.

154. Hobbes, *On the Citizen*, 41.

155. On the central role of anxiety in Hobbesian thought, see William Sokoloff, "Politics and Anxiety in Thomas Hobbes's *Leviathan*," *Theory and Event* 5:1 (2001), http://ezpro.cc.gettysburg.edu:2221/journals/theory_and_event/v005/5.1sokoloff.html.

156. Fisher, *Vehement Passions*, 114.

157. The emphasis Hobbes places on divine retribution is an important part of some definitions of loyalty. Thus, Horace Bushnell argues in an 1864 sermon that it is impossible to construct a government without some reference to "a Supreme Being," in part because humans require something more than "enforcement" to create a robust sense of allegiance and obligation: "Enforcement creates fear but never obligation. True obligation towers above all enforcement" ("Popular Government by Divine Right," 289).

158. That fear might also compel rational behavior is a part of Philip Pettit's argument in *Made with Words: Hobbes on Language, Mind, and Politics* (Princeton, N.J.: Princeton University Press, 2008), 60-66.

159. Hume, *Treatise*, 517-519. On Hume's account of promises, see Annette Baier, "Promises, Promises, Promises," *Postures of the Mind: Essays on Morals* (Minneapolis: University of Minnesota Press, 1985), 174-206.

160. Ibid., 522.

161. J. L. Austin defines commissive speech, a subset of the performative, as those speech acts that "commit the speaker to a certain course of action." Among the examples Austin lists (of which there are thirty-three) are "promise," "covenant," "contract," "undertake," "swear," "consent," "declare for," "vow," "engage," "embrace," and "give my word" (*How to Do Things with Words* [Cambridge, Mass.: Harvard University Press, 1962], 157-158).

162. The political oaths I have been examining differ from the kind of performatives Judith Butler traces in *Excitable Speech: A Politics of the Performative* (New York: Routledge, 1997) in that they are specifically state-sanctioned means of interpellating individuals into carefully circumscribed roles as citizens. While it is true that the performative violence she traces also operates politically to interpellate subjects into the community—or mark them as marginal in the same—the kind of coerced performance of the oath carries with it a different kind of politics, one that is conservative and paranoid and intolerant of precisely that which it seeks to safeguard.

163. Fitz James O'Brien, "The Prisoner of War," *Harper's Monthly* 24 (February 1862), 348.

164. J. T. Trowbridge, *Cudjo's Cave* (Tuscaloosa: University of Alabama Press, 2001), 323; all subsequent references will be to this edition and indicated parenthetically in the text. Not all readers were moved by Trowbridge's excesses. The reviewer for the *North American Review* admits to "a feeling of relief" upon emerging from *Cudjo's Cave*. The novel's success—the review observes that it "has had a great sale"—could be explained, he wrote, by the fact that it "is happily adapted to the excitement of the hour, and is entertaining from the rapidity of its incident and the animation of its style" ("Trowbridge's *Cudjo's Cave*," *North American Review* 98 [April 1864]: 614-616). Part of its "excitement" might have come from parallels readers could draw between the novel and the real-life exploits of Parson Brownlow, a Tennessee minister imprisoned by the C.S.A. for his support of the Union. On Brownlow, see Smith, *No Party Now*, 105.

165. For another example, see "On the Kentucky Border," *Harper's Weekly*, February 1, 1862, 70–71.

166. Trowbridge's position may have correlated to what propagandists maintained should be the norm, but not everyone during the Civil War was as scrupulous as Carl. Although Mark Twain was in the Confederacy, his account in "The Private History of a Campaign That Failed" (*Century* 31 [December 1885]: 193–204) offers a telling alternate view of how individuals understood military oaths, establishing the ongoing importance of the issues Trowbridge engages in *Cudjo's Cave*.

167. Luciano, *Arranging Grief*, 20.

168. Fischer, *Vehement Passions*, 99.

169. Hyman, *Era of the Oath*, 37–38.

170. Palmer, *Oath of Allegiance*, 9, 10, 11. For a different objection to the oaths, one predicated on the assumption that all oaths of allegiance are invalid, see Lysander Spooner, *No Treason: The Constitution of No Authority and a Letter to Thomas F. Bayard*, ed. James J. Martin (Colorado Springs, Colo.: Ralph Myles, 1973), 34–43.

171. Palmer, *Oath of Allegiance*, 22.

172. Hyman, *Era of the Oath*, 33.

173. William H. Ruffner, *The Oath: A Sermon on the Nature and Obligation of the Oath, With Special Reference to the Oath of Allegiance, Delivered Presbyterian Church Lexington, VA, March 27, 1864* (Lexington, Va.: Printed at the Gazette Office, 1864), 11.

174. P. S. Atiyah, *Promises, Morals and Law* (New York: Oxford University Press, 1981), 18.

175. Lawson, *Patriot Fires*, 3.

176. Robert Penn Warren, *The Legacy of the Civil War* (Lincoln, Neb.: Bison Books, 1998), 3–4.

177. Smith, *Ethnic Origins of Nations*, 38–39.

178. Wilson, *Patriotic Gore*, xxxii.

2 / One Big Happy Family, Again?

1. James Russell Lowell, "E Pluribus Unum," *Atlantic Monthly*, February 1861, 238.

2. Wald, *Constituting Americans*, 47.

3. Edward A. Pollard, *The Lost Cause: The Standard Southern History of the War of the Confederates* (New York: Bonanza, n.d.), 43–44.

4. Jefferson Davis, *The Rise and Fall of the Confederate Government*, 2 vols. (New York: D. Appleton, 1881), 2:581; Jaffa, *New Birth of Freedom*, 236.

5. John William Draper, *History of the American Civil War* (New York: Harper, 1867), 3:669.

6. Whitman, *Complete Poetry and Collected Prose*, 9.

7. Foner, *Reconstruction*, 185.

8. Sidney Andrews, "Three Months among the Reconstructionists," *Atlantic Monthly*, February 1866, 240–241. According to Indiana congressman George W. Julian, "if the voice of the loyal millions could be faithfully executed today, treason would be made infamous, traitors would be disenfranchised, and the loyal men of the South, irrespective of color, would hold the front seats in the work of reconstruction" (*Speeches on Political Questions* [New York: Hurd and Houghton, 1872], 346).

9. Michael Walzer, *Obligations: Essays on Disobedience, War, and Citizenship* (Cambridge, Mass.: Harvard University Press, 1970), 194–195; Nancy Cott, *Public*

Vows: A History of Marriage and the Nation (Cambridge, Mass.: Harvard University Press, 2000), 8–18.

10. Werner Sollors, *Beyond Ethnicity: Consent and Descent in American Culture* (New York: Oxford University Press, 1987), 112.

11. Lincoln, *Speeches and Writings, 1859–1865*, 404.

12. Wald, *Constituting Americans*, 68.

13. On this tension, see Gregory Jackson, "'A Dowry of Suffering': Consent, Contract, and Political Coverture in John W. De Forest's Reconstruction Romance," *American Literary History* 15:2 (Summer 2003): 294; Wald, *Constituting Americans*, 68–69.

14. Nina Silber, *The Romance of Reunion: Northerners and the South, 1865–1900* (Chapel Hill: University of North Carolina Press, 1993), 45; Mary Louise Kete, *Sentimental Collaborations: Mourning and Middle-Class Identity in Nineteenth-Century America* (Durham, N.C.: Duke University Press, 2000), 119.

15. Karen Keely, "Marriage Plots and National Reunion: The Trope of Romantic Reconciliation in Postbellum Literature," *Mississippi Quarterly* 51 (Fall 1998): 621.

16. Jackson, "'Dowry of Suffering,'" 282–283.

17. Stanley Cavell, *Pursuits of Happiness: The Hollywood Comedy of Remarriage* (Cambridge, Mass.: Harvard University Press, 1981), 23.

18. Ibid., 31, 18, 19.

19. James Russell Lowell, "Editor's Table: Discipline," *Harper's New Monthly Magazine* 24 (January 1862), 261.

20. Foner, *Reconstruction*, xxvi.

21. Fahs, *Imagined Civil War*, 107. James Russell Lowell says "we prove our good breeding by making no trouble [when ordered by a person in authority of lower social standing], and quietly submitting to the order, even when we think that it is not as judicious as it might be" ("Editor's Table," 261).

22. Don Herzog, *Happy Slaves: A Critique of Consent Theory* (Chicago: University of Chicago Press, 1989), 143, 225.

23. Allen, *Talking to Strangers*, 68.

24. Jackson draws a contrary conclusion, claiming that De Forest manifests "opposition to the Hobbesian contract," an argument that he bases on a reading of family affect ("'Dowry of Suffering,'" 292). Yet a closer analysis of wartime political rhetoric suggests that the kind of feeling associated with the political family was neither as rational nor as focused on sympathy as Jackson's analysis would suggest.

25. Alan Keenan, *Democracy in Question: Democratic Openness in a Time of Political Closure* (Stanford, Calif.: Stanford University Press, 2003), 12.

26. The scholarship on the role of literature in the construction of national identity is vast, crossing numerous disciplinary boundaries. Among the most pertinent to this argument are Benedict Anderson, *Imagined Communities: Reflections on the Origin and Spread of Nationalism* (London: Verson, 1991); Wald, *Constituting Americans*; Lauren Berlant, *The Anatomy of National Fantasy: Hawthorne, Utopia, and Everyday Life* (Chicago: University of Chicago Press, 1991); Rogers Smith, *Stories of Peoplehood: The Politics and Morals of Political Membership* (Cambridge: Cambridge University Press, 2003); Doris Sommers, *Foundational Fictions: The National Romances of Latin America* (Berkeley: University of California Press, 1993).

27. Lauren Berlant, *The Queen of America Goes to Washington City: Essays on Sex and Citizenship* (Durham, N.C.: Duke University Press, 1997), 57.

28. James E. Gargano, ed., *Critical Essays on John William De Forest* (Boston: G. K. Hall, 1981), 35.

29. Ibid., 33.

30. Eve Kornfeld, *Creating an American Culture: A Brief History with Documents* (New York: Bedford/St. Martin's, 2001), 8.

31. Marianne Noble, *The Masochistic Pleasures of Sentimental Literature* (Princeton, N.J.: Princeton University Press, 2000), 64.

32. Susan Warner, *The Wide Wide World* (New York: Feminist Press at CUNY, 1987), 12.

33. Lauren Berlant, "The Female Woman: Fanny Fern and the Form of Sentiment," in *The Culture of Sentiment: Race, Gender, and Sentimentality in Nineteenth-Century America*, ed. Shirley Samuels (New York: Oxford University Press, 1992), 268.

34. See Cott, *Public Vows*, 10–17.

35. Henry James calls Lillie "trifling" in an anonymous 1867 review in the *Nation*. Howells praises the "light, strong way" De Forest manages his tale, lauding how De Forest "treat[s] the war really and artistically" ("Miss Ravenel's Conversion from Secession to Loyalty," *Atlantic Monthly*, July 1867, 121). See Wilson, *Patriotic Gore*, 685; Aaron, *Unwritten War*, 173.

36. Jackson concurs, claiming "De Forest found the sentimental particularly salient for staging the contradiction of consent and coercion at citizenship's core" ("'Dowry of Suffering,'" 277).

37. De Forest, *Miss Ravenel's Conversion*, 11; all subsequent references will be to this edition and indicated parenthetically in the text.

38. Harriet Stowe, *Uncle Tom's Cabin, or; Life among the Lowly* (New York: Penguin, 1981), 624.

39. Enlistment poems, like Horatio Alger's "Mother, May I Go?" or Nancy Priest's "Kiss Me, Mother, and Let me Go," sought to control the maternal resistance to the war (Fahs, *Imagined Civil War*, 108).

40. "Mother, Can I Go?" *Harper's Weekly*, March 22, 1862, 187. On the importance of convention in a related genre, the call-to-arms poem, see Jessica Forbes Roberts, "A Poetic *E Pluribus Unum*: Conventions, Imperatives, and the Poetic Call-to-Arms in Frank Moore's *Rebellion Record*," *ESQ* 54 (2008): 171-197.

41. J. T. Trowbridge, *The South: A Tour of Its Battle-Fields and Ruined Cities* (Hartford, Conn.: L. Stebbins, 1866), 160.

42. Ibid., 585.

43. Ibid., 103.

44. Jean Starobinski, *1789: The Emblems of Reason*, trans. Barbara Bray (Charlottesville: University of Virginia Press, 1982), 102–105.

45. Trowbridge, *South*, 103, 587.

46. Herman Melville, *Battle-Pieces and Aspects of the War* (New York: Prometheus Books, 2001), 245.

47. Nabers, *Victory of Law*, 30.

48. Bertram Wyatt-Brown, *Southern Honor: Ethics and Behavior in the Old South* (New York: Oxford University Press, 1982), xv.

49. Thomas, *American Literary Realism*, 33.

50. Ibid., 34. See Wade Newhouse, "Reporting Triumph, Saving a Nation: 'Interesting Juxtapositions' in John W. De Forest's Civil War," *Studies in American Fiction* 32

(Autumn 2004): 165–166, for a related argument based on a reading of Mrs. Larue's unruly category bending.

51. The dilemma De Forest depicts in this scene, particularly as it relies on promises, recalls Hume's claim that promises are especially useful for creating obligations between strangers. See Hume, *Treatise*, 519.

52. Amanda Claybaugh, *The Novel of Purpose: Literature and Social Reform in the Anglo-American World* (Ithaca, N.Y.: Cornell University Press, 2007), 93–99.

53. De Forest wrote a history of Connecticut Indians in which he concluded that their eventual disappearance and defeat were the result of their own "barbarism" (*History of the Indians of Connecticut from the Earliest Known Period to 1850* [Hartford, Conn.: Wm. Jas. Hamersley, 1851], 190).

54. Charles G. Leland, "Bone Ornaments," *Continental Monthly* 2 (July 1862): 5; Samuels discusses other fictional representations of Southern women's savagery (*Facing America*, 81–82). Taking bones as mementoes was not just the stuff of fiction; Henry Bellows brought home "the hip bone of a loyal hero" from Bull Run (Fredrickson, *Inner Civil War*, 103).

55. Drawings like this were common in Northern periodicals, as the association of Confederate soldiers with existing assumptions about Native savagery added fuel to charges that Union troops were desecrated on the battlefield (Frost, *Never One Nation*, 20–21).

56. Martha Finley, *Elsie Dinsmore* (Nashville, Tenn.: Cumberland House, 2000), 226.

57. One could connect Ravenel to the figure of the "authoritarian doctor" Noble locates in many sentimental novels (*Masochistic Pleasures*, 102).

58. Charles Lyell, *Principles of Geology* (Chicago: University of Chicago Press, 1990), 1:165.

59. Here the father-daughter bond, rather than that between husband and wife, constitutes the family, but the dynamics nonetheless make overt the connections between family and government. On these tendencies in U.S. politics, see Cott, *Public Vows*, 10–18.

60. Norton, *Considerations*, 15.

61. Richard Brodhead, *Cultures of Letters: Scenes of Reading and Writing in Nineteenth-Century America* (Chicago: University of Chicago Press, 1993), 13-47.

62. Nelson, "'No Cold or Empty Heart,'" 39. De Forest stresses that Ravenel is an amateur mineralogist, but still remarks that he is writing articles for the scientific community.

63. Draper, *Thoughts on the Future Civil Policy*, 241, 239.

64. Draper, *History of the American Civil War*, 3:669. Dorothy Ross notes: "The problematic that ran through [Draper's] account was republican rather than romantic, not spiritual realization but historical decline. The 'Great Republic' was like all nations, a 'transitory,' 'vanishing' form" ("'Are We a Nation?': The Conjuncture of Nationhood and Race in the United States, 1850–1876," *Modern Intellectual History* 2:3 [2005]: 343).

65. Draper, *History of the Civil War*, 3:670, 673, 670, 671, 666, 671.

66. Ravenel's instructions mirror those being offered to freed people in various conduct manuals published during the period. On the "burdened individuality" they helped to shape, see Saidiya Hartman, *Scenes of Subjection: Terror, Slavery, and Self-*

Making in Nineteenth-Century America (New York: Oxford University Press, 1997), 125–163.

67. Smith, *Ethnic Origins of Nations*, 171–172. Smith's argument pertains particularly to the role of such social sciences as archaeology, anthropology, sociology, and history, but given De Forest's explicit connection between theory and practice in the novel, it seems plausible to expand Smith's original list.

68. Draper, *Thoughts on the Future Civil Policy*, 251–252. For critic Wade Newhouse, "individuality becomes an illusion" in such arguments, "surrendered to an imaginary political collective in the service of postwar American nationalism"; on his view, *Miss Ravenel's Conversion* "establishes a model of subsuming personal interests in those of an abstract nationhood" ("Reporting Triumph," 177).

69. Draper, *Thoughts on the Future Civil Policy*, 264.

70. De Forest's interest in science is mirrored in Draper, who claims that only "three powers" "can organize the world—theology, literature, science." Science is the best choice for social organization, he concludes, because "it admits of universal communion" (*Thoughts on the Future Civil Policy*, 250).

71. John W. De Forest, *Kate Beaumont* (State College, Pa.: Bald Eagle Press, 1963), 424.

72. John W. De Forest, *The Bloody Chasm* (Freeport, N.Y.: Books for Libraries Press, 1972), 201, 145.

73. Both nations found justification for their actions in the Bible. "The Bible, on one side of Mason and Dixon's line, is the great bulwark of slaveholding; on the other, the great arsenal of liberty," so one signal advantage of the war, Henry Bellows averred, would be its melting of "the chains of superstition and prestige and custom" (*Advantage of Testing*, 18, 19).

74. Gaines Foster, *Moral Reconstruction: Christian Lobbyists and the Federal Legislation of Morality, 1865–1920* (Chapel Hill: University of North Carolina Press, 2002), 23, 20.

75. On the Confederate materials, see Elizabeth Fox-Genovese, "Days of Judgment, Days of Wrath: The Civil War and the Religious Imagination of Women Writers," in *Religion and the American Civil War*, ed. Randall M. Miller, Harry S. Stout, and Charles Reagan Wilson (New York: Oxford University Press, 1998), 229–230. Henry Ward Beecher's 1863 sermon "The Ministration of Suffering" provides a fine example of Northern pulpit practices. After the war, "organized religion offered another battleground of acrimonious controversy" (Paul Buck, *The Road to Reunion, 1865–1900* [Boston: Little, Brown, 1937], 58).

76. Michael Rogin, *Ronald Reagan, The Movie and Other Episodes in Political Demonology* (Berkeley: University of California Press, 1987), 87, 90.

77. *The Gates Ajar* was immensely popular, selling 180,000 copies in the United States and England, 4,000 in its first few weeks alone.

78. Elizabeth Stuart Phelps, *Three Spiritualist Novels: The Gates Ajar (1868); Beyond the Gates (1883); and The Gates Between (1887)* (Urbana: University of Illinois Press, 2000), 7; all subsequent references to all three of the *Gates* novels will be to this edition and indicated parenthetically in the text.

79. Michael Wheeler, *Death and the Future Life in Victorian Literature and Theology* (New York: Cambridge University Press, 1990), 126; Drew Gilpin Faust, *This Republic of Suffering: Death and the American Civil War* (New York: Vintage,

2008), 177–181. These two models of heaven were, Wheeler argues, both important to nineteenth-century culture but "difficult to reconcile" (*Death and the Future*, 4). John J. Kucich argues for three versions of heaven in nineteenth-century America in "The Politics of Heaven: The Ghost Dance, *The Gates Ajar*, and *Captain Stormfield*," in *Spectral American: Phantoms and the National Imagination*, ed. Jeffrey A. Weinstock (Madison: University of Wisconsin Press, 2004), 102. On Phelps's materiality, see Lori Merish, *Sentimental Materialism: Gender, Commodity Culture, and Nineteenth-Century American Literature* (Durham, N.C.: Duke University Press, 2000), 90.

80. Elizabeth Stuart Phelps, *Chapters from a Life* (Boston: Houghton Mifflin, 1897), 97. Lyde Cullen Sizer points out that Phelps lost a lover during the conflict, and this grief provided a spur to her writing (*The Political Work of Northern Women Writers and the Civil War, 1850–1872* [Chapel Hill: University of North Carolina Press, 2000], 264). More Americans were killed in the Civil War than any other U.S. war. On average, there were 182 deaths for every 10,000 people. The Union lost a greater number of troops, but the Confederacy's losses were proportionally higher (Cott, *Public Vows*, 78).

81. Phelps, *Chapters*, 96.

82. See Grace Elizabeth Hale, *Making Whiteness: The Culture of Segregation in the South, 1890–1940* (New York: Pantheon, 1998), 80. For Southern writers, this distinction was often nonexistent; for its influence on women writers of the period, see Sarah Gardner, *Blood and Irony: Southern White Women's Narratives of the Civil War, 1861–1937* (Chapel Hill: University of North Carolina Press, 2003), 65.

83. Henry Ward Beecher, "Sources and Uses of Suffering," in *Plymouth Pulpit: Sermons Preached in Plymouth Church, Brooklyn* (Boston: Pilgrim Press, 1875), 4:161.

84. Phelps, *Chapters*, 98.

85. See Nancy Schnog, "'The Comfort of My Fancying': Loss and Recuperation in *The Gates Ajar*," *Arizona Quarterly* 49 (Autumn 1993): 131–133.

86. Gottfried August Bürger, "Lenora," *Old Guard* 4 (June 1866): 359–364. This poem appeared in numerous nineteenth-century anthologies, including the *Old Guard* in June 1866. This is not the translation used in *The Gates Ajar*, however.

87. One finds comparable arguments throughout the postbellum period. Jane Thrailkill notes that reviewers of "The Yellow Wallpaper," for example, "knew that complete absorption into one's perceptual experience—whether it pertained to wallpaper, battle, or a short story—had the makings of pathology" (*Affecting Fictions: Mind, Body, and Emotion in American Literary Realism* [Cambridge, Mass.: Harvard University Press, 2007], 121).

88. Whereas I find the cross-racial and gender identifications the characters playfully understand as imbued with a radical potential, Elizabeth Young links this scene to the earlier incident in which Mary's rebelliousness is disciplined (*Disarming the Nation*, 70).

89. Barnes, in *States of Sympathy*, demonstrates a parallel operation relative to the power of sympathy in early national texts.

90. Lisa Long, *Rehabilitating Bodies: Health, History, and the American Civil War* (Philadelphia: University of Pennsylvania Press, 2004), 68; Samuels, *Facing America*, 84.

91. Mrs. Bland's gruesome fate may have been informed by the notorious July 1861

death of Frances Longfellow, wife of poet Henry Wadsworth Longfellow, who died from injuries sustained when her dress caught fire. In *Chapters*, Phelps notes that it is "a privilege full of affectionate sadness" to recall her friendship with the famous poet (153). While she does not mention his wife's death, the publicity it drew leaves no doubt that she would have been familiar with the horrible event.

92. This reading is influenced by Teresa Goddu's discussion of the relationship between the slave narrative and the gothic (*Gothic America*, 131–140).

93. Henry Ward Beecher, *Sermons* (New York: Harper and Brothers, 1868), 269.

94. Wald, *Constituting Americans*, 66.

95. That Abraham Lincoln was rumored to have dabbled in spiritualism while in the White House complicates this claim; see Russ Castronovo, *Necro-Citizenship: Death, Eroticism, and the Public Sphere in the Nineteenth-Century United States* (Durham, N.C.: Duke University Press, 2001), 169–171.

96. Horace Bushnell, *The Spirit in Man: Sermons and Selections* (New York: Scribner's Sons, 1910), 163.

97. For an argument that correlates citizenship, death, and activity in a distinctly different way, see Castronovo, *Necro-Citizenship*, 25–61.

98. Horace Bushnell, "Our Obligations to the Dead," in *Building Eras in Religion*, 353.

99. Faust, *This Republic of Suffering*, 187.

100. Gail K. Smith, "From the Seminary to the Parlor: The Popularization of Hermeneutics in *The Gates Ajar*," *Arizona Quarterly* 54 (Summer 1998): 113. Phelps's theory of biblical language overlaps with the one Bushnell more famously propounded; both share the belief that gospel truths are best conveyed in an evocative and metaphoric language to capture the figurative nature of religion. On Bushnell and language, see Glenn Hewitt, *Regeneration and Morality: A Study of Charles Finney, Charles Hodge, John W. Nevin, and Horace Bushnell* (Brooklyn: Carlson, 1991), 127.

101. Bonnie Honig, *Democracy and the Foreigner* (Princeton, N.J.: Princeton University Press, 2001), 109, 113.

102. Bushnell, "Doctrine of Loyalty," 574–575.

103. Horace Bushnell, "Popular Government by Divine Right," 288.

104. On submission in Phelps, see Thomas, *American Literary Realism*, 116–120; Schnog, "'Comfort of My Fancying,'" 127–154.

105. Castronovo, *Necro-Citizenship*, 33.

106. In his satirical representation of heaven, written in response to the *Gates* novels, Mark Twain takes direct aim at the idea that heaven is like the United States, as a functionary in his less-than-ideal heaven asks, "'Where is America? What is America?' The under clerk answered up prompt and says—'There ain't any such orb'" (*Extract from Captain Stormfield's Visit to Heaven* [New York: Harper and Brothers, 1909], 17).

107. Elizabeth Stuart Phelps, *The Oath of Allegiance and Other Stories* (Boston: Houghton Mifflin, 1909), 30–31. "The Oath of Allegiance" became the title story for a 1909 volume of short stories and first appeared in the *Atlantic Monthly*.

108. Ganz, "Binding the Will," 579.

109. Berlant, *Queen of America*, 27–28.

3 / Pledging Allegiance in Henry James

1. Blight, *Race and Reunion*, 217.

2. According to Bronson Howard's *New York Times* obituary (August 5, 1908), *Shenandoah* was "the greatest success" by the "dean of American playwrights."

3. Bronson Howard, *Shenandoah: A Military Comedy*, 19–20, http://www.gutenberg.org/etext/13039.

4. Jennifer James, *A Freedom Bought with Blood: African American War Literature from the Civil War to World War II* (Chapel Hill: University of North Carolina Press, 2007), 86.

5. Grant, *North Over South*, 62.

6. Howard, *Shenandoah*, 24–25.

7. Brooks, *Melodramatic Imagination*, 27–62.

8. Wilson, *Patriotic Gore*, xvi.

9. James, *Freedom Bought with Blood*, 85–86.

10. Constance Fenimore Woolson, *Women Artists, Women Exiles: "Miss Grief" and Other Stories*, ed. Joan Myers Weimer (New Brunswick, N.J.: Rutgers University Press, 1988), 144.

11. Henry James, *The Complete Notebooks of Henry James*, ed. Leon Edel and Lyall Powers (New York: Oxford University Press, 1987), 9.

12. Critics disagree about the importance of the Civil War to James and *The Bostonians*: see Wilson, *Patriotic Gore*, 654–665; Aaron, *Unwritten War*, 110–120; Silber, *Romance of Reunion*, 118–119, 186–187; Peter Rawlings, *Henry James and the Abuse of the Past* (New York: Palgrave, 2005).

13. Lionel Trilling calls this "the novel's crucial scene" yet surprisingly merely notes that Ransom lectures Verena about the meaning of the war, concluding that James seeks to establish that "the danger of the battle had never been so great as the sexual danger of his present civil situation" (*The Opposing Self: Nine Essays in Criticism* [New York: Viking, 1955], 115). See, as well, Millicent Bell, *Meaning in Henry James* (Cambridge, Mass.: Harvard University Press, 1991), 139; Leland Person, "In the Closet with Frederick Douglass: Reconstructing Masculinity in *The Bostonians*," *Henry James Review* 16 (Autumn 1995): 296; Richard Godden, *Fictions of Capital: The American Novel from James to Mailer* (New York: Cambridge University Press, 1990), 29; Michael Anesko, *"Friction with the Market": Henry James and the Profession of Authorship* (New York: Oxford University Press, 1986), 89; Thomas, *American Literary Realism*, 53–87. Janet Bowen, who details how architecture provides James with a critical means of explaining his "sense of being an outsider in his own homeland," nonetheless ignores this domineering building ("Architectural Envy: 'A Figure Is Nothing without a Setting' in Henry James's *The Bostonians*," *New England Quarterly* 65 [1992]: 6).

14. Henry James, *Literary Criticism: Essays on Literature; American Writers; English Writers* (New York: Library of America, 1984), 518, 528.

15. Ibid., 516.

16. Leon Edel, *Henry James: The Conquest of London, 1870–1881* (Philadelphia: J. B. Lippincott, 1962), 389.

17. Richard Brodhead, *The School of Hawthorne* (New York: Oxford University Press, 1986), 8. Merging Hawthorne's romance, which takes up issues of history and "the vexed nature of group life," with the romance of reunion, which seeks to evade such vexations in sentimental reconciliation, James reveals the naïveté of the latter's

assumptions and conclusions (Stacey Margolis, *The Public Life of Privacy in Nineteenth-Century American Literature* [Durham, N.C.: Duke University Press, 2005], 17).

18. Anesko, *"Friction with the Market,"* 85.

19. Nathaniel Hawthorne, *The Blithedale Romance* (New York: Penguin, 1983), 2.

20. Walter Benn Michaels, "Local Colors," *MLN* 113 (1998): 734. While I agree that the novel explores the impact of the Civil War on gender, I will show that this is a means to a broader exploration of American culture, rather than an end in itself. Silber notes that James's novel does not fit the formula neatly, especially given the use of "the virile and masculine Basil for the romantic lead" (*Romance of Reunion*, 119).

21. See Butler, *Excitable Speech*; Eve Kosofsky Sedgwick, *Touching Feeling: Affect, Pedagogy, Performativity* (Durham, N.C.: Duke University Press, 2003).

22. Henry James, *The Question of Our Speech; The Lesson of Balzac: Two Lectures* (Boston: Houghton Mifflin, 1905), 10, 52; see Caroline Levander, "Bawdy Talk: The Politics of Women's Speech in *The Lecturress* and *The Bostonians*," *American Literature* 67 (1995): 467–485; Joyce A. Rowe, "'Murder, What a Lovely Voice!': Sex, Speech, and the Public/Private Problem in *The Bostonians*," *Texas Studies in Language and Literature* 40 (1998): 158–183; Thrailkill, *Affecting Fictions*, 226.

23. William James, *The Varieties of Religious Experience* (New York: Penguin, 1982), 340; all subsequent references will be to this edition and indicated parenthetically in the text. For a useful discussion of William James's differentiation between the martyr and the fanatic, see Jennifer Fleissner, *Women, Compulsion, Modernity: The Moment of American Naturalism* (Chicago: University of Chicago Press, 2004), 128.

24. Associating war and religion, James develops a claim he made in passing in 1897, that the Civil War was a conflict between "the fanatics of slavery" and abolition, itself a kind of fanaticism (*The Monument to Robert Gould Shaw: Its Inception, Completion, and Unveiling, 1865-1897* [Boston: Houghton Mifflin, 1897], 75).

25. James's interest in fanaticism can be linked back to the representation of Hollingsworth in *The Blithedale Romance*, as Robert Levine helpfully reminded me.

26. James, *Freedom Bought with Blood*, 87.

27. Henry James, *The Bostonians* (New York: Penguin, 2000), 30; all subsequent references will be to this edition and indicated parenthetically in the text.

28. Cited in Fisher, *Vehement Passions*, 33.

29. Trilling dismisses the idea that James was interested in female reform, suggesting that the topic was just a means of approaching deeper social issues (*Opposing Self*, 110). Greg Zacharias observes that the question of the novel's actual subject has been debated since the novel's initial appearance in the *Century* (*Henry James and the Morality of Fiction* [New York: Peter Lang, 1992], 49). Among the many critics who have treated this topic, a few are especially useful: Sara Davis, "Feminist Sources in *The Bostonians*," *American Literature* 50 (1979): 570–587; Judith Fetterley, *The Resisting Reader: A Feminist Approach to American Fiction* (Bloomington: Indiana University Press, 1978), 101–153; Alfred Habegger, "Henry James's *Bostonians* and the Fiction of Democratic Vulgarity," in *American Literary Landscapes: The Fiction and the Fact*, ed. F. A. Bell and D. K. Adams (New York: St. Martin's Press, 1988), 102-121; Fleissner, *Women, Compulsion, Modernity*, 123–160.

30. Irving Howe, "Introduction," in *The Bostonians* (New York: Modern Library, 1956), xxvi.

31. This is not to suggest, of course, that James was entirely blind to the historical conditions of either the women's rights movement or the politics of Reconstruction. My claim is, rather, that he manipulates these issues to get at his more fundamental concern, the damage done to the social fabric through the tyranny of fanaticism.

32. Friedrich Nietzsche, *Will to Power*, trans. Walter Kaufman (New York: Vintage, 1968), 35.

33. Edel, *Henry James Letters*, 4:682–683.

34. Henry James, *Literary Criticism: French Writers; Other European Writers; The Prefaces to the New York Edition* (New York: Library of America, 1984), 1138.

35. Commonly held to be a caricature of Sara Peabody, James was chastised by his brother William for "the Birdseye sacrilege," to use William Dean Howells's phrase (Anesko, *"Friction with the Market,"* 99).

36. Sedgwick effectively but briefly links James's aesthetics of shame, the excitement of slave narratives, and the Civil War (*Touching Feeling*, 65).

37. "Abolitionist martyrology," the sacrifice of a white life for black freedom, celebrated "the glorious army of martyrs"—like Lovejoy and Shaw—who died for the cause (Fredrickson, *Inner Civil War*, 153–154).

38. Menand, *Metaphysical Club*, 373–374.

39. Both sides accused the other of fanaticism—the South pointing to fiendish designs of Puritans, Radical Republicans, and abolitionists, the North to aristocratic despots and slave drivers. The Reverend W. G. Eliot observed in a published sermon that shrill and rigid partisanship had hastened the nation to war: "Fanatics at the North declared that every slave State was a pandemonium; fanatics at the South rejoined that Eden itself would be an imperfect abode without the peculiar institution" (*Loyalty and Religion*, 6). Looking back to the Civil War at the end of *The Fanatics* (1901), Paul Laurence Dunbar observed, "they were all fanatics" (*The Fanatics* [New York: Copley, 2001], 196).

40. Notebook entries on the novel point to James's original idea to focus on Verena as the heroine of the book, using her name as title (*Complete Notebooks*, 12–20, 30).

41. It could have been informed as well by the novels of George Eliot, which take up the issue of promising. See Ganz, "Binding the Will," 565–602; Randall Craig, *Promising Language: Betrothal in Victorian Law and Fiction* (Albany: State University of New York Press, 2000).

42. Speech is not just a concern for the characters, as James's narrator is unsure about how to represent Ransom's accent. "Although Verena's voice is silenced, the one voice we never hear is Ransom's," a fact that complicates, for Michaels, "the often asked question of whether Ransom speaks for James" ("Local Colors," 735).

43. Deborah Esch, "Promissory Notes: The Prescription of the Future in *The Princess Casamassima*," *American Literary History* 1 (Summer 1989): 319.

44. Miller, *Speech Acts in Literature*, 104.

45. Sedgwick considers the role of the performative in the prefaces to the New York edition and, more passingly, *The Golden Bowl* (*Touching Feeling*). The most sustained examination is J. Hillis Miller, *Conduct as Literature: Speech Acts in Henry James* (New York: Fordham University Press, 2005).

46. Thomas, *American Literary Realism*, 66.

47. Sedgwick, *Touching Feeling*, 74.

48. J. L. Austin, *Philosophical Papers* (New York: Oxford University Press, 1961), 242.

49. Ibid., 239.

50. According to Thomas, "Olive's idealized bond demands a perpetual renewal based on mutual trust" (*American Literary Realism*, 66).

51. Ganz, "Binding the Will," 580.

52. Henry James, *The Complete Stories, 1864–1874* (New York: Library of America, 1999), 24, 26–27.

53. On these popular tales, see Fahs, *Imagined Civil War*, 130.

54. Kirk Savage, *Standing Soldiers, Kneeling Slaves: Race, War, and Monument in Nineteenth-Century America* (Princeton, N.J.: Princeton University Press, 1998), 167. On the tension between memory and forgetting in the national imagination, see Anderson, *Imagined Communities*, 204.

55. Savage, *Standing Soldiers*, 5.

56. Oliver W. Holmes Jr., *Speeches* (New York: Little, Brown, 1891), 2. Anderson links nationalism to "synchronic novelty"—"substantial groups of people . . . think of themselves as living lives *parallel* to those of other groups of people"—that is, in part dependent on an oscillation of forgetting and memory (*Imagined Communities*, 188).

57. Holmes, *Speeches*, 11, 3; see also Blight, *Race and Reunion*, 96.

58. Theodore Roosevelt, *American Ideals, and Other Essays Social and Political* (New York: G. P. Putnam's Sons, 1897), 3.

59. The phrase is taken from a poem written by Oliver Wendell Holmes Sr. for the dedication of Memorial Hall (*New York Times*, October 7, 1870).

60. Anderson, *Imagined Communities*, 204.

61. Bainbridge Bunting, *Harvard: An Architectural History* (Cambridge, Mass.: Belknap Press of Harvard University Press, 1985), 86.

62. One faculty member and 1,311 Harvard students and graduates enlisted in the Union army, and 257 students enlisted in the Confederate army (ibid., 299; Menand, *Metaphysical Club*, 15). The lives and deaths of 95 of these students were elaborately memorialized in the two-volume 1866 *Harvard Memorial Biographies*, edited by Thomas Wentworth Higginson.

63. The series was issued in 1887 as a four-volume set entitled *Battles and Leaders of the Civil War*. See Blight, *Race and Reunion*, 164, 174.

64. Ann Bigham stresses the "dramatic display" of Basil's "patriotic manhood" in this scene, drawing an important connection between "union-making at the national scale" and "heterosexual union" ("Touring Memorial Hall: The State of the Union in *The Bostonians*," *Arizona Quarterly* 62 [Autumn 2006]: 14–16).

65. Wilson, *Patriotic Gore*, 12. Wilson focuses exclusively on the religiosity of the Southern Lost Cause, but many of his insights are germane to the Northern postwar experience as well. The closing scene in Music Hall, Anesko notes, offers a "deliberate parallel to the oldest of New England's civic rituals—the public conversion of a visible saint," but does so to indicate the lamentable vulgarization of the tradition's modern incarnation (*"Friction with the Market,"* 97). This historical parallel is further complicated by the other saints in the novel, the fallen soldiers and the abolitionists.

66. Foner, *Reconstruction*, 34.

67. Many Civil War memorials struggled to balance individual and communal

sacrifice; while early monuments usually were comprised of a simple tablet or obelisk, later monuments often depicted a common soldier in his battle gear, although not fighting or dead (Savage, *Standing Soldiers*, 162–208).

68. Lynn Wardley, "Woman's Voice, Democracy's Body, and *The Bostonians*," *ELH* 56 (1989): 654.

69. Savage argues that the use of names in monuments simultaneously condenses and particularizes the monument's meaning (*Standing Soldiers*, 162).

70. Susan Mizruchi also observes the shift in narrative perspective, although she concludes that "neither the 'braver' and 'heroism' at Memorial Hall, nor the delicate pre-autumnal wasting of the land at Marmion, can be considered the work of a historicizing consciousness" (*The Power of Historical Knowledge: Narrating the Past in Hawthorne, James, and Dreiser* [Princeton, N.J.: Princeton University Press, 1988], 169).

71. On Holmes and Civil War memory, see Fredrickson, *Inner Civil War*, 219–221; Menand, *Metaphysical Club*, 3–4.

72. Ernst Renan, "Qu'est-ce qu'une nation?" in *Nationalism*, ed. John Hutchinson and Anthony D. Smith (New York: Oxford University Press, 1994), 17.

73. Luciano, *Arranging Grief*, 174. Russ Castronovo develops a similar point, arguing that monuments "support the work of nation-building by creating, through the manipulation of a mythical past, a feeling of national belonging" (*Fathering the Nation: American Genealogies of Slavery and Freedom* [Berkeley: University of California Press, 1995], 109–110).

74. Benedict Anderson, "Replica, Aura, and Late Nationalist Imaginings," in *The Spectre of Comparisons: Nationalism, Southeast Asia, and the World* (London: Verso, 1998), 56–57.

75. Wardley, "Woman's Voice, Democracy's Body," 655.

76. Sharon Cameron's discussion of Harvard's Soldiers' Field (which James claims in *The American Scene* is "like some flat memorial slab that waits to be inscribed"), mourning, and James's "parody of writing that leads to its erasure" demonstrates that James's interest in the relationship between memory and memorials in not limited to *The Bostonians* (*Thinking in Henry James* [Chicago: University of Chicago Press, 1991], 68, 16).

77. Friedrich Nietzsche, *On the Advantage and Disadvantage of History for Life*, trans. Peter Preuss (Indianapolis: Hackett, 1980), 16, 17.

78. Margaret Higonnet maintains that "realist authors like James . . . use women for their critique of militarism." Her example—"Story of a Year"—supports her further claim that the vehicle for these critiques is often irony ("Civil Wars and Sexual Territories," in *Arms and the Woman: War, Gender, and Literary Representation*, ed. Helen Cooper, Adrienne Munich, and Susan Squier [Chapel Hill: University of North Carolina Press, 1989], 92–93).

79. Luciano, *Arranging Grief*, 174.

80. Ransom's other assertion—Music Hall has for him "a kind of Roman vastness," complete with "the *vomitoria* that he had read about in descriptions of the Coliseum"—completes the historical circle, invoking, as did Booth, the assassination of Caesar (333–334).

81. Sometimes called the Little Civil War, the violence in the Dakota Territory, instigated by tardy federal annuity payments, lasted approximately six weeks, ending after the battle at Wood Lake. In a series of military trials, 303 Dakota were convicted

and sentenced to death; on December 26, 1862, the largest execution in U.S. history took place when thirty-eight of the condemned were hanged.

82. Nell Irvin Painter, *Standing at Armageddon: The United States, 1877–1919* (New York: Norton, 1987), 163.

83. Jackson, "'Dowry of Suffering,'" 294.

84. Faust, *This Republic of Suffering*, 37.

85. Shelley Streeby, *American Sensations: Class, Empire, and the Production of Popular Culture* (Berkeley: University of California Press, 2002), 221, 227; Frost, *Never One Nation*, 26–29.

86. Charles Sumner, *Are We a Nation?* (New York: n.p., 1867), 7, 2.

87. American Indian metaphors were also used to characterize perceived threats from immigration or labor movements (Jeffory Clymer, *America's Culture of Terrorism: Violence, Capitalism, and the Written Word* [Chapel Hill: University of North Carolina Press, 2005], 58–59).

88. Gaines Foster, *Ghosts of the Confederacy: Defeat, the Lost Cause, and the Emergence of the New South* (New York: Oxford University Press, 1985), 66.

89. Christopher Castiglia, *Bound and Determined: Captivity, Culture-Crossing, and White Womanhood from Mary Rowlandson to Patty Hearst* (Chicago: University of Chicago Press, 1996), 11.

90. Joseph Tussman, *Obligation and the Body Politic* (New York: Oxford University Press, 1960), 24.

91. Cited in Crane, *Race, Citizenship, and Law*, 189.

92. Ibid.

93. Stanley, *From Bondage to Contract*, 175–217.

94. Cott, *Public Vows*, 62.

4 / Loyalty's Slaves

1. Foster, *Ghosts of the Confederacy*, 146.

2. Belle Kearny, *A Slaveholders Daughter* (New York: Abbey Press, 1990), 224.

3. Silber, *Romance of Reunion*, 180, 178–185; Painter, *Standing at Armageddon*, 141–169; Amy Kaplan, *The Anarchy of Empire in the Making of U.S. Culture* (Cambridge, Mass.: Harvard University Press, 2002), 121–145. Samira Kawash discusses the impact of both the Spanish-American War and the Civil War on Chesnutt's *The Marrow of Tradition* (*Dislocating the Color Line: Identity, Hybridity, and Singularity in African-American Literature* [Stanford, Calif.: Stanford University Press, 1997], 85–123).

4. Savage, *Standing Soldiers*, 163, 158, 155–157, 161. Savage goes on to argue that sentimentalized slave nostalgia was dropped from the Southern program of memory because the South craved national acceptance; as slavery no longer fit the nation's "self-image," even its sentimental form had to be abandoned. Savage underestimates, however, the genuinely national appeal of the "loyal slave." Transferred to other media—early film or advertising—the trope persisted well into the twentieth century. For other studies of "loyal slave" monuments, see especially Paul Shackel, *Memory in Black and White: Race, Commemoration, and the Post-Bellum Landscape* (New York: AltaMira Press, 2003), 77–112; Caroline Janney, "Written in Stone: Gender, Race, and the Heyward Shepherd Memorial," *Civil War History* 52 (June 2006) 117–141.

5. Blight, *Race and Reunion*, 355.

6. Fletcher, *Loyalty*, 7.

7. Trowbridge, *South*, 589–590.
8. Young, *Black Frankenstein*, 14.
9. Blight, *Race and Reunion*, 287.
10. Foner, *Reconstruction*, 230, 231. Despite the egalitarian impulse of the Radicals' ideas, it would be wrong, Foner importantly clarifies, to assume that they were free of the period's common racial prejudices.
11. For an overview of the implications of the Fourteenth Amendment for American literary practice, see Nabers, *Victory of Law*.
12. Foner, *Reconstruction*, 447.
13. Hartman, *Scenes of Subjection*, 60.
14. For a history of the antebellum loyal slave, see Micki McElya, *Clinging to Mammy: The Faithful Slave in Twentieth-Century America* (Cambridge, Mass.: Harvard University Press, 2007), 4–10. George Boulukos provides the Atlantic prehistory of the figure, linking it to antebellum representations, in *The Grateful Slave: The Emergence of Race in Eighteenth-Century British and American Culture* (New York: Cambridge University, 2008), 233–245. During the war years, Northern dime novels sometimes relied on faithful slaves to "fortify ... a Unionist sentiment," while Confederate literature more consistently included stories of loyal slaves to defend Southern policies and values (Streeby, *American Sensations*, 215). Drew Gilpin Faust notes that Confederate ideology did not match reality, for "slaves were anything but consistently loyal to the peculiar institution and their masters" (*Creation of Confederate Nationalism*, 71).
15. My point here is informed by Anthony Smith's argument in *Ethnic Origins of Nations*, 208.
16. Although some ex-slaves did remain loyal to their former masters, my interest in this chapter is with the trope of the "loyal slave" and the ways in which it was used to establish particular claims about race relations and citizenship rights.
17. MacPherson, *For Cause and Comrade*, 47–48.
18. Foster, *Ghosts of the Confederacy*, 122–123.
19. Katharine Prescott Wormeley, *The Other Side of War: with the Army of the Potomac: letters from the Headquarters of the United States Sanitary Commission during the Peninsular Campaign in Virginia in 1862* (Boston: Ticknor and Fields, 1889), 102; Sherwood Bonner, *Like Unto Like* (Columbia: University of South Carolina Press, 1997), 14-15; Stephen Crane, *Prose and Poetry* (New York: Library of America, 1984), 112.
20. Walter Benn Michaels, *The Shape of the Signifier: 1967 to the End of History* (Princeton, N.J.: Princeton University Press, 2004), 21.
21. Richard Posner, ed., *The Essential Holmes: Selections from the Letters, Speeches, Judicial Opinions, and Other Writings of Oliver Wendell Holmes, Jr.* (Chicago: University of Chicago Press, 1997), 89.
22. On Holmes, see Blight, *Frederick Douglass' Civil War*; Blight, *Race and Reunion*; Fredrickson, *Inner Civil War*, 168–170, 218–221; Aaron, *Unwritten War*, 161–162; Menand, *Metaphysical Club*, 36–38.
23. Silber, *Romance of Reunion*, 180.
24. Menand contends that Holmes survived the Civil War by embracing uncertainty (*Metaphysical Club*, 37).
25. Fletcher, *Loyalty*, 517–520.

26. On the issue of Twain's allegiance, see Neil Schmitz, "Mark Twain, Traitor," *Arizona Quarterly* 63 (Winter 2007): 25–37.

27. Mark Twain, *A Connecticut Yankee in King Arthur's Court* (New York: Modern Library, 2006), 115–116.

28. See Taylor, *Cavalier and Yankee*, 303. Caroline Lee Hentz swears that she had "never *witnessed* one scene of cruelty or oppression," but had been, to the contrary, "touched and gratified" by the master's "affectionate kindness and care" and the slave's matching "loyal and devoted attachment" (*The Planter's Northern Bride* [Chapel Hill: University of North Carolina Press, 1970], 5).

29. See Wald, *Constituting Americans*, 50.

30. Adam Smith, *The Theory of Moral Sentiments* (Indianapolis: Liberty Fund, 1984), 9.

31. Ibid., 139, 52, 86. Julie Ellison finds in Smith's hierarchical argument a set of fundamental assumptions about masculinity that structure the argument (*Cato's Tears and the Making of Anglo-American Emotion* [Chicago: University of Chicago Press, 1999], 10–12).

32. Smith, *Theory of Moral Sentiments*, 73–74.

33. Ibid., 21.

34. Christopher Castiglia, *Interior States: Institutional Consciousness and the Inner Life of Democracy in the Antebellum United States* (Durham, N.C.: Duke University Press, 2008), 124.

35. Anderson, *Imagined Communities*, 149.

36. Lincoln's apocryphal comment that *Uncle Tom's Cabin* started the Civil War aside, the novel mobilized Southern authors to pen literary works to celebrate their culture and institutions. The open exhortation of "The Duty of Southern Authors," for example, urged readers to bend their talents to "the establishment of a *Southern* literature," for "it is the literature of a country that gives her people a position among the nations of the earth" (W.R.A., "The Duty of Southern Authors," *Southern Literary Messenger* 23 [October 1856]: 241). For two recent discussions of how Stowe's novel influenced the depiction of race in the United States, see Gillian Brown, *Domestic Individualism: Imagining Self in Nineteenth-Century America* (Berkeley: University of California Press, 1990), 38–60; Robert S. Levine, *Martin Delany, Frederick Douglass, and the Politics of Representative Identity* (Chapel Hill: University of North Carolina Press, 1997), 58–98.

37. Stowe, *Uncle Tom's Cabin*, 50–51.

38. James Lane Allen, "'Uncle Tom' at Home in Kentucky," *Century* 34 (October 1887): 854; all subsequent references will be indicated parenthetically in the text.

39. In conflating fact and fiction, Allen repeats rhetorical strategies used in Confederate materials during the war, especially those written for schools and newspapers (Faust, *Creation of Confederate Nationalism*, 62–63).

40. Jacqueline Goldsby traces a parallel, but differently inflected, tension between fact and fiction (or form) in Douglass's preface to Ida B. Wells's *Southern Horrors*. She notes that "'Fidelity' is a cagey complement for Douglass to pay" to Wells, one that becomes even more ambivalent when juxtaposed against the loyal slave trope under investigation here (*A Spectacular Secret: Lynching in American Life and Literature* [Chicago: University of Chicago Press, 2006], 75).

41. Henry Wonham, *Playing the Races: Ethnic Caricature and American Literary Realism* (New York: Oxford University Press, 2004), 17; Goldsby discusses the popularity of exaggerated "coon" images and the "pastoralism of the plantation past" (*Spectacular Secret*, 255).

42. Butler, *Excitable Speech*, 68.

43. On the homoerotic intonations of Allen's fiction, see Caroline Gebhard, "Reconstructing Southern Manhood: Race, Sentimentality, and Camp in the Plantation Myth," in *Haunted Bodies: Genders and Southern Texts*, ed. Anne Goodwyn-Jones and Susan Donaldson (Charlottesville: University of Virginia Press, 1997), 132–155. In stories of wartime loyalty, like Grace King's "Bayou L'Ombre: An Incident of the War" (1887), the male slave entrusted with the care of his master's family fulfills his duty faithfully: "He knew all about the war; Marse John had told him. He knew what Marse John meant when he left the children to him, and Marse John knew what to expect from John" (*Harper's Monthly* 75 [July 1887], 275).

44. It is folly to think that government finds its authority in consent, Fitzhugh argued, for "all governments must originate in force, and be continued by force. The very term, government, implies that it is carried on against the consent of the governed" (*Cannibals All!* 243).

45. Anna Julia Cooper, *A Voice from the South* (New York: Oxford University Press, 1988), 222–223.

46. George Washington Williams, *History of the Negro Race in America, 1619–1880* (New York: G. P. Putnam's, 1883), 1:x. Even as black soldiers fought in conflicts on the western frontier; at Wounded Knee, South Dakota; or overseas in Cuba and the Philippines, depictions of loyal slaves became more prevalent; part of its work, then, was to make the case for the denial of African American rights regardless of patriotic service.

47. Frederick Douglass, *Autobiographies* (New York: Library of America, 1994), 874; all subsequent references will be to this edition and indicated parenthetically in the text. The visit took place in June 1877. Among his reasons for including the incident, Douglass explains, is how it was reported in newspapers at the time.

48. David Blight, "'For Something beyond the Battlefield': Frederick Douglass and the Struggle for the Memory of the Civil War," *Journal of American History* 75 (March 1989): 1169.

49. My point here is similar to Hartman's, when she observes that the "separate-but-equal doctrine effected the cordoning off of public space for the health and happiness of the greater body of Americans" (*Scenes of Subjection*, 170).

50. Kevin Gaines, *Uplifting the Race: Black Leadership, Politics, and Culture in the Twentieth Century* (Chapel Hill: University of North Carolina Press, 1996), 75.

51. Booker T. Washington, *Up from Slavery: An Autobiography* (New York: Penguin, 1986), 221. According to McElya, Washington "offered plantation nostalgia as evidence of contemporary 'patience' and a lack of 'resentment' among black southerners for past and present wrongs" (*Clinging to Mammy*, 36).

52. Hsuan Hsu, "Literature and Regional Production," *American Literary History* 17 (Spring 2005): 54–55.

53. One white supremacist group, the Knights of the White Camelia, required members to swear a racial loyalty oath, promising to protect the purity of the white race (Holland, *Body Politic*, 154).

54. Cited in Susan Gillman, *Blood Talk: American Race Melodrama and the Culture of the Occult* (Chicago: University of Chicago Press, 2003), 76.

55. Claudia Tate, *Domestic Allegories of Political Desire: The Black Heroine's Text at the Turn of the Century* (New York: Oxford University Press, 1992).

56. Charles Chesnutt, *The Journals of Charles W. Chesnutt*, ed. Richard Brodhead (Durham, N.C.: Duke University Press, 1993), 139–140.

57. Ibid., 140, 139.

58. Ibid., 139; Joseph R. McElrath Jr. and Robert C. Leitz III, eds., *To Be an Author: Letters of Charles Chesnutt* (Princeton, N.J.: Princeton University Press, 1997), 80.

59. Helen Chesnutt, *Charles Waddell Chesnutt: Pioneer of the Color Line* (Chapel Hill: University of North Carolina Press, 1952), 57.

60. Brodhead, *Cultures of Letters*, 207. That there were actual examples of "such characters" posed a distinct challenge for African American writers and thinkers of the period; W. E. B. Du Bois likewise admits that "the moral integrity of the Negro race" had been deeply scarred by the caste system introduced during Reconstruction, encouraging and rewarding the "gross flatter of white folk," especially "lying to appease and cajole them" (*Black Reconstruction in America, 1860–1880* [New York: Free Press, 1998], 702). See Keckley, *Behind the Scenes*, 99, 176.

61. Charles Chesnutt, *The Colonel's Dream* (New York: Harlem Moon, 2005), 24; all subsequent references will be to this edition and indicated parenthetically in the text.

62. Wiley Cash provides a reading of French's "liberal racism" that complements my own analysis ("*The Colonel's Dream* Deferred: A Reconsideration of Chesnutt's Liberal Racist," *American Literary Realism* 37 [2004]: 24).

63. Charles Chesnutt, *Stories, Novels, and Essays* (New York: Library of America, 2002), 30; all subsequent references to *The Marrow of Tradition* and to Chesnutt's stories will be to this edition and indicated parenthetically in the text.

64. Charles W. Chesnutt, *Essays and Speeches*, ed. Joseph R. McElrath Jr., Robert C. Leitz III, and Jess S. Crisler (Stanford, Calif.: Stanford University Press, 1999), 138.

65. William James, *Psychology: The Briefer Course* (New York: Dover, 2001), 16. Chesnutt's familiarity with the rudiments of Jamesian psychology is by no means a certainty, although James did publish essays in periodicals with which Chesnutt was familiar during the 1890s.

66. Ibid.

67. On the historical riot and Chesnutt's retelling, see Kawash, *Dislocating the Color Line*, 103–109; Gillman, *Blood Talk*, 98–100; Bryan Wagner, "Charles Chesnutt and the Epistemology of Racial Violence," *American Literature* 73 (2001): 311–337; Richard Yarborough, "The Wilmington Riot in Two Turn-of-the-Century African American Novels," in *Democracy Betrayed: The Wilmington Race Riot of 1898 and Its Legacy*, ed. David Cecelski and Timothy Tyson (Chapel Hill: University of North Carolina Press, 1998), 225-251. Thomas Dixon's *The Leopard's Spots: A Romance of the White Man's Burden 1865-1900* (New York: Grosset and Dunlap, 1902) offers a very different account of the riot.

68. Crane reads this scene as introducing a notion of contract at odds with "a naturally positivistic social order" that would require no such obligation (*Race, Citizenship, and Law*, 200). This analysis, however, understates the extent to which obligations and responsibilities inhered in the paternalistic system celebrated by the Southerners

depicted in the novel. It is not necessary, in other words, to have a fully theorized notion of contract for mutual obligations to exist.

69. Smith, *Theory of Moral Sentiments*, 52. Smith shares the idea that we have particular esteem for the wealthy with Hume, even referencing the *Treatise of Human Nature* in his footnotes.

70. Smith, *Theory of Moral Sentiments*, 52–53.

71. Scarry, "Consent and the Body," 878.

72. Gregg Crane suggests that Jerry is Carter's "loyal vassal," which overlooks the prudential nature of the character's choice (*Race, Citizenship, and Law*, 200).

73. See especially Brodhead, *Cultures of Letters*; Eric Sundquist, *To Wake the Nations: Race in the Making of American Literature* (Cambridge, Mass.: Belknap Press of Harvard University Press, 1993).

74. Howells's first review of Chesnutt's work appeared in the *Atlantic Monthly*, May 1900, and the disappointed reaction to *The Marrow of Tradition* appeared in the *North American Review* (December 1901). See Lorne Fienberg for a very different reading of the collection ("Charles W. Chesnutt's 'The Wife of His Youth': The Unveiling of the Black Storyteller," *ATQ* 4 [1990]: 219-237).

75. The standards for recognizing the legality of slave marriages varied from state to state in the years after the Civil War, but one could easily consider how these differing understandings of the contractual status of persons living under the conditions of slavery might impact Chesnutt's representation of the marriage vow. As Crane makes clear, Chesnutt's legal training influences his understanding of ethical dilemmas (*Race, Citizenship, and Law*, 184–190).

76. Tate, *Domestic Allegories*, masterfully details the political strategies deployed in late-nineteenth-century novels by African American women. Sundquist stresses the importance of marriage, observing that "marriage was a sign of communal healing," captured by Chesnutt in the reunion of "scattered or racially divided black families" (*To Wake the Nations*, 300). Hartman argues that "the articulation of black politics at the site of the family is often consistent with the regulatory efforts of the state" (*Scenes of Subjection*, 157).

77. In a letter of February 13, 1897, Chesnutt proposed to Walter Hines Page that "The Wife of His Youth" and "A Matter of Principle" could be published together under the title "The Blue Veins." Alternatively, three stories—"The March of Progress," "The Wife of His Youth," and "A Matter of Principle"—could be grouped under the title "Forward, Back, and Cross Over." Chesnutt's proposed clusters were offered in response to Page's idea that the *Atlantic* pair "The Wife of His Youth" and "The March of Progress" as "they both illustrate interesting phases of the development of the negro race" (Chesnutt, *Charles Waddell Chesnutt*, 78, 77). None of the plans materialized, and the *Atlantic* published "The Wife of His Youth" in July 1898.

78. McElrath and Leitz, *To Be an Author*, 115.

79. Sundquist, *To Wake the Nations*, 299–300.

80. Wonham, *Playing the Races*, 167; Sollers, *Beyond Ethnicity*, 159–160.

81. Wonham, *Playing the Races*, 168.

82. Castronovo, *Necro-Citizenship*, 241.

83. One could argue, with Tate, that the difference between Harper's and Chesnutt's works has much to do with the gender conventions being represented; in Tate's

analysis, male texts depict the frustration of "the hero's desire for public respect" rather than the heroine's desire for respectability (*Domestic Allegories*, 108).

84. Gillman, *Blood Talk*, 22.

85. William D. Howells, *An Imperative Duty* (New York: Harper and Brothers, 1892), 132.

86. As an early diary entry indicates, Chesnutt was attuned to the habits of mind and narrative that Americans had adopted about slavery: "There is something romantic, to the Northern mind, about the southern Negro, as commonplace and vulgar as he seems to us who come into contact with him every day. And there is a romantic side to the history of this people. Men are always more ready to extend their sympathy to those at a distance, than to the suffering ones in their midst" (quoted in Brodhead, *Cultures of Letters*, 192).

87. Wyatt-Brown, *Southern Honor*, 15.

88. Gillman, *Blood Talk*, 82.

89. As Kevin Gaines explains, "elite blacks also devised a *moral economy* of class privilege, distinction, and even domination *within* the race" (*Uplifting the Race*, 17).

90. Goldsby, *Spectacular Secret*, 54.

91. Ryder's phrase suggests to Wonham that he could be "claiming a measure of independence from responsibilities that attach to his former identity," especially as "Chesnutt leaves it unclear whether Ryder's acknowledgement of Liza Jane implies a renewal of their antebellum marriage vows, or simply an enlargement of his moral vision" (*Playing the Races*, 168).

92. David Hume, *An Enquiry Concerning the Principles of Morals* (Charleston, S.C.: BiblioBazaar, 2007), 125.

93. Atiyah, *Promises, Morals, and the Law*, 43. Bracketing the questions about identity the tale raises—how much change is required before a person is no longer identical with himself or herself—one could also associate Liza Jane's exorbitant loyalty with the "politics of transfiguration," which Paul Gilroy has argued resist the norms of Western rationality (*The Black Atlantic: Modernity and Double-Consciousness* [Cambridge, Mass.: Harvard University Press, 1993], 37).

94. Atiyah, *Promises, Morals, and the Law*, 37. Notably, Liza Jane assumes that only the loss of Sam's reason—if he were to be "out'n his head, so he could n' 'member his promise"—would prevent him from undertaking a similarly exhaustive search; this alternate configuration of what constitutes the reasonable demonstrates that the tension in "The Wife of His Youth" is between completely distinct and separate conventions about the parameters of allegiance.

95. Penelope Tucker argues that Chesnutt's promises rely on the strict moral code of reform writers to mark the moral value of African Americans and their collective worth as citizens ("The Culture of Promises: Literary Ethics and American Cultural Politics, 1820–1870" [Ph.D. diss., Harvard University, 2002], 10).

96. Chesnutt, *Essays and Speeches*, 120.

97. Michael Elliott, *The Culture Concept: Writing and Difference in the Age of Realism* (Minneapolis: University of Minnesota Press, 2002).

98. Dunbar, *Fanatics*, 131, 312.

99. Paul Laurence Dunbar, *Folks from Dixie* (New York: Dodd, Mead, 1898), 186; all subsequent references will be to this edition and indicated parenthetically in the text.

100. Brook Thomas, *Plessy v. Ferguson: A Brief History with Documents* (New York: Bedford, 1996), 24.
101. Elliott, *Culture Concept*, 72.
102. Young, *Black Frankenstein*, 155.
103. Ibid., 14.
104. My reading of Arendt has been influenced here by Honig, *Political Theory*, 76–125.
105. Victoria Earle Matthews's 1893 "Aunt Lindy" presents a similar argument. See as well Dunbar's *The Fanatics*, an adaptation of the reconciliation romance.
106. On changing ideas about the body during Reconstruction, see Holland, *Body Politic*, 93–168.
107. Allen, *Talking to Strangers*, 25–46.
108. James, *Monument to Robert Gould Shaw*, 85. As with Dunbar's story, the incident is not without its more complicated interpretation. In a letter to his brother Henry, William James notes, "The thing that struck me most in the day was the faces of the old 54th soldiers, of whom there were perhaps thirty or forty present, with such respectable old darkey faces, the heavy animal look entirely absent, and in its place the wrinkled, patient, good old darkey citizen." Commenting on this letter, Elizabeth Samet notes, "The 'good old darkey' is the stuff of nostalgia," especially as the reduction of the soldiers to "docile bodies" strips them of "political agency" (*Willing Obedience*, 177). Samet's reading overlooks James's emphasis on their role as citizens, a position he compromises by qualifying the reference.

5 / Philosophies of Loyalty

1. Josiah Royce, "Race Questions and Prejudices," in *Race Questions, Provincialism and Other American Problems* (New York: Macmillan, 1908), 6; all subsequent references will be to this edition and indicated parenthetically in the text.
2. Franz Boas, "Race Problems in America," *Science* 29 (May 1909): 839.
3. W. E. B. Du Bois, *The Souls of Black Folk* (New York: Library of America, 1990), 16.
4. James E. Cutler, *Lynch-Law: An Investigation into the History of Lynching in the United States* (New York: Longmans, Green, 1905), 225.
5. For more on the philosophical community at the turn of the century, see T. J. Jackson Lears, *No Place of Grace: Antimodernism and the Transformation of American Culture, 1880–1920* (Chicago: University of Chicago Press, 1994); Frank Lentricchia, "Philosophers of Modernism at Harvard, circa 1900," *South Atlantic Quarterly* 89 (1990): 787–834; Menand, *Metaphysical Club*; Bruce Kuklick, *The Rise of American Philosophy: Cambridge, Massachusetts 1860–1930* (New Haven, Conn.: Yale University Press, 1977).
6. Kuklick, *Rise of American Philosophy*, 309. One exception is Morton White, who notes that Royce's thought has been overlooked in part because of intellectual fashion. Connecting his ideas about a modified provincialism and loyalty to an idealist metaphysics, Royce "lost allies in social philosophy as he had lost them in the philosophy of history. American social thought at the turn of the century was breaking away from the rigidities of absolutistic metaphysics and much more sympathetic to the pluralism of James and the relativism of Dewey" (Morton White, *Science and Sentiment in America* [New York: Oxford University Press, 1972], 236).

7. Kuklick, *Rise of American Philosophy*, 308–309.

8. In the appendix detailing books of interest relative to "The Negro Race Problems," Alain Locke lists Royce's work, along with contributions by fifty-six other authors on the sociological dimension of the problem (*The New Negro: Voices of the Harlem Renaissance* [New York: Simon and Schuster, 1997], 448–449).

9. On Royce's fiction, an 1886 novel, *The Feud at Oakfield Creek*, see Walter Benn Michaels, "Frank Norris, Josiah Royce and the Ontology of Corporations," in Bell and Adams, *American Literary Landscapes*, 122–151.

10. Noble, *Masochistic Pleasures*, 295.

11. Lauren Berlant, *The Female Complaint*, 107-144; Elaine Scarry, *The Body in Pain: The Making and Unmaking of the World* (New York: Oxford University Press, 1985); Hortense Spillers, "Mama's Baby, Papa's Maybe: An American Grammar Book," *Diacritics* 17 (Summer 1987): 77–80; Michael Warner, "The Mass Public and the Mass Subject," in *Habermas and the Public Sphere*, ed. Craig Calhoun (Cambridge, Mass.: MIT Press, 1992), 377–401.

12. "To The Reader," *Journal of Speculative Philosophy* 1 (1867): 1. On the journal's importance to American philosophy, see Menand, *Metaphysical Club*, 253, 268.

13. G. W. F. Hegel, *The Philosophy of History*, trans. J. Sibree (New York: Dover Books, 1956), 86.

14. John S. Mackenzie, *An Introduction to Social Philosophy* (Glasgow: James Maclehose and Sons, 1890), 7.

15. D. H. Meyer, "American Intellectuals and the Victorian Crisis of Faith," *American Quarterly* 27 (March 1975): 602–603.

16. Louis J. Budd, "Altruism Arrives in America," *American Quarterly* 8 (March 1956): 4; David M. Tucker, *Mugwumps: Public Moralists of the Gilded Age* (Columbia: University of Missouri Press, 1998). On both sides of the Atlantic, the Ethical movement was specifically interested in education; Felix Adler brought a particular zeal to the issue of moral education for the young. For more on Adler's career, see Horace L. Friess, *Felix Adler and Ethical Culture* (New York: Columbia University Press, 1981).

17. *Ethics and Religion: A Collection of Essays by Sir John Seeley, Dr. Felix Adler, Mr. W. M. Salter, Prof. Henry Sidgwick, Prof. G. Von Gizycki, Dr. Bernard Bosanquet, Mr. Leslie Stephen, Dr. Stanton Coit and Prof. J. H. Muirhead*, ed. Society of Ethical Propagandists (London: Swan Sonnenschein, 1900), vii.

18. Speaking to a preliminary meeting of the Cambridge University Ethical Society, Henry Sidgwick began his remarks by noting that he was "not at all sanguine as to the permanent success of such a society," particularly given the lofty goals it had set for itself (*Ethics and Religion*, 109).

19. Adler contributed two essays to *Ethics and Religion*, "Freedom of Ethical Fellowship" and "The Ethical Bond of Union," and was an activist for education reform along Ethical lines throughout his life.

20. For recent discussions of American racial violence, see Goldsby, *Spectacular Secret*; Stewart E. Toldnay and E. M. Beck, *A Festival of Violence: An Analysis of Southern Lynchings, 1882–1930* (Urbana: University of Illinois Press, 1995); W. Fitzhugh Brundage, *Lynching in the New South: Georgia and Virginia, 1882–1930* (Urbana: University of Illinois Press, 1993); Trudier Harris, *Exorcising Blackness: Historical and Literary Lynching and Burning Rituals* (Bloomington: Indiana University Press, 1984).

21. Robyn Wiegman, *American Anatomies: Theorizing Race and Gender* (Durham, N.C.: Duke University Press, 1995), 86, 81.

22. Josiah Royce, *Philosophy of Loyalty* (Nashville, Tenn.: Vanderbilt University Press, 1995).

23. Royce, "Provincialism," in *Race Questions*, 86.

24. Sollors, *Beyond Ethnicity*, 181.

25. While Royce mentions many possible forms of loyalty in *Philosophy of Loyalty*—national, domestic, religious, commercial, and professional, to list a few—he never offers race as a viable basis for genuinely loyal relations.

26. American attitudes toward Japan were complicated at the beginning of the twentieth century given Japan's recent display of military prowess; widespread beliefs about Japanese culture, especially its emphasis on obedience and authority; and the popularity of Asian art and philosophy. See Lears, *No Place of Grace*, 85–149.

27. White, *Science and Sentiment*, 235.

28. See Cutler, *Lynch-Law*, 278.

29. Gaines, *Ghosts of the Confederacy*, 10–11.

30. A best-selling Southern author as well as ambassador to Italy during the Wilson administration, Page owed his renown in the postbellum period to his sentimental novels of the Old South and his stance as an adamant apologist of lynching and other forms of racial violence.

31. Thomas Nelson Page, *The Negro: The Southerner's Problem* (New York: Charles Scribner's Sons, 1904), 208.

32. Ibid., 36.

33. For a related argument, see Young, *Black Frankenstein*, 56–60.

34. Page, *The Negro*, 38.

35. For a full treatment of this mythic figure, see Sandra Gunning, *Race, Rape, and Lynching: The Red Record of American Literature, 1890–1912* (New York: Oxford University Press, 1996), 3–17; Wiegman, *American Anatomies*, 95–113.

36. Page, *The Negro*, 38, emphasis added.

37. Ibid.

38. The role of newspapers in articulating responses to lynching is detailed in Goldsby, *Spectacular Secret*, 16–20, 46–104.

39. Page, *The Negro*, 43.

40. Goldsby, *Spectacular Secret*, 23.

41. Smith, *Theory of Moral Sentiments*, 136.

42. See Castiglia, *Interior States*, 122–125.

43. Ross, "'Are We a Nation?'" 345.

44. Fitzhugh provides an important exception here.

45. Hentz, *Planter's Northern Bride*, 500.

46. Blight, *Race and Reunion*, 220.

47. Dismissing the rumor, Higginson's biographer, Tilden Edelstein, held "he had come to give greater credence to Page's account of slavery than Theodore Weld's or Mrs. Stowe's" (Gebhard, "Reconstructing Southern Manhood," 151).

48. Elliott, *Culture Concept*, 67.

49. Thomas, *Plessy v. Ferguson*, 34.

50. Page's fictional "history" of Reconstruction is paralleled in the daily press by the impact of fiction on reports of the Spanish-American War, where the conventions

of sentimental romance were deployed to stabilize the response of readers to U.S. imperialism. The case of a prominent young Cuban woman (the "Cuban Jan of Arc") imprisoned on suspicion of aiding the revolutionaries was "virtually scripted ... as a romance novel," in which the heroine is said to have been "imprisoned for resisting the lustful advances of a Spanish officer." "As in the old Romances," a writer for the *New York Journal* observed, "there is no uncertainty as to which way our sympathies should turn" (Kaplan, *Anarchy of Empire*, 109).

51. Thomas Nelson Page, *Red Rock: A Chronicle of Reconstruction* (New York: Charles Scribner's Sons, 1932), vii; all subsequent references will be indicated parenthetically in the text.

52. James, *Freedom Bought with Blood*, 59.

53. Robert S. Levine, *Dislocating Race and Nation: Episodes in Nineteenth-Century American Literary Nationalism* (Chapel Hill: University of North Carolina Press, 2008), 76.

54. Frederick Douglass was an outspoken critic of attempts to incite fear over what he called the "new crime" (Blight, *Frederick Douglass' Civil War*, 231).

55. Goldsby, *Spectacular Secret*, 69.

56. Michael Hatt, "Race, Ritual, and Responsibility: Performativity and the Southern Lynching," in *Performing the Body/Performing the Text*, ed. Amelia Jones and Andrew Stephenson (New York: Routledge, 1999), 80.

57. Recognizing this general problem, the New Negro movement of the 1920s also worked to reconstruct the trope of the black body; while their efforts were diffuse, one overarching tendency, much noted in the criticism, was toward depicting an educated, bourgeois, almost race-less minority that might represent African Americans more broadly. See Henry Louis Gates Jr., "The Trope of a New Negro and the Reconstruction of the Image of the Black," in *The New American Studies: Essays from Representations*, ed. Philip Fisher (Berkeley: University of California Press, 1991), 319–453.

58. Johnson, *Critical Difference*, 3.

59. That the black body has been subject to particular exposure and exploitation, rhetorical as well as physical, has been amply established in ante- and postbellum texts; in pointing to the ways in which this figure was closed to alternate interpretations, then, I am challenging those critics who have suggested the rhetorical possibility of constructing other kinds of black bodies within the context of nineteenth- and early-twentieth-century narrative. Considering the dilemmas faced by authors depicting their experiences under slavery, Lindon Barrett has argued that "in giving an account of slavery and 'themselves,' [the] paramount task [confronting ex-slave narrators] is to reproduce the experiences and trials of a 'body'—their bodies—in a medium necessarily antithetical to that project" ("African-American Slave Narratives: Literacy, the Body, Authority," *American Literary Realism* 7 [Spring 1995]: 423). Success could only be achieved, Barrett concludes, if writers could "make their bodies appear for their readers, since to be an African American or slave is to be foremost a body and to be fixed in a particular kind of space" (ibid., 424). Similarly, Karen Sanchez-Eppler has urged that the manipulation of the language of sentimentality permitted black authors to "rhetorically create an authorial body" and to co-opt the reader's body (*Touching Liberty: Abolition, Feminism, and the Politics of the Body* [Berkeley: University of California Press, 1993], 24).

60. Karen Halttunen, "Humanitarianism and the Pornography of Pain in Anglo-American Culture," *American Historical Review* 100 (April 1995): 326.

61. Elizabeth Clark, "'The Sacred Rights of the Weak': Pain, Sympathy, and the Culture of Individual Rights in Antebellum America," *Journal of American History* 82 (September 1995): 486.

62. Hartman, *Scenes of Subjection*, 4.

63. For another instance in which Royce configures "an utterly disembodied entity" as the solution to political tensions, see "Corporate Fiction," in Walter Benn Michaels, *The Gold Standard and the Logic of Naturalism: American Literature at the Turn of the Century* (Berkeley: University of California Press, 1987), 181–214.

64. Josiah Royce, "On Certain Psychological Aspects of Moral Training," *International Journal of Ethics* 3 (July 1893): 424.

65. John J. McDermott, ed., *The Writings of William James* (Chicago: University of Chicago Press, 1977), 10.

66. Onora O'Neill, "Ethical Reasoning and Ideological Pluralism," *Ethics* 98 (July 1988): 711.

67. Royce's position is complicated further by the inconsistent 1896 ruling in *Plessy v. Ferguson*, which maintained that racial distinctions both were and were not the function of physical characteristics. See Walter Benn Michaels, "The Souls of White Folks," in *Literature and the Body: Essays on Populations and Persons*, ed. Elaine Scarry (Baltimore: Johns Hopkins University Press, 1988), 185–209.

68. Josiah Royce, *The Problem of Christianity* (New York: Macmillan, 1913), 1:viii–ix.

69. Ibid., 1:ix.

70. Michaels, *Gold Standard*, 190.

71. Royce nonetheless did maintain that "some races are more teachable than others," although he believed that such judgments needed to be deferred until "centuries of opportunity to be taught" had passed (43-44).

72. W. E. B. Du Bois, *The Autobiography of W. E. B. Du Bois: A Soliloquy on Viewing My Life from the Last Decade of Its First Century* (New York: International, 1975), 148.

73. Ibid., 144. Herbert Aptheker points out that Royce was Du Bois's professor for this composition course (W. E. B. Du Bois, *Against Racism: Unpublished Essays, Papers, Addresses, 1887-1961*, ed. Herbert Aptheker [Amherst: University of Massachusetts Press, 1988], 16). Full attention to Du Bois's *Autobiography* suggests that Tommy J. Curry's claim that here Du Bois "speaks against Royce's sensibilities to the problem of lynching" is somewhat simplistic ("Royce, Racism, and the Colonial Ideal: White Supremacy and the Illusion of Civilization in Josiah Royce's Account of the White Man's Burden," *Pluralist* 4:3 [Fall 2009]: 34).

74. Nahum Chandler notes that "nearly every commentator on Du Bois's study ... since its first publication in 1909, has remarked or called attention to this passage" ("The Souls of an Ex-White Man: W. E. B. Du Bois and the Biography of John Brown," *New Centennial Review* 3 [Spring 2003]: 185).

75. W. E. B. Du Bois, *John Brown* (New York: Modern Library, 2001), xxv; all subsequent references will be to this edition and indicated parenthetically in the text. The volume took Du Bois four years to finish, even though his publishers nagged him regularly (Dominic Capeci Jr. and Jack Knight, "Reckoning with Violence: W. E. B. Du Bois and the 1906 Atlanta Race Riot," *Journal of Southern History* 62 [1996]: 762). Du

Bois relied heavily on the numerous treatments of Brown's life that appeared around the turn of the century and the fiftieth anniversary of the Harper's Ferry raid: Elijah Avey's *The Capture and Execution of John Brown; A Tale of Martyrdom* (1906), Richard J. Hinton's *John Brown and His Men* (1894), or Jonathan Wingate Winkley's *John Brown, the Hero; Personal Reminiscences* (1905). A full biography of works on the life of this contested American is vast, even at the end of the nineteenth century.

76. Shamoon Zamir, *Dark Voices: W. E. B. Du Bois and American Thought, 1888–1903* (Chicago: University of Chicago Press, 1995), 14.

77. Capeci and Knight trace Du Bois's personal crisis in the wake of the 1906 Atlanta race riot, claiming that his failure to act decisively affected his principles for advancing his race and for assessing the efficacy of Hegelian philosophy, both changes influencing the biography in significant ways. "Reflecting his own post-riot changes," they claim, "Du Bois recast Brown as a modern, tragic hero" ("Reckoning with Violence," 759).

78. In Du Bois's narrative of the life of John Brown, it is possible to detect the lingering influence of Prussian historian Heinrich von Treitschke, whose heroic romantic nationalism influenced Du Bois deeply during his studies in 1892–1894 in Berlin (Cornel West, *The American Evasion of Philosophy: A Genealogy of Pragmatism* [Madison: University of Wisconsin Press, 1989], 140).

79. Hale, *Making Whiteness*, 68.

80. Ralph Waldo Emerson, *Ralph Waldo Emerson: The Oxford Authors*, 137.

81. Locating Du Bois in the tradition of American pragmatism, West concludes that *Souls of Black Folk* "can be viewed as being in the Emersonian grain," although Du Bois critically "subverts the Emersonian theodicy by situating it within its imperialist and ethnocentric rhetorical and political context" (*American Evasion*, 142, 143).

82. Du Bois, *Black Reconstruction*, 714; all subsequent references will be to this edition and indicated parenthetically in the text.

83. Gillman, *Blood Talk*, 163.

84. On the relationship between ethical accounting and economic practices in Chesnutt, see Kawash, *Dislocating the Color Line*, 86–88.

Afterword

1. James, *Literary Criticism: Essays on Literature; American Writers; English Writers*, 427–428.

2. Frank Sullivan, "Uncivil Thoughts on the Civil War," *New York Times*, November 13, 1960.

3. Wilson, *Patriotic Gore*, ix.

Index

abolitionism: on black body, 204–205; in *The Bostonians*, 111, 112, 113, 135, 246n35; martyrology of, 246n37

abstraction: abstract nationhood, 142, 231n76, 241n68; allegiance predicated on abstract principle or ideal, 102; blacks seen as unable to form abstract bonds, 148; in *The Bostonians*, 14, 112–113; in citizenship, 177–178; for countering racial hate, 180; domestic sentiment versus abstract loyalty, 25–26, 29; in moral reasoning, 182, 183, 184; Royce on, 15, 181–182, 186, 205–206; in white loyalty, 142

Adams, Henry, 220

Adams, John Quincy, 2

"Address to the Young Men's Lyceum of Springfield, Illinois" (Lincoln), 46–47

Adler, Felix, 184, 257n16, 257n19

Adventures of Huckleberry Finn (Twain), 149

African Americans: assumptions about deviancy of, 195; black American body, 181, 186, 193, 199, 204–207, 259n57, 259n59; Black Laws, 216; compromise of 1876 abandons, 74; conduct manuals for freedmen, 170; Du Bois on Reconstruction and, 212; equal rights for, 149, 155, 158, 170, 196, 252n46; family in literature of, 157; intraracial prejudice among, 165–166, 167; Jim Crow laws, 113, 140, 141; mass migration to the North, 194; *Miss Ravenel's Conversion from Secession to Loyalty* on race, 82–83; Page on, 195–199; race loyalty for, 156, 165; representations in literature, 151; sexual violence against white women, 196–199, 202–203; Supreme Court cases limit rights of, 155; sympathy and loyalty deployed against, 143; uplift ideology, 155–156, 158, 167, 170; violence against, 74, 151. *See also* lynching; slavery

alcohol abuse, 76

Alcott, Louisa May, 40–43

Alexander, William T., 154

allegiance: anomaly of American, 23, 24–25, 31; anxiety about verifying, 115; Bellamy on sentiment and national, 2–3; black and white distinguished, 155; conflicts between, 171; Du Bois on, 212, 217; loyalty as alternative to sympathy for, 3–4, 4–5, 21–23, 39, 55, 60, 142, 146, 186; loyalty oaths for formalizing, 7–8, 23–24, 46–48; multiplicity of ideals of, 224n13; obsessive, 110; Pledge of Allegiance, 1, 3, 7, 9; predicated on abstract principle or ideal, 102. *See also* loyalty

Allen, Danielle, 178

Allen, James Lane, 148–151, 155
altruism, 183
Anderson, Benedict, 124, 147–148, 247n56
Andrews, Sidney, 62
"Anecdote of the Jar" (Stevens), 116
Anesko, Michael, 247n65
anxiety, 50–51, 53, 115, 121
Aptheker, Herbert, 260n73
Arendt, Hannah, 24, 48, 51–52, 177, 235n150, 235n151
Aristotle, 2, 18
Atiyah, P. S., 171
Atlanta Constitution, 137
Austin, J. L., 54, 116, 118, 236n161

"Barbara Frietchie" (Whittier), 43
Barnes, Elizabeth, 2, 21
Barrett, Lindon, 259n59
Battle-Pieces (Melville), 73
"Battles and Leaders of the Civil War" series, 200, 247n63
Bayard, James A., 47
"Bayou L'Ombre: An Incident of the War" (King), 252n43
Beecher, Henry Ward: on the flag, 35; on gigantic dishonesties, 45; home and battlefield compared by, 88; reaction to "Marse Chan," 200; on sacrifice, 93–94; "The Sources and Uses of Suffering," 88; on Southern secession, 30, 31–32
Bellamy, Francis, 1–3, 7, 9, 224n10
Bellows, Henry: on loyalty versus self-interest, 36; on oaths, 44–45; on religion and Civil War, 241n73
Bense, James, 229n34
Berlant, Lauren, 4, 67, 99, 181
Beyond the Gates (Phelps), 90, 97–98
Bigham, Ann, 247n64
black Americans. *See* African Americans
Black Laws, 216
Black Reconstruction in America (Du Bois), 210, 211, 212
Blight, David, 141
Blithedale Romance (Hawthorne), 105–106, 244n17
Bloody Chasm, The (De Forest), 84–85
Boas, Franz, 179
body, the: abstractions for evading prejudice based on, 181; African American, 181, 186, 193, 199, 202, 204–207, 259n57, 259n59; in "Nelse Hatton's Vengeance," 175; race without, 208; racialized bodies, 189–194, 196; Royce on seeing beyond, 180; white, 198, 199, 201. *See also* lynching
Bond and Free (Howard), 151
"Bone Ornaments" (Leland), 76–77, 240n54
Bonner, Sherwood, 143
Booth, John Wilkes, 130, 131
Bostonians, The (James), 103–136; on abolitionism, 111, 112, 113, 135, 246n35; *Blithedale Romance* compared with, 105–106; on causes as closed systems, 108; central question about commitment, 114; on Civil War's aftermath as captivity narrative, 14–15, 131–136, 139; on fanaticism, 14, 103, 104, 108–113, 115; final sentence of, 136; on gender, 106, 245n20; on language, 114–122; on Manichaean oppositions, 136; marriage at end of, 106; Memorial Hall scene, 104, 109, 124–130, 244n13; Music Hall scene, 130–131; as national novel, 103–104; original publication of, 124; on promises, 116–122; and "The Question of Our Speech," 107; reunion romances compared with, 103, 106, 121–122; rhetoric of conversion, 121; on women's rights, 108–109, 110, 111, 112, 114, 129, 132–133, 135, 136, 245n29
Bowen, Janet, 244n13
Bronks, William, 87
Brooks, Peter, 49, 102, 103
Brown, John, 27, 210–217
Brown, Wendy, 225n20
Brown, William Wells, 151
Brownson, Orestes, 223n9
Bürger, Gottfried August, 89, 242n86
Bushnell, Horace: on biblical language, 243n100; changes his views on loyalty, 231n73; on the dead calling on us to do our duty, 94; "The Doctrine of Loyalty," 32, 38, 229n44; on extreme conditions needed for loyalty, 94; on flag as symbol, 34–35; on government as requiring Supreme Being, 236n157; on lack of local patriotism in the North, 31; on loyalty and law, 38; on loyalty as Old World, 32; on loyalty requiring repudiation of rebellion, 97; on nation and family, 36–37, 70, 232n86;

"Reverses Needed," 94; on sympathy with Southern rebels, 29
Butler, Benjamin, 58
Butler, Judith, 236n162

Cable, George Washington, 158
Cahan, Abraham, 167
Calhoun, John C., 229n38
Cameron, Sharon, 248n76
Cannibals All! or Slaves without Masters (Fitzhugh), 28–29
Capeci, Dominic, Jr., 261n77
Castiglia, Christopher, 147
Castronovo, Russ, 167, 248n73
Cavell, Stanley, 64, 91
Centennial Exposition (1876), 9
Century Magazine, 124, 200
Chandler, Nahum, 260n74
Chesnutt, Charles, 157–172; *The Colonel's Dream*, 159–161, 168; Du Bois contrasted with, 216; on ethical approach to human relationships, 157; on family as model for nation, 157; on habit and character, 161, 253n65; "Her Virginia Mammy," 171–172; interest in bonds between people, 171; legal training of, 254n75; loyal slave trope opposed by, 156–157, 158–159; on loyalty, 157; "The March of Progress," 254n77; *The Marrow of Tradition*, 159, 161–164, 254n74; "Mars Jeems's Nightmare," 161; "A Matter of Principle," 254n77; moral revolution as goal of, 158, 172; on Northern narrative of slavery, 255n86; on place, consent, and morality, 163, 170; "A Plea for the American Negro," 172; "Uncle Wellington's Wives," 165; "The Web of Circumstance," 161; "The Wife of His Youth," 15, 164–171, 254n77; *The Wife of His Youth and Other Tales of the Color Line*, 164
Chicago Inter-Ocean, 137
Chicago Tribune, 194
"Chiefly About War-Matters" (Hawthorne), 13, 24–27, 42
"Chrismus on the Plantation" (Dunbar), 176
Civil Rights Cases (1883), 155, 174
Civil War: and American exceptionalism, 221–222; centennial of, 221; *Century Magazine* War Series, 124; comes to be seen as miscommunication, 101; continuity through, 4, 221; cultural value of emotion declines during, 20–21, 63; death ratio in, 242n80; demonstrating loyalty in the North, 43–48; Du Bois on, 210, 215–216; fanaticism seen as cause of, 246n39; fiftieth-anniversary celebrations of, 211–212; Frederickson on development of loyalty during, 5–6; Harvard faculty, students, and graduates in, 247n62; in Hawthorne's "Chiefly About War-Matters," 24–27; home and battlefield compared in literature of, 87–88; James influenced by, 104, 106; literary production following, 220–221; loyalty as alternative to sympathy in discourse of allegiance during, 3–4, 4–5, 21–23, 39, 55, 60, 142, 146, 186; loyalty oaths in, 7, 23–24, 46–48; marital dispute compared with, 62; and memory, 122–130; monuments, 123, 137–138, 247n67; as mythic origin of American nation, 221; Native Americans in, 132; passivity and authority in Union prosecution of, 36; patriotism changed by, 59; as pivotal moment in American history, 219; Pledge of Allegiance inspired by, 7; private propagandizing of loyalty during, 38–39; as purification of the nation, 220; rational loyalty versus indulgent sympathy and, 6, 13, 14; reinterpreted as nonideological, 143; religion's prominence in era of, 86; resists representation, 220; Revolutionary history contested in, 31–32; sentimentality in disseminating moral norms in wartime North, 39–43; soldiers as cogs in wheel, 143–144; Spanish-American War finalizes reconciliation, 137
Clark, Elizabeth, 205
Claybaugh, Amanda, 76
Cleveland, Grover, 133
Colonel's Dream, The (Chesnutt), 159–161, 168
Columbian World Exposition, 1
Columbus Day Programme (Columbian Exposition), 1–2, 3, 6–7
conduct manuals, 170

Confidence-Man, The (Melville), 58
Connecticut Yankee in King Arthur's Court, A (Twain), 144–145
consensus: techniques for creating, 124; Union assertions about, 23
consent: absolute devotion to nation and, 151; affective, 20–21; Bushnell on, 37; coerced, 14, 62, 65, 135; in Confederate theory of government, 22; ex-slaves and, 139; *Federalist* XXII on, 19; government's origins in force and, 252n44; in Locke's theory of government, 18–19; in *Miss Ravenel's Conversion from Secession to Loyalty*, 77, 79–80, 85; in *Moby-Dick*, 17–18, 19–20; place and, 163, 170; plantation reconstructed as site of, 141; in reunion romances, 14; revocable, 57; of Southerners to rejoining United States, 22; subordinated to force in Civil War, 26; voluntary oath-taking and, 24
constancy, 122–123
Constitution, U.S.: Beecher on the flag and, 35; Fifteenth Amendment, 140, 141; Fourteenth Amendment, 19, 140, 141, 155; loyalty as faithfulness to, 38; on oaths of public officials, 19
contamination, racial, 147–148
contracts: Hobbes on political, 53, 66; law versus morals, 11–12; in Locke's theory of government, 19; in *Moby-Dick*, 18; nuptial model of, 63; in postbellum narrative, 10; promises compared with, 10–11; and sentimental versus realist fiction, 13; temporal dimension of, 11, 19; and "The Wife of His Youth," 165
Conway, Moncure, 37
Cooper, Anna Julia, 151
Cooper, James Fenimore, 133
Copperheads, 38, 232n90, 234n122
Crane, Gregg, 10, 135, 253n68, 254n72, 254n75
Crane, Stephen, 143
Crimmins, Mary, 194–195
Cudjo's Cave (Trowbridge), 55–57, 236n164, 237n166
Curry, Tommy J., 260n73
Curtis, G. Ticknor, 33, 231n67
Cutler, James, 180

Dakota conflict of 1862, 76, 131, 248n81

Darwin, Charles, 80
"Dash for Liberty, A" (Hopkins), 154
David, Jacques-Louis, 72
Davis, Jefferson, 22, 34, 38, 61, 91, 92
Davis, Varina, 30
Dawes Severalty Act (1887), 132
Dean, Janet, 131
De Forest, John: *The Bloody Chasm*, 84–85; on fiction and nation, 67; *History of the Indians of Connecticut from the Earliest Known Period to 1850*, 240n53; *Kate Beaumont*, 84; on *Uncle Tom's Cabin*, 66. See also *Miss Ravenel's Conversion from Secession to Loyalty*
De Man, Paul, 47–48, 225n30
Democratic Party: compromises offered by, 46; Copperheads, 38, 232n90, 234n122
dime novels, 132, 250n14
"Doctrine of Loyalty, The" (Bushnell), 32, 38, 229n44
Douglass, Frederick: on Brown, 214, 216; on consent, 135; on loyalty and abolition, 38; preface to Wells's *Southern Horrors*, 251n40; on reunion with Captain Auld, 154, 252n47; on words for stimulating blows, 44
Draper, John William: on centralization and the nation, 82, 240n64; *History of the American Civil War*, 61–62, 82; on local patriotism in North, 30; on organic nation, 223n9; on science, 241n70; *Thoughts on the Future Civil Policy of America*, 82; on war in learning subordination, 84
Dred (Stowe), 36, 177
Du Bois, W. E. B., 209–217; on abstraction, 15; on agency, 217; on allegiance, 212, 217; and Atlanta race riot of 1906, 261n77; on black flattery of whites, 253n60; *Black Reconstruction in America*, 210, 211, 212; on Chesnutt and Dunbar, 156; on ethical standards in history, 212–213; Hegel's influence on, 213–214; on implication of Civil War for black Americans, 210; *John Brown*, 209, 210–217, 260n75; on loyalty, 209, 212; *The Philadelphia Negro: A Social Study*, 210, 211; on problem of color line, 179, 209; and Royce, 187, 209–210, 211, 260n73;

on slavery, 212, 216; *The Souls of Black Folk*, 179, 209, 211, 261n81; on traditional narratives of Civil War, 215–216

Dunbar, Paul Laurence, 172–178; "Chrismus on the Plantation," 176; direct engagement with Civil War heritage, 173; Du Bois contrasted with, 216; on ethical approach to human relationships, 157; on family as model for nation, 157; *The Fanatics*, 173, 216, 246n39; loyal slave trope opposed by, 156–157, 172; on loyalty, 157; "The Lynching of Jube Benson," 175; "Nelse Hatton's Vengeance," 15, 173–178

duty: honor versus, 74–75

Eliot, George, 99, 246n41
Eliot, W. G., 37, 44, 246n39
Ellis, Edward, 132
Elsie Dinsmore (Finely), 79, 81
Emerson, Ralph Waldo, 32, 59, 212
emotions: affective religion, 93; cultural value of declines during Civil War, 20–21, 63; language's effect on, 61; national affect, 68–69; Page appeals to, 197; plantation narratives on, 151, 157; race and capacity for, 198; rebellion linked with self-interested emotionalism, 89; reunion romances on voluntary emotional reconciliation, 63; Royce associates with mob-spirit, 186, 187, 195; Royce on affect-based moral reasoning, 181–182; Southerners associated with, 142; symmetry between head and heart, 90; and violence, 20; women's emotionality, 71. *See also* sentiment

empirical evidence about race, 189, 191
Encyclopedia Britannica, 212
equal rights: for African Americans, 149, 155, 158, 170, 196, 252n46; Bellamy on, 2; for women, 108–109, 110, 111, 112, 114, 129, 132–133, 135, 136, 245n29

Esch, Deborah, 116
Ethical movement, 183–184, 257n16
Ethics and Religion (Society of Ethical Propagandists), 183, 257n19
exceptionalism, American, 222

Fahs, Alice, 6, 220, 229n38, 231n76

family: in African American literature, 157; *The Gates Ajar* on, 62, 90–91, 95–96; nation compared with, 36–37, 62–64, 70, 81, 157; patriarchal, 167; in plantation narrative, 175; in "The Wife of His Youth," 165, 167

fanaticism: *The Bostonians* on, 14, 103, 104, 108–113, 115; in *The Gates Ajar*, 99; William James on, 107, 116, 245n24; seen as cause of Civil War, 246n39; sentiment of beauty in, 128

Fanatics, The (Dunbar), 173, 216, 246n39
Faust, Drew Gilpin, 234n121, 250n14
Federalist XXII, 19
Fields, James T., 26
Fifteenth Amendment, 140, 141
Finely, Martha, 79
First Duty of the Citizen, The (1863), 43
Fisher, Philip, 3, 48, 57
Fitzhugh, George, 28–29, 252n44
flag, the, 25, 34–35, 102
Fletcher, George, 10, 48, 139, 144, 226n33, 226n34
Fliegelman, Jay, 20
Foner, Eric, 250n10
Fool's Errand (Tourgée), 106
Fourteenth Amendment, 19, 140, 141, 155
Frederickson, George, 5–6, 36, 230n58, 231n61, 234n129, 246n37
Fukuyama, Francis, 221

Gaines, Kevin, 255n89
Ganz, Melissa, 12, 120
Gates Ajar, The (Phelps), 85–99; *The Bostonians* compared with, 103; catechism in, 94–95; on condolence system, 88–89; double infantilization in, 98; family and nation compared in, 62; on family ties persisting beyond the grave, 90–91, 95–96; on flexible identification and reunification, 91–92; on heaven, 87, 93, 95, 243n106; on loyalty as depending on death, 94; material objects in, 87; *Miss Ravenel's Conversion from Secession to Loyalty* compared with, 85–86; on necessity of death, 96–97; popularity of, 241n77; rebellion linked with self-interested emotionalism by, 89; recognition in, 64–65; remarriage in, 91; repetition in, 94; as reunion romance, 14, 62,

85; on sacrifice, 93–94; on sympathy and nuanced moral relations, 112; on violence in everyday life, 92–93
Gates Between, The (Phelps), 98
General Amnesty Act (1872), 74
Gettysburg Address, 35, 94
Gilroy, Paul, 255n93
Goddu, Teresa, 243n92
Goldsby, Jacqueline, 170, 251n40
Gone with the Wind (Mitchell), 7–8
Gurowski, Adam, 30

habit, 161
Hale, Edward Everett, 13, 48–51
Harper, Frances, 167
Harper's Weekly: on loyalty and nation, 33–34; "Mother Can I Go?," 70, 239n39; on Native Americans and Confederacy, 132, *133*; "Old Mr. Secesh, from his Housetop in Richmond, Va.," *28*; "Some Specimens of 'Secesh' Industry," *77, 78*
Harris, Elijah, 194–195
Hart, Albert Bushnell, 209
Hartman, Saidiya, 141, 170, 205, 252n49
Harvard University: faculty, students, and graduates in Civil War, 247n62; Memorial Hall, 104, 109, 124–130, *126*, 244n13
Hatt, Michael, 204
Hawthorne (James), 105, 219
Hawthorne, Julian, 228n30
Hawthorne, Nathaniel: on anomaly of allegiance, 23, 24–25, 31; on appropriate thoughts in time of civil war, 43–44; *Blithedale Romance*, 105–106, 244n17; "Chiefly About War-Matters," 13, 24–27, 42; James's *Hawthorne*, 105, 219; on loyalty versus sentiment, 25, 34
Hayes, Rutherford B., 74
Hayne, Robert, 34
Heaven Our Home (Bronks), 87
Hegel, Georg Wilhelm Friedrich, 182, 213–214
Hentz, Caroline Lee, 199–200, 251n28
"Her Virginia Mammy" (Chesnutt), 171–172
Herzog, Don, 65–66
heteronormativity, 50, 232n86
Higginson, Thomas Wentworth, 200
Higonnet, Margaret, 248n78

Hill, Walter, 148
Hirschman, Albert, 109, 228n30
History of the American Civil War (Draper), 61–62, 82
History of the Colored Race in America (Alexander), 154
History of the Indians of Connecticut from the Earliest Known Period to 1850 (De Forest), 240n53
History of the Negro Race in America, 1619–1880 (Williams), 154
Hobbes, Thomas: on coercive consent, 14, 65; *Leviathan*, 53, 65; on oaths and promises, 52–54, 236n157; *On the Citizen*, 52–53; on political contract, 53, 66
Holland, Catherine, 230n58
Holmes, Oliver Wendell, Jr., 11–12, 123–124, 127, 143–144
Honig, Bonnie, 96
honor: duty versus, 74–75; as self-regarding, 169
Hopkins, Pauline, 154
Hosmer, James K., 30
Howard, Bronson, 100–102, 103, 143, 244n2
Howard, James, 151
Howe, Irving, 110
Howells, William Dean, 10, 168, 220, 239n35, 254n74
Hume, David, 54, 171, 227n10, 254n69
Hunter's Escape, The (Ellis), 132

Imperative Duty, A (Howells), 168
Indian Jim (Ellis), 132
individualism, 82, 182
"In God We Trust," 86
"In the Cotton Country" (Woolson), 103
Introduction to Social Philosophy, An (Mackenzie), 183
Iola Leroy (Harper), 167
Ironclad Oath, 47

Jackson, Gregory, 238n24, 239n36
Jackson, Stonewall, 43, 221
Jamaica, 191–192
James, Alice, 113
James, Henry, 100–136; on abstract commitment, 142–143; Chesnutt compared with, 159; on Civil War and memory, 122–124; Civil War's influence

on, 104, 106; contract as influence on works of, 10; does not experience combat, 220; *Hawthorne*, 105, 219; on Lowell's allegiance, 104–105; on loyalty, 32–33, 105; on *Miss Ravenel's Conversion from Secession to Loyalty*, 239n34; "The Question of Our Speech," 107; "A Story of a Year," 122–123. See also *Bostonians, The*
James, Henry, Sr., 32–33, 231n61
James, William: and *The Bostonians*, 106; and Chesnutt, 253n65; on democratic citizenship, 178, 256n108; and Du Bois, 209; on fanaticism in Civil War, 245n24; on habit, 161; in *Journal of Speculative Philosophy*, 182–183; on plasticity, 205–206; on religious experience, 125; on religious zeal, 107–108, 116; and Royce, 180, 256n6; *The Varieties of Religious Experience*, 107–108
Japan, 190–191, 258n26
Jim Crow laws, 113, 140, 141
John Brown (Du Bois), 209, 210–217, 260n75
Johnson, Barbara, 42, 204
Journal of Speculative Philosophy, 182–183
Julian, George W., 237n8

Kantorowicz, Ernst, 144–145
Kate Beaumont (De Forest), 84
Keckley, Elizabeth, 30
Keely, Karen, 63
Kemble, E. W., 149–150, *152*, *153*, 176
Kierkegaard, Søren, 50
King, Grace, 252n43
Knight, Jack, 261n77
Knights of the White Camelia, 252n53
Kuklick, Bruce, 180–181

Lacan, Jacques, 50–51
language: *The Bostonians* on, 114–122; James on, 106–107; as limited for safeguarding nation's security, 51; performative, 48, 50–51, 54, 106–107, 115, 116, 118–119, 124, 217; political power of, 43–44; referential instability, 61, 65; Royce on material implications of, 207; vehemence of Southern speech, 71–72
Larcom, Lucy, 39

Last of the Mohicans, The (Cooper), 133
Lawson, Melinda, 22, 38, 231n66, 235n146
Lee, Robert E., 29, 221
Leland, Charles G., 76–77, 240n54
"Lenora" (Bürger), 89, 242n86
Letters to a Gentleman in Germany (Lieber), 199
Leviathan (Hobbes), 53, 65
Levinson, Sanford, 23, 24, 234n133
liberalism, 35
Lieber, Francis, 45–46, 82, 223n9, 199, 234n129
"Ligeia" (Poe), 96
Like Unto Like (Bonner), 143
Lincoln, Abraham: apotheosis of, 221; assassination of, 130, 131; denounced as traitor to Constitution, 38; Gettysburg Address, 35, 94; on his oath of office, 45; on loyalty oaths, 46–47; nation and family compared by, 62; on negative speech, 44; and spiritualism, 243n95; on *Uncle Tom's Cabin*, 251n36; on words and meaning, 61
Lippard, George, 96
Locke, Alain, 181, 257n8
Locke, John, 14, 18–19, 20, 66
Longfellow, Frances, 242n91
Lost Cause ideology, 221
"Love and Loyalty" (Alcott), 40–43
Lowell, James Russell, 13, 22, 61, 65, 104–105, 238n21
Loyal National League, 45–46
Loyal Publication Society, 46, 234n129
loyal slave narrative, 137–178; African American resistance to, 151, 156–157; black rapist compared with loyal slave, 197; in denial of African American rights, 252n46; dissemination of, 151; as at heart of Civil War memory, 141, 146; as integral to postbellum national fantasy, 145–146; "Nelse Hatton's Vengeance" reverses, 173, 175; nostalgic veneer acquired by, 15; in reconstruction of racialized American nation, 141–142; uplift ideology reinforces, 155–156; "The Wife of His Youth" inverts, 165, 170–171
loyalty: abolition of slavery associated with, 38; as absolute allegiance, 102; as alternative to sympathy in discourse of allegiance, 3–4, 4–5, 21–23, 39, 55, 60,

142, 146, 186; balance between head and heart, 37; Chesnutt and Dunbar on, 157; in *A Connecticut Yankee in King Arthur's Court*, 144–145; De Forest distinguishes sympathy from, 69–70; De Forest on discipline and, 83–84; and democratic values, 32; demonstrating in the North, 43–48; as depending on death, 94; discipline and obedience become hallmarks of, 65; domestic sentiment versus abstract, 25–26, 29; Du Bois on, 209, 212; Emerson on, 32, 212; emphasis on corporate whole, 5; enduring influence of, 60; of ex-slaves, 139–140; extreme conditions needed for, 94; as faithfulness to Constitution, 38; to the flag, 102; Frederickson on Civil War development of, 5–6; geographical morality distinguished from, 69; increasing formalism of, 102–103; indulgent sympathy versus rational, 6, 13, 14, 22–23, 30, 142, 144; institutionalization of submission as, 99; James on, 32–33, 105; and liberalism, 35; loyal mothers, 69–70; to loyalty, 186, 187, 188; as melodramatic vow, 103; in "Memorial Day 1898," 137, *138*; narrative structure associated with, 10; in national identity, 59–60; nationalization of, 102, 142; to national state, 65; as nurturing fanaticism, 99, 103; philosophies of, 179–217; Pledge of Allegiance and, 1; pledging one's, 45–46; Potter Committee investigates, 44; private propagandizing during Civil War, 38–39; race, 156, 165; regenerate versus degenerate, 33; in relationship of individual to God, 96–97; religious devotion compared with, 36, 86; replaces sympathy in postbellum narratives, 67; Royce on, 184–185, 186, 187–188, 207, 208; versus self-interest, 33–34, 35–36; sentimentality in disseminating moral norms in wartime North, 39–43; shifting importance of certainty for, 144; slavery associated with, 15; in South in 1865, 62, 75–76; as synecdoche, 5; test oaths for affirming, 7–8; unequal understandings of, 139; what does it look like, 43; white, 137–138, 142. *See also* loyal slave narrative; loyalty (test) oaths; patriotism; treason

loyalty (test) oaths: *The Bostonians* on, 116; coerced, 57–58; in colonial New England, 46, 234n131; elimination of, 73–74; enduring influence of, 60; individual will expressed in, 51; as ineffectual defense against treason, 51; in *Miss Ravenel's Conversion from Secession to Loyalty*, 75; Northern anxiety about, 72, 119, 121; premise of, 47; in Reconstruction South, 7–8; repetition in, 9, 64; Southern resistance to, 73; "Taking the Oath of Allegiance," 72–73, *73*; in Union during Civil War, 7, 23–24, 46–48; of white supremacist groups, 252n53

"Loyal Woman's No, A" (Larcom), 39
Luciano, Dana, 9, 35, 57, 128
Lyell, Charles, 80
lynching, 185–186; *Chicago Tribune* gathers statistics on, 194; and loyalty, 188; narratives about, 194–195; Page defends, 196, 198–199, 258n30; in *Red Rock*, 202–204; Royce on, 185, 186; Southerners see as appropriate response, 204, 207
"Lynching of Jube Benson, The" (Dunbar), 175
"Lynching of Negroes, The" (Page), 201
Lynch-Law (Cutler), 180

Mackenzie, John, 183
"Man without a Country, The" (Hale), 13, 48–51, 52, 57, 235n146
"March of Progress, The" (Chesnutt), 254n77
marriage: in African American women's fiction, 254n76; Civil War compared to marital dispute, 62; companionate, 165; nuptial model of contract, 63; slave marriages, 165, 254n75; slavery compared with, 135–136. *See also* remarriage
Marrow of Tradition, The (Chesnutt), 159, 161–164, 254n74
"Marse Chan" (Page), 150, 200
"Marseillaise" (song), 44
"Mars Jeems's Nightmare" (Chesnutt), 161

"Master, The" (Kemble), 150, *152*
"Matter of Principle, A" (Chesnutt), 254n77
"Meaning of the Four Centuries, The" (Bellamy), 1, 9
melodrama, 103, 108, 119, 169–170
Melville, Herman: *Battle-Pieces*, 73; *The Confidence-Man*, 58. See also *Moby-Dick*
Memorial Day, 124
"Memorial Day 1898" (cartoon), 137, *138*
Memorial Hall (Harvard University), 104, 109, 124–130, *126*, 244n13
memory: Civil War and, 122–130; loyal slave narrative as at heart of Civil War, 141, 146; in Reconstruction narratives, 50; of slavery, 135. See also monuments
Meyer, D. H., 183
Michaels, Walter Benn, 208, 246n42
Miller, J. Hillis, 116
Miss Ravenel's Conversion from Secession to Loyalty (De Forest), 68–85; on authority and consent, 77, 79–80; *The Bostonians* compared with, 103; on discipline and loyalty, 83–84; double infantilization in, 98; duty replaces honor in, 74–75; *Elsie Dinsmore* compared with, 79, 81; family and nation compared in, 62, 70, 81; *The Gates Ajar* compared with, 85–86; "Love and Loyalty" compared with, 233n101; on new parameters of national allegiance, 74; promises and oaths in, 74–76; on race, 82–83; recognition in, 64–65; remarriage in, 14, 63–64, 80, 83; as reunion romance, 14, 62, 76; science and politics associated in, 80–82, 99; Southerners depicted as savages in, 76–77; two parts of, 68, 71
Mitchell, Margaret, 7–8
Mizruchi, Susan, 248n70
Moby-Dick (Melville): Bushnell's views compared with, 37; consent as modeled in, 17–18, 19–20; oaths in, 17–18, 24, 51
monuments: Civil War, 123, 137–138, 247n67; to loyal slaves, 138, *139*; narrative of national sacrifice in, 125; Nietzsche on monumental history, 129
"Morella" (Poe), 96
"Mother Can I Go?" (*Harper's Weekly*), 70, 239n39
Mulford, Elisha, 82, 223n9

Mullin, Robert, 231n73

Nabers, Deak, 36
nation: absolute devotion to, 151; abstract nationhood, 142, 231n76, 241n68; American literary nationalism, 66; Bellamy on sentiment and national allegiance, 2–3; Civil War as mythic origin of American, 221; Civil War as purification of American, 220; Civil War in emergence of American nationalism, 59; family compared with, 36–37, 62–64, 70, 81, 157; fiction in shaping national community, 66; idealization in devotion to, 50; James and Union nationalism, 104–105; loyal slave narrative as integral to postbellum national fantasy, 145–146; loyalty to national state, 65; mythos of common origins and descent, 21; national affect, 63–69; organic conception of, 3, 223n9; race conflated with nationality, 208; race loyalty versus loyalty to, 156; racism and nationalism contrasted, 147–148; religion in American national mission, 86; returning "home" to the, 72; Royce on provincialism and, 187; Southern nationalism, 23, 27–29, 229n35, 229n38; Strong on American want of nationality, 24; tension between local and national, 80, 86, 187. See also patriotism
Native Americans: in Civil War, 132; Dakota conflict of 1862, 76, 131, 248n81
Negro, The: The Southerner's Problem (Page), 196
Negro in the American Rebellion, The: His Heroism and Fidelity (Brown), 151
"Nelse Hatton's Vengeance" (Dunbar), 15, 173–178
Newhouse, Wade, 241n68
New Negro movement, 259n57
newspapers, 194, 203
New York Draft Riots, 21
Nietzsche, Friedrich, 19, 110, 129
Noble, Marianne, 66
No Party Now; but All for our Country (Lieber), 46
Norton, Charles Eliot, 1, 36, 81
nullification crisis, 34

"Oath of Allegiance, The" (Phelps), 98–99, 243n107
Oath of Allegiance to the United States, The, Discussed in Its Moral and Political Bearings (Palmer), 58
Oath of the Horatii (David), 72
oaths: Bellows on lax attitude toward, 44–45; in *The Bostonians*, 106; of government officials, 19, 227n9; Hobbes on, 52–54; Lincoln on his, 45; in *Miss Ravenel's Conversion from Secession to Loyalty*, 74–76; in *Moby-Dick*, 17–18, 24, 51; promises contrasted with, 52; repetition in, 9, 64; for solving problems of uncertainty, 54; taken under false pretenses, 54; temporal dimension of, 9, 47–48, 49, 50; in Union literature, 54–57. *See also* loyalty (test) oaths
O'Brien, Fitz James, 54–55
Ohio Hegelians, 67, 182
Old Guard (newspaper), 232n90
Olmstead, Frederick Law, 229n38
O'Neill, Onora, 206
On the Advantage and Disadvantage of History for Life (Nietzsche), 129
On the Citizen (Hobbes), 52–53
Osgood, Samuel, 34
O'Sullivan, John L., 22, 228n22, 234n129

Page, Thomas Nelson, 195–199; lynching defended by, 196, 198–199, 258n30; "The Lynching of Negroes," 201; "Marse Chan," 150, 200; *The Negro: The Southerner's Problem*, 196; as novelist, 258n30; *Red Rock: A Chronicle of Reconstruction*, 201–204; Royce on, 195–196, 207; on sexual violence against white women, 196–199, 202–203
Page, Walter Hines, 166, 254n77
Paine, Thomas, 21
Palmer, Benjamin, 27–28, 58
Patriotic Gore (Wilson), 102
patriotism: Civil War changes, 59; discipline and obedience become hallmarks of, 65; as indistinguishable from its absence, 42; individualism versus, 82; loyalty supplanted by, 32; Northern loss of local, 30–31; Northern versus Southern conceptions of, 101; versus personal bonds of affection, 173; as reasonable, 32, 37; Royce on provincialism and, 187; totalizing implications of, 129
Peabody, Sara, 246n35
Phelps, Elizabeth Stuart: *Beyond the Gates*, 90, 97–98; on biblical language, 243n100; on fiction and nation, 67; *The Gates Between*, 98; loses lover in Civil War, 242n80; "The Oath of Allegiance," 98–99, 243n107; on *Uncle Tom's Cabin*, 66. *See also Gates Ajar, The*
Philadelphia Negro, The: A Social Study (Du Bois), 210, 211
Philosophy of Loyalty, The (Royce), 182, 185, 187–188, 206, 258n25
plantation fiction: on abolitionism, 113; African American response to, 156–157; Chesnutt on, 158–159; Douglass's autobiography challenges, 154; Du Bois's *John Brown* contrasted with, 216; and Dunbar's dialect poetry, 172; on emotions, 151, 157; family in, 175; "Nelse Hatton's Vengeance" rejects, 176; notion of loyalty in, 15; as outlet for nostalgic sentimentality, 139; as polemical, 151; racial violence fueled by, 194; *Uncle Tom's Cabin* and, 148–149
Planter's Northern Bride, The (Hentz), 199–200
"Plea for the American Negro, A" (Chesnutt), 172
Pledge of Allegiance, 1, 3, 7, 9
Plessy v. Ferguson (1896), 155, 201, 260n67
Poe, Edgar Allan, 96
Political Science (Woolsey), 11
Pollard, Edward A., 61, 64, 70
Potter Committee, 44
Principles of Geology (Lyell), 80
"Prisoner of War, The" (O'Brien), 54–55
Problem of Christianity, The (Royce), 208
promises: Arendt on, 51–52, 177; in *The Bostonians*, 116–122; coerced, 118; contracts compared with, 10–11; and forgiving, 177; Hume on, 54; in literary texts, 8–9; in Locke's theory of government, 19; melodramatic, 103; in *Miss Ravenel's Conversion from Secession to Loyalty*, 74–76; and narratives of loyalty, 10; in national identity, 59–60; and personal freedom,

171; Pledge of Allegiance, 1, 3, 7, 9; politics and faculty of making, 24; repetition in, 9; in romances of reunion, 14; temperance pledges, 76; temporal dimension of, 9, 19, 24; in "The Wife of His Youth," 170–171. *See also* oaths
"Provincialism" (Royce), 186, 187, 193
Puritans, 46

"Question of Our Speech, The" (James), 107

race: without bodies, 208; and capacity for emotion, 198; Du Bois on Brown and, 216; loyalty, 156, 165; *Miss Ravenel's Conversion from Secession to Loyalty* on, 82–83; nationality conflated with, 208; racial contamination, 147–148; racialized bodies, 189–194, 196; racialized sympathy, 146, 175, 181, 197, 198, 199–201; racial violence, 156, 180, 194–195, 196–199, 201–204; Royce on problem of, 179, 188–195, 207–209. *See also* African Americans; racism
"Race Problems in America" (Boas), 179
Race Questions and Other Matters (Royce), 181
"Race Questions and Prejudices" (Royce), 180, 185, 188, 189, 195, 208, 210
racism: Chesnutt on, 158; hardens resistance to Civil War, 21; intraracial prejudice, 165–166, 167; nationalism contrasted with, 147–148; as philosophical problem for Royce, 179–180; race theories as, 189; as reconstructed with the nation, 221; sympathy in organizing and camouflaging, 4, 147–148; uplift ideology reinforces, 155–156; white supremacy, 156, 164, 172, 174–175, 178, 252n53
rationality: alcohol abuse and irrationality, 76; balance between head and heart, 37; Chesnutt and Dunbar on loyalty and, 157; indulgent sympathy versus rational loyalty, 6, 13, 14, 22–23, 30, 142, 144; patriotism as rational, 32, 37; sexual violence against white women affects white male, 197–198; symmetry between head and heart, 90; sympathy tempered by, 187; women seen as illogical, 70–71
realism: contract in postbellum narrative, 10; literature of 1860s and, 220; rise after Civil War, 219, 221, 222; sentimentality during rise of, 4, 13
reason. *See* rationality
Reconstruction: Du Bois on, 211–212; efficacy of memory in narratives of, 50; end of, 221; Hobbesian model of contract in, 66; longing for prewar structures and assumptions in, 221; loyal slave narrative in, 141, 142; Page's depiction of, 201, 202; promises and oaths in postbellum narrative, 9; racism reconstructed with the nation, 221; radical utopian vision of, 141; sentimental fiction in, 66–67; test oaths in, 7–8
Red Badge of Courage, The (Crane), 143
Red Rock: A Chronicle of Reconstruction (Page), 201–204
religion: affective, 93; civil, 183; loses its position in moral adjudication, 183; loyalty compared with religious devotion, 36, 86; as loyalty to God, 97; prominence in Civil War era, 86; religious zeal, 107
remarriage: in *The Gates Ajar*, 91; in *Miss Ravenel's Conversion from Secession to Loyalty*, 14, 63–64, 80, 83; recognition in, 64, 85; in "The Wife of His Youth," 165
Renan, Ernst, 128
reunion romances: analogy of marital and political union in, 14; *The Bostonians* compared with, 103, 106, 121–122; characteristics of later, 100, 101; consolidation of female collective identity in, 67; differences within, 99; facticity of, 71; family and nation compared in, 62; *The Gates Ajar* as, 14, 62, 85; "Love and Loyalty" compared with, 40; *Miss Ravenel's Conversion from Secession to Loyalty* as, 14, 62, 76; that include the dead, 98; on voluntary emotional reconciliation, 63
"Reverses Needed" (Bushnell), 94
rights. *See* equal rights
Rogin, Michael, 86, 221

romances of reunion. *See* reunion romances
Roosevelt, Theodore, 124, 215
Ross, Dorothy, 240n64
Rousseau, Jean-Jacques, 66
Royce, Josiah, 179–195; on abstraction, 15, 181–182, 186, 205–206; address to Ethical Society, 179, 184–185; on affect-based moral reasoning, 181–182; on black body, 204, 205–206; and Du Bois, 187, 209–210, 211, 260n73; and Ethical movement, 184; lack of scholarly attention to, 180, 256n6; on loyalty, 184–185, 186, 187–188, 207, 208; on lynching, 185, 186; on material implications of language, 207; on Page, 195–196, 207; *The Philosophy of Loyalty*, 182, 185, 187–188, 206, 258n25; on plasticity, 205–206; *The Problem of Christianity*, 208; "Provincialism," 186, 187, 193; on race problem, 179, 188–195, 207–209; *Race Questions and Other Matters*, 181; "Race Questions and Prejudices," 180, 185, 188, 189, 195, 208, 210; on racial prejudice as philosophical problem, 179–180; on sympathy, 186–187, 188, 194, 195, 205, 206, 207
Ruffner, William H., 58

sacrifice: in *The Bostonians*, 110, 114, 125, 126, 127, 130; and Chesnutt on black fidelity, 158; citizenship entails, 178; *The Gates Ajar* on, 93–94; on home front, 87–88; honorable, 169; Lincoln calls for, 47; loss of Northern local patriotism as, 30, 31; in "Love and Loyalty," 40, 41, 42; loyalty sufficient to motivate, 32; versus self-interest, 36; in "'Uncle Tom' at Home in Kentucky," 151; in "The Wife of His Youth," 168, 169
Samet, Elizabeth, 227n4, 256n108
Sanchez-Eppler, Karen, 259n59
Savage, Kirk, 123, 137, 248n69, 249n4
"Saving His Master" (Kemble), 150, *153*, 176
Scarry, Elaine, 20, 163, 181
Sedgwick, Eve Kosofsky, 41, 246n45
self-interest, 33, 35–36, 65, 89
"Self-Reliance" (Emerson), 32

sensation fiction, 57
sentiment: abstract loyalty versus domestic, 25–26, 29; balance between head and heart, 37; Bellamy on national allegiance and, 2–3; class hierarchy of moral, 163; in disseminating moral norms in wartime North, 39–43; hierarchy of affective states, 39; Henry James on, 110; in monuments to faithful slaves, 138; Northern national, 30–31; political, 21; in postbellum schemes for denying African American claims, 151; power of reconciliation narratives, 154–155; Royce's redefining relationship between mind and heart, 182; sentimentality during rise of realism, 4, 13; vicariousness in, 41. *See also* sentimental fiction; sympathy
sentimental fiction: commercial world and home contrasted in, 28; in Confederate nationalism, 232n97; generic mission of, 67; in Reconstruction, 66–67; submission to authority in, 36; sympathetic identification in, 88, 92; in Union nationalism, 39
Seward, William H., 71
sexual violence against white women, 196–199, 202–203
Shenandoah: A Military Comedy (Howard), 100–102, 103, 108, 123, 137, 143, 244n2
Sidgwick, Henry, 257n18
Sigourney, Lydia, 36
Sizer, Lyde Cullen, 242n80
Slaughterhouse Cases (1873), 155
slavery: *The Bostonians* on national memory of, 135; care for elderly slaves, 160; as cause of Civil War, 102–103; divisions caused by, 154; Du Bois on, 212, 216; Fitzhugh's *Cannibals All! or Slaves without Masters*, 28–29; loyalty associated with abolition, 38; loyalty of ex-slaves, 139–140; marriage compared with, 135–136; monument to faithful slaves, 138, 139; negro servitude distinguished from, 61; obscured difference between freedom and, 170; in *The Planter's Northern Bride*, 199–200; sentimentalizing slave origins, 168, 255n86; slave marriages,

165, 254n75; submission to external authority compared with, 15, 143; violence against slaves, 204. *See also* abolitionism; loyal slave narrative
Smith, Adam, 2, 28, 146–147, 162, 199, 254n69
Smith, Anthony, 21, 59, 241n67
Smith, Gail K., 95
Society of Ethical Propagandists, 183
"Soldier's Faith, The" (Holmes), 143–144
Sollors, Werner, 62, 167, 187
songs: in Confederate nationalism, 234n121; seen as treasonous, 44
Souls of Black Folk, The (Du Bois), 179, 209, 211, 261n81
"Sources and Uses of Suffering, The" (Beecher), 88
South, The: A Tour of Its Battle-Fields and Ruined Cities (Trowbridge), 71–74
Southern Horrors (Wells), 251n40
"Southern Matron" (anonymous), 200
Spanish-American War, 137, 258n50
speech. *See* language
Spillers, Hortense, 181
states' rights doctrine, 132, 229n38
Stephens, Alexander, 86
Stevens, Thaddeus, 141
Stevens, Wallace, 116
Stillé, Charles J., 44
"Story of a Year, A" (James), 122–123
Stowe, Harriet Beecher: *Dred*, 36, 177; on sympathy, 21, 69; *Uncle Tom's Cabin*, 39, 66, 148–149, 151, 176–177, 199, 251n36
Strong, George Templeton, 24
submission to authority, 15, 36, 143
Sullivan, Frank, 219
Sumner, Charles, 38, 132, 141
Sundquist, Eric, 166, 254n76
Swedenborg, Emmanuel, 87
sympathy: affective consent, 20–21; Bellamy on sentiment and national allegiance, 2–3; bodies disrupt, 147; *The Bostonians* on, 111–112; and class, 175; conservative dimension of, 146–147; De Forest distinguishes loyalty from, 69–70; as destabilizing, 30, 230n46; in *The Gates Ajar*, 88–89; hierarchical model of, 146, 148; loyalty as alternative to, in discourse of allegiance, 3–4, 4–5, 21–23, 39, 55, 60, 142, 146, 186; loyalty replaces in postbellum narratives, 67; as metaphor, 5; national affiliation couched in terms of, 2; in organizing and camouflaging racism, 4, 147–148; racialized, 146, 175, 181, 197, 198, 199–201; rational loyalty versus indulgent, 6, 13, 14, 22–23, 30, 142, 144; with the rich, 146–147, 254n69; Royce on, 186–187, 188, 194, 195, 205, 206, 207; for slaves, 21; Adam Smith on, 2, 146–147, 162, 199; in Southern nationalism, 28, 29; with Southern rebels, 21, 27, 29–30; tempered by rationality, 187; for those of same race, 175

"Taking the Oath of Allegiance" (*The South: A Tour of Its Battle-Fields and Ruined Cities*), 72–73, 73
Tate, Claudia, 157, 254n83
temperance, 76
test oaths. *See* loyalty (test) oaths
Theory of Moral Sentiments, The (Smith), 2, 147, 199
Thinking Bayonet, The (Hosmer), 30
Thomas, Brook, 10, 13, 75, 117, 247n50
Thomas, George, 30
Thoreau, Henry David, 36
Thoughts on the Future Civil Policy of America (Draper), 82
Thrailkill, Jane, 242n87
Tourgée, Albion, 106, 200; *Fool's Errand*, 106
treason: allegiance to state and, 25; Constitution's definition of, 227n18; criticizing the government as, 234n122; as failure to understand citizenship, 145; James's *Hawthorne* as, 105; Lincoln seen as traitor, 38; loyalty oaths as ineffectual defense against, 51; refraining from patriotic utterances as, 42; sympathy for Southern rebels as, 21, 27, 29, 44; Thomas accused of, 30; wrong feeling as, 69
Treitschke, Heinrich von, 261n78
Trilling, Lionel, 244n13, 245n29
Trowbridge, J. T.: *Cudjo's Cave*, 55–57, 236n164, 237n166; on loyalty of ex-slaves, 139–140; *The South: A Tour of Its Battle-Fields and Ruined Cities*, 71–74
trust, 11, 23, 119, 121
Tucker, Penelope, 255n95

Twain, Mark: *Adventures of Huckleberry Finn*, 149; *A Connecticut Yankee in King Arthur's Court*, 144–145; contract as influence on work of, 10; does not experience combat, 220; on heaven and America, 243n106; on military oaths, 237n166
"Two Gentlemen of Kentucky" (Allen), 150

"'Uncle Tom' at Home in Kentucky" (Allen), 148–151
Uncle Tom's Cabin (Stowe), 39, 66, 148–149, 151, 176–177, 199, 251n36
"Uncle Tom without a Cabin" (Hill), 148
"Uncle Wellington's Wives" (Chesnutt), 165
uplift ideology, 155–156, 158, 167, 170

Vallandigham, Clement, 49, 234n122, 235n146
Varieties of Religious Experience, The (James), 107–108
Victor, Metta, 67
violence: against African Americans, 74, 151; and alcohol abuse, 76; and emotions, 20; *The Gates Ajar* on everyday, 92–93; and Nietzsche on contracts, 19; racial, 156, 180, 194–195, 196–199, 201–204; sexual violence against white women, 196–199, 202–203; against slaves, 204; in Southern rhetoric, 71; state's authority to deploy, 130. *See also* lynching

Wald, Priscilla, 62, 94
Wardley, Lynn, 127, 128
Warner, Michael, 181
Warner, Susan, 67, 90
Warren, Robert Penn, 59
Washington, Booker T., 155–156, 252n51
Washington, George, 31–32, 46
Wealth of Nations, The (Smith), 146
"Web of Circumstance, The" (Chesnutt), 161
Webster, Daniel, 34, 101

Wells, Ida B., 251n40
West, Cornel, 261n81
Wexler, Laura, 224n14
"What Can I Do?" (*Harper's Monthly*), 43, 233n111
Wheeler, Michael, 241n79
White, Morton, 256n6
White, Samuel, 138
white supremacy, 156, 164, 172, 174–175, 178, 252n53
Whitman, Walt, 4, 62, 67
Whittier, John Greenleaf, 43
Wide Wide World, The (Warner), 67, 90
Wiegman, Robyn, 185–186
"Wife of His Youth, The" (Chesnutt), 15, 164–171, 254n77
Wife of His Youth and Other Tales of the Color Line, The (Chesnutt), 164
Williams, George Washington, 154
Wilson, Edmund, 59, 102–103, 220, 247n65
women: *The Bostonians* on women's rights, 108–109, 110, 111, 112, 114, 129, 132–133, 135, 136, 245n29; in Butler's Order 28, 58; displaying their loyalty, 43; fierce rhetoric of Southern, 77; James on important of tone for, 107; loyal mothers, 69–70; modes of constraint in postbellum narratives, 67; seen as illogical, 70–71; sexual violence against white, 196–199, 202–203
Wonham, Henry, 167, 255n91
Wood, Fernando, 33, 231n67
Wood, Gordon, 231n63
Woolsey, Theodore, 11, 226n38
Woolson, Constance Fenimore, 103
Wormeley, Katherine, 143
Wyatt-Brown, Bertram, 74, 169

Yekl: A Tale of the New York Ghetto (Cahan), 167
Young, Elizabeth, 41, 176–177, 242n88
Youth's Companion, 1, 6–7

zeal, 26, 103, 104, 107, 108, 110, 112

About the Author

Elizabeth Duquette is an associate professor in the Department of English at Gettysburg College. This is her first book.

www.ingramcontent.com/pod-product-compliance
Lightning Source LLC
Chambersburg PA
CBHW032002220426
43664CB00005B/115